I0029424

COGNITIVE APPROACHES TO CULTURE

Frederick Luis Aldama, Patrick Colm Hogan, Lalita Pandit Hogan, and Sue Kim, Series Editors

Affective Ecologies

Empathy, Emotion, and
Environmental Narrative

Alexa Weik von Mossner

THE OHIO STATE UNIVERSITY PRESS
COLUMBUS

Copyright © 2017 by The Ohio State University.
All rights reserved.

Library of Congress Cataloging-in-Publication Data

Names: Weik von Mossner, Alexa, author.
Title: Affective ecologies : empathy, emotion, and environmental narrative / Alexa Weik
    von Mossner.
Other titles: Cognitive approaches to culture.
Description: Columbus : The Ohio State University Press, [2017] | Series: Cognitive
    approaches to culture | Includes bibliographical references and index.
Identifiers: LCCN 2016056888 | ISBN 9780814213360 (cloth ; alk. paper) | ISBN 0814213367
    (cloth ; alk. paper)
Subjects: LCSH: Ecocriticism. | Affect (Psychology) in literature. | Environmentalism—
    Psychological aspects. | Empathy in literature. | Cognitive psychology.
Classification: LCC PN98.E36 W45 2017 | DDC 809/.93353—dc23
LC record available at https://lccn.loc.gov/2016056888

Cover design by Martyn Schmoll
Text design by Juliet Williams
Type set in Adobe Minion Pro

Cover image: Boris Bugla

♾ The paper used in this publication meets the minimum requirements of the American
National Standard for Information Sciences—Permanence of Paper for Printed Library
Materials. ANSI Z39.48–1992.

9 8 7 6 5 4 3 2 1

For Michael

CONTENTS

ACKNOWLEDGMENTS

THIS BOOK has been in the making for quite some time, and it would not have been possible without the support and valuable feedback I received from a great many people. My special thanks go out to those who took it upon themselves to read parts or the entirety of the manuscript and whose astute comments have greatly helped me in developing and refining my ideas: Ursula Heise, Sylvia Mayer, Scott Slovic, Hubert Zapf, Thomas Austenfeld, Tina Bisogno, Brigitte Hipfl, Marie Körner, Salma Monani, and Carina Rasse. An earlier version of the present manuscript was submitted as *Habilitationsschrift* at the University of Klagenfurt, and I want to thank the committee members and reviewers in particular for their time and critical engagement with my work. I also want to thank my students at the University of Fribourg and the University of Klagenfurt, who over the years have helped me think through some of the issues I discuss in individual chapters. And I am grateful to the many friends and colleagues who have given me valuable input at conferences and in their feedback to earlier publications related to the larger project of this book.

Some of the early ideas for the book were developed during my time as Carson Fellow at the Rachel Carson Center for Environment and Society in Munich. I want to thank Christof Mauch and Helmuth Trischler for the generous support I received from the Center and for the opportunity to establish and curate the Green Visions film series, which not only allowed me to discuss environmental documentaries with their directors and a great number of scientific experts but also gave me the opportunity to acquire empirical data on how such films engage diverse audiences. The RCC also supported an international workshop that provided a wonderful opportunity to discuss a range of theoretical approaches to cinematic affect and emotion with leading ecocritical film scholars whose work informs many of the chapters in this book. I want to thank Pat Brereton, Joe Heumann, David Ingram, Adrian Ivakhiv, Robin Murray, Nicole Seymour, Belinda Smaill, Janet Walker, Bart Welling, and David Whitley for three days of intense and focused discussion and for their wonderful contributions to the edited volume that emerged from that workshop and that in many ways was a stepping stone for the present book. I also want to thank the other fellows at the Rachel Carson Center for the incredibly rich and multifaceted intellectual input I received during my time there.

Research for this book was also supported by a Fellowship for Advanced Researchers from the Swiss National Science Foundation. I want to thank the English Department at the University of Klagenfurt for granting me a year-long leave of absence and Ursula Heise for inviting me to spend that time as visiting researcher at the University of California, Los Angeles. I extend my gratitude to the English Department for hosting me and for granting me access to the university's outstanding research facilities. I was extremely lucky in that my stay happened to coincide with the Sawyer Seminar in the Environmental Humanities, organized by Ursula together with Jon Christensen and Michelle Niemann and funded by the Mellon Foundation. My ideas were greatly enriched by my regular participation in the seminar and our wide-ranging discussions about issues that concern scholars in the environmental humanities. I am particularly grateful for the opportunity to present my own research in this forum and want to extend my special thanks to Allison Carruth, Heather Houser, Dolly Jørgensen, Sverker Sörlin, and to so many others who shared their work, among them Joni Adamson, Stacy Alaimo, Hannes Bergthaller, Dipesh Chakrabarty, Elizabeth DeLoughrey, Thom van Dooren, Greg Garrard, Dale Jamieson, Jorge Marcone, Linda Nash, and Catriona Sandilands. They all have all greatly enriched my thinking on environmental narrative.

I would like to extend my sincere thanks to Kristen Rowley at the Ohio State University Press, who, quite simply, has been the best editor one can possibly imagine, and to Frederick Aldama and Patrick Hogan, who from the very first moment were enthusiastic about the project. I also want to thank the other editors of the series and Rachel F. Van Hart, who has done a wonderful job getting the manuscript into its final form.

My gratitude goes out to the editors and publishers who have granted me permission to draw on previously published materials. Portions of chapter 1 were taken from "Environmental Narrative, Embodiment and Emotion," which first came out in *The Handbook of Ecocriticism and Cultural Ecology*, edited by Hubert Zapf (Berlin: De Gruyter, 2016), 534–50. In chapter 3, I use passages from "Mysteries of the Mountain: Environmental Racism and Political Action in Percival Everett's *Watershed*," *Journal of American Studies of Turkey* 30 (Fall 2009): 73–88. Chapter 5 includes some material from "Facing *The Day After Tomorrow*: Filmed Disaster, Emotional Engagement, and Climate Risk Perception," an essay first published in *American Environments: Climate–Cultures–Catastrophe*, edited by Christof Mauch and Sylvia Mayer (Heidelberg: Universitätsverlag Winter, 2012), 97–115. It also includes some revised material from "Science Fiction and the Risks of the Anthropocene: Anticipated Transformations in Dale Pendell's *The Great Bay*," which was first published in *Environmental Humanities* 5 (2014): 203–16.

Finally, I want to express my deep gratitude to my family and friends in the United States and Europe for putting up with me over so many years. To my mother, Barbara, my father, Peter, my sister, Jo, and to that bright young lady Hera who calls me *Tante* and makes me smile. To Chris and Herrmann and Dani and Tina and Marie (again). And to Boris, for being not only a wonderful friend but also a gifted artist who creates the most stunning images such as the one on the cover of this book. I cannot imagine a better illustration of the close relationship between perception, emotion, and environment.

As always, my last words are reserved for my husband, Michael. Thank you for your unwavering love and support, your stubborn optimism, and your unparalleled sense of humor. Thank you for making life worth living. None of this would have been possible without you.

Environmental Narrative, Embodiment, and Emotion

ON THE first pages of Cormac McCarthy's *The Road*, a nameless man wakes up in the woods next to a sleeping child. It is dark and cold, and both the darkness and the coldness have a brutal and unnatural intensity to them, signaling "the onset of some cold glaucoma dimming away the world" (2006, 3). The man touches the child's chest for a moment, feeling it rise and fall "with each precious breath;" then he raises himself in his "stinking robes and blankets" (3), his mind flashing back to the nightmare he just had about a monstrous translucent creature, well adapted to a life in utter darkness. As he walks out to the road in the first light of day, readers are cued to imagine the environment he beholds as he gazes through his binoculars at "the valley below. Everything paling away into the murk. The soft ash blowing in loose swirls over the blacktop" (4). They are invited to enact the visual perception of "segments of road down there among the dead trees," as the man looks out "for anything of color. Any movement. Any trace of standing smoke" (4). But there is nothing to be seen, and so the man just sits there, "holding the binoculars and watching the ashen daylight congeal over the land" (4).

The post-apocalyptic scene that opens McCarthy's Pulitzer Prize–winning novel is brimming with visual imagery that signals abandonment, death, and decay, allowing readers to create a vivid mental image of a barren and lifeless environment. Other sensual perceptions are also evoked—the feel of air so cold that the "ashen daylight" appears to harden and turn to ice, the touching of the child's chest, the stink of their dirty clothes, and the utter lack of natural sounds—each contributing to readers' understanding that this environment is dead, lacking sunlight, warmth, and life, devoid of food and potentially lethal. All of this plays out on the purely imaginary level, cued by verbs, nouns, and adjectives of movement and sensual perception.

Now consider the same moment in John Hillcoat's 2009 film adaptation of the novel, which relies on cinematic modes of narration to make the scene perceptually and emotionally salient. The first thing to note is that it is preceded by a dream-like flashback to an earlier time. Hillcoat opens his version of the story with a series of light-suffused shots showing lush green, colorful blossoms, a smiling woman (Charlize Theron), and a man (Viggo Mortensen) stroking the head of a healthy looking horse in the golden glow of the setting sun. The soundtrack features bird voices and the buzzing of insects, completing on the auditory level the visual impressions of a hot summer day. The lighthearted music score further supports the positive affective valence of the images and it is only when a closing screen door slowly darkens the view that things begin to change. The music continues across the cut to the nocturnal interior of the house, but now it seems arrested on a single note, sounding increasingly ominous as the man is woken by flickering light that penetrates the curtains. He looks outside and runs to the bathroom to fill the tub with water. The woman is awake now too, holding her pregnant belly. As the camera moves closer and the distant muffled shouts of humans become more audible, viewers are cued to focus their attention on the look of horror on the woman's face. The narrative then jumps forward to the moment that opens the novel: the man awakens from his dream, touching the chest of the child next to him with his hand. The image is almost devoid of color now, drowning everything in shades of brown and gray. The protagonists' dirty winter clothes and the presence of discolored ice suggest that it must be very cold, and the sight and sound of a waterfall next to their makeshift bed further strengthens that perception. We see the man's breath misting as he gets up and stumbles to the opening of what looks like a cave. Outside, the world is just as gray as inside, and the only thing to be seen is charred mountains and dead trees as far as the eye can reach.

The relationship between the two sequences and the ways they have been realized no doubt poses many interesting questions about transposition and authenticity in intermedia adaptation, but that is not my concern here. My concern is with the ways in which both narratives appeal to our sensual perception and embodied cognition—if in very different ways—in order to immerse us into their storyworlds and engage us in the gruesome tale they tell about environmental disaster and human suffering.[1] Cognition is embodied because it "is deeply dependent upon features of the physical body of an agent" (Wilson and Foglia 2011, para. 1), and cognitive scientists like the Italian neurologist Vittorio Gallese have suggested that processes of *embodied simulation* play a crucial role in our engagement with the world as well as in aesthetic response (2015, 442). Both reading and watching are highly embodied activities not only in that we need our senses in order to be able to perceive things, but also in that our bodies act as sounding boards for our mental simulations of storyworlds and of characters' perceptions, emotions, and actions within those virtual worlds. When we read that McCarthy's nameless protagonist "lowered the glasses and pulled down the cotton mask from his face and wiped his nose on the back of his wrist" (2006, 4), we literally map those movements onto the motor cortices of our brains as the mental processing of action verbs activates the respective neurons.[2] When we watch the expression of horror on Charlize Theron's face in the film adaptation, we inevitably engage in affective mimicry and feel vaguely anxious as a result of the simulation, although we do not see what she sees.[3] Even more intriguing, there is evidence that we use our bodies not only to understand human characters, but also for our grasping of the environments that surround them, including the deliberations, emotions, and actions of nonhuman agents and even the movements of inanimate objects (Currie 2011; Freedberg and Gallese 2007). More crucial still, philosophers (M. Johnson 1994; 2014) and psychologists (Mar and Oatley 2008; Decety and Cowell 2014) have shown that embodied cognition plays an important role in the simulation of social experience and moral understanding.

This is why throughout this book I will argue that embodied cognition is of particular relevance for our theoretical and practical investigations of environmental narratives and the emotional responses they cue in readers and viewers. Environmental narrative, broadly defined, includes any type of narrative in any media that foregrounds ecological issues and human–nature relationships, often but not always with the openly stated intention of bringing about social change. Focusing on the American cultural context—and predominantly on American literature and film—I will suggest that an ecocritical approach that draws on the insights of cognitive science and the equally interdisciplinary field of cognitive cultural studies can give us a better understanding of how we interact with such narratives on the mental and affective level in ways that are both biologically universal and culturally specific. How do we experience the characters, events and environments we encounter in literature and film on the sensory and emotional level? How do environmental narratives invite us to care for human and nonhuman others who are put at risk? And how do we relate to the speculative futures presented to us in ecotopian and ecodystopian texts and films? These are the central questions that are explored in the three parts of *Affective Ecologies,* questions that are important not only for ecocritics but for anyone with an interest in the rhetorical strategies and persuasive power of environmental narratives.

EMBODIED COGNITION AND THE ANALYSIS OF NARRATIVE

Throughout this book, I will frequently draw on empirical research in cognitive science in order to support the theoretical arguments and close readings I offer in individual chapters. What I will present in these chapters could be called a cognitive ecocritical approach to narrative emotion, though I am not attached to labels. The term "cognitive" is often misunderstood or unjustly narrowed down to some version of computationalism or connectionism, which treat the mind as a disembodied information processor or neural network.[4] In this unduly simplistic view of cognitive science, the diversity of approaches within the larger field is often neglected, and the same is true for the considerable differences within the group of so-called "second-generation" neuroscientists who work within the larger framework of embodied cognition.[5] Despite such differences, neurologists such as Antonio Damasio (1994, 1999, 2003, 2010), Joseph LeDoux (1996), Marco Iacoboni (2009), Vilayanur Ramachandran (2010), and Vittorio Gallese (2005, 2014) all stress the central importance of the feeling body and its mental representation in human experience and reasoning, As Damasio declares in *Descartes' Error,* "the organism interacts with the environment as an ensemble: the interaction is neither of the body alone nor of the brain alone," which is why "mental phenomena can be fully understood only in the context of an organism's interacting in an environment" (1994, xxvii). Understanding the mind as both *embodied* (in a physical body) and *embedded* (in a physical environment), this view of the mind embraces the first two of the so-called 4E's of embodied cognition, which states that the mind is *embodied, embedded, enactive,* and *extended.* It does not necessarily embrace the second two *Es,* whose proponents can mostly be found in philosophy departments.[6]

While the first two *Es,* and the related research in neuroscience and cognitive psychology, are of central importance to my argument throughout the book, I am somewhat more skeptical about the notion that the mind is enactive and extended. I will occasionally draw on moderate forms of enactivist thought, which posits that consciousness arises *exclusively* in a body's inter-action with its environment, and I also embrace the fifth *E* (or *A*) that has recently been added by some researchers to the 4E approach, namely that the mind is emotional or affective.[7] However, I will not take up the related, and much more radical, idea forwarded by philosophers such as Daniel Hutto (2000), Andy Clark (2005, 2010), and Alva Noë (2010) that minds are *extended*.[8] The notion that "the content of our thoughts is determinable by features of the environment, and that the proper faculties of cognition are not limited to the brain and neuronal system, or even the body as a whole, but that they are spread out into the environment" (Clark and Chalmers 1998, 18) might look immediately attractive for ecocritics because of the great impor-tance it attributes to the environment. However, in my view it simply does not offer a convincing argument against neuroscientific simulation theories that place the mind *inside* the experiencer as her body interacts with her environment.[9]

Over the past two decades, humanities scholars have begun to draw increasingly on theories of embodied cognition and the neuroscience of per-ception, attention, mental processing, and emotional response.[10] In the field of literary studies, postclassical narratologists in particular have begun to reevaluate storytelling in the light of these new insights.[11] The last decades of the twentieth century already saw some recognition of reading practices though reception theory and reader-response criticism (Barthes 1974; Booth 1961; Eco 1979; S. Fish 1980; Iser 1978; Jauss 1982).[12] For most of these crit-ics, however, textual interpretation is a disembodied mental activity that is first and foremost linguistic in nature. Early work in the emerging field of cognitive narratology, similarly, mostly ignored the role of the body in liter-ary reading, as it was influenced by computational approaches in cognitive science and predominantly focused on information processing (Crane 2000; Hart 2001; Palmer 2004; Richardson and Steen 2002; Spolsky 1993; Turner 2006; Zunshine 2006).[13] The physical and emotional dimensions of literary reading were first explored by psychologists such as Keith Oatley (1992, 1999, 2002) and Raymond Mar (with Oatley, Hirsh, de la Paz, and Peterson 2006; with Oatley 2008; with Oatley and Peterson 2009; with Oatley, Dijikic, and Mullin 2011), and Richard Gerrig (1993), as well as by literary scholars such as David Miall, who frequently collaborates with the psychologist Don Kui-ken in order to examine reading practices empirically (Miall 1988, 1989; Miall and Kuiken 1994a, 1994b, 2001). In more recent years, cognitive narratologists such as Patrick Colm Hogan (2003, 2011a, 2011b) and Suzanne Keen (2007, 2010) have focused on the affective dimensions of our engagement with liter-ary texts. Peter Garratt (2016), Marco Caracciolo (2013a, 2013b, 2014, 2016) and Anežka Kuzmičová (2012, 2013, 2014, 2015) are among the literary scholars that have tried to integrate insights from cognitive neuroscience with those of phenomenological and enactivist philosophy, resulting in a strong focus on embodiment and environmental situatedness. Within film and media studies there exists an even richer tradition of cognitive approaches that includes philosophers such as Noël Carroll (1999, 2003) and William Seeley (Carroll and Seeley 2013, 2014) and film scholars such as Torben Grodal (2009), Carl Plantinga (2009a), Greg Smith (2003), and Murray Smith (1995). Embodiment and the affective dimensions of cinematic response play central roles in such approaches, which draw heavily on the insights of second-generation cognitive science for their analysis of the visual and narrative dimensions of film.

In the cognitive sciences, there is also growing recognition of the central part that narratives of all kinds play in processes of meaning making, as is attested by the film- and literature-related work of psychologists such as Ed Tan (1995, 1996), Arthur Shimamura (2013), Jeffrey Zacks (2015), Marco Iacoboni (with Zanna Clay 2011), and Vittorio Gallese (with Hannah Wojciehowski 2011; with Michele Guerra 2014). Such researchers have begun—often in collaboration with humanities scholars—to explore not only the ways narrative is processed in the brain but also what larger social repercussions such processing may have. In the coda to *Imagining Minds* (2010), literary scholar Kay Young and neurologist Jeffrey Saver assert the centrality of narrative to how we understand the world and ourselves. "When we choose to be in the company of a story by reading a novel or seeing a film," they explain, "the narrative sets itself off as a narrative, not as a part of our lives. . . . However, the storytelling we experience as an event in life can lose its appearance as narrative by virtue of its integration in life" (2010, 186). According to this definition there are two types of narrative, one that we consciously consume and one that is part of the texture of our lives. And yet the two modes are bound to overlap and influence each other.[14] Storytelling plays a central role in memory formation and counterfactual thinking; it is what allows us to communicate events we have experienced or imagined to others, who can then in turn imaginatively simulate those events and therefore share our experience to some degree. This might happen in everyday life or on the pages of a novel or film script. As Patrick Colm Hogan has shown, the creative imagination of authors is a function of simulation that "is continuous with our ordinary cognitive processes of counterfactual thinking" (2013, xiii).[15] Functionally, the brain does not really differentiate between consciously constructed and consumed narratives and other, less conscious forms of narrativization. "Whether we experience events in real life, watch them in a movie, or hear [or read] about them in a story," explains Zacks, "we build perceptual and memory representations in the same format" (2015, 150). This is why we can learn from stories in ways that impact the narratives of our everyday lives.[16]

Narrative, then, is a means for making sense of the world; not only of the imaginary world on the pages of a book or on the silver screen of a movie theater, but also of the actual world in which we live out our lives. In David Herman's influential definition, it is "a basic human strategy for coming to terms with time, process, and change—a strategy that contrasts with, but is not inferior to, 'scientific' modes of explanation that characterize phenomena as instances of general covering laws. Science explains how in general water freezes when . . . its temperature reaches zero degrees centigrade; but it takes a story to convey what it was like to lose one's footing on slippery ice on a late afternoon in December 2004, under a steel-grey sky" (2007a, 3). Herman's example encompasses both modes of narrative—the one that structures our present and past experiences and the one that we consciously construct and consume in storytelling. The second one arguably is already an example of an *environmental* narrative because it focuses on the conveyance of the sensual experience of and physical interaction with one's environment: the experience of losing one's footing on slippery ice on a winter day. That conscious experience of one's environment tends to be subjective and unique and therefore involves what cognitive scientists call *qualia*. As Janet Levin explains, the term *qualia* is "most commonly used to characterize the qualitative, experiential or felt properties of mental states" (1999, 693). In his essay "What Is It Like to Be a Bat?" the philosopher Thomas Nagel puts the problem in simpler terms: qualia are the sense or feeling of "what it is like" for someone to undergo conscious experience (1974, 435). A narrative, in Herman's example, is different from a scientific account in that it will allow those who receive it to imagine that sense or feeling of *what it is like* to lose one's footing on slippery ice. It will cue recipients—be they viewers, listeners, or readers—to simulate that sense or feeling in their minds, using their own real-world experiences as models and their own bodies as sounding boards for the simulation. Psychological research suggests that the events we mentally simulate in response to a story can continue to impact our emotions, attitudes, and behaviors after we have finished engaging with it (Mar et al. 2011; D. Johnson et al. 2013). To date, only very little of this exciting research has made inroads into ecocriticism or the environmental humanities more generally. This is remarkable not only because these fields have always been more open to scientific approaches than many other critical discourses within the humanities, but also because scholars working in these fields are often so intent on changing human–nature relationships for the better.

ECOCRITICISM AND THE STUDY OF AFFECTIVE AND EMBODIED COGNITION

From its inception in the early 1990s, ecocriticism has placed great trust in the ability of environmental narratives to have lasting effects on the attitudes and behaviors of their readers. Many ecocritics have also had an eye on perceptual and affective processes in that context, asserting that they are important not only in the production of environmental narratives but also for their societal effects. Lawrence Buell, for example, claims in *The Environmental Imagination* that for nature writers like Henry David Thoreau and John Muir "aesthetics was continuous with environmentalism" and that "a deeply personal love and reverence for the nonhuman led, over time, to a deeply protective feeling for nature" (1995, 137). That sensual pleasure and personal love for the nonhuman found expression in texts such as Thoreau's *Walden,* which, according to Buell, had an affective impact not only on specific readers but on American society as a whole. This implies that the affective and propositional understanding of readers—and even that of non-readers—can be shaped or at least influenced by environmental narrative.

Buell's belief in the emotional valence and social efficacy of nature writing and other environmentally oriented texts is shared by many environmental writers and critics. Scott Slovic has argued that Thoreau and other American nature writers were "constantly probing, traumatizing, thrilling, and sooth-ing their own minds" in order to sensually and affectively immerse readers in very similar ways into the natural environments they depicted and thereby provoke some kind of "awakening" or heightened modes of "awareness" (1996, 352). In her introduction to *The Cambridge Companion to Literature and the Environment,* Louise Westling points out that "mid-twentieth-century works such as Aldo Leopold's *Sand County Almanac* urged an ethics of nature and wildlife preservation, and Rachel Carson's *Silent Spring* dramatized the dev-astating ecological effects of pesticides, creating a national uproar that helped to launch the American environmental movement and spread its influence around the world" (2014, 5). The urging in Leopold's *Sand County Almanac,* the probing in Thoreau's *Walden,* and the dramatization Westling detects in Carson's *Silent Spring* all belong to a repertoire of rhetorical and narrative techniques that aim to engage readers sensually and emotionally and thereby move them to action. The belief that the use of such narrative techniques in environmental nonfiction has had tangible effects on individual American readers and the larger public sphere is common among ecocritics. There tends to be more ambiguity and disagreement when it comes to the question of what genres of fiction in literature and film are most effective in changing our perceptions of and attitudes toward nonhuman nature—and to the issue of whether works of art should be expected to do that at all. Nevertheless, there is a certain consensus that emotionally powerful renderings of human–nature relationships play an important role in our engagement with environmental narrative and that such engagements can have substantial repercussions in the real world.

Much of the evidence we usually rely upon for such assertions is anecdotal and/or phenomenological, as in the case of evolutionary literary scholar Jonathan Gottschall's acknowledgement that he finished McCarthy's *The Road* "flopped in a square of sunlight on my living room carpet, the way I often read as a boy. I closed the book and trembled for the man and the boy, and for my own short life, and for my whole proud, dumb species" (2013, xvi). What Gottschall describes here is one highly trained and critical reader's unabashedly emotional response to a fictional narrative. As it is the case for all readers, his experience of the novel is embedded in his previous experiences and knowledge of the world, and so his emotional response to its ending is not solely a response to the fictional fates of its characters. When Gottschall trembles for the man and the boy, his emotional response concerns the storyworld of the novel; when he does the same for his "own short life, and for [his] whole proud, dumb species," however, he moves beyond the fiction in his imagination, making the connection to his own existence and even to the future of all of humanity on the actual planet Earth. Of the end of the novel, he writes, "everything is precarious. The whole ecosystem is dead, and it's not clear whether the people can survive long enough to recover" (xvi). Gottschall's concern is not explicitly ecocritical, but he does suggest that while science cannot answer what will happen to McCarthy's virtual world, it "*can* help explain why stories like *The Road* have such power over us" (xvii). That power involves making a reader consider the potential real-world relevance of the fictional events he has experienced vividly and in an emotionally salient way, and Gottschall suggests that scientific research—including neuroscience, cognitive psychology, and evolutionary biology—can give us a better understanding of how certain narratives impact readers in ways that resonate beyond the immediate reading experience.

There are at least three other possible routes within environmental criticism to approaching these issues, all of them sharing some theoretical ground with the approach I am developing here: ecophenomenology, material ecocriticism, and ecocritical appropriations of affect theory. The first is based on the recognition of the value of phenomenological thinkers for ecocritical readings. Of particular relevance is the work of European philosophers such as Edmund Husserl, Martin Heidegger, and Maurice Merleau-Ponty, which focuses on our physical dwelling in place and claims that it is only as spatially and temporally embodied beings that perception and understanding can take place.[17] Louise Westling has argued for the particular relevance of Merleau-Ponty because, unlike Heidegger, he was able to embrace physical similarities between humans and other animals, suggesting that "all beings exist intertwined and in constant interaction with the flesh of the world around them" (Westling 2012, 127). As Westling points out, Merleau-Ponty was constantly engaged with the science of his day: Gestalt psychology and neuroscience during the 1930s and 1940s; physics and evolutionary biology during the following decade. Today, his work informs much of the enactivist strand within embodied cognition, which embraces all four of the 4Es—positing that the mind is embodied, embedded, enactive, and extended—and also places great emphasis on the experiential and affective components of meaning making (Kukkonen and Caracciolo 2014).

The early enactive thought first developed by Franciso Varela, Evan Thompson, and Eleanor Rosch in *The Embodied Mind* (1991) also informs some work within the diverse field of material ecocriticism.[18] As Serenella Ioviono and Serpil Oppermann explain in their introduction to *Material Ecocriticism,* ecocritics who ride "the new materialist wave of thought" (2) are interested in "the emerging dynamics of matter and meaning, body and identity, being and knowing, nature and culture, bios and society . . . not in isolation from each other but through one another, matter being an ongoing process of embodiment that involves and mutually determines cognition, social constructions, scientific practices, and ethical attitudes" (2014, 5). Material ecocriticism is not the first approach within environmentally oriented literary and cultural studies to have challenged the Cartesian division between body and mind, nature and culture. Cultural ecology, for example, as it has been conceived and developed by the German literary scholar Hubert Zapf, "considers the sphere of human culture not as separate from but as interdependent with and transfused by ecological processes and natural energy cycles" (2008, 851).[19] However, in the material ecocritical approach, nature and culture are seen not only as interdependent, but as an inextricable and inescapable "mesh." Not only is all cognition necessarily embodied and embedded, the body itself also becomes a site of interpretation. There are literally no boundaries in this approach to embodiment, which also takes cues from quantum physics.[20] Mind is understood as "a medium in which we are corporeally situated and from which we are simply unable to extricate ourselves without ceasing to exist" (Abram 2014, 303) and sympathy as a "mode of natural causality" that "names not only an inner psychological state but, more fundamentally, an impersonal ontological infrastructure, an undesigned system of affinities"

(Bennett 2014, 239). Neither minds, nor bodies, or even sympathies are confined to an individual experiencer in this approach. It is all out in the open, shared and constituted in the interaction of everyone and everything.[21]

This interest in the manifold and complex interactions, exchanges, and circulations between narratives, bodies, and environments is echoed within recent affect theory, which couches its insights in a similarly dense jargon and also shares in the conceptual unwillingness to accept boundaries of any kind. Affect, declare Melissa Gregg and Gregory Seigworth in their introduction to the *Affect Theory Reader*, "is found in those intensities that pass body to body (human, nonhuman, part-body, and otherwise), in those resonances that circulate about, between, and sometimes stick to bodies and worlds, *and* in the very passages or variations between these intensities and resonances themselves" (2010, 1). Ondine Park, Tonya Davidson, and Rob Shields's introduction to *Ecologies of Affect* traces the history of affect studies back to Deleuze's 1978 lectures on Spinoza, in which he revived the Latin concept of *affectus,* defining it as a change in one's "force of existing" (2011, 4). The affective dimension of experience, in this definition, is nothing more and nothing less than an "increasing and decreasing capacity to act" (4) and necessarily involves a wide range of feelings. Ecocritics have found the work of affect theorists such as Brian Massumi (2002), Sara Ahmed (2004), Lauren Berlant (2008), and Sianne Ngai (2007) productive for the analysis of how the affects produced by a nonfiction text such as Carson's *Silent Spring* circulate in the public sphere (Lockwood 2012), how narrative fiction envisions the endangerment and technologization of both human bodies and environmental systems (Houser 2014), and how a TV series such as *Northern Exposure* structures its narrative around an ambiguous and protracted affective state such as irritation (Goldberg 2015). There is a growing interest within the field in theorizing our affective engagements with environmental narratives, and an engagement with theoretical work on affect offers one way to do this.

Like ecophenomenology and material ecocriticism, affect studies approaches tend to be firmly anchored in European traditions of philosophical thought, even as they recognize the relevance of contemporary cognitive science. Acknowledging that "phenomenology, trauma studies, psychoanalytic theory, queer theory, and microhistories of the social are just some of the domains where emotion has been a key analytic for several decades," Houser maintains that "two commitments stand out to affiliate accounts of affect in these areas as well as in the cognitive sciences, aesthetics, and political philosophy: determining how objects and events rise to attention in our personal worlds and how attachments, detachments, and commitments form from that attention" (2014, 5). That certainly is true, but it does not change the fact that affect studies' relationship to the insights of contemporary cognitive science is at best tenuous and that the latter often defines and utilizes its conceptual terms in very different ways.

To date there are only a handful of ecocritical scholars who draw on the insights of cognitive science in their work, and even references to the work in cognitive narratology and film theory are rare to find within environmentally oriented scholarship. Nancy Easterlin—the first to speak of a "cognitive ecocriticism" (2010, 257)—has pointed out that this is remarkable, since "knowledge of human perception, cognition, and conceptual articulation is more crucial to the key issues underlying ecocriticism than it is perhaps to any other area of contemporary literary study" (2012, 92). Moreover, as both Erin James (2015) and Markku Lehtimäki (2013) have suggested, cognitive narratology offers valuable analytical tools for ecocritics who are interested in the formal aspects of representations of environment. Econarratology, as James defines and develops it in *The Storyworld Accord* (2015), draws on contextual and cognitive strands within narrative theory and carefully maps out the overlaps between that work and various ecocritical endeavors, while also demonstrating the relevance of such an interdisciplinary approach for the critical analysis of postcolonial literature. Easterlin's *A Biocultural Approach to Literary Theory and Interpretation* (2012) uses insights from cognitive and evolutionary science in her analysis of "human way-finding" (90) and the embodied nature of human experience.[22]

Such interdisciplinary approaches can bring out previously neglected aspects of the narrative strategies that writers use to create immersive environments for readers. At the same time, they can also highlight the importance of such environments for plot and character development, a point that tends to be downplayed in much of narratology. So far, there has been very little interest in environmental questions and issues within cognitive narratology, and so this field stands to learn much from ecocritical analysis. As James has observed, "*all* narrative texts, even those that do not seem to be interested in the environment in and of itself, offer up virtual environments for their readers to model mentally and inhabit emotionally" (2015, 34). The same is true for narrative films and their viewers. Open-minded dialogue between cognitive cultural studies and ecocriticism therefore stands to benefit both sides in the investigation of narrative.

In this book, I aim to contribute to and further promote such dialogue. I will be considering film as well as literature and, on the final pages, will also briefly turn to transmedia and digital narratives. In doing so, I will pay attention to a number of issues that have been of concern for scholars with an interest in the relationship between cultural texts and the environment, among them environmental justice, animal studies, ecological citizenship, and eco-science fiction, and I will suggest that cognitive approaches to literature and film can greatly enrich our understanding of such issues. While they can in no way replace other ecocritical approaches, they can complement them, especially when it comes to questions of perception, embodiment, and emotion, which are highly relevant for the larger questions environmentally minded scholars tend to ask. An approach to environmental narrative that builds on this multifaceted work in cognitive science and cognitive cultural studies cannot only help answering Lehtimäki's important question about how techniques for consciousness presentation can "be leveraged to suggest how characters' experiences both shape and are shaped by their engagement with aspects of the natural world" (2013, 137); it can also give us a better understanding of the ways in which environmental narratives engage readers and viewers on the perceptual, cognitive, and emotional level and what consequences such engagement may have. Such an improved understanding, it seems to me, is of particular importance to ecocriticism, and to the environmental humanities more generally, precisely because research in this interdisciplinary field is so strongly invested in questions around the multifaceted interactions and interdependencies between human subjectivity, culture, and the natural environment. Easterlin suggests that "the sooner ecocritics begin to grapple with the how and why of the mind's constructions, the sooner they will be able to formulate a workable epistemological stance and promote an informed awareness of the dynamic and mutually modifying sets of relationships—the ecologies—that shape life on Earth" (2012, 93).

Affective Ecologies aims to explore some of those hows and whys, and my hope is that it will be useful not only to ecocritics and scholars in the cognitive humanities, but also to those involved in environmental or science communication. The scientist-turned-filmmaker Randy Olson reminds us that humans are narrative creatures, so even scientists need "narrative intuition" if they want to communicate their findings effectively (2015, 20). In Olson's view, such intuition entails the knowledge of the basic rules of narrative, but I would argue that it is just as important to understand *how* we engage with narratives and *why* it is that they can impact us so deeply.

THE STRUCTURE OF THE BOOK

Part I of *Affective Ecologies* explores the sensory and affective experiences cued by the American environments we find in literature and film. Chapter 1, entitled "Captivating Evocations: Literary Topophilia and Narrative Perspective," introduces the neuroscientific concept of *liberated embodied simulation* (Gallese and Wojciehowski 2011) and explores the role of simulation processes in readers' sense of transportation and immersion into literary storyworlds. The chapter will look at two forms of environmental narrative that have often been hailed for their awareness-raising abilities—nature writing and environmental fiction. John Muir's *The Mountains of California* (1894) and Bonnie Nadzam's novel *Lamb* (2011) will serve as examples of such narratives, and they will also provide an opportunity to engage with claims made by scholars such as Richard Gerrig and Patrick Colm Hogan that there is no qualitative difference between fiction and nonfiction when it comes to processes of narrative transportation and readers' affective engagement with the storyworld that is evoked by a literary text.

Chapter 2, "Touching Sights and Sounds: Embodiment, Emotion, and Cinematic Environments," will then turn to film, exploring the ways in which audiovisual texts evoke environments in the embodied minds of viewers and how they make such environments, and their characters' relationships to them, emotionally salient. After offering some theoretical insight into the role of embodied simulation in the viewing of film, it will explore how cinematic environments come to life for viewers on the emotional level in a variety of film genres. A cognitive reading of Jan De Bont's *Twister* (1996) will demonstrate that *moving* environments are central to both enjoyment and narrative understanding in the disaster film genre. It will also explore the question of whether knowing that the storyworlds presented to us are *authentic* matters for our affective engagement. Josh Fox's fracking-documentary *Gasland* (2010) will provide the basis for a discussion of the relevance of the fiction/nonfiction divide for viewers' emotional responses to filmic representations of environments and human–nature relationships.

Part II of the book focuses on the moral dimensions of our empathic engagements in environmental narratives that are concerned with issues of exploitation, abuse, and injustice. Entitled "Imagining the Pain: Strategic Empathy and the Environmental Justice Narrative," chapter 3 introduces the concept of *"authorial strategic empathizing"* (2010, 82) as it has been developed by Suzanne Keen, exploring how environmental justice narratives engage readers' empathy strategically to make a moral argument about people who have been wronged. The chapter will briefly look at Helena Maria Viramontes's *Under the Feet of Jesus* (1995) as an example of a text that offers an *insider view* on environmental injustice in the sweltering heat of the orchards of Southern California, discussing how such a narrative perspective implicates readers affectively in what is being told. Percival Everett's *Watershed* (1996) will serve as an example of a text that uses a different narrative strategy, aligning readers not with the victims of environmental injustice, but with an outsider who tries to help them—an outsider who himself belongs to a disenfranchised minority group. The chapter then turns to Michael Apted's *Thunderheart* (1992) and Benh Zeitlin's *Beasts of the Southern Wild* (2012) in order to demonstrate that the same two basic forms of strategic empathizing—the insider and the outsider perspective—can also be found in film and that they can be equally successful in cueing moral allegiance to the victims of environmental injustice.

Chapter 4, "Beyond Boundaries: Imaginary Animals and the Intricacies of Trans-species Empathy," will continue the investigation of strategic empathizing in environmental narratives, now turning to cultural texts that focus on nonhuman animals. Questions around anthropomorphism and animal emotions will loom large in this chapter, which uses evidence from affective neuroscience and cognitive ethology—the study of animal minds—to explore the psychological mechanisms behind our emotional responses to the animals we encounter in literature and film. The chapter will look at Louis Psihoyos's documentary *The Cove* (2009) and Michael Apted's biopic *Gorillas in the Mist* (1988) to show how strategic empathy has been employed by filmmakers to align viewers with human characters who fight for nonhuman others. It will also consider literary texts as well as animated films such as George Miller's *Happy Feet* (2006), which purport to offer an *insider perspective* on animal experience, centering their stories on heavily anthropomorphized nonhuman protagonists. Whether such portrayals cue trans-species empathy in their audiences, and whether there is any potential value in them beyond mere entertainment, is another issue that the chapter will explore.

Part III of *Affective Ecologies* will investigate our embodied experience of speculative future environments in eco(dys)topian narratives and the negative and positive emotions cued by such narratives in order to promote more sustainable lifestyles in the Anthropocene. Chapter 5, entitled "Troubling Futures: Climate Risk and the Emotional Power of Dystopia," is interested in the emotional dimensions of risk perception as it pertains to transnational and global environmental problems such as climate change. Introducing the "affect heuristic" developed by the psychologist Paul Slovic and his collaborators, the chapter explores how popular science books make use of dystopian storytelling to make their arguments emotionally salient, cueing negative emotions such as fear, anger, and guilt. The chapter will also consider dystopian novels that either cue a range of negative emotions or, as in the case of T. C. Boyle's *A Friend of the Earth* (2000), approach the issue through a layer of irony and satire, thereby providing emotional distance from the nightmarish scenarios they describe. The final section of the chapter will consider the ways in which Hollywood films have presented ecodystopian scenarios to provide audiences

with entertaining viewing experiences, discussing whether any of these different affective stances can potentially promote social change.

Chapter 6, "Alluring Visions: Hope, Desire, and the Affective Appeals of
Ecotopia," is concerned with a range of *positive* emotions that might be cued
when utopian narratives manage to avoid the much more problematic feeling of boredom. Andrew Dobson's concept of *ecological citizenship* (2003)
serves as a touchstone for the chapter's consideration of the potential value
of critical ecotopian narratives in instigating social change. Considering Kim
Stanley Robinson's speculative novel *Pacific Edge* (1988), it explores what—if
anything—ecotopian scenarios, and readers' embodied simulation of them,
can contribute to political imaginations of ecological citizenship and environmental sustainability. The chapter will conclude with a discussion of James
Cameron's *Avatar* (2009), a film that follows the narrative conventions of the
classical utopia and then makes its evocation of an ideal world exciting by
endangering it. The fact that *Avatar* became the most successful film in history
invites an exploration of the exact nature of the enticing world it depicts and
the technical means by which it transports viewers into that alternative world,
providing them with an emotionally salient virtual experience. The conclusion
of the book will widen the scope of its exploration in a brief consideration of
digital technologies that allow for even greater immersion than 3-D film and
then closes with some thoughts on the importance of empirical research in the
investigation of the affects and effects of environmental narratives.

PART I

Sensing Place

CHAPTER 1

Captivating Evocations

Literary Topophilia and Narrative Perspective

IMAGINE YOU ARE reading a book. What is it that you actually do, and what happens to you if it is a book that "works" for you in the sense of it being able to captivate your attention? We read books under different circumstances and within very different environments—even on very different media. You may have selected a shady spot in your garden and brought a nice cup of coffee to enjoy, looking forward to spending a few relaxing hours with a good read. Or you might be standing up in a crowded subway train on your way to work, having your back poked at irregular intervals by some fellow passenger who needs to get past you. You may not even be holding a bound paper copy of the book, but an electronic reading device, or you might be reading it on your computer in a lecture hall when you are supposed to be focusing on other things. In each of these situations, with various degrees of perfection, the same thing happens: you read the words that an author put there for you or anyone else to read—you accept, so to speak, an invitation—and as a result the narrative that has congealed on the page comes to life in your mind, opening up an alternative world for you to experience imaginatively.

This partial or near-complete shifting of attention away from our present environment and toward the events that play out within the virtual environment of a literary text is a process that the psychologist Richard Gerrig has called *transportation*. In *Experiencing Narrative Worlds*, Gerrig likens the process to an imaginary journey in the course of which the reader's mind travels *"some distance from his or her world of origin"* ([1993] 1998, 13).[1] Drawing on Gerrig, psychologists Melanie Green and Timothy Brock define transportation as "an integrative melding of attention, imagery, and feelings" (2000, 701) with the result that "the reader loses access to some real-world facts in favor of accepting the narrative world that the author has created" (702). Importantly, the narrative worlds that captivate our attention do not have to be fictional. Gerrig maintains that the illusion of transportation is "neutral with respect to the issue of fictionality" and that even very simple forms of narrative can tease us to make some kind of imaginative journey ([1993] 1998, 7). Consider what just happened as you were reading the first paragraph of this chapter. Assuming that you accepted my "invitation" by focusing your attention on the words of the text, you probably imagined someone (or possibly even yourself) in a sunny garden, enjoying a cup of coffee with a good book, followed by the simulation of the situation of someone trying to read his novel in the crammed and persistently shaking environment of a subway train and that of a student who stares absentmindedly at the screen of her laptop. You may not have imagined *what* these people were reading because my text didn't mention that. And you may not have imagined their environments in much detail because I didn't provide you with a whole lot of vivid description. But I did offer you *some* perceptual cues, mentioning shade, a garden, coffee, a crowded train compartment, people who poke your back, and the like, and since you have experience with these things and know how they *feel,* you were able to form mental images—however hazy and incomplete—that allowed you to "see" the situations I described.

Most narratives, however, will offer more fodder for their readers' imagination. Literary scholars such as Elaine Scarry and Marco Caracciolo have likened literary narratives to "instruction manuals" (Caracciolo 2013a, 83) that contain "a set of instructions for mental composition" (Scarry [1999] 2001, 244) and invite readers to follow those instructions.[2] The metaphor of the instruction manual is an interesting one because it stresses the active role of the reader as someone who *performs* the narrative, as Gerrig would put it ([1993] 1998, 12). Just like actors on a stage, Gerrig proposes, readers engage in acts of simulation during which "they must use their own experiences of the world to bridge the gaps in texts" and must invest their own emotions in order to "give substance to the psychological lives of characters" (17). This suggests that the mental performances of readers will be idiosyncratic to some degree, because they are fueled by their own personal experiences, by their historical and socio-cultural contexts, and, as Anežka Kuzmičová has convincingly shown, by their immediate reading environments (2015).[3] But there will also be similarities across readers. Like instruction manuals, literary narratives "'invite' their readers to entertain certain imaginings (and not others)" (Caracciolo 2013a, 83), and the physiological processes that allow readers to entertain such imaginings are similar in all humans.[4] These processes can be explained through the concept of *embodied simulation,* which involves, in the words of David Freedberg and Vittorio Gallese, "the activation of embodied mechanisms encompassing the simulation of actions, emotions and corporeal sensation" (2007, 197). What each of us imagines when reading about a person sitting with a good book in a shady spot of her garden will be very different in terms of detail and appearance, depending on our personal experiences and cultural background. And yet—unless we for some reason exhibit an aberrant response—it will involve the embodied simulation of someone who has sought shelter from the sunlight and is now transfixed by the words on the pages or screen.

In this chapter, I will take a closer look at how exactly narrative environments are evoked for readers and how both the environments themselves and characters' relationships to them are imbued with affective meaning. My first example will come from the rich tradition of American nature writing, a genre that has often been hailed for its attention to environmental detail. Nature writers are masters in providing readers with literary "instruction manuals" that allow them to imaginatively experience landscapes they might never have personally seen. Many of them go further than that. They also want to convey to the reader their own "affective ties with the material environment"—a bundle of sensations that the American geographer Yi-Fu Tuan famously termed *topophilia* (1974, 93)—in the hope that this will lead to greater awareness. The second section of the chapter will explore how one classic text—John Muir's *The Mountains of California* (1894)—invites readers to vividly imagine and therefore *feel* the environment it so famously describes. It will pay particular attention to the role played by narrative style and perspective in the effectiveness of this "invitation" and the consequences for reader engagement. The final section will continue this interest in style and perspective while also putting pressure on Gerrig's claim that narrative transportation is "neutral with respect to the issue of fictionality" ([1993] 1998, 7). Bonnie Nadzam's novel *Lamb* (2011) is a story about a somewhat unusual nature retreat that puts a question mark not only behind the oft-asserted superiority of realist style when it comes to the vivid evocation of nature but also behind naïve celebrations of topophilic attachments. Before I get to any of these texts and issues, however, I first want to elaborate on the ways in which concepts of liberated embodied simulation and related mirror neuron research shed new light on our theoretical understanding of how readers engage with environmental narrative.

SENSING LITERARY ENVIRONMENTS: EMBODIED SIMULATION, PERCEPTION, AND EMOTION

In one of ecocriticism's foundational texts, Cheryll Glotfelty and Harold Fromm's edited volume *The Ecocriticism Reader*, Neil Evernden complains that since Descartes, westerners have accepted that they are not only "not a part of an environment, we are not even part of a *body*. We, the 'real' us, is concentrated in some disputed recess of the body, a precious cocoon, separate from the world of matter" (1996, 98). Two years earlier, in 1994, the neuroscientist Antonio Damasio published his influential book *Descartes' Error*, in which he declares that the Cartesian mind-body split that for so long dominated western thinking is fatally flawed. Damasio famously argued that cognition cannot be separated from emotion, just as perception, attention, and awareness cannot just be located within the mind or even the nervous system alone but takes place in the whole body as it interacts with its environment (1994, xvii). While Evernden was right, then, in stating that the Cartesian tradition has made it difficult for westerners to understand themselves as embodied, embedded, and affective beings, there is by now a plethora of research within cognitive science and related disciplines that challenges this understanding and thus can enrich environmentally oriented scholarship.

Within the philosophical branch of the field, scholars with an interest in the lived experience of the world frequently draw on the thought of phenomenologists like Edmund Husserl and Maurice Merleau-Ponty, on J. J. Gibson's ecological psychology of perception, and on the work of American pragmatists like Charles Sanders Peirce, William James, and John Dewey. Many of these phenomenologist and enactivist thinkers explore the interface between philosophy and neuroscience inspired by Francisco Varela's call for an interdisciplinary research program he called "neurophenomenology" (1996).[5] On the neuroscientific side, Damasio and Gallese both belong among the researchers who have engaged with phenomenological and pragmatist thought in their deliberations about the relationship between body, mind, and environment.[6] In *Descartes' Error*, Damasio draws on William James's perspective on feelings as a read-out of body states when developing his hypothesis of an "as-if-body-loop" that allows for bodily feelings to be simulated rather than actual, thus foreshadowing the simulation process that a group of neuroscientists around Giacomo Rizzolatti would later attribute to the mirror neuron system—by now one of the most influential, and most contested, findings in cognitive science.[7]

Mirror neurons are cells in our brains that fire both when we carry out an action and when we watch another person carrying out the same action, allowing us to understand the other person's action on a visceral level.[8] Just as important for cultural studies scholars is the finding that the same neurons are also activated when we watch an actor perform the action in a movie or when we read in a novel about a character engaged in that action (Iacoboni 2009, 5). This is perhaps more intuitive in the case of film, where we watch actors perform movements much like we would in real life—a point I will take up in chapter 2. But how is it possible that reading about a character's movements produces the same kind of activation in the mirror neuron system when the only thing we truly "see" is the famous black dots on the white page? The answer lies in the way in which action-related words are processed in our brains. As Gallese sums up the empirical results of several functional neuroimaging (fMRI) studies:

> Silent reading of words referring to face, arm, or leg actions, or listening to sentences expressing actions performed with the mouth, the hand, and the foot, both produce activation of different sectors of the premotor cortex. . . . These activated premotor sectors coarsely correspond to those active during the execution/observation of hand, mouth, and foot actions. Thus, it appears that the MNS [mirror neuron system] is involved not only in understanding visually presented actions, but also in mapping acoustically or visually presented action-related linguistic expressions. (2011, 443)[9]

In the case of reading (or listening), the perception of movement thus plays out on the imaginary level, with our brains reacting much in the same way they would respond to directly perceived or personally performed movement.

Importantly, the mirror system does not only help us recognize the *actions* of others, real and imagined, but also in the attribution of mental states such as *sensations, attitudes,* and *emotions.*[10] "The perception of pain or grief, or of disgust experienced by others," explain Rizzolatti and Corrado Sinigaglia, "activates the same areas of the cerebral cortex that are involved when we experience these emotions ourselves" (2008, xii). Such "feeling with" another person is what we call empathy, and for many researchers our capacity for an empathic response lies at the heart of intersubjectivity. Mirror neurons therefore offer, as neurologist Marco Iacoboni has suggested, "for the first time in history, a plausible neurophysiological explanation for complex forms of social cognition and interaction" (2008, 5–6).[11] They also offer a plausible neurophysiological explanation for Gerrig's observation that we use our own emotions to "give substance to the psychological lives of characters" (17) and for the notion that narrative texts are "instruction manuals" that guide readers' experience of stories.

Needless to say, the use of mirror neuron research in literary studies does have its caveats. As Kuzmičová points out, "in each attempt at fusing literary theoretical speculation with experimental cognitive science, one could identify a host of methodological problems, starting from the fact that the stimuli used in cognitive experiments usually do not bear the slightest resemblance to literary narrative" (2014, 276). Like Kuzmičová, I have chosen to accept most of these problems as a natural part of any interdisciplinary inquiry.[12] While there is reason to be skeptical about naïve celebrations of mirror neurons, empirical research can nevertheless help in substantiating theoretical approaches to narrative.[13] Like all works of art, suggests philosopher William Seeley, literary texts are at heart "communicative devices. They are stimuli intentionally designed to trigger, induce, or evoke perceptual, affective, and cognitive responses sufficient to enable . . . readers to recover their content from information carried in their surface structure" (2016, 270).[14] This is why scientific research on human perception and cognition has proven helpful for narratologists who investigate the communicative properties of literary texts without losing sight of what David Miall calls their "literariness" (2006, 3)—the aesthetic and imaginative qualities that distinguish literature from everyday discourse.[15]

Patrick Colm Hogan, for example, draws on Damasio's clinical research to develop a *perceptual account* of emotion in literary reading. In this account, our emotional response to a literary work is "some version of an empathic response" (2011a, 55) that is triggered by *imagined* perception. Rejecting the appraisal account of emotion that is at the heart of many other simulation theories in literary reading, Hogan argues that "our emotional responses are generated by . . . concrete imaginations and emotional memories, not by inferences as such" (56).[16] I will follow Hogan's perceptual account in this book, accepting that our emotional responses are first and foremost triggered by (real and imagined) perceptions. As in Gerrig's work on transportation and performance, the issue of fictionality is irrelevant in this account, as is the fact that we are not responding to direct perceptual triggers. Instead, our affective response to a literary text is determined by emotional memories we have retained of previous experiences (real and imagined) and by the *vivacity* of the things we imagine while reading.

For a definition of vivacity, Hogan looks to literary scholar Elaine Scarry, who has claimed that it "comes about by reproducing the deep structures of perception" ([1999] 2001, 9). What is simulated in literary reading, argues Scarry, "is not only the sensory outcome (the way something looks or sounds or feels beneath the hands) but the actual structure that gave rise to the perception; that is, the material conditions that made it look, sound, or feel the way it did" (9). There are at least two features of narratives, then, that enable readers to experience what Scarry calls "non-actual, mimetic perception" (9): one is a vivid account of sensory outcomes, the other the evocation of the material conditions that give rise to those outcomes. In the first case, the text cues readers to empathetically share a character's sensations. As Suzanne Keen attests in *Empathy and the Novel,* there is very robust evidence—in part from mirror neuron research—that "readers feel empathy with (and sympathy for) fictional characters" (2007, vii). While empathy refers to a reader's capacity to simulate a character's emotional state (feeling *with*), sympathy denotes that reader's feelings of interest, compassion, and care for that character (feeling *for*). We will see that the latter is often (though not always) a result of the former, but for Scarry's first point, empathy is more crucial because it allows us to understand *what it is like* to undergo a certain sensual experience. Just as the mirror neurons in our brains are activated when we read words that refer to actions, they also respond to words that refer to a character's perception or affective state.[17]

Coming at this phenomenon from an enactivist perspective, Caracciolo suggests that readers relate to the subjective experience of a character either through consciousness-attribution or through consciousness-enactment (2014, 110). In the case of *consciousness-attribution,* the character's words, facial expressions, and actions are rendered from a third-person perspective, and the reader attributes mental states to that character, much like she would in real life. This is what psychologists call mindreading or Theory of Mind (ToM), a process that, according to the cognitive literary scholar Lisa Zunshine, has not only evolutionary relevance but also explains our predilection for reading fiction (2006, 4).[18] In the case of *consciousness-enactment,* the reader is given direct access to a character's consciousness, sharing his perceptions, sensations, thoughts, and emotions, either because the narrative is told from a first-person perspective or because a third-person narrator uses the character as focalizer. This is not possible in real life, yet most readers will find it quite natural to inhabit a literary character's mind. In both cases—consciousness attribution and consciousness enactment—readers will map the sensations, emotions, and movements of a character onto their own brains, thereby understanding, and literally *feeling,* their interaction with the character's environment, its pleasures, and its pain.

This blurring of the distinction between one's own body and that of another—real or imagined—is what Gallese calls embodied simulation. "The sharp distinction, classically drawn between first- and third-person experience of acting and experiencing emotions and sensations," he writes, "appears to be much more blurred at the level of the neural mechanisms mapping it" (2010, 442). Rather than a form of pretense, as critics of the simulation approach have claimed, it must be understood as a "non-conscious, pre-reflective functional mechanism of the brain–body system, whose function is to model objects, agents and events" (Gallese 2014, 3–4).[19] When we engage with narrative art forms such as literary texts, Gallese and the literary scholar Hannah Wojciehowski explain in a cowritten article, "our embodied simulation becomes *liberated,* that is, it is freed from the burden of modeling our actual presence in daily life. . . . Through an immersive state in which our attention is focused on the narrated virtual world, we can fully deploy our simulative resources, letting our defensive guard against daily reality slip for a while" (2011, 19; emphasis mine). This is another way to describe the subjective experience that Gerrig and others who follow his terminology call "transportation." *Transportation* is a misleading term of sorts because it suggests that something moves from point A to point B, and it has led scholars to speculate on whether that something is the reader's consciousness (Ryan 2001, 104) or perhaps her "virtual body" (Caracciolo 2014, 160).[20] In reality, however, nothing at all is transported during the reading process. We only experience the *illusion* of transportation as we focus our attention on the words of a narrative and, as a result, engage in processes of liberated embodied simulation.

The research on embodied simulation also sheds light on Scarry's second claim, which is particularly important for the consideration of environmental narratives: that imagination in literary reading is not limited to the sensory outcomes experienced by characters but also includes "the material conditions that made it look, sound, or feel the way it did" ([1999] 2001, 9). Scarry's readings are strikingly original and poetic, but despite her claims to the contrary, she shows little interest in the insights of contemporary cognitive science in her investigation of how literary art evokes mental images that communicate the solidity and movement of material objects. Research on embodied simulation in language understanding suggests that we do not only *see* such objects before some inner eye but that we literally feel them. Neuroscientist Arthur Jacobs and literary scholar Raoul Schrott explain that "reading the sequence of letters that makes up the word 'radish' causes various sensory-response areas of the brain to become active, while 'ball' also causes movement centers to be active, and 'kiss' serves those that deal with emotions. The brain actually experiences events it is actually only reading about, and this power of simulation (mimesis, reliving) is an important basis of immersion, the neuronal substratum of the 'cinema of the mind'" (2014, 130). How much mimetic detail we need to be able to simulate the perceptual feel of a narrative environment depends on previous experience and related emotional memories—an issue I will take up in later sections of the chapter. But there is no question that we need *some* information about that environment of a narrative in order to experience it vividly.

Narratologists have come to refer to such environments as storyworlds. "In trying to make sense of a narrative," explains David Herman,

> interpreters attempt to reconstruct not just what happened but also the sur-
> rounding context or environment embedding storyworld existents, their
> attributes, and the actions and events in which they are involved. Indeed,
> the grounding of stories in storyworlds goes a long way towards explain-
> ing narratives' immersiveness, their ability to 'transport' interpreters into
> places and times that they must occupy for the purposes of narrative com-
> prehension. Interpreters do not merely reconstruct a sequence of events and
> a set of existents, but imaginatively (emotionally, viscerally) inhabit a world
> in which things matter, agitate, exalt, repulse, provide grounds for laughter
> and grief, and so on—both for narrative participants and for interpreters of
> the story. More than reconstructed timelines and inventories of existents,
> then, storyworlds are mentally and emotionally projected environments in
> which interpreters are called upon to live out complex blends of cognitive
> and imaginative response. (2005, 570)

Herman's argument is in agreement with the theoretical assumptions of much of ecocriticism: that the narrative environments are as important to our understanding of given narrative as are the characters or plot lines; that they may in fact play a central role in both character and plot development. The econarratological approach that Erin James develops in *The Storyworld Accord* (2015) demonstrates the relevance and usefulness of the storyworld concept for ecocritical analysis. Modeling and inhabitation of storyworlds, argues James, "is an inherently *environmental* process, in which readers come to know what it is like to experience a space and time different from that of their reading environment" (2015, xi). Both of Scarry's claims about the vivacity of mimetic sensual perception are of relevance for the imaginary experience of storyworlds that James sees at the heart of the econarratological project. The vivid description of a protagonist's sensations will help readers imagine *what it is like* to experience that alternative world. However, the emotional and visceral inhabitation of a storyworld is also depended on the vivid evocation of the material conditions that provoke that sensual experience.

Such evocation may be channeled through the mind of the protagonist or it may be given independently. Readers can simulate perceptual experience, argues Caracciolo, "even in the absence of fictional characters to which they could attribute that experience" (2014, 103). This is an important point that begs the question of whose perceptual experience we simulate whenever we are not bound to the qualia of a character. For Caracciolo, it is the reader's own virtual body that is transported into the narrative world and that then does what he calls *hypothetical* perceiving (103).[21] But as readers we rarely believe that a virtual version of our own bodies is physically present in the storyworld of a narrative. There are other, and I think better, ways to account for our ability to simulate perception in the absence of a perceiving character. One has been provided by the narratologist James Phelan, who has argued that narrators can be focalizers (2001, 289). Against accounts that claim that narrators cannot personally perceive the storyworld on which they report because they are "never part of the diegesis" (Prince 2001, 47), Phelan asserts that such a limitation of the epistemological abilities of narrators "fails to explain their ability to influence the perception of *narratees,* implied audiences, and flesh and blood readers" (2001, 51). In Phelan's account, it is the narrator's perception that readers simulate in moments when the text doesn't invite them to engage with the perceptual experience of a fictional character. This thought is productive not only for the analysis of a fictional text such as Nadzam's *Lamb,* which features an ambiguous narrative voice that at times conveys a decidedly experiential feel of the novel's virtual environment. It is helpful also for a better understanding of the narrative strategies of nature writing, which often renders environmental experience from a first-person perspective. A typical example is John Muir's *The Mountains of California,* which boasts an abundance of mimetic sensory content, enabling readers to imaginatively see, hear, smell, touch, taste, and therefore *feel* its title-giving material object. Muir's sometimes rapturous writing about the California mountains invites us to turn our attention to "the self-consciousness of the narrator" (Phelan 2001, 52) and to the way both material objects and subjective sensual experience are conveyed in ways that allow readers to come into imaginative contact with an environment that once existed (and, in different form, continues to exist). "The crucial point about nature writing," observes ecocritic Thomas J. Lyon, "is the awakening of perception to an ecological way of seeing" (2001, x). That makes it an ideal starting point for an investigation of the role played by embodied simulation and imaginary perception in our affective engagement with environmental narrative and of the narrative impact that such engagements can have on readers' attitudes.

SENSING THE ENVIRONMENT: THE AFFECTIVE APPEALS OF MUIR'S *MOUNTAINS OF CALIFORNIA*

John Muir was a very emotional and, at the same time, a very strategic writer. His nature essays bear witness to his topophilic attachment to the Sierra Nevada and other "wild" places in the American West, and yet they are almost always written with a very specific purpose. That purpose was, writes ecocritic Terry Gifford, "to encourage his readers to share his sense of religious awe and respect for nature in order to want to participate in its conservation" (2006, 49). Awe is a word that Gifford frequently uses in his comments on Muir's writing style, and although it can only be found occasionally in Muir's own texts, it describes well the mixture of amazement, enthusiasm, and reverence that pervades them as he tries to convey both the material qualities and the sensual experience of the California wilderness.

Conveying the material qualities and sensual feel of a natural environment in a way that enables readers to imaginatively experience them is not an easy task, but if nature writing is any indication, intimate knowledge of and personal passion for that environment are what enables authors to succeed in it. Tuan describes topophilia as something "vivid and concrete" (1974, 4), and such topophilic attachment fuels the literary imaginations of many nature writers, regardless of whether the environments they engage with are woodlands, mountains, or deserts. Patrick Hogan reminds us that "the reader's simulation [of a narrative world] is presupposed by the author's simulation, for the author incorporates a receptive simulation in anticipating the emotional effect of the work" (2013, 6). In the case of a nonfiction genre such as nature writing, the author's simulation during the writing process involves the vivid memory (often aided by notes) of concrete experience. The task is to put those memories into words in a way that will allow readers to simulate it in vivid and emotionally engaging ways. Muir was no stranger to the creative difficulties that can arise when the tools available do not seem adequate to that task. Gifford reminds us that his "early frustration at the limits of human discourse arose out of a deep sense of the richness of relations in the natural world he wanted to mediate" (Gifford 2011, para. 10). He often struggled with translating his experiences to the page, and yet he ended up writing down hundreds of thousands of words in the hope that this would lead his fellow Americans to develop a topophilic attachment to the Sierra Nevada and other wilderness areas he sought to protect.

Muir became a celebrated nature writer and environmental activist only relatively late in life, and although he was a rich man by any definition when he died, he started out from a position of emotional poverty. Leaving behind a traumatic childhood in Scotland and years of abuse as a "plowboy" on his father's farm in Wisconsin, he spent four years at the University of Wisconsin to study "chemistry . . . mathematics and physics, a little Greek and Latin, botany and geology" and then decided to exchange that campus for the much larger and extensive one of "the University of the Wilderness" (Muir 1913).[22] After some time in Canada, his legendary one thousand-mile walk from Indiana to Florida, and a brief stint in Cuba, Muir came to California in 1868 to explore Yosemite Valley. Over the years he wrote numerous magazine articles about his long walks across the Western mountain ranges as well as the geological and natural history of the region. He was already in his mid-fifties when he assembled some of his earlier writings in *The Mountains of California,* the first of several books and, according to environmental historian Donald Worster, "the best of the bunch, an enduring classic of American nature writing" (2011, 339).

A typical example of Muir's style, *The Mountains of California* mixes the recounting of personal experience with scientific observation and rapturous celebration. Readers are directly addressed in the very first sentence of the book: "Go where you may in the bounds of California," writes Muir, "mountains are ever in sight, charming and glorifying every landscape" (1894). He then asks readers to situate themselves imaginatively on "the summit of any of the peaks or passes opposite San Francisco" on a "clear spring day" and proceeds to describe what they will see:

> At your feet lies the Central Valley, glowing golden in the sunshine, extending north and south farther than the eye can reach, one smooth, flowery, lake-like bed of fertile soil. Along its eastern edges rises the mighty Sierra, miles in height, reposing like a smooth, cumulus cloud in the sunny sky, and so gloriously colored, and so luminous, it seems to be not clothed with light, but wholly composed of it like the outer wall of some celestial city. Along the top, and extending a good way down, you see a pale, pearl-gray belt of snow; and below it a belt of blue and dark purple, marking the extension of the forests; and along the base of the range a broad belt of rose-purple and yellow, where lie the miner's gold-fields and the foothill gardens. (1894, para. 2)

The passage is an "instruction manual" in the most obvious way, instructing readers to simulate the *visual* appearance of the California landscape in their minds. With the exception of the term "celestial," nearly every word contributes to the creation of visual imagery. Not only does it describe the quality of the light (it's sunny) and the dominant color impression of the valley (it's golden), the text also conveys the appearance of its flatness and large extension (farther than the eye can see) as well as the contrast with the colorful towering wall of the mountains, which seem solid (mighty) and insubstantial (seemingly composed of light) at the same time.[23]

The cognitive literary scholar Gabrielle Starr reminds us that while several kinds of nonvisual imagery can be found in literary texts, "visual imagery, like visual activity, plays perhaps the largest sensory role in our imaginative economies and is often experienced as having the greatest vivacity" (2010, 277). Even readers who have never seen the Central Valley or the Sierra Nevada have a decent chance at creating a vivid image of it in their minds, because Muir provides them with powerful visual imagery. Scarry has argued that writers such as Homer use qualities like "radiant ignition" ([1999] 2001, 77) and "rarity" (89) to make solid objects seem so vibrant and airy that they suggest movement. Muir seems to be just after this effect when he writes that the Sierra is "so gloriously colored, and so luminous, it seems to be not clothed with light, but wholly composed of it" (1894). The mountain range here loses its solidity to a degree that, to the experiencer, it seems to aspire to the sky—and indeed to heaven. The passage also suggests movement in the form of a slowly wandering gaze that first scans the extent of the valley from side to side, then moves up to the mountains, scans sideways again along the range, and slowly down until it reaches the foothills. It explicitly asks readers to imagine *themselves* standing there, and so this is one of the rare instances where readers— following the instructions of the text—are indeed likely to project their own virtual bodies into its imaginary environment, as Caracciolo has suggested. Yet we can also explain the phenomenon in terms of focalization. "Determining focalization," writes Phelan, "is just a matter of answering the question *who perceives?*" (2001, 58), and in this case the reader is explicitly invited to become the perceiver as indicated by the use of the second-person pronoun. This is a common feature of guidebooks and other nonfiction genres that seek to provide readers with a sense of immediacy and self-involvement. As ecocritic Scott Slovic remarks with reference to the work of nature writer Barry Lopez, the choice of the second person offers the author "a way to make his experience the reader's as well" (1992, 160). While readers will always simulate narrative worlds and events in their minds, narrative perspective inflects the vivacity of that simulation. Slovic suggests that "occasional shifts into the second person serve as attempts to bridge the distance between author and reader, to make the anecdote particularly tangible for the reader" (160). All of this applies to Muir's use of direct address in the opening passage of *The Mountains of California,* which serves to "transport" readers quickly into the narrative world and to seduce them into wanting to learn more.

Whether that attempt at seduction is successful depends on a number of factors, among them readers' willingness to focus their attention on the text and their personal predilection for nature descriptions. A contemporary college student might find Muir's style outdated and his subject matter boring, experiencing low levels of transportation and immersion and therefore a low degree of sensual and emotional involvement. As Philip Mazzocco and his collaborators have shown, individual "transportability" into a narrative world can vary considerably among actual readers, and such variations predict not only emotional engagement but also attitude and belief change in response to stories (2010, 361). Readers may actively resist a given text, they may be distracted, or they may happen to dislike detailed nature descriptions for their lack of dramatic action. In such cases, it is unlikely that they will feel transported into Muir's narrative world, which, as Mazzocco et al. note, involves an "integrative melding of attention, imagery, and emotion" (361). Unless, that is, they come across something that piques their interest.

It is important to note that the opening passage of *The Mountains of California* does not actually provide a very detailed description. We do not learn about any people or animals in the valley or about the crops, houses, and streets we are looking at. Nor do we receive information about the height and shape of the mountain peaks or the exact appearance of the foothill gardens. Instead, Muir provides us with strong sensual imagery that invites us to imagine a landscape that is beautiful and enticing. Rich descriptive detail can greatly aid in the mental effort of simulation—especially if readers are not personally familiar with the object described—but, as Kuzmičová has argued, "there is no straightforward relation between the degree of detail in spatial description on one hand, and the vividness of spatial imagery and presence on the other" (2012, 23). Rather, the illusion of presence arises from complex processes of sensorimotor simulation and resonance.[24] Muir is a master of detailed description, but in this opening passage, he uses a different narrative strategy. Rather than offering an accurate "snapshot" of the landscape, he provides readers with emotionally salient visual cues intended to evoke a sense of awe, beauty, and pleasure.

Aesthetic experience, argues Starr, always "engages the senses (as well as sensory analogues in imagination) and we are not indifferent to that experience. Sensory perceptions are blended with emotions, and with sensations of pleasure and displeasure—but aesthetic experience also engages personal experience, prior knowledge, and evaluative judgements" (2013, 18). Muir's description of the Central Valley as a "smooth, flowery, lake-like bed of fertile soil" that is "glowing golden in the sunshine" (1894, para. 2) evokes sensual perceptions that for most humans will be pleasing, not least because it suggests an environment that sustains human life. Just as important, however, is the affective valence of the reader's imaginary physical position. Easterlin cites research in ecological psychology finding "that the disposition of elements in the environment is often of more importance than the presence or absence of a specific feature (e.g., trees or water) to the affective and cognitive response of the organism" (2012, 121). With reference to a study by Stephen Kaplan (1992) on the human preference for savannah scenes, she concludes that "preference determination [is] relative to where the human subject imagined him- or herself to be situated within the scene" (Easterlin 2012, 121).[25] Muir situates his readers on a lofty height and thus in a perfect position to survey the landscape. Research on the power dynamics involved in such an "imperial gaze" goes back at least to Mary Louise Pratt, but Easterlin suggests that "the ability to assess the environment quickly" (2012, 121) is another important reason why we tend to find the top-down view from an airy height attractive.[26]

Arguably, the spatial distance that comes from such a position also contributes to a sense of pleasure because it avoids the sensation of scorching heat that is so typical of the Central Valley as well as a closer look at the labor performed on what at this time was mostly wheat fields.[27] Muir only implicitly addresses this issue when, in the following paragraph, he shifts readers' attention to his own persona and to an earlier time. "When I first enjoyed this view," he writes, "one glorious April day, from the summit of the Pacheco Pass, the Central Valley, but little trampled or plowed as yet, was one furred, rich sheet of golden compositæ, and the luminous wall of the mountains shone in all its glory" (1894, para. 3). This, in essence, is the same scene that he previously asked readers to imagine, making obvious the fact that he used his own real-world experience in the creation of the imaginary scene. Of course, what he recounts is remembered experience rather than immediate experience. His narrative persona nevertheless functions as the perceiving agent and thus as focalizer, inviting readers to see and—most importantly—*feel* along with him when he now expresses his misgivings about the agricultural development that has changed the face of the landscape. In the final chapter of the book, Muir will return to the Central Valley and openly complain about the fact that "of late years plows and sheep have made sad havoc in these glorious pastures, destroying tens of thousands of the flowery acres like a fire, and banishing many species of the best honey-plants to rocky cliffs and fence-corners" (1894, para. 3). Between these two peeks at the cultivated expanse of the valley lies an in-depth exploration of his beloved "Range of Light," which he was determined to protect from such human cultivation.

Muir had retained from his college days a passion for science, and so during much of the book he piles on facts and figures about the Sierra Nevada with an abundance of descriptive detail.[28] At the same time, he tried to instill in his readers a "loving conception" (Worster 2011, 339) of the natural world, and he regularly did this by gushing about the awe-inspiring beauty of the landscape, asking them to simulate his own awareness and topophilic attachment. An intriguing example is chapter 10 of *The Mountains of California*—the often-anthologized "A Wind-Storm in the Forests"—which aims to give readers a sense of *what it is like* to hold on to the top of a hundred-foot-tall Douglas spruce in the middle of a storm. Before he gets to that "beautiful and exhilarating" moment (1894, para. 6), however, Muir takes time to give readers an understanding of the elemental forces that shape the forests. "The mountain winds," he writes, "like the dew and rain, sunshine and snow, are measured and bestowed with love on the forests to develop their strength and beauty. . . . The snow bends and trims the upper forests every winter, the lightning strikes a single tree here and there, while avalanches mow down thousands at a swoop as a gardener trims out a bed of flowers" (1894, para. 1). The passage is characterized by the reverential posture that is so typical of Muir's prose and by what Gifford calls his "sentimental personifications" (2011). However, what he describes could also be considered a form of material agency, since forces such as the wind, snow, lightening, and avalanches all physically work on and shape the forest.[29] Even as he seems to suggest that a benevolent God-like figure controls the whole process, Muir without doubt recognized and respected the agency of nonhuman entities.

Even more important for my context here are the verbs that he uses to describe that agency. As Starr reminds us, several kinds of nonvisual imagery can be found in literary texts: "olfactory, concerning smell and sometimes taste; haptic, concerning grasp and touch; motor kinesthetic, concerning movement and sometimes proprioception (perception of one's own body position)" (2010, 275–76). Muir mostly uses visual imagery relating to movement and touch in this passage—the snow *bends* and *trims,* lightning *strikes,* and avalanches *mow down.* This brings me to Gregory Currie's intriguing claim that "some simulative processes are recruited to both personal empathy [with other humans] and empathy for objects" (2011, 86). Currie finds support for his position not only in the work of early Empathists such as Theodor Lipps (1903–1906) and Herbert Langfeld (1920), but also in an fMRI study conducted by Keysers et al., which shows that the secondary somatosensory cortex is activated not only in response to physical touch and the sight of other people being touched, but also by watching an inanimate object being touched by another inanimate object (2004, 339).[30] Gallese has coauthored several studies with the art historian David Freedberg that demonstrate the importance of embodied simulation in our understanding of motion representations, including the motion of inanimate objects. While most of these studies refer to visual perception, research on liberated embodied simulation suggests that action-related linguistic expressions will be processed in a similar way (Gallese 2010).[31] Reading that the snow *bends* and *trims,* lightning *strikes,* and avalanches *mow down* the forests will activate the somatosensory and motor cortices in readers' brains, regardless of the fact that these actions are attributed to nonhuman agents. Muir's use of personification thus contributes to the vivacity of the events he describes, allowing readers to understand on a visceral level the dynamism of nature.

Gifford has argued that "Muir travels into the world to physically enter the elements at their most dynamic, to learn about those processes from the heart of the storm, the earthquake, the waterfall, the avalanche, the ice flow, the mountain range" (2006, 20). That need is nowhere more obvious than in his recounting of his experience of riding a storm-battered tree in the dramatic climax of the chapter. After walking in the woods for hours in the storm, Muir finally picks "the tallest of a group of Douglas Spruces . . . rocking and swirling in wild ecstasy" (1894, para. 9). He climbs his chosen tree and stays there for the remainder of the storm:

> Never before did I enjoy so noble an exhilaration of motion. The slender tops fairly flapped and swished in the passionate torrent, bending and swirling backward and forward, round and round, tracing indescribable combinations of vertical and horizontal curves, while I clung with muscles firm braced, like a bobo-link on a reed. In its widest sweeps my tree-top described an arc of from twenty to thirty degrees, but I felt sure of its elastic temper. . . . My eye roved over the piney hills and dales as over fields of waving grain, and felt the light running in ripples and broad swelling undulations across the valleys from ridge to ridge, as the shining foliage was stirred by corresponding waves of air. (1894, para. 9–10)

Everything in this passage invites readers to simulate motion. Packed with visual and motor imagery, it helps them to both *see* and *feel* the situation: the big trees bending, flapping, and swishing in the storm, the rhythm and repetition of words—"backwards and forwards, round and round"—intensifying the sensation of motion. The first-person perspective allows readers to *also* share

Muir's subjective experience of that moment, simulating his exhilarating sensations of motion, touch, and proprioception as he "clings with muscles firm braced" to the elastic wood of the tree top, as well as his visual perception of the storm-battered forest. In case readers have never beheld such a sight, the text offers the metaphor of "fields of waving grain," cueing us to imagine wind gusts so mighty that the sturdy trees are swaying back and forth like feeble wheat.[32]

Embodied simulation is a pre-reflective functional mechanism of the brain–body system, and so not all of this will be entirely conscious. Kuzmičová rightly points out that we must not conflate embodied simulation with mental imagery (which by definition is conscious) although the two are closely related (2014, 279). She also reminds us of the fact that "the presence of an experiencer" is a prerequisite of what she calls "enactment-imagery" (282). Alan Palmer goes one step further, claiming that "events only have significance if they are *experienced by actors*. It is difficult to imagine a narrative that consisted entirely, for example, of descriptions of natural events in which no person was present to experience those events" (2004, 30). From an ecocritical point of view, this comes across as a deeply anthropocentric stance, and so it all hinges on the definition of what constitutes a person and on whether or not we consider the narrator an experiencer, as Phelan has argued we should. It is hard to dispute that it takes *some kind* of experiencing mind to tell a story about nature or anything at all, just as it takes one to perceive and mentally perform that story.

The presence of a protagonist in a given scene allows readers to relate to it differently than they would without a focalizer who is physically present in the storyworld. Had Muir not placed his experiencing I into the midst of the storm, readers would still be able to imagine the scene in accordance with his instructions, but they would not have the added thrill of simulating the subjective experience of someone who rides a tree in a storm. While on the first pages of his book Muir seeks to create immediacy by asking readers to imagine *themselves* being present in the landscape he describes, he now uses the bodily presence of his own younger self to allow them to come "as close as one possibly can to forgetting that the experience [is] in fact mediated by a string of words on a page" (Kuzmičová 2014, 283). Because there is no sharp distinction "between first- and third-person experience of acting and experiencing emotions and sensations . . . at the level of the neural mechanisms mapping it," as Gallese has explained (2010, 442), most readers will make no conscious distinction between simulating Muir's foregrounded subjective experience of riding the tree and the more oblique outer perspective also provided, which cues them to see a tiny figure on the wildly bending tree—like a bird on a

reed. This fluidity of perspective seems peculiar to the verbal arts, where readers and listeners are given considerable freedom not only in how they imagine the things described but also in the perspective they assume at any given
point.[33] In this case, it serves to increase the sense of wild and potentially
dangerous motion and the resulting emotional response. Both the bird-reed
metaphor and the metaphor of waving grain serve to diminish the solidity of
the material trees on the imaginary level, thus further enhancing the sensation
of motion in the reader's mind.

Although it was authentic, Muir's relating of his own visceral and spiritual
experience of the Sierra Nevada served a strategic purpose. His exhilaration
and awe were intended to be infectious, writes Gifford, "and would later provide the foundation for appeals to a commitment to conservation in his readers" (2006, 49). In this, he was spectacularly successful. Although he is rarely
ranked among the best nature writers, Muir certainly was one of the most
influential ones. His writings led thousands of Americans to visit Yosemite
Valley and other wilderness areas in the West, and they were instrumental
in his political battles for the conservation of these places, leading to the creation of several national parks and the founding of the Sierra Club. "More
than any comparable figure," writes his biographer Steven Holmes, "Muir's
cultural influence has been expressed in a series of vivid images of his personal relationships with particular natural places" (1999, 3). The sensual vivacity of those images allows readers to feel "transported" into the environments
he evokes for them, and recent research in social psychology suggests that
narratives "tend to be more persuasive when they elicit from recipients a state
of psychological transportation" (Mazzocco et al. 2010, 361). There is now a
substantial amount of evidence that readers who feel more transported and
thus more emotionally engaged exhibit greater attitude and belief change in
response to narratives.[34] A 2012 study by Green, Chatham, and Sestir shows
that a greater sense of transportation leads to stronger emotional engagement
and that this is true for both fiction and nonfiction, although the researchers
speculate that "it is possible that the emotional effects of a fictional story may
disappear more quickly than those of a factual story" (54–55). In the case of
Muir's creative nonfiction on the Sierra Nevada, the persuasive effects were
long term, aided by his activism in the political arena and by the fact that he
was integrated into a larger network of like-minded people who advocated
conservation.

Gifford argues that despite these political usages, "Muir's emphasis on the
sensual, on the value of direct experience, on his use of the imagination, and
on the need for a spiritual appreciation of scientific knowledge places his discourse in the realm of the aesthetic" (2006, 52). While I greatly appreciate

his thoughtful analysis of Muir's writings, I believe that the cognitive reading I have offered casts a critical light on Gifford's related claim that aesthetic
experience is "essentially noncognitive," leading "to an apprehension that goes
beyond the cognitive perception of a creative-destructive nature in which we
are embedded" (52). The notion of noncognitive experience strikes me as an
oxymoron, since experience per se is cognitive—even though, as we have seen,
not all cognition is necessarily conscious. Scott Slovic has argued that nature
writers "are constantly probing, traumatizing, thrilling, and soothing their
minds—and by extension those of their readers—in quest not only of consciousness itself, but of an *understanding* of consciousness" (1996, 352). One of
the chief preoccupations of such writers, he states, is the raising of awareness
of the natural world, and awareness means paying attention to one's conscious
experience. That experience can take place in a seemingly pristine wilderness area such as the Sierra Nevada, but for most of us, most of the time, it
unfolds in less pristine places where the boundary between nature and culture
is impossible to define. Raising awareness, therefore, also means paying attention to the ways in which the wilderness idea can be a sham.

In his seminal 1996 essay "The Trouble with Wilderness," the environmental historian William Cronon famously criticizes the notion of wilderness
for its reliance on a false dichotomy between nature and culture as well as its
dependence on American frontier nostalgia. Expanding on Cronon's critique,
ecofeminists have debunked the concept as a fundamentally male construct
that celebrates rugged (white) masculinity to the exclusion of other perspectives. In response to such criticisms, the past twenty years have seen the steady
incorporation of the work of women and minority writers into anthologies of
American nature writing.[35] In his contribution to the *Oxford Handbook of Ecocriticism* (2014), Richard Kerridge goes one step further, including both nonfiction and fiction under the umbrella term of nature writing and citing Jean
Sprackland's *Strands* as an example of "new nature writing," which is "concerned with the disorderly and dirty 'edgelands' between human society and
the natural wild, rather than with wilderness as separate space" (374). Bonnie
Nadzam's novel *Lamb,* to which I will now turn, similarly questions the validity of such binaries, and it also demonstrates that narratives must neither be
factual nor realist in order to vividly evoke natural environments. *Lamb* is a
story about the power of the imaginative worlds that can be induced and sustained by narrative even in the face of evidence to the contrary. Its title-giving
protagonist, David Lamb, is a narcissist and pathological liar, someone who
uses stories to seduce people into admiring him and to keep the gaping emp-
tiness at bay that threatens to swallow his fragile ego. The stories he tells are
about the unfathomable beauty and healing power of the Rocky Mountains,

about love and friendship, about a simple true life that can only be lived in the wilderness, away from the gray concrete of the city. They are well-tried stories within the nature-writing tradition at least since Thoreau and Muir, but nothing in this novel is ever what it seems to be. Neither Lamb's captive audience—the eleven-year-old girl Tommie, whom he abducts from her home outside Chicago to take to his cabin in the Rockies—nor the reader can ever be fully certain where the fiction ends and reality begins.

FASCINATING STORYWORLDS: PERSPECTIVES ON FACT AND FICTION IN BONNIE NADZAM'S *LAMB*

One of *Lamb*'s most striking features is the ambiguity of its narrative voice, which seems unreliable and knowledgeable, detached and involved, at the same time. I want to begin with a consideration of this feature, not only because it significantly inflects the evocation of the novel's urban and natural environments, but also because it emerges on the novel's very first page:

> We'll say this all began just outside of Chicago, in late summer on a residen-
> tial street dead-ending in a wall. It was the kind of wall meant to hide free-
> ways from view, and for miles in each direction parallel streets ended at the
> same concrete meridian. No trees on the lawn, no birds on the wires. North-
> ern shrikes gone, little gray-bellied wrens gone. Evening grosbeaks and elm
> trees and most of the oaks and all the silver brooms of tall grass and bunch
> flowers and sweetfern and phlox gone. Heartsease gone. About the tops of
> upturned trash bins, black flies scripted the air. (2011, 1)

At this point most readers will likely assume that they are dealing with a first-person narrator. This is suggested by the colloquial tone imitating oral speech and by the fact that the narrator is prefacing her/his story with a casual "we'll say," thereby pointing to the narrative's fictionality and potential unreliability. The "feel" of a first-person narrator is also created by the considerable ecological knowledge displayed in these first sentences, and by the implied complaint about the observed biodiversity loss in this suburban space located next to a busy thoroughfare. All of this suggests a consciousness that participates in the story, as a protagonist would, or at least one that will introduce herself/himself as a specific person that stands in some kind of relation to the people in his/her story. But none of this is the case. While the narrator clearly is a perceiving consciousness, s/he never reveals his/her identity and also never takes part in the story.[36]

Nadzam's narrator might therefore be understood as an instance of what the narratologist Harry Shaw has called "loose narrators"—auctorial narrators that at times seem to be able to enter the storyworld and thus directly perceive and experience whatever is happening there. Against strict differentiations between story space (in which protagonists go through events) and discourse space (in which narrators report on those events), Shaw argues that "such categorical distinctions are likely to fade at moments at which the narrator's presence seems overwhelmingly palatable. The narrator becomes much more than a reporter, peering over the hedge of an estate he cannot enter and telling us what transpires there. At such moments, narrators seem to break loose from the discourse space" (1995, 95).[37] Phelan is even more radical than Shaw, arguing that *all* narrators "can—and do—perceive, can and do act as our lenses on the story world, [even] without being physically present in it" (2001, 58). This is why, in his view, they can function as focalizers, allowing readers to simulate their perception at moments when no perceiving agent is located within the storyworld. This certainly is true for a nonfiction narrative such as Muir's *The Mountains of California,* which alternates between passages that feature Muir's younger self as an experiencer who is physically present in the storyworld and passages in which it is Muir's narrating I who acts as our lens on that world. The situation becomes trickier in the case of fiction, where storyworlds may be partially or wholly invented. But in the end, the same logic applies. Unless we follow Caracciolo's suggestion that it is the reader's own virtual body who engages in an act of "hypothetical perception" (2014, 103), we must assume that in Nadzam's opening scene it is the narrator whose perceiving "presence seems overwhelmingly palatable" (Shaw 1995, 95) and who chooses to provide us mostly with information about what *isn't* there.

A reader's imagination is literally teased in these first few lines as the narrator spells out the names of birds and plants, only to follow up with the information about their absence: "Northern shrikes *gone,* little gray-bellied wrens *gone.* Evening grosbeaks and elm trees and most of the oaks and all the silver brooms of tall grass and bunch flowers and sweetfern and phlox *gone*" (Nadzam 2011, 1). Even though most readers may not know these species well enough to have an exact picture in mind, the naming of birds, trees, and flowers nevertheless immediately evokes images of living nature, just to subtract them again with the very next word: *gone.* It is an interesting technique that in the smallest possible space conjures the image of both wilderness and its destruction. Despite its sparseness, the passage offers a clear "instruction manual," asking readers to imagine an environment that, with the exception of the lawn and the black flies, is devoid of nature, thereby instilling a sense of loss. There is something lacking in this environment, so much so that it is not even worth or possible to describe it in any detail. While readers' mental simulation of the scene may vary widely, it will most likely be one of deprivation—a theme that foreshadows the dramatic events of the story.

In the very next sentence, the narrator makes it obvious that s/he is relying on readers' faculties of mental simulation and previous experience in order to bring this story to life: "Imagine the corner of a house made of white brick and aluminum siding the color of yellow mud. Inside an old man sat in a dim-lit television room, tipped back his La-Z-Boy, a box of microwaved chicken balanced on his sunken chest" (2). The shift in narrative perspective is remarkable here, as the narrator suddenly uses present tense and addresses the reader directly, literally telling her what to imagine much in the way Muir does. The instruction manual is once again a minimalist one, including very few details and thus allowing for a lot of freedom in the reader's mental simulation of the visual appearance of the house. Just as abruptly, the narrative shifts back into past tense, closing in on the old man who we will later learn is David Lamb's father and who will be dead very soon.

Lamb is a fifty-four-year-old man in a major life crisis. Not only does his father die at the outset of the story, his wife has recently left him, his house is on the market, and his sexual relationship with his coworker Linnie is no longer new or exciting. David needs things to be new and exciting, and he needs them to revolve around himself. Whenever that doesn't happen and his grandiose self-image deflates, he creates a new narrative. His storytelling is as narcissistic as it is convincing, and this is true not only for the stories he constantly tells himself, but also for his emotional manipulation of others. In his desperation, he focuses his attention on the unassuming Tommie, whom he first meets in a parking lot after the funeral of his father, when she tries to scrounge a cigarette off him. Lamb looks at the "pale little freckled pig with eyelashes," her "ratty and chewed fingernails," and feels "a little sick" (2011, 10). Yet he immediately senses that the "ugly kid" (12) will be an easy victim for his charms and thus will provide him with much-needed adulation. On a whim, he pretends to abduct the girl, only to drive her to the run-down apartment building she calls home. "It wasn't kidnapping," he later tells himself (18), and apparently Tommie sees it the same way. From now on they meet regularly: the shy, introvert girl and the middle-aged man who uses stories much in the way an addict uses a drug.

Lamb looks at Tommie with a mixture of fondness, hate, and condescension, and he is convinced he can give her something she lacks. "Your face needs a line of broken-toothed mountains behind it," he tells her, "A girl like you needs a swimming hole. A river. Trees and clear skies" (25). Although Tommie is "practically the only living person" he knows (27), Lamb feels certain that the deadening concrete of the city will smother her life force and that she needs "something else to steer by. Something other than this. A person who—as it turned out—had both the resources and inclination to do so" (28). That person is he, and so he begins to feed the girl stories about his cabin in the wilderness, explicit instruction manuals for her young mind:

> He sat opposite her on the tailgate [of his car], his legs stretched out alongside hers, his boots at her hip. He cracked open his own soda; it hissed. "This is out in a high, wide valley," he said. "Okay? Really high. Thousands of feet."
> "Okay."
> "Can you see it?" He paused, drinking. "Acres of pale grass. Almost gray. Big knots of sliver brush. We call that sage."
> "I know that."
> "Good. Picture that. And one house. A little one, whitewashed. A slash of dark green half a mile off where the cottonwoods and tamarack grow by the river. Can you see all of that?"
> "Yes." (31–32)

Just like Muir in the opening of *The Mountains of California*, Lamb uses mostly visual imagery in his description of the valley, perhaps because he knows from experience that it is the most vivid in a listener's mind and therefore the most effective in storytelling. Also like Muir, he focuses on impressions of color and light, and he addresses his audience directly, asking Tommie to "see" and "picture" in her mind the objects he describes.

Kuzmičová reminds us that "the workings of . . . audial media are often environment-sensitive" (2015, 291) in that outward stimuli can interfere with processes of liberated embodied simulation when we listen to a story by demanding our sensory attention. Lamb shows awareness of this, too, instructing Tommie to close her eyes and asking whether she is paying attention before he proceeds to evoke a "small sliding window that looks out over the water tank for the old ragged horse we keep. And Tommie, let me tell you something: this is a horse you really love" (Nadzam 2011, 33). Again like Muir, Lamb instructs the girl to imagine her own physical presence in his idyllic storyworld, only that he goes so far as to also dictate her affective response. The similarities between this passage and Muir's text continue to the point that the invitation to feel transported into a colorful valley is part of a larger attempt at persuasion. Yet, what is different is not only that Lamb's audience is physically present but also that his act of narrative persuasion serves a self-centered purpose. Whereas Muir was using his alluring narrative to support nature conservation efforts, Lamb wants to instill in Tommie's young mind a desire to do—with him—exactly what he describes, and so he instructs her how to feel about his storyworld just like he instructs her how to hold the cigarette as he lights it, where to look on the road, and how to feel about *him*.

The narrator uses Lamb as a focalizer throughout this passage, and since readers have direct access to his consciousness through free indirect discourse, they likely will feel alarmed by his glances at the girl's "skinny bare legs" (31), his sudden impulse "to strike her, imprint her with a bruise in the shape of his hand" (29), and the fact that he calls himself "Gary," thus hiding his true identity. At this point in the story, it is impossible for them to determine what his motives are. His obsessively repeated intention is that he just wants to give the girl a glimpse of "what she was missing" (28), but he also entertains fantasies that suggest he is planning to abuse her once they are alone in the wilderness. Tommie's mind is not accessible to readers. Whereas they are invited to *enact* Lamb's consciousness, they can only ever *attribute* consciousness to the girl, using clues from her dialogue and behavior just as they would in real-life processes of mindreading. What is different from real life, however, is the unreliable focalization of such clues. Every attempt at attributing consciousness to the girl, and to explain her often sudden decisions, her passivity, and her seeming naiveté, is filtered through Lamb's obsessive urge to understand everything and everyone only in terms of himself. And although readers may quickly see through this psychological pathology, their cognition remains nevertheless bound to it.

One seeming exception to this rule occurs when Lamb drops Tommie off in front of her desolate apartment building at the end of their second meeting. The passage is told by an ambiguous voice that might belong to the consciousness of the narrator or (perhaps more likely) glimpse into Lamb's head as the narrator renders his thoughts in free indirect discourse:

> The dear girl. How could she not carry Lamb with her, all the grassy fields he painted hanging between her little face and the world, bright screens printed with the images he made for her: flashes of green and silver; huge birds circling in the wind; the brown eye of a horse; yellow eggs on a breakfast dish; the curve of their backs atop a weathered rail fence on a cool blue morning. (36)

Whether it is Lamb thinking of himself in the third person or the narrator commenting on the events is impossible to decide. And yet the speaker makes clear that the novel's title is not only synonymous with its protagonist's last name but applies to Tommie as well. The deprived girl emerges as a helpless victim of Lamb's devouring storytelling, defenseless against the enticing images of a good and simple life in the mountain wilderness he has planted into her mind. Packed with visual imagery, the passage describes with almost scientific detail the process of embodied simulation while at the same time allowing readers to simulate along with Tommie an imaginary experience of the Rocky Mountains. It is both an affective evocation of nature and a comment on storytelling's power to evoke nature in the minds of others in emotionally salient ways.

The narrator then shifts the focus back to Lamb, who looks on as Tommie waits "in the dirty yellow light for the elevator doors to open" (36). When she steps into the elevator, the narration follows her although Lamb can no longer see her. From now on everything she says, does, feels, and thinks is rendered a subjunctive mood, suggesting once again fictionality, speculation, and potential unreliability. We learn that "she'd travel up the nine floors with a skinny boy whose face was lumpy and red with acne. He lived on fourteen" (36). Lamb cannot really know this, nor can he know that Tommie "would stare ahead until the boy spat across the car to the dented steel wall upon which she had fixed her gaze" or that in response she "would shut her eyes, the bees and the white heads of flowers nodding in the warm daylight and the silhouette of Gary's baseball cap written across the inside of her skull" (36). The use of the subjunctive creates an epistemological ambiguity, suggesting that none of this is necessarily happening. When Tommie enters the apartment and engages in a brief dialogue with her indifferent mother about where she has been, this might represent Tommie's actual experience or be part of a fantasy that Lamb needs to justify before himself his strong desire to take the girl with him to the Rocky Mountains. It does not make a difference in terms of readers' neural responses. Even if they decide that they are enacting Lamb's imaginary enactment of Tommie's potential experience, and thus a fantasy, they will still engage in the same processes of liberated embodied simulation when they read that "Tommie would go into the bathroom and move all her mother's and Jessie's things out of the way and fill up the tub and sneak her mother's razor to shave her legs. First time" (38). And regardless of whether they believe that the eleven-year-old indeed shaves her legs for Lamb or whether they think this is something he makes up in his mind, if they suspect that the middle-aged man plans to abuse the girl, they will feel alarmed.

Free indirect discourse represents a character's thoughts and emotions in the narrator's voice and, as Blakey Vermeule notes, it "mines and focuses [readers'] attention" (2010, 77). *Lamb*'s narrator uses free indirect discourse frequently and ambiguously.[38] Readers are aligned with Lamb throughout the story, and this becomes increasingly uncomfortable because they will likely consider his thoughts and actions immoral. "Moral perversity," writes film scholar Murray Smith, "is an enduring subject of fictional representation, both filmic and literary" (1999, 219). What is crucial, however, is how readers/ viewers are positioned with respect to a morally transgressive agent. In this context, it is important to understand the difference between alignment and allegiance. Alignment, Smith explains, is a result of "our access to the actions, thought, and feelings of a character" (220). If we see the events from a certain character's perspective, we are aligned with that character in the sense that the character acts as focalizer. Allegiance, by contrast, refers to the way in which a narrative "elicits responses of sympathy" toward that character. Such responses are "triggered—if not wholly determined—by the moral structure" of the narrative (220). Typically, alignment with a character is combined with allegiance to that character, but world literature also teems with examples of morally ambiguous protagonists that challenge reader expectations.[39] The example that comes to mind immediately in comparison to *Lamb* is Vladimir Nabokov's *Lolita* (1955), but *Lamb*'s intentions are much less clear than Humbert's, and Tommie is depicted as much more passive than Dolores Haze.[40] In both novels, readers are aligned with morally transgressive protagonists, but while Humbert makes a bid for readers' sympathy by declaring that he truly loved the girl he calls Lolita, Lamb is not able to love, neither himself nor anyone else. Although he will never go further than a kiss, and although he will return Tommie home at the end of the story, the emotional cruelty with which he manipulates her into fulfilling his narcissistic needs complicates his romanticized vision of a wilderness retreat.

Nadzam clearly is aware of the tradition of American nature writing, and her novel participates in that genre while at the same time subverting its central assumptions about representational authenticity. "Let's say there were none of those truss towers of galvanized steel lining the highway this next day," suggests the narrator as the Lamb steers his truck toward the Rocky Mountains. "No telephone poles. No wires. Say that Lamb's truck and the highway were the only relics of the actual world. The road was overcome with native grasses and aromatic flowers, with wild onion and pusstoes. Soft gaping mouths of beardtongue, and mountain lover, and buckbush and drowsy purple heads of virgin's bower. Say it was like this that they crossed the Midwestern line beyond which the sky spreads itself open—suddenly boundless, suddenly an awful blue" (Nadzam 2011, 90). As in the opening scene, the narration here initially focuses on what *isn't* there, but this time it is the signs of human civilization that are missing—truss towers, telephone poles, wires. Readers are cued to imagine a space that is separate from human culture, a picturesque nature ready to be conquered (ironically, in a truck) on a convenient highway. Once again, the style of narration suggests that there is nothing definite about the scene. Not only does the narrator emphasize that the whole of it is imagined—a nod toward postmodern textuality—s/he also calls the truck and the highway "the only relics of the actual world," suggesting that the natural objects evoked are somehow nonactual, figments of someone's imagination. When Lamb and Tommie finally reach his little house in a high valley in the Rocky Mountains, he stops the car and wakes her up so she can behold what he promised her:

> In the new quiet, engine off, they could hear the rush of the river. A magpie sat on the rusted weather vane and blinked. No other houses in sight. Grass and a blue sawtooth horizon and trees and somewhere out behind those trees, nothing and nothing and nothing and nothing. Lamb opened the glove compartment and took out a small ring of keys.
>   "Just like you imagined?"
>   "But"—she was whispering—"I thought we were pretending." (120)

Lamb just laughs and feeds on Tommie's wonder and amazement in the face of a natural beauty that exceeds her most vivid simulations. It is *his* sensual impression of the sight of the "blue sawtooth horizon" and the sound of the "rushing river" that readers are simulating here (once again through free indirect discourse), and unlike in the previous passage, the actuality of the landscape is not called into question. Tommie's bewildered comment further stresses that this is no longer a mental simulation of the little house before the skyline of the mountains, but *the real thing.* And yet, the narrator's earlier comments suggest that there is something inauthentic to this whole journey and the affective experiences it provides.

The epistemological uncertainty continues throughout the second half of the novel, which chronicles Lamb's and Tommie's life in the mountains with early breakfasts over open fire, exhaustive wilderness walks, and nightly cuddling against the cold. Brimming with evocative nature descriptions of the American West, the narrative is filtered through Lamb's consciousness and thus through a mind that cannot appreciate anything that exists independently of him:

> He'd fed her well and told her stories and loved her up all the way through the dim-lit outskirts of Rockford, Iowa City, Omaha; across the national grasslands, stiff and pale in the increasing cold; over the continental divide as the sky shed itself in falling snow, and up to where there were no trees, no birds, no life but the slow force of rock rising up from a thin and frozen

crust of ground. Say this was all in hopes of glimpsing something beautiful. And is there anything wrong with that? (198)

There is, in fact, nearly everything wrong with what Lamb is doing, and this is one of many moments in which readers are challenged to respond to his rhetorical question with protest, just as they are cued to become increasingly critical of his rapturous insistence that this is "the most beautiful place on the planet" (124). As Nadzam has pointed out in an interview, Lamb's "response to nature and relationship with nature is—as is the case with most of the things he does—delusional and warped. . . . He buys the wrong flies for the fishing season; he purchases a ridiculous gun for what he considers light hunting (and never fishes or hunts). . . . Much of the West with which he identifies is made up of invasive weeds or species of plants so endangered he'd probably never actually see them out there" (Nadzam 2016, para. 2). Lamb's topophilia is a posture, a dazzling performance to ensure a constant flow of awe and admiration from a girl who has never been in nature before and who yearns for his guidance and attention. Just like Tommie, readers increasingly lose the ability to distinguish between fact and Lamb's delusional fiction as narcissistic fantasy and narrative reality merge into one inextricable mesh.

It is only toward the end of the story—when Tommie becomes physically sick and Lamb leaves her alone in the cold shed so he can have sex with his recently arrived lover, Linnie—that the narrative invites readers to fully withdraw their allegiance from Lamb. The couple's journey back to Chicago is depicted as feverish and confused, both of them in emotional turmoil, if for different reasons. The final moment of the novel shows the enamored girl running desperately to catch up to Lamb's truck, "her shrinking pale white face twisted in anguish and bobbing unevenly behind him in the rearview mirror" (275). It is a scene of emotional cruelty that illustrates the perfidious ways in which narcissists dispose of their lovers once they have no more use for them. Although it does not offer any direct insight into Tommie's subjective experience, it cues readers to feel compassion for the little girl who for weeks has lived in a world that Lamb constructed for her and who now is coldly abandoned. "Simulation has consequences," writes Patrick Hogan, "because it engages emotional systems" (2013, 4). Simulating Tommie's "pale white face twisted in anguish" (Nadzam 2011, 275) as it is literally shrinking in Lamb's egocentric gaze will "trigger activity in emotional brain centers such that [readers] end up experiencing the emotion associated with those facial gesture and bodily postures" (Clay and Iacoboni 2011, 317). There are many messages that one can take away from such embodied simulation, but one is that the imaginary evocation of nature can be abused like any other persuasive discourse. The fact that topophilic storytelling is disingenuous does not necessarily lessen its evocative power, and in *Lamb* it is not only Tommie but also the reader who is in constant danger of succumbing to its charms.

CONCLUSION

In this chapter, I have explored the role of embodied simulation in readers' imagined experience of literary environments. Richard Gerrig and Patrick Hogan are both right, I believe, when they claim that there is no difference between fiction and nonfiction in terms of transportation and imagined perception. Rather, it is the skillful use of sensory imagery that activates the sensorimotor cortices in readers' brains and thus ensures vivid imagined perception and, as a result, a distinct affective experience of the evoked environment. Just as important for readers' imaginings are the sensations and emotions that characters feel in response to the storyworld. The embodied simulation of a protagonist's conscious experience allows readers to get a sense of *what it is like* to be in that environment, leading to an empathetic affective response. As Keen has pointed out, "narrative emotions are tied up with fictional characters because those actants normally play the role of active agency in plots, but they also belong to the readers who respond to the techniques of storytelling with curiosity, suspense, and surprise. They are shared across the narrative transaction by authors who seek to evoke feelings in readers employing the powers of narrativity" (2015, 152). The powers of narrativity can be employed by writers of fiction and nonfiction alike. Muir often places his own younger self into the storyworld he presents in order to allow readers to simulate a human's physical presence in the forests of the Sierra Nevada and therefore make their embodied simulation of sensory and affective experience more vivid. Nadzam's novel offers a meta-account of embodied simulation, having her characters mentally perform enticing landscapes and making it impossible for readers to decide when they are simulating a character's actual experience and when they are simulating that character's mental simulation of experience.

These postmodern ambiguities, however, are not the only potential differences between Muir's nature writing and Nadzam's fictitious wilderness retreat. Another important difference in how we respond to the imaginary environments of fiction and nonfiction is related to the way in which a text is indexed and then marketed to readers. While Muir's readers would probably have been outraged to learn that he never actually experienced the environments he describes, a fictional text such as Nadzam's does not have to be true to any actually existing environment (though it can be) in order to be authentic. Indexing a work as nonfiction involves certain claims about its relationship to actuality. Chapter 2 will explore these issues further in relation to documentary and fiction film, and it will also pay attention to the similarities and differences in our cognitive engagement with the environments we find in audiovisual media. While first-person narration and free indirect discourse are decidedly literary modes of representation that cannot be transferred easily into the medium of film, there are filmic modes of narration that arguably are just as effective in communicating not only the material qualities of objects but also character's subjective experience of them, inviting viewers to engage in processes of liberated embodied simulation.

CHAPTER 2

Touching Sights and Sounds

Embodiment, Emotion, and Cinematic Environments

IMAGINE YOU ARE watching a film. What is it that you actually do, and what happens to you if it is a film that "works" for you in the sense of it being able to captivate your attention? You may experience a gradual disappearance of your physical environment and a sense of transportation into the alternative world of the film. The sensual presence of that storyworld may be so vivid and immersive that you almost forget where you are as you mentally simulate the events presented to you on the screen. This may result in distinct physical reactions: your heart rate and other bodily processes change as you duck into your seat during suspenseful passages and jolt backwards in response to moments of startling surprise. Or you find yourself helplessly crying as you watch characters you care for suffer or die.

Clearly, some elements of this experience are quite similar to that of reading an immersive novel. Just as clearly, however, there are also some rather dramatic differences. Whereas literature consists of linguistic structures that, upon decoding, cue us to imagine the appearance of storyworlds as well as the sensations, thoughts and actions of characters, film offers us actual sight and sound. That addition has some rather drastic consequences. A literary text, as I have discussed in the previous chapter, is full of informational gaps when it comes to the evocation of a character's environment, even in moments when it is of great importance. The text might offer a very detailed description of the environment, and yet there are countless elements that remain unclear, such as the exact spatial relations among objects and people, or the exact number, color, and shape of things that are not in the focus of the narrator and/or the character. Film cannot afford such vagueness. The fact that filmmakers have to provide viewers with images means that they have to make very concrete decisions about the storyworlds they present, such as the spatial relations between characters, the exact time of the day, and the numbers, shapes, and colors of even the most mundane object in the visual composition of a given scene, the so-called mise-en-scène. This is why the names of an army of location managers, production designers, painters, carpenters, drapesmasters, greensmen, props masters, and (often) computer animation specialists can be found on the final credits of any major movie production. If it wasn't for them, we would end up with cinematic environments not unlike the one we find in Lars von Trier's *Dogville* (2003): drastically impoverished and almost theatrical settings that only contain objects that are of central importance to the plot. Such a cinematic experiment has its own charms, but it won't fulfill most viewers' expectations. Unlike when they pick up a novel, the majority of people expect an immersive *sensual* experience when they buy a movie ticket or flip on their computer or television set to watch a film.

The experience of film is much closer than reading to our sensual perception of the actual world, which is why it has been used by neuroscientists to study event cognition (Zacks, Speer, and Reynolds 2009), memory (Hasson et al. 2008), consciousness (Naci et al. 2014) and dynamic changes in attention (Bezdek et al. 2015). And yet, it would be a mistake to assume that watching a film is *the same* as real-world perception.[1] Whereas in real life our perception and emotion systems are confronted with a massive array of unstructured data, movies are what film scholar Noël Carroll calls "criterially prefocused" (2003, 70). Watching a film, Carroll explains, differs from real-life perception in that "the filmmakers have already done much of the work of emotionally organizing scenes and sequences for us through the ways in which [they] have foregrounded what features of the events in the film are salient" (68). In the literary realm, foregrounding involves linguistic and stylistic features that guide reader attention (Miall and Kuiken 1994a). In the case of film, cinematography, lighting, mise-en-scène, editing, and sound design, together with a range of effects that are added during postproduction, all crucially influence how viewers perceive a given scene. While film *mimics* natural perception, a good part of what plays out on the screen in fact differs dramatically from the way we normally perceive the world around us.

In this chapter, I will be concerned with such foregrounding techniques and with their influence on our understanding of cinematic environments and the depiction of human–nature relationships. The first section will offer some theoretical insight into the cognitive study of film, paying particular attention to the role of liberated embodied simulation in film reception. The second section will consider the ways in which cinematic environments come to life for viewers on the emotional level and will look at a heterogeneous group of film genres that derive their box office appeal not least from the featuring of intriguing environments. While some of those film genres have been the subject of ecocritical scrutiny, relatively little attention has been payed to the ways in which foregrounded or outright *active* environments engage viewers' embodied minds in ways that simulate movement and provoke strong emotional responses. The third section will therefore turn to the disaster film genre and to Jan De Bont's 1996 blockbuster *Twister* to demonstrate how such active cinematic environments are evoked in the minds of viewers. It will also explore the related question of whether knowing that the storyworlds presented to us are *authentic* matters for our affective engagement. The chapter will conclude with a discussion of the relevance of the fiction/nonfiction divide for the cultural representations of environments and human–nature relationships—an issue that will remain important throughout the remaining chapters of the book.

CINEMATIC ENGAGEMENT OF THE SENSES: MOTION, ATTENTION, AND FOREGROUNDING

In chapter 1, I began my exploration of the relevance of neuroscientific research on human perception and embodied simulation for the study of our engagement with environmental narrative. The Italian neuroscientist Vittorio Gallese, one of the most influential figures in simulation research, has coined the term *experimental aesthetics* for empirical work on cultural artifacts (2015, 2), which helps answer some of the questions humanities scholars tend to ask about representation, aesthetics, and reception.[2] As I have explained in the previous chapter, Gallese understands our engagement with cultural texts as a liberated form of the mental simulation processes that we constantly use to navigate our world. It is *embodied* because it involves brain areas, such as the premotor cortex, that are also active when our bodies engage in actual movement. And it is *liberated* because the simulation is offline, so to speak— the brain regions are active although there is no corresponding movement in our bodies. Processes of liberated embodied simulation play a central role in readers' vivid imaginings of literary environments and characters' relationships to them. It is what allows us to imaginatively experience a storyworld that we cannot actually touch or see. The same process is also at the heart of our visceral reaction to the environments we encounter in visual media. "We live in relation to other people, objects, and landscapes that are present in our real world," writes Gallese, "but we live as well in relation to people, objects, and landscapes that are part of the imagined worlds produced by the arts. Both kinds of relationships are rooted in our brain–body system. If we aim to grasp the basis of the complex multimodality these relationships imply, we will have to get back to the brain in its own body" (2016, 3). The multimodal relationships between people, objects, landscapes, and our embodied brains are particularly complex in the case of film, which not only provides narrative (like literature) or visual information (like a painting) but also sound and, most importantly, motion.

Cinematic experience depends on motion in more than just one way. As Gilles Deleuze once put it, "cinema not only puts movement in the image, it also puts movement in the mind" (2000, 366). The biology of the human brain, and the limitations of its processing capacity, are what enables us to see actual movement in motion pictures.[3] The philosopher Katherine Thomson-Jones reminds us that the impression of movement in a projected filmstrip

> is currently understood to rely on two psychological mechanisms: critical flicker fusion, which involves our seeing a rapidly flashing light as a continuous beam, and apparent motion, which involves our seeing motion in a rapidly changing visual display. Thanks to the first mechanism, the movie seems to be continuously illuminated—rather than flashing rapidly in response to the opening and closing of the projector shutter every 1/48th second. Thanks to the second mechanism, there appears on the screen a persistent moving image—rather than a succession of static images. (2013, 116)

Film quite literally is a motion picture in this sense, and its earliest forms became popular precisely because they enabled audiences to watch movement. The first of Eadweard Muybridge's zoopraxiscope discs, dating back to 1879, showed a galloping horse on the Palo Alto race track.[4] Although it was not yet a film in the narrower sense, the device readily exploited the physiological mechanisms Thomson-Jones describes to create the illusion of movement in the mind of viewers. It was an illusion that fascinated people who up to this point had only seen still photography and other motionless forms of representation. The short filmstrips that soon filled kinetoscopes and other early exhibition devices in New York City and elsewhere in the United States all featured humans, animals, and other objects of the natural world in motion.[5]

As cinematic technology developed and thrived, filmmakers became increasingly sophisticated in adjusting their motion pictures to the cognitive capacities of viewers. Neuroscientist Tim Smith and colleagues point out that "the Hollywood style of moviemaking, which permeates a wide range of visual media, has evolved formal conventions that are compatible with the natural dynamics of attention and humans' assumptions about continuity of space, time, and action" (Smith, Levin, and Cutting 2012, 107). The history of film has been a history of developing technical means that trick our brains into a powerful response with the aim to create highly immersive film-viewing experiences.[6] Single-run film strips shot from a static camera soon gave way to longer formats that combined several shots from different perspectives into increasingly complex visual narratives. From D. W. Griffith's infamous *Birth of a Nation* (1915) onward, an increasingly standardized set of filming and continuity editing techniques has been working in concert with those technological innovations toward creating the illusion of spatial and temporal unity and achieving transparency with regard to the cinematic techniques themselves.[7] That it is an *illusion* becomes clear once we consider that a continuity editing convention like the "match on action"—a character runs to a door and the next shot shows him running up a staircase—does not require the door and the staircase to be in the same shooting location or even to be shot on the same day. The only world in which the two objects belong to the same continuous space and time might be the fictional world of the film, but few viewers will even notice the cut in between.[8]

It is in this sense that the filmic means are transparent. Most film viewers will not pay any attention to cuts, camera movements, or sound design in a mainstream Hollywood production or even most of documentary film unless they are specifically asked to do so.[9] Their minds almost automatically ignore that technical layer of the film and cut straight through to its content: to the characters and their story. And yet, continuity editing and other cinematic techniques are what guides viewers' attention, telling them where to look and what to notice. Over 90 percent of shots in Hollywood films have been shown to adhere to continuity editing rules (Bordwell, Staiger, and Thompson 1985; Levin and Wang 2009) and visual attention plays a critical role in the perception of continuity across cuts (Smith, Levin, Cutting 2012, 9). A film's guidance of viewers' visual attention through camera movement, mise-en-scène, lighting, editing, and sound design is comparable to the function of a literary narrator that guides readers' attention through focalization and other narrative techniques.[10] And like literary texts, films are full of narrative gaps. While the photographic image of a cinematic environment offers more visual information than viewers will be able to process and retain, there are countless other areas where they have to use their imagination and revert to their own memories in order to make sense out of what is presented to them. When a character runs out of a house and then leaves his car in the next shot in order to step into a store, viewers must fill in the gap, namely the drive from the house to the store. They are constantly invited to make inferences in this way, to speculate about where things might lead, what might have happened in the meantime in some place that was not shown on the screen, or simply how a character might be feeling in a given scene. Unlike literature, film rarely gives direct insight into a character's consciousness (the exception to this rule is the use of voiceover). Most of the time, viewers have to use Theory of Mind and processes of embodied simulation to infer from characters' dialogue, body postures, and facial expressions what they might think or feel.[11]

This brings me to the second way in which films *move* viewers: by touching them emotionally. The cognitive film scholar Carl Plantinga has asserted that "affect and emotion are fundamental to what makes films artistically successful, rhetorically powerful, and culturally influential" (2009a, 5), and so we do well in paying attention to the ways in which films cue affective responses. Viewers' embodied simulation of characters' motions and emotions is perhaps most central to their involvement in a film, but this should not lead us to disregard the role of cinematic environments in cueing viewer emotion. As Siegfried Kracauer observes in his *Theory of Film,* it is not only a "face on the screen" that can "attract us with a singular manifestation of fear or happiness," but a "street serving as the background to some quarrel or love affair may rush to the fore and produce an intoxicating effect" ([1960] 1997, 303). In Kracauer's account, that unexpected "rushing to the fore" of the background is more or less unintended by the filmmaker. It is a moment in which the viewer's attention shifts away from both protagonist and narrative and toward the surrounding cinematic environment. Such unintended—and highly idiosyncratic—moments of shifting attention may indeed happen during the viewing of any film, and they often depend on previous personal experiences and the cultural context of individual viewers. Yet, most of the time the sudden shift of attention, experienced as a "rushing to the fore" of the cinematic environment, is a result of cinematic foregrounding and therefore a response that has been deliberately cued by the filmmakers through the ways in which certain aspects of the environment are made salient.

SETTING, LANDSCAPE, AND NARRATIVE:
THE AGENCY OF CINEMATIC ENVIRONMENTS

Ecocritical film scholars have only just begun to address the affective dimensions of cinematic environments, and only very few of them have engaged with cognitive film theory in their work.[12] Within cognitive film studies, the analytical emphasis has tended to be on characters and on a range of other cinematic features, such as music and editing.[13] There has only been very limited attention to the emotional impact of cinematic environments and their role in character and plot development. One of the few cognitive approaches to consider the emotional impact of cinematic environments, at least indirectly, has been developed by Ed Tan and Nico Frijda. In their theoretical essay on "Sentiment in Film Viewing" (1999), the two psychologists differentiate between empathetic "F emotions" and nonempathetic "A emotions." The first group consists of "responses to the fictional world" of a film, including "sympathy, compassion, and admiration" (52). The second, *non*empathetic group of emotions can be enjoyed "regardless of what they mean to the protagonist's fate and feeling," including "the sight of a majestic landscape" (52). In Tan and Frijda's understanding, our emotional responses to imagery portraying "an environment in which one feels tiny and insignificant" or other visually overwhelming landscapes are therefore *independent* from our investment in character and narrative (62), and such responses are by definition nonempathetic. According to the authors, such imagery can trigger two kinds of response: "On the one hand, the stimulus may be attractive and call forth fascination. . . . On the other, it may have a repellent quality, eliciting a tendency to shiver and look for shelter" (62).

While I am intrigued by Tan and Frijda's cognitive approach to the affective appeals of landscape imagery that in other contexts would be called *sublime*, I believe it falls short of describing the very complex role that cinematic environments can and do play in a wide range of films and how they engage viewer emotions.[14] In a way, it reproduces an argument made by Martin Lefebvre in *Landscape and Film* about the difference between the "setting" of a film, which is subjected to the needs of the narrative and the much more autonomous "filmic landscape" (2006b, 22). According to Lefebvre, filmic landscape emerges in moments when the natural environment ceases to be the background setting for the foregrounded action and becomes "*a space freed from eventhood*" that invites contemplation (22). In the history of American cinema, filmmakers have often used spectacular landscape shots to direct viewer attention toward the environment that surrounds characters and potentially creates what Kracauer calls "an intoxicating effect" ([1960] 1997, 303). Pertinent examples include movies set in "exotic" locales, such as Sydney Pollack's *Out of Africa* (1985) and Michael Apted's *Gorillas in the Mist* (1988), but landscape shots are also an integral part of the iconography of epic Western films, from John Ford's *Stagecoach* (1939) to Sam Peckinpah's *The Wild Bunch* (1969) and Kevin Costner's *Dances with Wolves* (1990). The typical Western film would be unthinkable without stunning images of the arid Southwest, and spectacular panoramas of visually enticing landscapes also play a central role in countless other films that celebrate American environments.

Ecocritics have acknowledged such celebrations for the attention they draw to the environment, but they have also problematized them for their lack of ecological depth and historical authenticity.[15] Beth Berila, for example, suggests that the "scenic vistas and panoramic shots of mountains, forests, and water" in Robert Redford's 1992 film adaptation of Norman Maclean's novella *A River Runs Through It* (1976) "encourage viewers to see the vistas merely as objects of beauty" (2010, 117).[16] Berila criticizes Philippe Rousselot's Oscar-winning cinematography with its "sweeping panoramic shots" of "Montana's spectacular natural beauty" for its aestheticizing distance that encourages a thoughtless consumption of visual beauty and a "carefree enjoyment without responsibility" (119). It is the same kind of surveying gaze that I have already discussed in chapter 1 with reference to the opening of John Muir's *Mountains of California* (1894), with the difference that in this case the medium offers *actual* panoramic sights instead of imagined sights. The reason why viewers tend to find such sights beautiful and pleasurable might be explained in terms of power (Pratt 1992) or evolutionary conditioning (Kaplan 1992; Easterlin 2012). Such feelings of pleasure might be further intensified by a matching music score and an elegiac editing pace to produce what Plantinga has called "synesthetic affect" (2009a, 156): the affective tones of different filmic elements—such as image, sound, pacing, etc.—are matched in a way to produce a certain overall effect.[17] However, Berila is not interested in exploring *why* we enjoy the spectacular landscape shots in Redford's film. She takes it as a given that they position "the spectator in a dominating and consuming relationship with the landscape, instead of locating humans as part of a larger ecosystem" as is the case in the activist environmental justice documentaries that she also considers (2010, 127). She thus criticizes exactly the lack of narrative connection and contextualization that Lefebvre celebrates as autonomy—the moment in which the cinematic landscape becomes a pure spectacle.

I will return to Berila's criticism of Redford's film, but before I do so, I first want to put some pressure on the claim that cinematic environments—in whatever way they are shot and presented—can and do ever gain independence from a film's narrative. Lefebvre asserts that

spectators watch [a] film at some points in the narrative mode and at others in the spectacular mode, allowing them to follow the story and, whenever necessary, to contemplate the filmic spectacle. It is necessary, however,
to emphasize that one cannot watch the same filmic passage through both
modes at the exact same time. . . . This is why it can be said that the spectacle
halts the progression of narrative for the spectator. . . . When I *contemplate*
a piece of film, I stop following the story for a moment, even if the narrative
does not completely disappear from my consciousness. . . . Said differently,
the contemplation of filmic spectacle depends on an "autonomizing" gaze.
It is this gaze which enables the notion of filmic landscape in narrative fiction
(and event-based documentary) film; it makes possible the transition from set-
ting to landscape. The contemplation of the setting frees it briefly from its
narrative function. (2006b, 29)

What Lefebvre describes here is essentially the viewer's shifting of attention
away from the characters and their story and toward the landscape that envel-
ops them. I agree that attention is crucial for viewers' engagement with cinematic environments, but I have my qualms with several of the claims Lefebvre
puts forward here.

One of my qualms concerns his use of the term "landscape," which I find
unduly limiting and therefore unhelpful.[18] Film setting entails a good deal
more than just natural landscapes; it in fact refers to *any* kind of environment
that surrounds characters and in part enables (or limits) what they can do.
When viewers' attention shifts away from a character and toward the surrounding environment, the latter need not be a landscape in any traditional
(or natural) sense.[19] Elements of urban and/or interior environments, even
highly claustrophobic ones, are as likely the object of viewers' shifting attention as grand, sweeping natural landscapes. Lefebvre's notion of landscape
also seems to overstress the *visual* to the exclusion of other central factors in
the emergence of cinematic environments, most crucially sound. He rightly
points out that something happens to viewers when they "look at the natural
environment as if it were framed" (2006a, xv), but he does not fully acknowledge that shot size and selection are only two of several factors that guide
viewer attention. As I have already pointed out, most viewers will attend to
a specific part of a cinematic environment because camera position, lighting,
visual depth, mise-en-scène, music, and sound *all* serve to prefocus attention
and evoke a range of emotional responses in them—not only direct emotional
responses to the environment itself but also emotions in relation to a protagonist's fate *within* that environment. Unsurprisingly, motion is often key for
such shifts in attention. For evolutionary reasons we tend to focus our gaze on

things that move within our vision field, and such sudden shifts in attention are not dependent on the naturalness of the moving object.[20]

My second and related qualm with Lefebvre's account concerns his strict division between narrative and what he calls the "visual *spectacle*" of cinematic landscape (2006b, 28). It is somewhat limiting to assume that viewers' minds operate in a binary mode that forces them to shift back and forth between a "narrative mode" and a "spectacular mode" of viewing, which are mutually exclusive. Not only is there no empirical evidence for such a dual model of film reception, it also neglects the many ways in which spectacle and narrative can influence and reinforce one another in a wide range of films. As Geoff King has observed, "spectacle can have an impact similar to that of driving linear narrative: it has the potential to reinforce, almost physiologically, whatever the narrative asserts" (2000, 34). Clearly, the overall effect of the film will depend on what exactly it *is* that the narrative asserts. This is a point I will return to. First, however, I want to make an argument for the integration of narration and spectacle and suggest that there is no need or necessity for a cinematic environment to become autonomous from plot and story. In fact, we might recognize its great importance for character and plot development precisely at the point when we see it in functional and ecological *relation* to them without necessarily speaking of *subordination*.

There are at least two narrative functions of cinematic environments that neither Tan and Frijda nor Lefebvre really account for, functions that are of central importance for our emotional responses to film. The first is their role in what Greg Smith has called "mood cues." Filmmakers frequently use the environment that surrounds a character to set the general *mood* for a certain scene or sequence, thereby preparing the viewer for stronger and more immediate bursts of emotion. Smith explains that "a mood is a preparatory state in which one is seeking an opportunity to express a particular emotion or emotion set" (2003, 38). He uses Steven Spielberg's *Raiders of the Lost Ark* (1981) to illustrate how mood cues work in the movies: "The opening sequence of the film follows Jones through the jungle and into a booby-trapped cave in search of a golden statue. The mood is suspenseful, apprehensive of the imminent attacks of jungle savages or the swift triggering of hidden death traps" (2003, 45). Together with the foreboding music score and a cacophony of animal voices, the jungle environment, which "is full of deep shadows" (45), is key to creating suspense in this sequence, preparing the viewer emotionally for a sudden startle response and the brief spike of fear that comes with it.[21]

In Lefebvre's terms, the environment here still functions as setting because it serves the narrative. However, this does not change the fact that it is also quite spectacular and that viewers are likely to shift their sensual attention away from the human protagonists and toward the surrounding environment at times, scanning it for movement or any sign of an impending attack. As the cognitive film scholar Henry Bacon points out, our perception of space in film tends to be "governed by concerns related to characters, starting from their narrative centrality, which crucially guides our construction of the story world" (2011, 38). The opening of *Raiders of the Lost Ark* takes advantage of this tendency and also strategically uses low-key lighting, according to Smith, Levin, and Cutting, a way of giving "viewers fewer options of where to look," leading to an "increas[ed] control over viewers' attention" (2012, 109). The result is a suspenseful and yet playful mood that prepares viewers not only for the more exciting scenes that will follow once the protagonists have stepped into the cave, but also for the film as a whole.

Of course, viewers *know* on some level that these images were shot by a film team and that what they see is actors and a series of special effects in what must be a partially natural and partially built environment. That is what most of them would answer if someone interviewed them afterward. However, this knowledge has little effect on their emotional responses to the events on the screen. As neuroscientist Jeffrey Zacks explains, "Your eyes and ears are telling you that something exciting is happening in front of you and your brain is preparing to react. Of course, you *know* it's just a movie. But large parts of your brain don't process that distinction" (2015, 4). This is why viewers feel suspense, excitement, and mild fear as they simulate Indiana Jones' experience of the enigmatic and dangerous environment. Plantinga calls this phenomenon *conditional realism*. The spectator is on some level aware of the fictionality of the presented events, and yet she "has emotions and affects in response to [them] that suggest that she perceives and responds to a fictional world in some of the same ways she would perceive and respond to the actual world" (2009b, 239–40). How effective Spielberg's opening scene is in creating such conditional realism depends to a large degree on the presentation and internal consistency of the presented world.[22]

The fact that the scene is filmed by a moving subjective camera is crucial not only for the guidance of viewer attention but also for their sense of immersion. As Michele Guerra points out, the use of camera movement in film emphasizes the viewer's sense of presence within the shot (2015, 151). While viewers rarely assume that they *themselves* are physically present in the fictional storyworld of the film, the use of subjective shots facilitates *a sense of presence* that, in combination with empathetic care for characters, allows them to experience cinematic environments on the visceral level. Gallese's observation that "the sharp distinction, classically drawn between first- and third-person experience of acting and experiencing emotions and sensations, appears to be much more blurred at the level of the neural mechanisms mapping it" (2011, 442) is as relevant here as it is in relation to literary reading. Not only does it elucidate how we map the observed movements of people and objects onto our own bodies, it also explains why we react to them on the emotional level.

This brings me to the second narrative function of cinematic environments that is relevant for a consideration of their emotional impact on viewers: the fact that in some, if not all, films the diegetic space is not so much the passive *setting* for the action (or an autonomous landscape) as it is an *active agent* and thus *part* of the action. Bacon emphasizes that "what is of interest to the spectator is how the characters *relate* to their environment, what kin[d] of dangers and affordances it offers them, how the spatial relationship between people and objects is indicative of and shapes the dramaturgical situation" (2011, 38). Although he does not explicitly say so, this constitutes an ecological view of the relationship between film characters and their surroundings, and it also suggests that even in films in which the cinematic environment ostentatiously is "only" the setting, it limits or enables what characters can do.[23] Much of nonhuman nature, notes environmental historian Linda Nash, does not have agency in the sense of intentionality or choice, but the problem might actually lie with our somewhat narrow definition of agency. Nash suggests that "our narratives should emphasize that . . . so-called human agency cannot be separated from the environments in which that agency emerges" (2005, 69). This is true for Spielberg's *Raiders of the Lost Arc,* in which characters are quite literally chased by their environment, and it is also true for Redford's *A River Runs Through It.* David Ingram observes in *Green Screen* (2000) that Redford's film presents "the unspoilt wilderness in the film" as "a site of moral goodness and spiritual transcendence, in contrast to the corruptions associated with the small town" (27). Within the film's logic, the natural environment of Montana offers the protagonists various affordances that allow them to develop their characters and talents, whereas the corrupted space of the town curtails and endangers that development. This ideological use of a cinematic environment through the inclusion of visually stunning wide-angle shots was in turn instrumental in a conservation project for the Big Blackfoot River in western Montana that Redford advocated with *A River Runs Through It.*[24]

Both Ingram and Berila are highly critical of the film's gender politics and narrative strategies, and for very good reasons. But these strategies demonstrate that even in films that boast spectacular landscape cinematography, the featured environments—and the emotions they evoke in viewers—rarely are disconnected from its narrative. Bacon's mentioning of the "dangers and affordances" that cinematic environments offer to characters suggests not only that such environments possess material agency but also that they can influence the fates of characters in positive and negative ways (2011, 38). This puts a question mark behind Tan and Frijda's claim that cinematic environments cue what they call "A emotions"—nonempathetic emotions that can be enjoyed "regardless of what they mean to the protagonist's fate and feeling" (1999, 52). The emotions we feel in response to a cinematic landscape are in fact rarely disconnected from our concern for the protagonist's fate. This becomes particularly obvious when we consider film genres in which the cinematic environment plays a more obvious role for narrative arcs and viewer engagement. Psychological studies such as Alfred Hitchcock's *Rope* (1948) and Sidney Lumet's *12 Angry Men* (1957) take advantage of the emotional pressure inherent in small spaces and reproduce their claustrophobic feel for viewers by limiting their visual experience to one single set and a limited range of camera movements. Suspense and thriller films also frequently make use of such spatial limitations, especially when they impede characters' ability to hide, move, or escape, as is the case in David Fincher's *Panic Room* (2002) or Rodrigo Cortés's *Buried* (2012). More interesting still, in my context, are horror films like Stanley Kubrick's *The Shining* (1980) and Mikael Håfström's *1408* (2007), which feature environments that are haunted and therefore threatening for the protagonists. In the disaster film genre, finally, such active environments take center stage, quite literally forcing protagonists to behave in certain ways by brute, natural force. It is to this genre and the emotional thrill it offers to which I will now turn.

MOVING ENVIRONMENTS: MOTION AND EMOTION IN FILM DISASTER

Disaster films have a long and lively history in American cinema.[25] In his 1977 article, "The Bug in the Rug: Notes on the Disaster Genre," Maurice Yacowar differentiates between eight different types of disaster film, arguing that "the most common disaster type pits a human community against a destructive form of nature" (2012, 313).[26] This destructive form of nature may come in the form of animals (genetically modified or not), in the form of hostile elements, or in the form of "an atomic mutation" (314). It remains open to debate how "natural" atomic mutants really are, but what interests me here is the second subtype, the attack by the elements, which Yacowar traces from John Ford's *The Hurricane* (1937) and other popular flood movies to films about volcanic eruptions and quakes such as William Dieterle's *Volcano* (1950) and Mark Robson's *Earthquake* (1974). We could easily extend the list to include a streak of natural-disaster movies from the 1990s, among them Roger Donaldson's *Dante's Peak* (1997), Mick Jackson's *Volcano* (1997), and Jan de Bont's *Twister* (1996). In more recent years, the "Natural Attack" type of the disaster genre seems to have lost a little of its allure, but films like Roland Emmerich's *The Day After Tomorrow* (2004) and *2012* (2009) prove that they can still do well at the box office.

Unless they happen to be shooting during an actual natural disaster, the "destructive forms of nature" at work in these movies' storylines force film-makers to manipulate their footage of pre-filmic environments with a range of cinematic techniques in order to make them more hostile and therefore more thrilling for viewers. *Twister*, for instance, includes dozens of animated tornadoes and hundreds of digital sky-replacement shots in order to create a "dark nature" that drives its protagonists to various spectacular actions. Donaldson's *Dante's Peak* adds a digital peak to a large hill near the old mountain mining town of Wallace in Idaho to make it look like a volcano and a flood of SFX lava and pyroclastic flows that keep scientists and locals on their toes throughout the film. Emmerich's sci-fi spectacle *2012* upgrades its panoramic shot of Yellowstone National Park with a mind-boggling CGI eruption of the area's famed super-volcano. In all these films, computer animation and more traditional forms of special effects transform pre-filmic environments into active participants in the film's narrative. They are interesting in the context of this book because they replicate on an audiovisual level a phenomenon that I have described in chapter 1 with regard to Muir's *The Mountains of California:* that the embodied simulation of *motion* can greatly contribute to narrative pleasure and to the degree in which we feel immersed in a given storyworld. Muir's autobiographical recounting of "A Wind-Storm in the Forest" contains a passage in which his younger self rides the top of a Douglas spruce during a thunderstorm. The tree is "bending and swirling backward and forward, round and round, tracing indescribable combinations of vertical and horizontal curves" while Muir is clinging to it "with muscles firm braced, like a bobolink on a reed" (1894). I argued in chapter 1 that the passage invites readers to simulate motion. Packed with visual and motor imagery, it helps them to the see and feel the big tree bending, flapping, and swishing in the storm, while the first-person perspective allows them to also (and at the same time) share Muir's subjective experience of that moment, simulating his exhilarating sensations of motion, touch, and proprioception as he "clings with muscles firm braced" to the elastic wood of the treetop. Much the same happens to viewers when they behold motion in film.

The film scholar Vivian Sobchack has differentiated between four basic kinds of cinematic motion: (1) the movement of humans, animals, and objects within the frame; (2) the editing, and therefore the movement, between the images; (3) the zoom, that is, the optical movement of the camera lens; and (4) the movement of the camera (1982, 317). These modes of movement not only guide attention, as I have discussed in the first section of this chapter, but they also play a role in viewers' embodied simulation of motion. The movement of people and objects is perhaps the most obvious form of cinematic motion, and all the "Nature Attacks" films I have mentioned use special effects and/ or animation to make not only protagonists but also large parts of their surroundings move in very swift ways. In a cowritten article, Gallese and Guerra remind us that embodied simulation "is characterized by the capacity to share meaning of actions, basic motor intentions, feelings and emotions" and proceed to assert its importance "in the experience of many 'action-packed' movies" (2012, 193). In their view, it is not only moving objects that facilitate embodied simulation in the movie theater but also the three other forms of cinematic movement that Sobchack mentions: editing, focus, and, most importantly, camera motion. In a more recent paper, the authors present evidence from an empirical high-density EEG (Electroencephalogram) neuroscientific study on camera movement, concluding that the use of a Steadicam has a particular pronounced effects on viewers' motor cortex activation (Gallese and Guerra 2014, 103).[27] Other forms of camera movement, such as zooming, tilting, panning, or dolly-type shots, had a less extreme, but still detectable, effect on viewers' brain activity.[28] Clearly, this holds true for film viewing in general, but it has particular relevance for disaster movies because in such films the camera movement crucially adds to the movement of objects and people, thereby heightening viewers' sense of immersion in the threatening environment featured in the film.

Take the example of *Twister*, in which a group of scientists risks their lives to get measurements from inside a tornado. The first of their storm chases, about thirty minutes into the film, is a good example of how the various forms of cinematic movement collaborate in the creation of a thrilling "nature attack." Motion within the frame dominates this sequence as the team around Bill Harding (Bill Paxton) and his estranged wife, Jo (Helen Hunt), races in a convoy of trucks toward a tornado that was only added to the frames in postproduction. The long and winding shape of the animated twister dances on the ground with remarkable grace, its elegant motion attracting viewer attention and cueing emotions of fascination and awe. Since at this point the "force of nature" is still too far away to give viewers a sense of its velocity, it is the human actors in their speeding trucks who bring movement to the sequence. But they are not alone. Music, sound, editing, and especially camera movement greatly help in making the chase fast paced and exciting for viewers.[29]

The cross-cutting between shots is getting increasingly quicker and almost every single one of those shots is taken from a moving camera. Traveling shots from three different cameras mounted on camcars racing in parallel to Harding's truck are alternated with subjective shots from the interior of the truck and shots taken from cameras mounted to the truck's sides and bottom as it speeds along a muddy dirt track to get into the twister's pathway.[30]

Everything in this scene is geared toward making viewers feel like they are part of the action. Not only do they automatically map the movements and emotions of the protagonists onto their own bodies through processes of emotional contagion and embodied simulation, the subjective shots from inside the truck—and especially those from the side and from underneath the truck—also give them a sense of speed. A quick zoom toward the dashboard tells them on the cognitive level that the car is going 75 miles per hour on this uneven road, and the more visceral information they receive on the visual and aural level suggests that this is true (though it most likely isn't; the footage is undercranked to create the illusion of a higher speed).[31] It is unlikely that viewers will literally project themselves and their own bodies into the shot (which at times would place them above or below the truck), but as Zacks has pointed out, once our "eyes and ears are telling [us] that something exciting is happening" in front of us, our brains are "preparing to react" regardless of our understanding that we aren't affected by it (2015, 4). Geoff King explains well how such scenes work on viewers' bodies: "Big widescreen cinema claims to fill the viewer's vision. Multichannel hi-fi sound . . . adds significantly to the impression of immersion in a three-dimensional experience. Viewers are assaulted by a brand of spectacle that might amount to sheer pace and kinetics; to loudness that can be felt as bodily vibration, and brightness that makes the eyes contract. . . . The viewer is sold the illusion of being transported into the world on-screen" (2000, 33). Although he does not draw on any neuroscientific research on embodied simulation, King stresses the importance of the viewer's physical involvement in the visceral *experience* of spectacular film.

As an audiovisual medium, film can only ever reach two of our senses directly—sight and hearing—but it manages to engage all other senses on the imaginary level.[32] Vision, explains Gallese, "is far more complex than the mere activation of the visual part of the brain. Vision is multimodal: it encompasses the activation of somatosensory, emotion-related and motor brain networks; these play out in endocrine systems" (2015, 4). Not only can images "make you sweat" (4), but the multimodality of vision also allows for the activation of a range of other physical responses: "The observation of touch activates the somatosensory cortex" (4). Watching moments of physical touch (pleasant and unpleasant) therefore adds a tactile and affective dimension to the observed.[33] Although nothing physically touches the viewer's body (unless she happens to sit in a 4DX theater), the combination of sight and sound gives her a vivid sense of touch. This phenomenon is not only what makes love and sex scenes so captivating for viewers, it also allows for the visceral experience of a catastrophic environment.[34]

The final part of the first storm chase sequence in *Twister* illustrates this well. Once the tornado is directly behind the truck as planned, the movement of the protagonists is stopped abruptly by a narrow bridge that blocks their way. At this point in the sequence it is their immediate surroundings that provide most of the motion. Pieces of dirt and debris are flung at their faces as they run and then crawl to take shelter underneath the bridge while the twister unleashes its full force. As De Bont puts it in his director's comments on the DVD version of the film, "everything is moving" within the frame, and the frantic editing pace further adds to the impression of pervasive motion while the protagonists now try to remain still, clinging desperately to a pier of the bridge. Close-ups of their weather-beaten faces allow viewers to empathize with their feelings of fascination and fear through involuntary mechanisms of facial feedback and emotional contagion. As Plantinga notes, "the prolonged concentration on the character's face is not warranted by the simple communication of information about character emotion. Such scenes are also intended to elicit empathetic emotions in the spectator" (1999, 239). The quick pacing of De Bont's film does not allow for "prolonged concentration" but in this case frequency makes up for duration. No less than eleven close-ups within less than two minutes invite viewers to simulate not only the dangerous physical situation of the protagonists but also their emotional reactions to it.

Like Muir's recollection of the wind storm in the forest, the film here offers both a sensual impression of the dangerous tornado that cues *direct* emotions of fascination and fear, and the protagonists' emotional reaction to it, which cues *empathetic* emotions of fascination and fear. In this context, it is interesting to consider what Murray Smith has called the "twofoldness" of spectator response to film characters (2011, 277). As Plantinga explains, "twofoldness is a dual response that takes film characters as simultaneously 'real' in some sense (they are assumed to have bodies, intentions, goals, desires, and feelings) but also as fictional constructs (they are played by actors and famous movies stars, are costumed, read lines from a script, etc.)" (2015, 300). Viewers' empathetic response is thus conditional, and it, to a good degree, depends on the *sensed authenticity* of what they see. De Bont remembers in his DVD commentary that during the filming of the first twister encounter the set was so dominated by the powerful wind machines—among them a Boeing 707 jet engine—that Paxton and Hunt could barely hear the commands they needed in order to produce the right facial expressions at the right moment. "I had to act out a tornado," he explains, and since "obviously there's nothing there . . . I had to tell them what is going on . . . so that they had something to react to."[35] It is thus simulated emotion expressions and the sensual spectacle of a simulated storm that, in combination with the disturbing sound and racing editing pace, treat viewers to the exhilarating experience of a virtual tornado. As Mick LaSalle notes in his review for the *San Francisco Chronicle*, "Virtually everything in 'Twister' is fake. But the effects . . . are so expertly accomplished that it doesn't matter. . . . It looks real, and De Bont keeps the action coming so fast that there's no time to question it" (1996). The fact that the brief close-ups of emotion expressions are immediately juxtaposed with shots of the highly active environment that causes them greatly aids in creating the overall affective charge of the scene. This, too, is a case of *synesthetic affect* (Plantinga 2009a, 156), in which several filmic elements collaborate to create an emotional effect.

King calls the flood of sights and sounds in "Nature Attack" films such as *Twister* an "assault" on the viewer's senses, suggesting that such "moments of spectacle may offer . . . the illusion of a more direct emotional and experiential impact" than less spectacular stretches of narrative film (2000, 36). Unlike Lefebvre, however, he does not suggest that this makes moments of cinematic spectacle autonomous or independent from the film's narrative. Instead, he argues that narrative and spectacle act in concert in *Twister,* as the film presents elemental force "as both lethal danger and potential source of redemption, precisely the role played by the wilderness and its occupants in the classic American frontier tradition" (2000, 18). Like Redford's *A River Runs Through It, Twister* has been read as a modern frontier narrative that portrays nature as an untamed space where white heterosexual men can prove themselves and develop their virtues. As ecocinema scholar Pat Brereton points out, *Twister's* rugged protagonist is portrayed as superior to the scientists in a competing team because he "can read nature's signs without the often faulty aid of complicated technological devices. Simply by sniffing the earth and observing the sky, he can intuitively predict much more about the impending twister than by using an array of scientific instrumentation" (2005, 66). Clearly, the reading of *Twister* as a masculinist frontier story is complicated by the presence of Helen Hunt's character, who is at least as courageous as her male counterparts. It is also complicated by the fact that the protagonists are scientists who want to explore nature rather than to tame or control it. But this does not change the fact that, as in Redford's film, the spectacle of nature is tied to the film's narrative and larger ideological underpinnings.

The combination of visceral spectacle and morally uplifting narrative is what makes the film attractive for a mass audience, precisely because it features relatable (if flat) characters that struggle and succeed in their interaction with an exciting and dangerously active environment that only very few people would appreciate encountering in their day-to-day lives. "Cinematic spectacle," writes King, "claims to provide something marked as distinct from [our] quotidian environment, something special, more intense and filled with the large-scale illusion of presence" (2000, 33). *Twister* creates such an intense environment and enables viewers to feel its excitement through the bodies of daring protagonists while clinging firmly to the much safer environment of their theater seats. The same is true for other films in the "Nature Attack" category, such as Emmerich's *The Day After Tomorrow,* which combines spectacular scenes of weather-related disaster with a melodramatic storyline, all the while lecturing viewers about the great risks associated with abrupt climate change. Such disaster scenes need not be scientifically accurate, nor does the natural spectacle itself have to be authentic—as I have argued, the very condition of a dangerously active nature precludes filming the actual thing. This leads us to the question I want to explore in the final section of this chapter: whether the authenticity of cinematic environments is relevant in any way for viewers' emotional response to them and whether there is any difference in this regard between fiction and nonfiction film.

FEELING REAL: ENVIRONMENTAL AUTHENTICITY AND EMOTION IN FICTION AND NONFICTION FILM

When films are shot on location, write Elena Gorfinkel and John Rhodes in *Taking Place* (2011), they "take actual places—take images of actual places, record impressions of the world's surface—and archive them on celluloid" (viii). A film like *A River Runs Through It* indeed records impressions of the actual places in Montana where it was filmed. The same is true for *Twister,* which was shot on location in Oklahoma. Although the filmmakers added a mix of dirt, ice, and debris to the scenery (some of it brought in from other states) and the weather phenomena were mostly added in postproduction, many shots show the actual Oklahoma landscape in 1995 and therefore "archive" it on celluloid in the way that Gorfinkel and Rhodes suggest.[36] However, authenticity often plays only a minor role, not only when filmmakers elevate nature to a protagonist within the narrative but also when it comes to the selection of shooting locations. For economic, political, practical, and, not least, aesthetic reasons, the makers of fiction films often have one environment stand in for another. In the case of *A River Runs Through It,* the shooting had to take place on the Gallantin River near Livingston, Montana, because the Big Blackfoot River, on which both the novella and the film are set, was too polluted to allow for filming (Ingram 2000, 29). This gives the film's evocation of nostalgia for a bygone time a somewhat bitter twist, but unless viewers are intimately familiar with the area, it is unlikely that they will notice the substitution. There are also more notorious examples of cinematic inauthenticity, such as David Lean's *Doctor Zhivago* (1965), in which the filmmakers exchanged Spain for Siberia, covering miles and miles of Spanish countryside in white marble dust at the height of summer to create a Russian winter landscape. Or take John Ford's *The Searchers* (1956), in which the famed sights of Monument Valley have been miraculously transferred to Texas.

However, even such remarkable replacements seem to have very little impact on viewers' emotional responses to the portrayed environment. In most cases they will not notice them, and if they do, they may not care. The shooting locations of the popular CBS show *Northern Exposure* (1990–1995) in Kittitas County, Washington, have become something of a pilgrim site for fans who are undeterred by the fact that the show's setting in Alaska is quite central to its narrative.[37] And the devotees of science fiction film are perfectly aware that earthly places will have to stand in for the ecologies of foreign planets, one of the latest examples being the substitution of Wadi Rum in southern Jordan for the surface of Mars in Ridley Scott's *The Martian* (2015).[38] It seems that viewers today do not expect environmental authenticity in fiction formats any more than the audiences of the early days of audiovisual entertainment. Many studio productions of the 1930s and 1940s featured spectacular matte paintings instead of real skies, and almost everything else was specifically built for the film. The history of film animation—from the first Disney features to James Cameron's hybrid science-fiction epos *Avatar* (2009) and beyond—tells us that we in fact do not need *any* actual place at all in order to react emotionally to a cinematic environment (I will return to this point in chapters 4 and 6). Our emotional investment in fiction films does not seem to depend very much on the actual places that are "archived" in it. What matters is whether the depicted environment looks convincing and is consistent in the context of the narrative.

In the case of nonfiction film the situation is very different. Film scholars with a special interest in documentaries have long debated the differences between fiction and nonfiction film—and the latter's exact relationship to reality. It is notoriously difficult to draw a clear line between the two modes of film, and when it comes to the depiction of cinematic environments it is particularly difficult to sustain.[39] Yet most viewers would feel betrayed if they learned that the spectacular landscapes they see in a nature documentary were filmed in a different location or that the wild animals featured in them are in fact tame and trained for the part. Even more than nature writing, nature film promises the vivid evocation and presentation of *authentic* natural environments, allowing viewers to explore and feel them from afar. As the environmental historian Gregg Mitman points out in *Reel Nature* (2009), "nature films . . . have sought to capture and recreate an experience of unspoiled nature" (3), regardless of the fact that, like all other modes of filmmaking, "the camera lens must impose itself, select its subject, and frame its vision" (4). Replacing one environment for another would break the unwritten contract between the makers and viewers of such films.[40]

The same is true for documentaries more generally. The authenticity of the depicted places, actors, and events is of great importance to the meaning of a nonfiction film, precisely because it is not understood by the viewer as fiction. Noël Carroll has argued that "films come labeled . . . or indexed" either as fiction or nonfiction film and that as viewers we thus expect a certain kind of film when we buy a ticket to see it (1996, 287).[41] When we buy a ticket for a documentary, we expect to see authentic protagonists and environments, unless a sequence has been specifically denoted as re-enactment. As Plantinga puts it, a nonfiction film "asserts, or is taken by the spectator to assert, that the states of affairs it presents occur or occurred in the actual world" (1996, 310). It is this assertion of actuality that Dirk Eitzen sees at the heart of our emotional response to documentary film. Rather than calling nonfiction a mode, Eitzen suggests that we should simply consider it "a *discourse of consequence*" (2005, 192). His central example is Robert Gardner's *Forest of Bliss* (1985), a documentary about India that at one point shows an emaciated dog that "is set upon by a pack of more-robust dogs. The lone mongrel tries to run away, but the pack catches it and brings it down" (2005, 183). Eitzen reports that "even in a fiction film, seeing an event like this would be profoundly disturbing. Seeing it in a documentary, I found it practically unbearable" (183). His emotional response was modulated by his knowledge that these events were *authentic*. The dog in the film was actually attacked by the other dogs and no disclaimer was added that no animals were harmed during the making of this film.

I will return to Eitzen's display of empathy and compassion for a dog in distress in chapter 4, when I discuss trans-species empathy and our emotional response to animals on film. Right now, I am interested in Eitzen's claim that the actuality and consequential nature of the things we see in nonfiction film are constitutive for our emotional response. To see the relevance of this claim, we only need to consider the heated public controversies around an environmental documentary like Josh Fox's *Gasland* (2010), which tackles the "hot" political and economic issue of natural gas drilling by hydraulic fracturing—or "fracking"—in the United States.[42] It was a letter from a natural gas company offering to lease his family's land in Milanville, Pennsylvania, to drill for gas that led Fox to embark on a project that would later be nominated for an Academy Award and also become the target of vicious attacks from the oil and gas industry. The film is framed as an inquiry into the "truth" of natural gas fracking and the risks and dangers it might pose to the environment and the animals and people who live in it. It shows miles and miles of authentic American landscape that have been affected by the drilling activities, using zooms, pans, and other forms of camera movement as well as accompanying scientific and technical information to direct viewer attention toward the devastation. Its most notorious shots, however, all show American citizens who can light their tap water on fire because of the methane it contains. As far as special effects in fiction films go, those moments of burning water are pretty unspectacular, and yet most viewers will recoil, move back in their seats, when watching the protagonists jump backward to escape the flare that is leaping at them from their faucet. While the bodily movement itself is an involuntary startle response, it is the viewer's conviction that there is no special effect involved that makes these scenes emotionally salient, not only because there are real-world consequences for the people portrayed in the film but also because, theoretically at least, the viewer herself could be affected.

Much of the controversy around the film has focused on those moments of burning tap water.[43] The Independent Petroleum Association of America founded the front group Energy In Depth in response to the film and created a web page that lists factual inaccuracies in *Gasland*. It also produced the documentary *Truthland* (2011), which rebuts several of *Gasland*'s claims, above all the relation it draws between fracking and groundwater contamination.[44] *Truthland* is staged as a "teacher and farmer's" inquiry into "the real truth" of the issue.[45] She admits that what she has seen in *Gasland* is "pretty scary" but is quick to add that "scary movies do not always tell the truth." Well aware that it is *Gasland*'s claim to actuality that makes the film emotionally powerful, the makers of *Truthland* try to debunk the truth content of its most spectacular claim, presenting evidence that natural gas occurs independently of any fracking activities in so-called burning springs in Kentucky and West Virginia.[46] The goal behind the film is to convince viewers that the evidence presented in *Gasland* is misleading and therefore *inconsequential* in the actual world. In fact, Energy In Depth went so far as to send an open letter to the Academy of Motion Picture Arts and Sciences shortly before the award ceremony to suggest that while the Oscar-nominated film has value as "an expression of stylized fiction," it fails to comply with the Academy's "Special Rules for the Documentary Awards" and should therefore be withdrawn from the documentary feature category (quoted in Keegan 2010).[47] This is a remarkable attempt to re-index *Gasland* as fiction in the eyes of the public. Viewers who believe the argument will likely feel much less emotionally affected by the fracking landscapes they see in Fox's film, regardless of the fact that those landscapes, as well as the burning water faucets, are authentic.[48]

The issue of environmental authenticity is therefore a tricky one in any form of ecocinema. The makers of the most consciously environmentalist fiction film will exchange one location for another for any number of reasons or transform pre-filmic environments beyond recognition if it fits the needs of the narrative and heightens the film's emotional impact on viewers. Documentary film is more "truthful" when it comes to the actual places it archives on film, but even wildlife documentaries have been known to show manipulated environments to make them more attractive to viewers. While this does not change the important role played by cinematic environments in our affective responses to film, it does complicate ecocritical arguments because—much like in the case of actors—there often is a discrepancy between the actual environment that is filmed and the environment it "plays" on the screen. Such complications do not render ecocritical analysis mute, but they need to be taken seriously.

CONCLUSION

In this chapter, I have been concerned with filmic foregrounding techniques and the ways in which filmmakers guide viewer attention toward the cinematic environments that not only surround their protagonists but also circumscribe and sometimes determine their actions. Whereas the perceived authenticity of the depicted environment is of central importance for viewers' cognitive and affective response to documentaries, that importance is greatly diminished in the case of fiction films, which often are shot in locations that have little or no relationship to the environment depicted in the film. In both fiction and non-fiction film, however, the space that surrounds characters is much more than just a "background" for the foregrounded action. Like the literary environments I discussed in chapter 1, cinematic environments play an important role in our sense of immersion in a storyworld and in our embodied simulation of the protagonists' actions, thoughts, and emotions. Processes of embodied simulation even seem to play a central role in our direct response to all kinds of cinematic environments, regardless of their degree of authenticity, especially so if those environments are full of motion. Psychologist Davide Massaro and his collaborators state in a behavioral and eye-tracking study on the visual processing of artworks that "perhaps, even when contemplating a waterfall, embodiment is relevant" (2012, 13). Recent fMRI research suggests that we also map inanimate movement such as that of a waterfall (even one represented in art) onto the motor systems of our brain, simulating and thus understanding it in relation to our own bodies, regardless of the fact that our bodies are not actually capable of performing that particular kind of movement.

Such empirical evidence further substantiates Gregory Currie's claim that we can have "empathy for objects" (2011, 82), and puts a question mark behind Tan and Frijda's assertion that the emotions we feel in response to a visually overwhelming cinematic landscape are by definition nonempathetic (1999, 52).[49] The fact that we map the movements and collisions of observed objects onto the premotor cortices of our brains gives another dimension to the excitement we feel when watching the spinning movement of an animated tornado in *Twister*. And perhaps our empathy with objects goes even beyond mere embodied simulation to include an empathetic relation with another living being's struggle for survival. That we can feel with and for trees or even mountains will not come as a surprise to most environmentalists. That we might be invited do so in a movie suggests itself to anyone who has witnessed the destruction of Pandora's Hometree by humans in *Avatar*.

I will return to Cameron's film in part III of the book, when I discuss the affective appeal of utopian ecologies. Before I get to that, however, I want to give more thought to the role played by empathy in our engagements with out-group others within and beyond the human species boundary. Eitzen's account of his emotional response to the suffering of a dog in a documentary film reminds us that empathetic engagement with others does not stop at the human species boundary, and yet, it often is remarkably difficult for us to truly feel for other humans who we do not know well. There is ample research on empathy's "familiarity bias," demonstrating that it is much easier for us to empathize with those who are close to us not only in terms of personal relations but also in terms of gender, race, ethnicity, nationality, religion, and a range of other social markers. In part II I will demonstrate that this research has implications for our moral and ethical thinking about social and environmental justice, and that it also is relevant for the analysis of the narrative strategies of environmental justice stories in literature and film.

PART II

Feeling with Others

CHAPTER 3

Imagining the Pain

Strategic Empathy and the Environmental Justice Narrative

WHEN ROBERT HAWKS steps out of his mountain cabin in the middle of a snowstorm to have a look at the nearby creek, he immediately can "tell, even in its frozen state, that something [is] wrong" (Everett [1996] 2003, 166). As a hydrologist, it is Hawks's job to read landscapes and waterways, and so he sees instantly that the winter flow of the creek is much too low. Having barely recovered from a car accident on a patch of black ice, the protagonist of Percival Everett's novel *Watershed* cannot stop himself from following the frozen rivulet higher up the mountain until he finally stands in front of the reason for its reduced flow: "There, in the middle of nowhere on Dog Creek, was a dam, a real honest-to-goodness poured-concrete dam, and the gate of it did not open into the Dog, but instead led down the mountain in a direction ninety degrees opposed to it" (167). Stunned and suspicious, Hawks follows the raised pipeline that leads away from the dam until it opens onto a hillside: "I studied the land there . . . and then it hit me. . . . I was in Silly Man Canyon and from here the water fed down into the Plata, which ran through the Plata Creek Indian Reservation" (167). Hawks is so incensed by the discovery that he ends up camping out in the blizzard in search of the reason for the water diversion. Because he is a literary character and first-person narrator, readers are cued to sense and feel along with him, simulating in their minds his physical exhaustion in the icy weather and his moral outrage when he finally finds the secret government depot of biological weapons that has begun to leak into the groundwater and is now poisoning the Plata tribe. Seeing the situation through the eyes of a scientist who fully understands its horrific implications, readers are invited to empathize with his feelings of shock, disgust, and anger, and to later root for him when he joins the Plata Indians in a violent struggle for environmental justice.

In the first part of the book, I have investigated how literary texts and films evoke environments and how they make those environments emotionally salient through the use of narrative perspective and imagery that invites embodied simulation. In this chapter, I will continue that investigation with a consideration of environmental justice narratives and the ways in which they use readers' empathy strategically to make a moral argument about people who have been wronged. As Kristin Shrader-Frechette explains, "environmental justice occurs whenever some individual or group bears disproportionate risks, like those of hazardous waste dumps, or has unequal access to environmental goods, like clean air, or has less opportunity to participate in environmental decision-making" (2002, 3). There are many ways in which people can be affected, but they always involve a limitation of personal and communal agency due to class, gender, race, ethnicity, and a range of other social markers. In a democratic nation such as the United States, the social unevenness of environmental risk distribution constitutes a case of not only moral but also political and legal injustice, and since the emergence of the environmental justice movement in the early 1980s, affected communities have repeatedly taken the responsible parties to court.[1] However, as the literary scholar Julie Sze has pointed out, the environmental justice movement is "not only a political movement concerned with public policy issues of environmental racism;" it is also "a cultural movement interested in issues of ideology and representation" (2002, 163). The novels and films I will consider in this chapter participate in the cultural discourse around environmental injustice by foregrounding its political, legal, economic, and, above all, *moral* dimensions.

American ethnic literature, in particular, has produced powerful narratives about minority communities struggling with ecological degradation or with toxic environments. Examples range from Leslie Marmon Silko's *Ceremony* (1977) and Linda Hogan's *Solar Storms* (1995) to Toni Cade Bambara's *The Salt Eaters* (1980) and Helena Maria Viramontes's *Under the Feet of Jesus* (1995).[2] While these novels are indexed as fiction, their narratives gain emotional force through their direct or indirect references to actual cases of environmental injustice. Even though the characters and stories they present are fictitious, they allude to *similar situations* that have occurred—and have been consequential—in the actual world.[3] The novels' relationship to these authentic situations, people, and environments is therefore much more complex and ambiguous than that of nonfiction forms. And yet, the fact that they are based "on a true story" or allude to actual occurrences impacts readers who are aware of that connection. In this chapter, I will be interested not only in the affective dimensions of this complex relationship between fact and fiction, but also in how such narratives use our capacity for empathy strategically in order to encourage readers to feel moral allegiance with the victims of environmental injustice.

The first section will draw on Suzanne Keen's concept of "*authorial strategic empathizing*" (2010, 82) to make a theoretical argument about how environmental justice narratives invite readers to empathize and sympathize with out-group others who are at risk. Erin James has suggested that "sensory appeals, or *qualia,* are particularly powerful when they are filtered through a subjective consciousness informed by a different sociohistorical, material, and/or cultural context than that of the reader" (2015, 40). The section will use Viramontes's *Under the Feet of Jesus* as an example of a novel that filters its sensory appeals through the subjective consciousness of Hispanic migrant workers who get poisoned in the orchards of Southern California, discussing how such an *insider perspective* involves readers affectively in a situation of environmental injustice. The second section will then turn to Everett's *Watershed,* which uses a very different, and in certain ways more indirect, narrative strategy. Instead of aligning readers with the victims of environmental injustice, the novel presents its case through the eyes of an *outsider* who only slowly and begrudgingly learns to care for a Native American community that is put at risk by the American government. I will argue that this, too, constitutes a case of strategic empathizing, and one that is particularly interesting not only because of the novel's complex racial politics and frequent allusions to American history but also because of its postmodern form.

The third and last section will demonstrate that the same two basic forms of authorial strategic empathizing—what I will call the *insider perspective* and the *outsider perspective*—can also be found in film, though they are realized by different narrative means. Michael Apted's *Thunderheart* (1992) in certain ways parallels Everett's indirect approach on the cinematic level as it aligns viewers not primarily with the victims of environmental injustice but with someone who tries to help them. The last film I will consider—Benh Zeitlin's *Beasts of the Southern Wild* (2012)—is a particularly intriguing example not only of an insider perspective on environmental injustice, but also of a film that deftly merges fact and fiction. Featuring lay actors and original locations in the Louisiana bayous, it explores environmental injustice from the inside and through the consciousness of a child, thereby aligning viewers with a moral perspective that is unabashedly emotional and, at times, magical.

STRATEGIC EMPATHY AND MORAL JUDGMENT: ENVIRONMENTAL INJUSTICE AND NARRATIVE PERSPECTIVE

Our capacity for empathy is of central importance for our social relationships with others. Defined by psychologist Martin Hoffman as "an affective response more appropriate to another's situation than one's own" (2000, 4), empathy is what allows us to "slip into another person's shoes" and to experience some of her sensations, thoughts, and feelings. This is true not only in real life but also in our engagement with literature and film. Psychologists differentiate between *cognitive empathy*—also known as mind reading or Theory of Mind (ToM)—and *affective empathy*, which is the result of emotional contagion or, more generally, the complex processes of embodied simulation that Vittorio Gallese and Hannah Wojciehowski call Feeling of Body (FoB) (2011).[4] Cognitive empathy allows us to make logical inferences about another person's situation, thoughts, and emotions, while affective empathy allows us to understand that person's feelings and the situation she is in on a more visceral and often subconscious level. Both processes are crucial for our emotional understanding of others. As Hoffman explains, the two types of empathy "often occur together, as for example in the courtroom when a judge or jury member becomes aware of an absent victim's plight, imagines how the victim feels, and the resulting image triggers affective empathy" (2011, 231). In Hoffman's view it is affective empathy—and therefore processes of embodied simulation— that are of particular importance to moral reasoning and prosocial behavior. "Mature adult empathy," he explains, "has a meta-cognitive dimension: one is aware of the empathizing—that is, one feels distressed but knows this is a response to another's misfortune, not one's own, and has an idea of how the other feels" (231). Feeling along with the victim leads to what Hoffman calls *empathetic distress*. In many cases, it is so uncomfortable for the person experiencing it that it leads to helping behavior and other prosocial actions.[5]

The courtroom example that Hoffman offers makes clear that the person in distress does not have to be physically or even visually present to trigger an empathic response. Mere words are sufficient if the description is vivid enough to cue a strong embodied simulation in the mind of the listener or reader. This is why it has been argued by psychologists and philosophers alike that emotionally engaging literature can have *moral* effects on readers that go beyond the immediate reading experience. The philosopher Martha Nussbaum, for example, writes that literary texts can "wrest from our frequently obtuse and blunted imaginations an acknowledgment of those who are other than ourselves, both in concrete circumstances and even in thought and emotion" (1997, 111–12). Research in the psychology of fiction suggests that such wresting can have some very concrete effects on people's attitudes and behaviors in the actual world. A 2009 study by Raymond Mar, Keith Oatley, and Jordan Peterson found that fiction exposure "predicted performance on an empathy task" and "that exposure to fiction was positively correlated with social support" (407). Reading engaging fiction allowed subjects to perform better on an empathy task (watching short clips of people in ordinary situations and guessing what is going on between them) than not reading or the reading of nonfiction.[6]

Such research is particularly interesting in light of what Hoffman calls empathy's "familiarity bias" (2000, 22). Psychologists Jean Decety and Jason Cowell explain: "at times, empathy guides moral judgment, yet other times empathy can interfere with it" (2014, 337). Empathy can interfere with moral judgment because we tend to empathize most readily with those who are near and dear to us, or at least *like* us in the sense of belonging to the same social, ethnic, national, or religious group. It takes much more effort to feel empathy for members of an out-group, which is why the philosopher Jesse Prinz has argued that empathy "is so vulnerable to bias and selectivity that it fails to provide a broad umbrella of moral concern" (2011, 227). Prinz concludes that empathy does not have much "force in promoting action" (228) and that it therefore "cannot serve the central role in driving pro-social behavior" (229) that Hoffman attributes to it. In Prinz's view, empathy "has a place in morality, but other emotions may be much more important: emotions such as guilt and anger. When confronted with moral offenses, it's not enough to commiserate with victims. We should get uppity" (229). While Prinz may be right about this last point, I wonder about some of his reasoning here. Empathy is not normally considered a proper emotion, though it may lead to or be part of an emotional response. Also, the simulation of another person's situation need not (solely) lead to commiseration. It may as well lead to empathetic anger, to feelings of guilt (transgression guilt if one is personally responsible for a negative situation or bystander guilt if one has done nothing to help). It may also lead to disgust at the person who is responsible for the moral offense, or to other forms of empathetic distress. As I have demonstrated in *Cosmopolitan Minds* (2014a), narratives can invite readers to feel all of those emotions through an empathetic relation to fictional characters and the vivid simulation of the situations they are in.

The strongest barrier to feeling with and for others is *empathy inhibition*—the cognitive suppression of empathic distress for egoistical, economic, practical, ideological, or cultural reasons. As Patrick Colm Hogan has pointed out, in-group/out-group divisions are among the most important forms of empathy inhibition because they construct the other as stereotypically different and less worthy of an empathetic response (2011b, 177). Some scholars have claimed that fiction is in fact particularly suited for overcoming such identity-related forms of empathy inhibition, precisely *because* readers know that the characters are fictitious. Keen, for example, has argued that fiction "disarm[s] readers of some of the protective layers of cautious reasoning that may inhibit empathy in the real world" and so they might end up empathizing with and caring for a fictional character of a different nationality, ethnicity, race, or class that they never would have befriended in real life (2010, 69). Such out-group empathizing with fictional beings, however, may quickly reach its limitations. Dan Flory alerts us to the problem of "imaginative resistance" (2013, 41). With reference to the philosophical work of Tamar Gendler (2000, 2006), he explores the difficulties both readers and spectators may experience "in engaging in an imaginative act concerning a moral claim stipulated by a fictional narrative" (43), difficulties that may "make it impossible for us to imagine in the way the narrative directs us" (44). Such moments of imaginative resistance can also occur when we are invited to imagine a character belonging to an out-group, leading either to empathy inhibition or, perhaps even more interestingly, to imaginary inaccuracies concerning the identity of the fictional character.[7]

Politically minded writers and filmmakers often try to circumvent such forms of resistance by employing what Keen calls *authorial strategic empathizing* (2010, 82). Evoking Gayatri Spivak's notion of "strategic essentialism," Keen explains that "strategic empathizing occurs when an author employs empathy in the crafting of fictional texts, in the service of 'a scrupulously visible political interest'" (83).[8] The question is how empathy can be employed in ways that circumvent imaginary resistance due to in-group/out-group divisions. Patrick Hogan's concept of *situational empathy* is helpful in thinking about narrative strategies that try to get around imaginary resistance and empathy inhibition by inviting readers to become familiar with the *situation* of a character and with the character's thoughts and feelings in response to that situation. Situational empathy, Hogan explains in *The Mind and Its Stories* (2003), involves a shifting or 'fusing' of perspectives in a process in which one draws on memories (and associated feelings) that are similar to what the other person (real or fictitious) goes through. By empathizing with the situations of people, we can approximate some of their feelings and concerns, even if these people are very different from ourselves. Situational empathy, therefore, can lead us to feel with members of an out-group with whom we do not share a great number of group-defining features (P. Hogan 2003, 140–46). While there is always the danger of what Keen has called "empathetic inaccuracy" (2010, 88), a basic understanding of such situations is possible.[9]

There are at least two ways in which authors can employ strategic empathizing to help readers to imaginatively experience the situation of a victim of injustice: They can align them with the victim himself—what I have called the *insider perspective*—or with someone who isn't directly affected but learns to care for the victim and his situation—this I have called the *outsider perspective*. As I have explained in chapter 1, in our engagement with literature, alignment is a result of our access to the consciousness, feelings, and action of a character. If we see the events from a certain character's perspective, we are aligned with that character in the sense that the character is the focalizer of the story. Such alignment often leads to moral allegiance when the narrative elicits sympathy toward that character, which in turn is "triggered—if not wholly determined—by the moral structure" of the narrative (M. Smith 1999, 220).[10] As has become clear in my discussion of Bonnie Nadzam's *Lamb*, narratives can align us with morally ambiguous or perverse protagonists that make us uncomfortable precisely because we are so closely aligned with them in terms of narrative perspective. When protagonists act *in accordance* with the moral structure of the narrative, however, we are likely to feel allegiance to them unless that moral structure strongly opposes our own moral beliefs.

According to Gendler, imaginative resistance on the part of the reader signals a failure of the author's authority (2006, 157–59) and thus a failure of authorial strategic empathizing. Like the risk of empathetic inaccuracy, the risk of imaginative resistance is unavoidable and it will vary with different readers and different groups of readers. And yet, strategic authorial empathizing can also be quite successful. A recent empirical study by psychologist Dan Johnson and colleagues (2013) offers a great example for how the use of narrative perspective can lead readers to feel allegiance to a character that does not belong to their in-group. Johnson and his team used a chapter from Shaila Abdullah's novel *Saffron Dreams* (2009) to test whether reading about a racist attack from the point of view of its Muslim victim has any effects on (non-Muslim) American readers' prejudices against Arabic-looking individuals. As the authors explain, the protagonist and first-person narrator of the novel "is an educated and strong-willed Muslim woman who is assaulted in a New York City subway station. She is also pregnant and exhibits extraordinary courage by standing up to her attackers' ethnic and religious slurs" (Johnson et al. 2013, 582).[11] The events are focalized through Arissa's consciousness, allowing readers to simulate her subjective experience. This use of an insider perspective to align readers with the experience of a victim of racial violence had significant effects on subjects' subsequent response to images of mixed-race individuals in the second phase of the experiment. Johnson et al. sum up their findings as follows: "The narrative was particularly effective at reducing implicit prejudice in low dispositional perspective-takers. Partially explaining this effect, the narrative appeared to provide a safe haven from intergroup anxiety so that they could use perspective-taking to reduce prejudice. These findings demonstrate the narrative's power to induce spontaneous empathy and perspective-taking and consequently reduce implicit and explicit prejudice" (2013, 578). In a follow-up publication (2013), Johnson highlights that these results correlated to a significant degree with readers' sense of transportation into the narrative world.[12]

Abdullah's novel indeed makes it easy for readers to simulate Arissa's subjective experience of her situation as she notices that "they were moving closer. I could feel it, and I tried to rush my pace. The muscles in my back tightened as I sensed their gained momentum, the footsteps matching mine" (2009, 61). Even presented out of context, as it is here, the passage invites readers to slip into Arissa's shoes and to simulate her dangerous situation, feeling empathetic fear as their own back muscles tighten and they imagine the alarming sound of footsteps coming closer in a deserted subway station. Howard Sklar argues in *The Art of Sympathy in Fiction* (2013) that sympathy results from two basic components: "the heightened awareness of the suffering of another" and "a judgment of the explicit or implicit unfairness of that suffering" (28). These two components are present throughout Abdullah's novel, and they are particularly prevalent in the chapter that Johnson et al. selected for their experiment. Not only does the narrative present the woman as vulnerable to her attackers and thus in need of protection because of her pregnancy, this vulnerability is combined with traits that invite sympathy and admiration when Arissa bravely turns around to face the young men who try to hold her responsible for the terrorist attacks on 9/11. When her attackers split open Arissa's coat with a knife and expose "the big bulge on [her] stomach" (Abdullah 2009, 62), her fear turns into anger and she confronts them with the fact that her husband—and thus the father of her unborn child—was among the people who died in the twin towers. Readers' awareness of the protagonist's suffering is thus combined with the realization that the infliction of this suffering is both immoral and profoundly unfair.

Given the findings of Johnson et al.'s study, we must assume that narratives that align readers with the victims of environmental injustice can have similar effects on some out-group readers at least, particularly so in cases

where authors use strategic empathizing to make such alignment emotionally salient. Viramontes's novel *Under the Feet of Jesus,* for example, invites
readers to share the experience of the Chicana girl Estrella, who, at the age of
fifteen, is forced to work in the orchards of California to help feed her family
of migrant workers. Readers learn that "the sun was white and it made Estrella's eyes sting like an onion, and the baskets of grapes resisted her muscles,
pulling their magnetic weight back to earth" (1995, 49). As I have explained
elsewhere (Weik von Mossner 2016), the vivid visual and motor imagery of
such sentences allows readers to mentally simulate Estrella's experience, giving
them a sense of *what it is like* to sink one's knees "in the hot white soil," and
then get up again, "row after row, sun after sun" (Viramontes 1995, 50). Even if
they aren't migrant workers themselves (they most likely aren't) most readers
will be able to empathize with Estrella's *situation.* In her ecocritical reading of
Under the Feet of Jesus, Christa Grewe-Volpp states that the novel "realistically
depicts the poor living conditions and the monotonous, hard field work of the
migrant pickers, their exploitation and their poisoning" and that it "sympa-
thetically sides with marginalized people" (2005, 64). Both the sympathizing
and the realism are of central importance for readers' involvement in the text
and for their experience of empathetic distress not only for Estrella but also
for other people *like* her. Henry James once claimed in his influential essay on
"The Art of Fiction" that "the only reason for the existence of a novel is that
it does compete with life" (1884), and it is in this sense that *Under the Feet of
Jesus* and many other environmental justice novels are realistic.[13]

Viramontes has dedicated her novel to her parents, "who met in Button-
willow picking cotton" in the San Joaquin Valley, and she has explained in an
interview that, in her view, literature is "great for prompting discussions about
certain social issues" (Romero 2010, para. 5). This commitment to fictional-
izing authentic experience in order to prompt a social discussion leads her to
tell her story from the point of view of the workers, using personal experience as inspiration for the fictional storyworld of the novel and the characters
that populate it. Grewe-Volpp notes that the narrative's multiple viewpoints
demand "active reader participation" (2005, 64). All of those viewpoints, however, belong to Estrella's family and other migrant workers. Even in situations
that involve a conflict between the workers and the dominant culture that
circumscribes their lives, readers remain consistently tied to the perspective
of the workers, gaining little or no insight into the thoughts and emotions
of those who mistreat them. As a result, readers' sympathies—even those of
out-group members—will likely lie with the workers rather than with the people who refuse to see their existential needs and their sheer humanity. As in
Abdullah's *Saffron Dreams,* readers are given ample opportunity to become

aware of the suffering of the novel's protagonists, who are portrayed as caring, virtuous, and hard-working individuals. Viramontes thereby invites readers to feel along with her sympathetic characters and to recognize the unfairness of their situation. Even in moments of aggression and outright violence—as in the climactic moment when Estrella uses a crowbar to threaten a white nurse who has failed to help her dying boyfriend—readers are likely to root for the desperate girl rather than for the indifferent nurse, judging Estrella's rage to be morally justified within the circumstances.[14]

Many narratives that deal with environmental injustice provide readers with such insider perspectives on the suffering of the affected communities. If the protagonist is not immediately involved, then she often belongs to the same community and therefore possesses an emotional connection to the related events.[15] Everett's *Watershed,* to which I will now turn, is an example of a narrative that approaches environmental injustice from a genuine outsider perspective, one that is particularly interesting because both the victims and the person who tries to help them belong to ethnic minorities. With Robert Hawks, the novel centers on an African American scientist who cannot help but get involved in the environmental justice struggle of a group of Native Americans because he empathizes with their situation and is morally outraged.

STRATEGIC EMPATHY AND THE OUTSIDER PERSPECTIVE ON ENVIRONMENTAL INJUSTICE: *WATERSHED*

One cannot write about strategic empathizing in *Watershed* without first addressing the novel's complex narrative structure. While it is consistently told from Hawks's perspective, it is a decidedly postmodern text that freely jumps back and forth between three different time planes and also intersperses fragments from nonfiction texts, such as scientific documents and legal treaties, both historical and fictitious. It starts out with a statement made in 1873 by the Congregational minister Edward Parmelee Smith about the impossibility of a "general Indian war" (Everett [1996] 2003, 1). From there it jumps, in media res, to the following declaration:

> My blood is my own and my name is Robert Hawks. I am sitting on a painted green wooden bench in a small Episcopal church on the northern edge of the Plata Indian Reservation, holding in my hands a Vietnam-era M-16, the butt of the weapon flat against the plank floor between my feet. There are seven other armed people sitting on the floor, backs against the

paneled walls, or pacing and peering out the windows—stained and clear—
at the armored personnel carrier some hundred yards away. . . . Out there,
there are two hundred and fifty police—FBI, all clad in blue windbreakers
with large gold letters, and National Guardsmen, looking like the soldiers
they want to be. (1–2)

The opening passage creates immediacy through the use of present-tense,
first-person narration, and in spite of its sparseness in terms of descriptive
detail, it is filled with visual and motor imagery that allows readers to get a
clear sense of Hawk's surroundings and situation.[16] Simulating that situation
in their minds, they might be forgiven for thinking that they are about to
embark on a thriller. They might also be forgiven for assuming that the protagonist is Native American. There is no information about Hawks's looks or
racial identity, and so readers cannot know that his insistence that his "blood
is [his] own" alludes to his utter refusal to be classified in racial terms. What
they do learn, however, is that he and a group of Indians are in very serious
trouble with the police and that—unlikely as it may seem in this dangerous
situation—he has a story to tell. Despite feeling "put out or annoyed or even
dismayed at having to tell this story," Hawks believes himself to be "the only
one who can properly and accurately reproduce it" (2). He is an unwilling sto-
ryteller, then, but one who believes in the power of true stories and who feels
compelled to speak because no one else would give "a fair representation of
the events" (2).

From this dramatic opening, the novel jumps back in time, offering several
short fragments from which we learn that Hawks is African American; that
both his father and his grandfather were actively engaged in the Civil Rights
Movement; and that this political engagement disrupted the family. We also
learn that Hawks has escaped to Plata Mountain to get away from Denver and
from his personal problems with Karen, the woman he has "been fucking" (4).
His narrative voice is laconic, ironic, and distant, as when he tells us that he
has decided to use this rather drastic term for his "interaction" with Karen,
"having found disfavor with the term *relationship*" (4). Relationships aren't
Hawks's strongpoint, and so it is with the same laconic voice that he narrates
in many interspersed flashbacks what it meant for him to grow up in a family of civil rights activists and how he was affected by the turbulent quarrels
with Karen that immediately preceded his arrival on Plata Mountain. Out of
this complicated structure, a narrative emerges that gives insight into Hawks's
personal history and psyche. As a result of his childhood experiences in a
racialized society, he has become a deeply antisocial, disconnected, and cyni-
cal man. We learn that he has chosen the profession of a hydrologist not least

because he believes it to be thoroughly apolitical and disinterested. Considering himself "an objective, hired gun" (152), he claims that he puts his scientific knowledge into the service of whoever pays his salary. About the rest of the world and the state it is in, he professes not to care.

Overwhelmed by his own inability to "extricate" himself from an unhealthy relationship, Hawks has taken a leave of absence from his university and moved into his cabin on Plata Mountain whose watershed he has been studying for years. In the solitude of the wintery landscape, he hopes "to fish and think and be alone" (4). However, this solitary retreat into nature does not last very long. Soon the scene gets crowded with all kinds of people, and Hawks is forced to realize that the ecological space of Plata Mountain is neither lonesome nor peaceful. He first meets Louise Small Calf, a dwarfish Plata Indian woman who fixes his broken truck and hitches a ride to the nearby lake and who later in the same night shows up half-frozen at the door of his cabin with no explanation of her actions in the meantime. Next, Hawks is confronted with the news that two FBI agents have been found dead in the lake and a number of state officials turn up at his door, all asking questions about Louise.

Like Nadzam's *Lamb, Watershed* ironizes the idea of the wilderness retreat as a place where one finds peace and quiet in an unspoilt nature free of humans. And like *Lamb,* it aligns readers with a flawed and in many ways unsympathetic protagonist who, as Hawks puts it himself, is "a smart-ass" (22): arrogant, cool, and unable to commit to a person or cause. Unlike *Lamb,* however, *Watershed* lets its protagonist speak for himself as a first-person narrator. By giving readers insight into his painful youth and the personal demons that haunt him, Hawks enables readers to construct explanations for his current behavior. "When you're older," his grandfather tells him when he is still a boy, "the police will stop you and search and, if they don't shoot you, they'll take you in and say you look like another 'nigger.' . . . It's happened to me. It's happened to your father. It will happen to you" (14). The finality and inevitability implied in such statements scare the young boy, but what disturbs him even more is that his grandfather later takes his own life after losing his license to practice medicine because of his political activism. Hawks has suffered, and he didn't deserve to suffer any more than any other boy. His distant attitude and dismissal of all affiliations is a coping mechanism—a maladapted one, perhaps, but one that is relatable for readers who have experienced painful losses themselves and/or are principally opposed to racial discrimination.

Unlike David Lamb, then, Robert Hawks increasingly invites sympathy as the story progresses, not only because readers develop an understanding of why and how he has become the man he is, but also because he changes his demeanor rather dramatically, becoming more and more engaged. When the FBI agents knock on his door to inquire about Louise Small Calf, Hawks almost instinctively lies to them. At this point, he knows very little about the situation on Plata Mountain, despite the many years he has spent studying its watershed. The only disturbing information he has received—aside from the murder of the two agents—is Louise's statement that "the mountain is dying" because "the river is no longer any good" (19). When she suggests that he should come to the reservation and meet her people, Hawks retreats into silence, unwilling to get involved. And yet, he not only protects Louise from the police but also defends her tribe against unjust allegations. When two white farmers want to know from him, the scientist, "whose water" it is, Hawks at first clings to his long-cultivated disinterest, claiming that he "only stud[ies] water" and that he does not "know whose it is" (30). But after one of the men blurs out that "them Injuns" are "just fuckin' greedy" (30), Hawks can no longer hold himself back, reminding him that "the treaty says it's theirs. They were here first" (30). He thereby makes clear that he in fact knows exactly whose water it is. Hawks is familiar with American water law in the arid West of the country, which—following for historical reasons Spanish (and essentially Moroccan) water law—adheres to the doctrine of prior appropriation.[17] The impatience in his words indicates that he is also aware of the Native American struggle for those rights.[18] His interlocutors sense this, too. "You're on their side," one of the men says and seems almost satisfied. "If I have to be on a side," Hawks answers coolly, "I guess it won't be yours" (Everett [1996] 2003, 30).

If pressed to takes sides, Hawks chooses that of the Plata Indians, suggesting not only to the farmers but also to readers that this is the legally and morally right side to be on. The fact that he speaks as the cool-headed scientist here only increases the persuasive power of his words and prepares readers for the revelation of the much greater injustice and outright assault on the lives of the Plata Indians that is revealed later on. "Fictional characters," writes psychologist Richard Gerrig, "are often introduced by their behaviors, rather than by explicit mention of the traits that (potentially) generate those behaviors" (2010, 360). Readers infer essential character traits from simulating those behaviors using cognitive empathy, or Theory of Mind. That is why in *Watershed* they quickly find out that Robert Hawks is not quite as distant as he declares over and over again that he is. His "over-the-top second order thinking" is, as he admits, "a detaching device" (Everett [1996] 2003, 11), but the more he insists on his detachment, the more readers realize that it doesn't match up with his behavior. His first-person narrative is therefore unreliable in an unusual sense, insisting on his indifference and reporting actions that suggest the contrary. Despite his repeatedly professed unwillingness to engage with racial or political issues of any kind, his curiosity about Louise and her people propels him ever deeper into her world. His interest further increases once he learns that some of the younger Plata Indians belong to a militant group called the "American Indian Revolution" (AIR)—one of many elements in the novel that aim at creating connections between its fictional storyworld and the actual history of minority groups in the United States.

Readers who already felt that the siege of the small church that opens the narrative was vaguely familiar will at this point recognize obvious parallels to the historical American Indian Movement (AIM) and its eventful history. William Handley has maintained that *Watershed* "is a novel in which history weighs heavily" (2005, 305), and this is true in multiple ways. The Native American novelist Sherman Alexie explains in his introduction to *Watershed* that "Everett fictionalizes the 1970s political battles on the Lakota Sioux Pine Ridge Reservation in South Dakota, combines them with fictional and real events during the 1960s civil rights battles for African Americans, and sets it all on a contemporary and fictional Indian reservation" (1996, ix–x). Everett himself, of course, writes in the acknowledgments section of his book that "the Plata Reservation and the Plata Nation presented in this work are fictitious and are meant to bear no direct or indirect resemblance to any existing place or people" ([1996] 2003, 202). However, reading Alexie's introduction, one shares Handley's suspicion about whether one should believe Everett, since interested readers will also detect parallels to the 1973 Wounded Knee Incident and the 1975 Pine Ridge Shootout—both sited in the South Dakota Pine Ridge Reservation.[19] And while the landscape around Plata Mountain might indeed be "complete fiction" (202), as Everett has also claimed, the environmental hazards generated by military sites to which American Indian communities are exposed to are far from fictitious.

The fact that in the novel the deadly contamination is brought into the reservation through a river is of particular significance, since contaminated water supply is one of the many ways in which environmental hazards have affected Indian reservations.[20] In 1980, the *Report of Women of All Red Nations* declared: "to contaminate Indian water is an act of war more subtle than military aggression, yet no less deadly" (qtd. in Brook 1998, 111). Viewed from this perspective, the U.S. government in Everett's novel has declared war on the Plata Indians; a war characterized by an extraordinary callousness. The government might not divert the toxic runoff from the leaking biological weapon depot onto reservation land *in order to* kill Native Americans, but their death is tacitly accepted as insignificant collateral damage.[21] Hawks's outsider perspective on these events is particularly intriguing because, next to Native Americans and Hispanics, black communities have had to bear the brunt of environmental risks and hazards in the United States. As sociologist Robert Bullard points out, "historically, toxic dumping and location of locally unwanted land uses (LULUs) have followed the 'path of least resistance,' meaning black and poor communities have been disproportionally burdened with these externalities" (1990, 3). Although we do not find an environmental justice battle in *Watershed*'s many flashbacks to Robert Hawks's youth as a black boy in Denver, the unbridled violence of American police officers that we encounter there is just another expression of the same ideology of callous neglect and institutionalized racism.[22]

His personal history of suffering makes it almost inevitable for Hawks to empathize with the *situation* of the Plata Indians and to need to find out more. As William Handley notes, "the desire to know more [becomes] a historical quest that leads Everett's narrator . . . to discern the connections and differences between African- and Native American experience under American colonialism" (2005, 305). Stacey Alaimo's ecocritical reading of the novel underlines the fact that, just as importantly, Hawks's quest also unveils the important continuities between the Civil Rights Movement and more recent struggles for environmental justice (2010, 66). Hawks cannot stop himself from noticing these continuities and from getting "involved" (Everett [1996] 2003, 187). And once he is emotionally involved, he begins to feel bystander guilt over his own inaction and apolitical stance. As both Hoffman (2000, 2011) and Prinz (2011) have noted, feelings of guilt and the related empathetic distress can be tremendous drivers of prosocial action. In Hawks's case it drives him to the moment that I have visited at the beginning of this chapter: the moment when he searches for evidence on Plata Mountain and finally stands before the concrete dam that the government has built in order to divert the poisoned water onto Indian land. It is the watershed moment in his life, and it demonstrates that empathy with a victim of injustice must not always lead to passive commiseration, as Prinz has claimed. In Hawks's case, it leads him to join the Plata's fight and to later crawl through a—perhaps contaminated—irrigation ditch to bring to safety a roll of film that will prove the government's illegal practices.

The reader is cued to feel along with Hawks and his growing concern and active engagement for a disenfranchised community that fights an institution that endangers and oppresses it. "What else am I supposed to do?" he responds when one of the Indians asks him why he risks his life for them (Everett [1996] 2003, 197). What stands behind this rhetorical question is a moral imperative, the imperative to leave behind his indifferent, apolitical stance and to do what is right. The fact that Hawks himself belongs to an oppressed minority group makes the story particularly rich and fascinating, but, for some readers at least, it might also stand in the way of easy identification and thus to the imaginative resistance I have discussed in the previous section. A 2012 study by Kaufman and Libby shows that out-group protagonists even tend to inhibit simulation processes in comparison to in-group protagonists. It also reveals that such prejudicial attitudes and resistances are reduced when the identity of the protagonist as an out-group member is only revealed late in the story's progression. In some of his other works, Everett has used that strategy, playing with the general tendency—especially of white readers—to assume, by default, that a protagonist whose racial and ethnic identity is not explicitly mentioned is white.[23] In *Watershed,* readers are early on made aware of Hawks's racial identity, yet the novel invites them in myriad other ways to question their own habits of racial stereotyping and categorization. The black man Hawks is a scientist who lives in the urban space of Denver, but he is also closely familiar with the Plata mountain range. As a hydrologist, he interacts with the natural environment in the objectifying way that we consider typical of (white) Western science. Yet, he also has an affective relationship to the mountain and, in an almost Thoreauvian manner, loves fishing and thinking—traits that run counter to stereotypical notions of African American relations to nature.[24] Many of the younger Plata Indians, on the other hand, have not grown up in close proximity with their ancestral lands but in Los Angeles or other big cities. They know nothing of Plata Mountain and thus ironically depend on the environmental knowledge of the black man Hawks.[25]

Despite, or perhaps because of, the novel's constant undermining of racial stereotypes, Hawks might prove a much more challenging identification figure for out-group members than the protagonist of Michael Apted's modern Western film *Thunderheart* (1992), who finds himself drawn into a very similar situation. Like *Watershed,* *Thunderheart* alludes to the historical clashes between the American Indian Movement and the American government, and just like Everett's novel, it focuses on a case of environmental injustice on reservation land. As we will see in the next section, *Thunderheart* exemplifies well that filmmakers, too, use strategic empathizing to engage viewers in a social and environmental justice argument. Carl Plantinga has noted that character engagement in fiction film "is rhetorical to the core; by cueing 'pro' and 'con' attitudes toward characters, filmmakers manipulate point of view, encourage audience desires for various narrative outcomes, and elicit particular spectator emotions" (2010, 34). Just as in the case of literature, such cueing of attitudes can involve both insider and outsider perspectives.

CONTAGIOUS FEELINGS: EMBODIMENT, EMOTION, AND MORALITY IN ENVIRONMENTAL JUSTICE FILMS

Cognitive film theory has produced a range of publications that focus on characters and spectators' emotional engagement with them. Plantinga and Murray Smith are among those who have given special thought to the moral dimensions of such engagement, and so in this section I will draw on their work in particular. By theorizing how spectators are aligned with complex characters—and how they may develop moral allegiances with them—these scholars offer insight into how films employ strategic empathy in order to make us sympathize with the victims of environmental injustice. In film, explains Smith, alignment "describes the process by which spectators are placed in relation to characters in terms of their access to their actions, and to what they know and feel" (1995, 82). With the exception of voice-over, films cannot render the consciousness of a character in the way a novel does. Alignment is achieved in different ways, ways that are specific to the medium of film. Smith proposes "two interlocking functions, *spatio-temporal attachment* and *subjective access* . . . as the most precise means for analyzing alignment. Attachment concerns the way in which the narration restricts itself to the actions of a single character. . . . Subjective access pertains to the degree of access we have to the subjectivity of characters" (83). Both of these interlocking functions are relevant for a consideration of how *Thunderheart* aligns viewers with Ray Levoi, an ambitious young FBI agent who is sent to the Bear Creek Indian Reservation in South Dakota to solve a murder case.

Unlike Everett, Michael Apted has been very open about his intention to fictionalize historical occurrences and thereby make a political statement with his film. From the outset, *Thunderheart* acknowledges that its portrayal of a fictional Native American community and its struggle for legal, social, and environmental justice "was inspired by events that took place on several Indian reservations during the 1970s." Combining genre elements of the Western and the thriller, the film has a documentary's attentiveness to detail and was shot almost entirely on location on the Pine Ridge Reservation where Apted also filmed his documentary *Incident at Oglala* (1992) about the life of AIM-activist Leonard Peltier. The documentary informs the fiction film in various ways. As Apted has put it, *Thunderheart* tries "in an entertaining way to educate people who would never see *Incident at Oglala*" (1993, 20). The most drastic decision in this regard is the creation of an—entirely fictional—mixed-blood protagonist so thoroughly Americanized that it is easy for non-Indian viewers to share his perspective. Val Kilmer plays Ray Levoi, an up-and-coming FBI agent who has been able to hide the fact that his father was a half-blooded Lakota Sioux from the world. This changes when Levoi is assigned to aid agent Frank Coutelle (Sam Shepard) in the investigation of the murder of Leo Fast Elk. It is suspected that the traditional Indian has been killed by Jimmy Looks Twice (John Trudell), a militant activist with the Aboriginal Rights Movement (ARM)—yet another thinly disguised fictional version of the American Indian Movement.

From the outset, the film aligns viewers with Levoi, who, despite his Native American ancestry, comes as a cultural outsider to a conflict he only gradually learns to understand. Viewers are attached to Levoi for almost the entirety of the film, following his actions and witnessing the actions of other characters only if they are in close proximity to him. Such a high degree of spatio-temporal attachment is relatively rare, and while it is not the equivalent of first-person narration in a literary text (which would limit the visual world to the character's subjective point of view) it is comparable to focalized third-person narration.[26] Although the film stays away from voice-over, it offers a significant amount of access to Levoi's subjectivity. One of the first scenes shows him at the FBI headquarters in Washington DC, as he receives his assignment. His gray suit, blue eyes, and blond, cropped hair make him look typical of a man of Anglo-Saxon decent, suggesting in no way that he is part Indian. The casting of Val Kilmer as Ray Levoi is not without its ironies here. Although most viewers at the time would have identified the Hollywood star as white, Kilmer is of partially Cherokee decent, thereby mirroring Levoi's ethnic identity on the level of the performer.[27] Levoi, however, seems uncomfortable with that identity. He lies when his superior asks him about his biological father, stating that he never knew him, when in fact he lived with him as a boy. After learning that he will go to South Dakota as "who [he is] . . . an American Indian Federal officer" (*Thunderheart* 1992), Levoi's highly controlled facial features erupt in an unbelieving laugh. Although viewers do not have direct access to his thoughts and emotions, they can easily read his mind in this scene, using cognitive empathy as well as processes of embodied simulation to decipher the visual information they receive from his tense body posture and face: Levoi does not *want* to go to South Dakota, least of all as an American Indian. While his reasons are not clear at this point, it is hard to miss that Levoi denies and despises that part of his ancestry.

Viewers' close alignment with Levoi in terms of both spatio-temporal attachment and subjective access is continued throughout the film with the effect that, together with Levoi, they become slowly familiarized with the situation on the Bear Creek Reservation. When the two FBI agents first arrive, Levoi is confronted with the grim reality of contemporary reservation life. Viewers are presented with a POV shot that shows the run-down houses, the poverty, and the sheer desperation. Coutelle, who has been in the area for a while, dryly comments that "we have the Third World slapped into the middle of America. . . . It used to be all theirs," referring to the pattern of dispossession and displacement that has marked the Native American experience. Levoi, however, is shocked speechless. Although he hides behind his dark sunshades, the close-ups of his frozen face in combination with the long shots of the reservation invite viewers to simulate his mixed feelings of repulsion and pity. While they may not be able to feel exactly *like* him because of their different personal histories and ethnic backgrounds, they will have a reaction of their own to the presented images, and they will be able to sense how Levoi feels in this situation through the use of cognitive and affective empathy. The fact that the fictitious Bear Creek Reservation is "played," so to speak, by the actually existing Pine Ridge Reservation and its impoverished inhabitants gives these images a documentary quality that makes them even more powerful for those who recognize their authenticity.

Mei Mei Evans has argued that the majority of "popular U.S. American cultural constructions of 'nature' serve[s] to empower some members of society while simultaneously disempowering others" (2002, 181). Beth Berila's critique of popular Hollywood movies, which I have discussed in the previous chapter, adds up to the same complaint. The spectacular landscape cinematography of such films, argues Berila, reduces "the landscape . . . to scenery" (2010, 121), with the result that "the racial, gender, and economic power dynamics that infuse relationships between human beings and nature" are occluded (127). *Thunderheart* demonstrates that this must not necessarily be the case. The film captures the impressive landscape of the South Dakota badlands in spectacular images, framing its protagonists within this unique ecological space. But the land around Wounded Knee not only makes for remarkable scenery or, as Martin Lefebvre would put it, for a spectacular "filmic landscape" (2006b, 22) that is disconnected from the narrative of the film; it is also an active participant in the story of the film. As the tribal policeman Crow Horse (Graham Greene) points out repeatedly in the film, the badlands are soaked with Indian blood, and the landscape also tells things about the murder to those who are attuned to it and able to listen.[28] Levoi, it is suggested, is too estranged from his Indian roots to understand anything the land says, but he soon starts to care enough about the people he meets to ask different questions.

Like Robert Hawks, Levoi undergoes a slow but steady transformation from detached and objective "hired gun" to someone who cares enough about the victims of injustice to risk his own life in order to help them. And in his case, too, the empathic engagement with a group of American Indians forces him to confront his own personal history. There are three people, in particular, that guide him in this process of transformation. One is Crow Horse, whose ironic punch lines not only provide a much-needed dose of comic relief to an otherwise dead-serious story, but who also helps Levoi—and the viewer—to see the murder case on Indian land through "Indian eyes." Levoi slowly begins to form an alliance with the tribal policeman, and he also develops feelings for Maggie Eagle Bear (Sheila Tousey), a schoolteacher and ARM activist who regards him with a combination of suspicion and spite. The third, and perhaps most important, catalyst in Levoi's transformation is Grandpa Sam Reaches (Ted Thin Elk), an enigmatic trickster figure who recognizes Levoi as "Thunderheart," a Native American hero slain during the 1890 Wounded Knee massacre who has been reincarnated to deliver the Sioux from their current troubles. Grandpa Reaches is also the one who takes away Levoi's dark shades by bartering for them, thereby quite literally taking away his protection and allowing him to *see* the environment and the people around him. As a result, Levoi develops a full-blown identity crisis and gets more and more involved in the bloody conflict within the Sioux community and a number of mysterious deaths.

It is this involvement that allows viewers to develop a moral allegiance to Levoi and invites them to side, together with him, with the victims of injustice. Allegiance, explains M. Smith, "depends upon the spectator having what she takes to be reliable access to the character's state of mind, on understanding the context of the character's actions, and having morally evaluated the character on the basis of this knowledge" (1995, 84). As Plantinga points out, it "is a deeper and more abiding psychological relationship with a character" than mere sympathy, "and it depends fundamentally on the spectator's moral intuitions elicited over the course of the narrative" (2010, 42). Like a literary text, a film has an internal moral structure that either supports or contradicts the behavior of a character. *Watershed* and *Thunderheart* each propose, in their way, that the Native American groups their protagonists get involved with are not criminals but people who are in a desperate situation. They are fighting for their rights and against those who threaten to kill them. Their acts of violence are therefore justified and morally permissible acts of self-defense. Once this is established, the protagonists' engagement on behalf of these endangered communities becomes a highly moral act of civil courage. This, in turn, strengthens viewers' emotional attachment to them, making them more likely to accept the protagonists' goals and the means by which they attempt to reach them. *Thunderheart* reaches its climax when Levoi and Crow Horse find test drilling sites for a government-sponsored uranium strip mine, which is polluting the water supply and killing people on the reservation. In the end, they can prove that, together with FBI-man Coutelle, the pro-governmental tribal president tried to cover up the ecological disaster with the murder of Leo Fast Elk and the framing of AIM activist Jimmy Looks Twice to discredit the organization.[29]

Thunderheart, like *Watershed,* thus ends with a transformed protagonist who has reached his immediate goals, providing closure for its narrative arc. It is, however, not an unambiguous happy ending. The woman Levoi has fallen in love with has been murdered, and he cannot stay on the reservation. The final scene of the film shows him on the crossroads to the reservation, ready to start a new life with a new identity. In its portrayal of the conflict between pro-governmental Indians, traditional ARM members, and government agents, *Thunderheart* is much more explicit than Apted's documentary. As Elise Marubbio has pointed out, "Part of *Thunderheart's* power lies in its open confrontation of several significant and controversial themes: colonialism, racism, and the violation of human rights" by the American government (2012, 51). Because a fiction film is much less likely to be attacked for false claims than a documentary, Apted felt that it was only possible to tell this story as fiction. He still was amazed that an American studio was brave enough to take it on since "fundamentally, the movie is saying that . . . the American government condoned murder and violence" (Apted 1993, 16). The resulting film keeps blurring the boundaries between fiction and nonfiction when he puts professional actor Val Kilmer in one shot with Ted Thin Elk, an untrained Sioux actor who basically plays himself, or when he models Levoi's love interest Maggie Eagle Bear after the murdered AIM activist Anna Mae Aquash. Most remarkable, perhaps, is his choice to cast John Trudell for the role of Jimmy Looks Twice, the Leonard Peltier-figure of the film.[30] During most of the 1970s, Trudell served as the chairman of the American Indian Movement, and he also figures prominently in Apted's documentary about Peltier. Together with the film's epigraph, these directorial choices all serve to remind viewers of the fact that what they see on the screen is not *really* fiction, and that they should share Levoi's outrage at the American government's treatment of American Indians.

Some critics have criticized Apted's choice of an outsider perspective as patronizing and generic.[31] Others have detected in the film a tendency to romanticize Indian spirituality or declared its semi-happy ending inauthentic.[32] Apted, however, has defended his directorial choices. "The truth of *Thunderheart,*" he has explained, "would have been incredibly depressing. The film would not have been allowed to be made had it been that depressing or it if had centered"—as his documentary did—"around an American Indian" (1993, 16). This, too, reminds us of some of the differences between a novel or a low-budget documentary film and a multi-million-dollar fiction production for the big screen. Making it into the multiplex almost always involves some serious creative negotiations and allowances. It is a conflict that politically committed filmmakers have to face, and one that we have to have in mind when we consider other Hollywood films that engage directly with environmental injustice, such as Steve Zaillian's *A Civil Action* (1998) and Steven Soderbergh's *Erin Brockovich* (2000). While *Thunderheart* was a box office failure and *A Civil Action* barely broke even with its production and marketing costs, *Erin Brockovich* has been remarkably successful.[33] Commercial success can never be reduced to just a simple formula, but keeping in mind Apted's comment about the impossibility—or rather the economic unfeasibility—of centering his film on an American Indian, we do have to acknowledge that both *A Civil Action* and *Erin Brockovich* feature protagonists who are white.[34] The same is true for the protagonists in the historical environmental justice cases on which these films are based, but given that the majority of such cases involve communities of color, it is a fact worth taking note of.

Just as relevant may be that these three films cue very different emotions in viewers. As Apted has pointed out, *Thunderheart*'s basic message is that the American government condoned murder and violence against American Indians. Together with its obvious references to the history of the American Indian Movement, that message cues emotions of anger and/or guilt, which does not exactly make for a feel-good movie to enjoy on a Saturday night. *A Civil Action* is not much more rewarding in this regard. Focusing on a historical case of groundwater contamination in Woburn, Massachusetts, it tells a David-versus-Goliath story in which Goliath mostly wins.[35] Not so in *Erin Brockovich,* which tells a story that is very similar to that of *A Civil Action,* but instead of witnessing the gradual decline of a big-shot attorney, viewers are cued to simulate Brockovich's (often highly comical) rise from impoverished single mom to spectacularly successful lawyer. I have discussed the narrative strategies of Soderbergh's film elsewhere (Weik von Mossner 2014d), suggesting that its success should prompt us to reconsider the rhetorical usefulness of melodramatic storylines in environmental justice narratives and the ways they make audiences *feel* about a film.[36] As Plantinga reminds us, "the most powerful ideological effects of any film—its capacity to persuade, change, or reinforce belief and value—will be bound up with the particular way in which it elicits emotions, for it is the emotions that have the potential to forge a place for the film in human memory and have the capacity to strengthen or alter ways of thinking and valuing" (2009a, 190).

Such emotions must not always be positive—some of the most powerful films elicit a good deal of negative emotions—but it is often a question of how such negative emotions are balanced with more gratifying ones. Plantinga's analysis of James Cameron's *Titanic* (1997) demonstrates that even profoundly sad events and storylines can be emotionally rewarding if they elicit "the emotions of elevation and admiration" as a result of the viewer's *moral evaluation* of a character's actions (2009a, 185). The last film I want to consider—Benh Zeitlin's *Beasts of the Southern Wild* (2012)—shows that even a film that offers an *insider perspective* on environmental justice and features minority actors can balance negative emotions with positive ones in a way that makes the experience both touching and highly entertaining.

THE INSIDER PERSPECTIVE: MIXED EMOTIONS IN *BEASTS OF THE SOUTHERN WILD*

Beasts of the Southern Wild is one of those rare independent films whose spectacular success surprises even the filmmakers themselves. It is also a movie that pushes the boundaries between fact and fiction further than any of the films discussed so far. Shot on location in the bayous of Louisiana and featuring local lay people, the low-budget production won the Grand Jury Prize at Sundance, the Golden Camera at Cannes, and numerous other international awards. Four Academy Award nominations further solidified the film's considerable critical and commercial success, which is the achievement of its young crew of filmmakers as much as it is that of the remarkable cast of locals who to no small degree shaped the narrative of the film. The most important contributions in this regard came from the New Orleans baker Dwight Henry, who plays the stubborn and deathly-ill Wink, and from Quvenzhané Wallis, who plays Hushpuppy, Wink's self-confident and fiercely creative daughter. Zeitlin encouraged Henry to channel his personal experiences as a "holdout" during Hurricane Katrina into his performance as Hushpuppy's father, a man who considers those who evacuate during a storm "a bunch of pussies" and who fires his shotgun at the clouds. Wallis's contribution is even more central to both the story and the look of the film. Zeitlin quickly learned that it was tremendously important to the six-year-old girl to understand her story from beginning to end. He sat down with her in regular sessions to tell "her the story like it was a folk tale or something" (Murray 2013, question 7). After getting her perspective, they used "her language and the way she thought about things to inform the script" (Murray 2013, question 7). Wallis's need for a chronological development of her character led the filmmakers to shoot the whole film in sequence, a highly unusual mode of feature film production that was only possible because of the small size, and resulting flexibility, of the film crew.[37]

That the narrative is to no small degree shaped by the mind of a black child has significant consequences for the way in which it engages viewers. Flory has suggested that non-black viewers "frequently have trouble imagining what it is like to be African American 'from the inside'—engaging black points of view empathically—because they do not understand black experience from a detailed or intimate perspective" (2008, 42). In Flory's view, the films of Spike Lee are particularly successful in engaging such viewers on the emotional level by inducing them to imagine black "characters 'from the inside' through providing detailed access to the context, reasons, and motivations for their actions and beliefs" (42). *Beasts of the Southern Wild,* too, aligns its viewers with its young black heroine through both spatio-temporal attachment and subjective access. Not only is Hushpuppy quite literally in every scene of the film, the filmmakers also give viewers access to her thoughts and emotions through the extensive use of voice-over and a remarkable number of close-ups that are proof of Wallis's considerable acting abilities. Perhaps because she was able to experience the development of her character sequentially, her facial features express a wide range of strong emotions, cuing viewers to feel along with her through processes of affective mimicry and emotional contagion. The objects of those emotions are both human—in particular Hushpuppy's father—and nonhuman elements of her immediate environment. Henry Bacon has observed that "what is of interest to the spectator is how the characters *relate* to their environment" and "what kin[d] of dangers and affordances it offers them" (2011, 38). The exploration of this complex material and psychological relationship between the protagonist and her environment is at the very heart of *Beasts of the Southern Wild.*

To some degree, the film is documenting the real state of affairs in the Louisiana bayous.[38] As Zeitlin has put it, the region is "right on the precipice of being wiped out and you feel death everywhere all the time" (Murray 2013, question 12). As a result of coastal erosion, at least 2,000 square miles of Louisiana marshland have disappeared over the past one hundred years, turning landmasses into open salt water and making the remaining land increasingly more vulnerable to storm floods and further erosion. In part, this is the result of natural ecological occurrences such as hurricanes. However, not only are hurricanes getting stronger and more frequent as a result of anthropogenic climate change, the effects of these hurricanes on the Louisiana wetlands are also greatly exacerbated by man-made river-control structures such as dams and levees. What we see represented in the film is, therefore, what ecocritic Rob Nixon has called "slow violence—a form of environmental injustice and violence that is dispersed across time and space" (2011, 1). In the film, this slow and long-distance mode of violence is embodied in the imposing levee that marks the outer boundaries of the Bathtub. "They built the wall that cuts us off," declares Hushpuppy, echoing the opinions of her father. "They think we're going to drown down here [but] we're going nowhere."

Zeitlin has acknowledged that his film exaggerates the height of the levee and the degree of the Bathtub's seclusion, and it is fair to say that it also exaggerates the cohesion, vibrancy, and resilience of its multiracial community. The real bayou region, Zeitlin has insisted, "is a place that defeats death. . . . It's always a battle—death is right there, and it's a place that's fighting it and beating it" (Murray 2013, question 12). His film is an attempt to fictionalize this wild battle with death—epitomized in the group's spectacular breeching of the levee with explosives so that the floodwater can leave the Bathtub. Their refusal to evacuate, the forced evacuation to an alien-looking emergency shelter, and eventually their return to the Bathtub—these are all plot turns that evoke the events around Hurricane Katrina, and so it is little wonder that *Beasts of the Southern Wild* has resonated with many viewers as a Katrina allegory that self-consciously celebrates hope, resilience, and community in post-Katrina Louisiana.[39] Others have criticized the film for its romanticizing depiction of extreme poverty and social dilapidation.[40] This depiction, however, is greatly complicated by the fact that we see the Bathtub and its resilient people from the perspective of a six-year-old who, as the narrative progresses, comes under extreme emotional distress.

What Hushpuppy calls "the prettiest place on earth" is often shown as strikingly beautiful but just as frequently exposed by the camera as dangerous, ugly, and decaying. Hushpuppy experiences her environment as active and alive, and she navigates it with a mixture of curiosity and inventiveness. What makes the movie special is that it does not differentiate on the visual level between actuality and the products of Hushpuppy's exuberant imagination. Most striking in this regard is her relationship to the extinct aurochs, which she first meets in the form of a tattoo on the thigh of her teacher and later imagines as enormous, boar-like creatures that can potentially destroy the world. They first emerge from the melting ice of the Arctic when Hushpuppy punches her father in the chest as an act of retaliation after he has, once again, abandoned her. It is because of his beginning heart failure that Wink collapses, but Hushpuppy's young mind makes different connections, placing the burden for everything—her father's illness, the terrible storm, the resulting flooding of the Bathtub, and the suffering of its human and nonhuman inhabitants—on her own small shoulders. Although they are consistently aligned with Hushpuppy's perspective, viewers soon understand that her highly moral view of the world is not necessarily reliable in the sense of giving an accurate interpretation of the state of affairs. They are unlikely to believe that Hushpuppy is responsible for her father's ailment or the terrible storm. Rather, it is a combination of other factors—factors that are beyond Hushpuppy's understanding but not the viewer's—that bring about the death and destruction that she sees all around her. However, not least because Wallis is such a gifted performer, most viewers will nevertheless empathize with her character, feeling sympathy for Hushpuppy's conviction that it is her personal responsibility to fix what she has broken because "the whole universe depends on everything fitting together just right."

Building his argument on David Hume's deliberations on the 'paradox of tragedy,' Plantinga has argued that filmmakers use various techniques to make the eliciting of negative emotions bearable and—in the end—enjoyable: first, in the narrative's most disturbing moments "painful affect is both attenuated in its effect *and* mixed with pleasurable affect"; second, in the course of the story, "negative emotions are gradually replaced by positive emotions"; and third, such positive emotions gain additional strength through what Plantinga calls "the spillover effect" (2009a, 187).[41] *Beasts of the Southern Wild* uses all three of these techniques to make its depiction of Hushpuppy's deprived living conditions painfully realistic and yet pleasurable to watch. Most frequently, it uses humor to attenuate the effect of negative emotions, such as in the moment when a deserted Hushpuppy cooks a can of cat food for herself with the help of a blowtorch. It is a disquieting scene, not only because close-ups of the sizzling cat food trigger a mixture of disgust and pity but also because throughout the whole process Hushpuppy imagines her mother, who has also abandoned her, sitting across from her and giving instructions. Yet, it is also a very funny moment, cuing amusement and admiration for the little girl's inventiveness and courage (not everyone is prepared to operate a large blowtorch in their living space). And although the film's ending is profoundly sad—Wink dies and makes Hushpuppy an orphan—such negative emotions are counteracted by viewers' admiration for the girl, who brings her father his favorite food minutes before he takes his last breath in order to "fix" what she has broken. The final close-ups of her face show her strong and serene in the midst of the Bathtub community while her voice-over tells us, "I see that I am a little piece of a big, big universe and that makes things right."

These last moments of the film arguably create what Plantinga calls a spillover-effect: "If strong negative emotions are accompanied by physiological arousal [such as crying], this arousal may contribute to the strength of the positive emotions experienced in the last . . . minutes of the film" (2009a, 187).[42] In other words, the viewer is so relieved at being released from the painful negative emotions cued earlier on that he "overshoots" in his positive response, feeling joy and relief in the face of Hushpuppy's apparent strength and the fact that she is being taken care of, regardless of the fact that her overall living situation in fact remains catastrophic. While it is not a feel-good movie in any traditional sense, *Beasts of the Southern Wild* offers an insider perspective on a situation of environmental injustice that mixes a good amount of pleasure into the pain.

CONCLUSION

In this chapter, I have explored the role of strategic empathy in our emotional engagement with out-group others in environmental narratives. I have differentiated between insider and outsider perspectives on issues of environmental justice, suggesting that narratives can either cue us to feel directly with the victims of injustice or indirectly, by aligning us with an outsider who learns to care about such victims. Keen has argued that there are three basic forms of strategic empathizing that writers can employ: *Bounded* strategic empathy is primarily addressed to readers of the writer's in-group (2010, 71), *ambassadorial* strategic empathy "addresses chosen others with the aim of cultivating their empathy for the in-group" (71); *broadcast* strategic empathy, finally, "calls upon every reader to feel with members of a group, by emphasizing common vulnerabilities and hopes through universalizing representations" (71–72). In practice, however, most politically oriented writers will use some form of broadcast empathy, which engages a potentially broad readership. American ethnic literature tends to address itself to a mixed readership consisting of members the depicted in-group as well as members of various out-groups. The novels I have discussed in the first two sections use strategic empathy in order to draw readers from various backgrounds into their stories, inviting them to simulate the thoughts, emotions, and actions of their protagonists through representations that are both universalizing and culturally specific. Viramontes's *Under the Feet of Jesus* uses an insider perspective that focuses on the experience of migrant workers, yet the novel conveys this experience in ways that allow all kinds of readers to simulate the protagonists' situation, drawing in part on their own personal experiences. Everett's *Watershed,* too, is very specific when it comes to the black and Native American experience that it represents, yet it aligns readers with a protagonist who helps members of an out-group because he empathizes with their situation and considers it the morally right thing to do.

Not least for economic reasons, the makers of commercial fiction films can very rarely afford to just address themselves to an in-group or chosen out-group. Even more than novelists, they tend to employ a cinematic variety of what Keen calls broadcast strategic empathy in order to involve a wide spectrum of viewers into the fates of their protagonists. In addition to the economics of film production, the use of this strategy may also serve political interests in the attempt to overcome people's imaginative resistance. Michael Apted's *Thunderheart* deliberately features a light-skinned, mixed-race protagonist to facilitate identification for non-Indian viewers. While some critics have been critical of that choice as well as of the casting of Val Kilmer for the role of Ray Levoi, both choices are geared toward engaging mainstream American audiences imaginatively and emotionally in an important aspect of Native American experience. Levoi's gradual development from cold-blooded outsider to a man who passionately cares about American Indians cues viewers to feel along and to see the ARM activists' struggle for social and environmental justice from his progressively more sympathetic perspective.

Beasts of the Southern Wild is perhaps the most daring narrative I have considered in this chapter. Hushpuppy likely belongs to an out-group for a large percentage of the film's viewers, regardless of their ethnic backgrounds, because she is a six-year-old child. Her perception of the world is radically different not only because it does not differentiate between "fact" and her self-created fiction (making her an unreliable narrator par excellence) but also because she makes very little distinction between human and nonhuman forms of life. In the opening sequence of the film, she is greatly interested to learn what birds and other animals might have to say to each other and to her. However, when she presses them to her ear she cannot help but realize that "they talk to each other in ways that [she] cannot understand." The film thus acknowledges boundaries between Hushpuppy's subjectivity and that of her nonhuman companions while at the same time also subtly destabilizing these boundaries, as, for example, when Hushpuppy's father announces "feed-up time" for the animals and his daughter alike, reminding her to "share with the dog."[43] Such negotiations between an empathetic interest in the continuities between human and nonhuman life-forms, and the acknowledgment that animals' cognitive abilities are fundamentally different from those of humans will be at the center of the next chapter, which explores questions around anthropomorphization and trans-species empathy.

CHAPTER 4

Beyond Boundaries

Imaginary Animals and the Intricacies of Trans-species Empathy

TOWARD THE END of Louie Psihoyos's Academy award-winning documentary, *The Cove* (2009), hundreds of dolphins are driven into a secret cove that is rigorously shielded from the public by local police and the fishermen who work there. The idyllic coastline near the Japanese seaside village of Taiji provides the scenery for a horrific visual spectacle as the fishermen over and over again drive their spears into the bodies of the trapped animals, the surrounding water turning bright red from gallons of dolphin blood. There is no commentary, no narration, just long minutes filled with images of relentless, brutal slaughter and the sounds of the dolphins as they try to writhe away from the boats or dive out of the water in frenzied motion, blood covering their sleek bodies. For viewers who care about dolphins, or about nonhuman animals more generally, this likely is the most disturbing and painful moment in a film that is filled with moments that are disturbing and painful to watch. It is the narrative climax of *The Cove*, the visual and auditory evidence that the filmmakers have been trying to get for months, plotting out clandestine operations to place hidden cameras and microphones into the cove so the world can see what is happening there. It is the evidence that the locals who harvest and process the dolphin meat want no one to see, perhaps because they know that such graphic display of animal suffering will cue very strong and very negative emotions in a great many viewers—especially so if the suffering animals displayed belong to a species that is celebrated and admired in marine parks around the world. Dolphins, to such viewers, are relatives of the movie star Flipper. They are remarkable, intelligent, and kind animals that like to play with humans and that are known to save them from danger. In other words: they are not something we kill and eat.

I will argue in this chapter that what makes the notorious slaughter scene in *The Cove* so painful to watch is a case of trans-species empathy, one of many cases in which human spectators—consciously or unconsciously—empathize with nonhuman animals, feeling their joy, their fear, their terror and pain. In doing so, I will argue against the assumption that our emotional responses to the display of animal emotions in literature and film can be explained by anthropomorphism alone. While some of the texts I will consider do make use of various degrees of anthropomorphism in order to engage their audiences, it is not a necessary condition for our empathic response to animals. Social psychologist Melanie Green has suggested that in order to transport people into a narrative world and make them care about the events they witness there, "it may be more important to have psychologically compelling characters than that those characters look like actual human beings" (2004, 253). Green does not seem to have nonhuman animals in mind when making that statement, but *The Cove* is one of many environmental narratives that feature characters who neither look like humans nor think or act like them and who nevertheless strongly appeal to human emotion.

Questions around anthropomorphism and animal emotions will loom large in this chapter, which uses evidence from affective neuroscience and cognitive ethology—the study of animal minds—to explore the psychological mechanisms behind our emotional responses to the animals we encounter in literature and film. The narratologist David Herman has argued that "scholarship on narrative can be informed by as well as contribute to the emergent, interdisciplinary field of critical animal studies" in its consideration of nonhuman characters and narrators (2011, 158–59). Critical animal studies is a relatively young branch of research that conceptualizes animal liberation as a social justice movement and stresses issues of inter-species exploitation, oppression, and recognition.[1] In addition to an activist orientation, the highly interdisciplinary field also has multiple theoretical dimensions.[2] As literary scholar Kimberly Benston explains, the proponents of critical animal studies view "human/animal relations as a problem for historical, sociological, and cultural analysis" and intervene "in biomedical animal studies by contesting assumptions of mentalistic and moral difference" (2009, 548). Like Herman, I believe that insights from critical animal studies can be helpful for the analysis of narrative representations of nonhuman minds, but I will suggest that research in cognitive ethology and affective science can complement such humanistic insights and inquires in important ways.[3] The first section of this chapter will draw on such research to explore what happens when we attribute consciousness to animals in life and in narratives and whether there are any non-anthropomorphic ways of doing so. It will also engage with the related issue of trans-species empathy, which allows us to feel with others across species boundaries, and address the question of why we tend to inhibit that capacity at times.

The second section will then use these theoretical insights to explore how the makers of *The Cove* make use of strategic empathizing in order to push an animal rights argument about the need to protect dolphins from slaughter and from enslavement in marine shows. In the previous chapter, I have explored the use of strategic empathizing by writers and filmmakers to cue readers to feel with and for the human victims of environmental injustice and to build moral allegiance to them. One way of doing this, I have suggested, is to focalize the narrative through the mind of an outsider who gradually learns to care about a group of people who have been wronged. In this section, I will argue that very similar narrative strategies have also been used to invite viewers to build moral allegiance with human characters who feel with, and fight for, nonhuman others who suffer and who do not deserve to suffer. Michael Apted's biopic *Gorillas in the Mist* (1988) will serve as my second example, demonstrating that strategic trans-species empathy has also been used in fiction film and to similar effect.

The last two sections of the chapter will be concerned with a mode of narration that seems much more radical and daring from a psychological and philosophical point of view, and that is nevertheless remarkably common not only in literary texts but also in film: the use of an *insider perspective* on animal experience. As Gérard Genette already pointed out in his *Narrative Discourse* (1980), "in fiction nothing prevents us from entrusting that role [of the narrative agent] to an animal" (244), and countless authors and filmmakers have undertaken exactly that, with varying degrees of success. Anthropomorphism is inevitable when nonhumans become narrative agents in human stories, and yet there is a wide spectrum of how it has been employed, reaching from novels that are presented from the first-person perspective of an animal to the anthropomorphic fantasies of Disney animation. All of these formats aim to engage us in various ways in the emotional lives of animals. What is of interest to ecocritics and cognitive scholars alike is why, exactly, it is that we care and whether there are any ethical and moral dimensions to such caring.

NARRATING ANIMALS: TRANS-SPECIES EMPATHY AND CONSCIOUSNESS ATTRIBUTION

The cognitive and affective abilities of animals do not always make a great topic for dinner conversations. It is a topic that can bring about tense faces and spoiled appetites, especially so if some of the plates on the table are heaped with meat. In *Why We Love Dogs, Eat Pigs, and Wear Cows* (2010), psychologist Melanie Joy asks her readers to imagine themselves in the middle of eating a generous portion of "savory stew" at a dinner invitation and to then trace their own emotional reactions upon the host's cheery announcement that the meal is made of "five pounds of golden retriever meat" (11). This announcement, she speculates, will turn most Americans' feelings of "pleasure to some degree of revulsion" (11–12). While it would not disturb them at all to learn that they are devouring beef (unless they are vegan or vegetarian, in which case they would not have touched the stew in the first place), the idea of eating a dog is culturally and emotionally unacceptable for Americans. Dogs are, as Donna Haraway has put it, a human "companion species" in the western cultural context (2003, 6) and therefore inedible.[4] Even when it comes to the cow, however, that hides behind the much less vibrant term "beef," Joy makes an interesting observation. "If you are like most people," she writes, "when you sit down to eat beef you don't envision the animal from which the meat was derived. Instead, you simply see 'food,' and you focus on its flavor, aroma, and texture. When confronted with beef, we generally skip the part of the perceptual process that makes the mental connection between meat and the living animal" (2010, 15). Vegans and vegetarians are much more likely to make that mental connection and to envision the living, breathing, and feeling animal behind the meat. It may be one of the reasons why they don't eat it.

Joy suggests that avoiding making the mental connection between meat and the animal that was slaughtered for it is a case of *empathy inhibition*. As I have discussed in chapter 3, empathy inhibition is the cognitive suppression of an affective empathetic response due to egoistical motives, cultural beliefs, or outright denial. In the case of meat, Joy explains, "the evidence strongly suggests that our lack of disgust [at eating certain animals] is largely, if not entirely, learned" (2010, 18).[5] Our belief system and the schemas it creates in our minds, "dictates which animals are edible, and it enables us to consume them by protecting us from feeling any emotional or psychological discomfort when doing so" (18). What is lacking in such situations is feelings of *empathetic distress,* according to psychologist Martin Hoffman, a strong prosocial motive (2000, 105). This lack is the result of what, following the terminology of Robert Jay Lifton, Joy calls *psychic numbing*—"a psychological process by which we disconnect, mentally and emotionally, from our experience" (2010, 18). Instead of feeling empathy, people are left with apathy, an apathy that is only shaken in moments when someone reminds them of the fact that the meat that they eat used to belong to the body of thinking, feeling, and suffering beings not unlike themselves. Literary scholar Erica Fudge sums up the central cognitive dissonance at the heart of human-animal relationships as follows: "We live with animals, we recognize them, we even name some of them, but at the same time we use them as if they were inanimate, as if they were objects. The illogic of this relationship is one that, on a day-to-day basis, we choose to evade, even refuse to acknowledge as present" (2002, 8).

It is not only when we think about meat production and consumption that the conscious experience of animals and their potential similarity to human experience becomes a dicey issue that many of us choose to evade. As Anat Pick has pointed out, "the concrete relations between human and nonhuman animals—increasingly since the age we call modernity—are an area of sharp separation" (2011, 1). There is a lot at stake in bridging that separation, not least because it has become deeply ingrained in western culture. Ecocritic Nandita Batra reminds us that "the most influential modern reinforcement of the dualist position came . . . from Descartes, whose 1637 *Discours de la mèthode* contained the notorious *bêtemachine* theory that animals were mere bodies, no more than automata" (2003, 156). Suggesting that animals have not only minds but also emotional lives that include the capacity to suffer, as the utilitarian philosopher Peter Singer and other animal-rights advocates have done, is in accordance with many of Charles Darwin's early insights, but it runs counter to the Cartesian separation between humans and beasts.[6] With reference to utilitarian philosophers Jeremy Bentham and John Stuart Mill, legal scholar Gary Francione explains the central axiom of the animal rights movement: "Humans and nonhumans may be different in many respects, but they are relevantly similar in that they are both sentient; they are perceptually aware and able to experience pain and pleasure" (2010, 7). Such a perspective on human–animal relationships puts into question not only deeply ingrained cultural practices but also the cherished belief that humans are special and somehow separate from other animal species roaming the surface of planet earth. And yet, from a scientific point of view, there is no longer any reason to doubt that it is correct.

Evolutionary biologist Marc Bekoff remembers in *The Emotional Lives of Animals* (2007) that when he started his research work in the 1970s, "researchers were almost all skeptics who spent their time wondering if dogs, cats, chimpanzees, and other animals felt anything" (xviii). Today, "the paradigm is shifting to such an extent that the burden of proof now falls more often to those who still argue that animals don't experience emotions" (xviii). The research field of cognitive ethology, founded by the American zoologist Donald Griffin in the early 1980s, has greatly contributed to this paradigm shift, which prompts us to understand nonhuman animals as sentient others who have emotions, thoughts, beliefs, rationality, and consciousness.[7] Fieldwork in cognitive ethology, Bekoff explains, "sometimes entails sitting back and watching, and sometimes involves indirect or direct interactions with the animals" (39). Bekoff acknowledges that "labs can be useful as controlled environments in which to conduct research on how animals' minds work," but suggests that "if you really want to know how animals live, think, and feel from their point of view, then you need to join them in their world" (38).

The corresponding lab work, conducted by affective neuroscientists such as Jaak Panksepp (1998) complements research in the field by giving us a better understanding of how animal brains function. In this context, it should be remembered that research on mirror neurons and their role in embodied simulation was first undertaken on macaque monkeys. While this opens up a whole other set of pressing questions about the use of animals in the lab— questions that have been addressed by critical animal studies scholars as well as by cognitive ethologists such as Bekoff—it rather forcefully reminds us that embodied simulation and related processes of affective empathy are not limited to humans.[8] Cognitive scientists like Gregory Berns try to get around the serious ethical problems related to conducting single-neuron research on animals by using fMRI to study the brains of awake and unrestrained dogs much in the way neuroscientists visualize activation patterns in human brains. The experiments, conducted in Berns's lab with dogs that were trained to lie still in an MRI scanner, reveal that "the same things that activate the human caudate, which are associated with positive emotions, also activate the dog caudate. Neuroscientists call this a functional homology, and it may be an indication of canine emotions. The ability to experience positive emotions, like love and attachment, would mean that dogs have a level of sentience comparable to that of a human child" (Berns 2013). Such empirical insights into the inner lives of animals call for a much more integrated study of embodied cognition. In recent years, there have been calls for the development of a "trans-species psychology" (Bradshaw and Watkins, 2006) and for a "cross-species understanding of empathy" (Panksepp and Panksepp 2013) that take note of these important continuities between human and nonhuman minds.[9] Such work in cognitive science is crucial, not least because it supports some of the claims made within critical animal studies. As psychologists Gay Bradshaw and Mary Watkins point out, "Recognizing the trans-species nature of psyche removes presumptions that allow animal objectification and undermines rationales used to withhold animals' rights" (2006, 76).

Taking the trans-species nature of psyche seriously also has far-reaching implications for the study of nonhuman characters in environmental narratives and the ways they engage audiences. Herman has suggested that examining nonhuman experience from a narratological point of view might prompt us to rethink "prior accounts of narrativity itself—accounts suggesting that part of what makes a text or a discourse amenable to being interpreted as a narrative is its focus on human or human-like characters" (2011, 158). Narratives do need actors of some kind, and emotionally engaging narratives tend to feature relatable characters. However, as scores of ecocritics have argued, it is a fallacy to assume that these characters have to be human, or even *like* humans.[10] Herman seems to agree, suggesting that narrative

> affords a bridge between the human and the nonhuman; stories provide this link not merely by allegorizing human concerns via nonhuman animals or engaging in anthropomorphic projections, but also by figuring the lived, phenomenal worlds—what the German-Estonian philosopher-biologist Jakob von Uexküll termed the Umwelten—of creatures whose organismic structure differs from our own. . . . By modeling the richness and complexity of "what it is like" for nonhuman others, stories can underscore what is at stake in the trivialization—or outright destruction—of their experiences. (2011, 159)

According to this account, the narrative representation of nonhuman consciousness has a moral and ethical dimension. Not only can it help us get a better understanding of what it is like to experience the world through a different set of senses, but we might also be led to conclude that conscious, thinking, and feeling beings deserve to be treated with more respect. Importantly, Herman points beyond mere anthropomorphism and the long tradition of casting allegorical animals in the role of humans, which reaches from Aesop's fables and a wide variety of fairy tales to George Orwell's *Animal Farm* (1945) and beyond. Such allegories have their cultural significance, but they do not give us a sense of what it is like to be a sheep, dog, fox, or pig since this is not really what they are after. What interests Herman is how the richness and complexity of nonhuman experience *can* be conveyed in a narrative that was created by a human mind.

Some would argue that it cannot be conveyed at all. In "What Is It Like to Be a Bat?" (1974), the philosopher Thomas Nagel famously argued that conscious experience exists in many animals and all mammals, and that each organism's qualia—the "subjective character of experience" (435)—must be unique. Speaking out against attempts to explain consciousness via objective and, in his view, reductionist means, Nagel turns to the bat as a mammal that without doubt has perception and experience, and yet, "bat sonar . . . is not similar in its operation to any sense we possess, and there is no reason to suppose that it is subjectively like anything we can experience or imagine. This appears to create difficulties for the notion of what it is like to be a bat" (436). In his article, Herman takes up Nagel's argument but suggests "an approach to the mind-narrative nexus premised on the continuity rather than the discontinuity between nonhuman and human experiences" (2011, 161). Even though some aspects of animal experience will remain impenetrable for human minds, we can approximate it, in part because there are important continuities between human and nonhuman experiences. In fact, such transspecies consciousness attribution is something we do all the time, be it in our day-to-day interaction with actual animals or in our imaginative engagement with the creatures we see represented in texts and audiovisual media, both fiction and nonfiction. The process is not so different from attributing consciousness to humans—real and represented ones—whose minds are not accessible to us. As the work of ethologist Jonathan Balcombe demonstrates, we even use it for a better understanding of bats.

In his 2010 book *Second Nature: The Inner Lives of Animals,* Balcombe recounts his experience of researching Mexican free-tailed bats that migrate north across the U.S. border to a range of limestone caves to bear and raise their young. Balcombe spent many hours listening to the cries that the bat pups sent out to help their mothers find them among millions of others pups in the vast and dark cave: "The bats' calls are partially audible to the human ear, but our brains process sounds at much lower speeds and lower frequency. By tape recording their calls at high speed and playing them back much more slowly, a whisper of faint blips and squeaks resolved into a constellation of unique cries. Perceptually, it was as if my hearing had become the mother bat's and I could now distinguish the insistent bellows of perhaps a dozen pups who happened to be within the range of the directional microphone" (2010, 10). Although Balcombe's use of technical equipment does not enable him to share the qualia of a bat, it does give him a better sense of *what it is like* for the bat mother to find her baby through its unique cry in the cacophony of voices.[11] By transforming his findings into a story, the ethologist Balcombe also becomes an ethographer and thus someone who aims to translate and mediate nonhuman experience to a larger audience by means of a narrative.[12] His readers, who simulate the sound of the "constellation of unique cries" in their minds in accordance with the instruction manual that he gives them, are even further removed from the bat's subjective experience. And yet, their mental simulation gives them a much better understanding of that experience than they had before.

Balcombe's nonfiction account thus helps readers get a sense of the physical and mental states of "creatures whose organismic structure differs from our own" (Herman 2011, 159). That we are able to imagine the creatures he describes suggests that processes of embodied simulation are not dependent on deliberate or crude forms of anthropomorphism: the bats here are not made to think and act like humans, as it would be the case in an allegory. If there is anthropomorphism in Balcombe's account—and there most certainly is—it is the self-reflective version of it that ethologists call *critical anthropomorphism*.[13] "Although it is true that we will never fully appreciate how another animal experiences the world," suggest Jesús Rivas and Gordon Burghardt in their contribution to *The Cognitive Animal* (2002), "by doing our best to accomplish this through applying critical anthropomorphism, including the full range of available scientific data, we will get closer to understanding the life of the animal" (11). Critical anthropomorphism, in this definition, is showing awareness of the inevitable anthropocentric bias of one's interpretation while at the same time doing one's best to put oneself "in the animal's shoes" as it interacts with its environment (11). Such an approach is common not only among cognitive ethologists and ethographers but also for writers of what Allan Burns has called "serious animal stories" (2002, 339).[14] As ecocritic Bart Welling has put it with reference to documentary film, such texts can provide their recipients "with heavily mediated but potentially transformative modes of access to the emotional lives of our nonhuman kin" (2014, 82). They can be transformative because the vivid display of emotions is contagious, not only within, but also across species boundaries.[15]

That this is the case will not come as a surprise to pet owners who have lived in close proximity with their nonhuman companions and who have experienced moments of shared emotions. There is, however, also scientific research to back up this personal and anecdotal evidence. A team of psychologists around Robert Franklin used fMRI to examine neural responses in (human) participants while they were presented with pictures of suffering humans and pictures of suffering dogs. They found "that viewing human and animal suffering led to large overlapping regions of activation previously implicated in empathic responding to suffering, including the anterior cingulate gyrus and anterior insula" (2013, 217). The results of the study indicate "that there are many overlapping [brain] regions in humans' empathic responses to viewing animal and human suffering, particularly in areas classically associated with empathic response" (225).[16]

This helps explain the forceful emotional response that the cognitive film scholar Dirk Eitzen has reported as a result of watching a suffering dog in Robert Gardner's documentary *Forest of Bliss* (1985). As I have explained in chapter 2, Eitzen uses his own emotional response to the film as evidence for his claim that documentary films involve our emotions in peculiar ways because we know that what we see on the screen is *consequential* in the actual world. He writes that seeing the pitiful dog being attacked relentlessly "by a pack of more-robust dogs" was "practically unbearable. I was literally nauseated. I wanted to turn away" (2005, 183). Later on in the essay, he records in more detail his physical response to the documented dog attack: "When I see a dog that is being attacked cringe before the fangs of its attackers, I cringe, too—not outwardly perhaps, but at least in those parts of my brain that know from experience what it feels like to cringe before a physical threat. This triggers a rush of adrenaline. It is partly what accounts for my extreme discomfort. It is partly why I feel such strong sympathy for the victim (and for underdogs, generally)" (190). What Eitzen describes here is a process of embodied simulation, leading to affective empathy, to sympathy and moral allegiance, to empathetic anger, and—of particular importance to Eitzen's argument—to a strong urge to become active on the dog's behalf, an urge "to hurl a stone at the attacking dogs" (190). Eitzen's empathizing with the dog leads to a complementary emotional response rather than a parallel one. Instead of feeling fear, the emotion exhibited by the dog, he feels anger and aggression against the attackers and an urge to protect the victim.[17] All this fits perfectly with Hoffman's account of the relationship between empathetic distress and prosocial action, regardless of the fact that the empathic engagement here crosses species boundaries. It also fits perfectly with the results of Franklin et al.'s fMRI study.

Eitzen claims that the desire to intervene is unique to documentary film, insisting that the emotional reaction he had in response to a shark attack in a fiction film was not accompanied by such a desire because he knew it was fictitious. This sounds reasonable since only in the case of nonfiction do we tend to assume that the things we are witnessing are *actually* happening to the protagonists, as opposed to mere play. Such assumptions about actuality might be the reason why books like Jonathan Safran Foer's *Eating Animals* (2009) and documentaries like Robert Kenner's *Food, Inc.* (2008) and Shaun Monson's *Earthlings* (2005), which unveil animal suffering in the food industry, have been credited with converting thousands of readers and viewers into vegetarians and vegans.[18] However, Eitzen's argument is nevertheless somewhat flawed. Not only is the fiction-nonfiction divide more complicated in the case of animal protagonists, as countless (authentically and involuntarily) falling horses in Western films could attest, the argument is also based on a poor comparison, since in his fiction example Eitzen empathizes with a human character (who is attacked by a shark), whereas in the documentary the object of his empathy is an un-anthropomorphized dog. One thing that this tells us is that anthropomorphism indeed is not a precondition for our ability to empathize with animals. While it may facilitate an empathetic response by making the animal seem more "like us," our ability to read the faces and bodies of animals is not predicated on deliberate anthropomorphization. In fact, Franklin et al.'s experiment showed "that perceiving [un-anthropomorphized depictions of] animal suffering elicits greater emotional responses than human suffering" (2013, 225). In order to make his comparison truly meaningful, Eitzen might have chosen a fiction film that also displays the suffering of an un-anthropomorphized animal like the documentary's dog.

What Eitzen also does not sufficiently account for is that fiction narratives can and do comment on real-world events, even bringing real-world aspects into their fictional storyworlds. While he is right that we feel differently about fiction and nonfiction, there are writers and directors who fuse the two modes in ways that unlock powerful emotional responses. I have discussed this issue with reference to environmental justice narratives in chapter 3. Here, I want to take it up again to shed light on our response to the suffering of animals on film and the effects that may have on viewers' emotional engagement and their inclination to intervene. As Franklin et al. point out, we tend to perceive animals as more helpless than adult humans, regardless of how wrong this might be in particular personal or historical circumstances. If this is paired with the depiction of an animal that we know well in the sense of sharing our lives with a member of the same species, we are even more inclined to become emotional.[19] Dogs and other companion animals have a long and successful history in fiction film, precisely because they are dear to our hearts. Filmmakers will debate long and hard whether they should let such nonhuman protagonists suffer and thereby risk alienating viewers.[20] However, this does not necessarily mean that the filmic depiction of suffering in animal species that we have less experience with evokes less empathy-related neural activation. The next section will suggest that our emotional engagement depends to a large degree on the charisma of the chosen animal and on the way it is depicted by the filmmakers. The films I have selected as examples do not center on what we would typically consider companion species, and yet they depict wild animals in ways that allow viewers to empathize with their plight and to develop strong moral allegiance to the human protagonists who try to save them.

FEELING FOR THEM: ANIMAL SUFFERING IN *THE COVE* AND *GORILLAS IN THE MIST*

The history of American cinema is filled with animals. From the galloping racehorse on Eadweard Muybridge's zoopraxiscope discs to Chris Renaud and Yarrow Cheney's *The Secret Life of Pets* (2016), they have been a constant presence in audiovisual entertainment. As Jonathan Burt reminds us, "Animals appear, with greater or lesser significance, in all genres . . . from wildlife films to Hollywood blockbusters, from scientific film to animation, as well as occurring in surrealist, avant-garde and experimental films, all of which use a multitude of different formats and technologies" (2002, 17–18). More often than not, such animal actors are cast in supporting roles, playing sidekicks, subordinates, or simply a means of transportation. Many of them are pets or otherwise domesticated creatures. But there has also been a place for wildlife in American film, often constituting a clear and present danger for human protagonists and an opportunity to prove their superiority. David Ingram has observed that "from the silent era of Hollywood film to the 1960s, wild animals tended to be represented in imperial narratives celebrating the conquest of nature by heroic European or American males. The wild animal was an obstacle to this narrative of progress, and was accordingly demonized as excessively savage and monstrous" (2000, 69). However, Ingram also detects another trend in American film, one that started in the 1950s in response "to rising popular interest in the conservation of wild animals" (69). This trend was, and continues to be, particularly pronounced in nonfiction films such as wildlife documentaries.[21] Wildlife films often have considerable affective appeal, and some of them, like *The Cove*, have been spectacularly successful not only at the box office but also in terms of raising awareness for conservation issues and animal rights.

The Cove centers on the former dolphin trainer and activist Ric O'Barry, who, together with the filmmakers, embarks on a quest to document the dolphin hunting operations in Taiji. In the 1960s, O'Barry was responsible for capturing and training the five female dolphins who starred as Flipper in the TV series of the same name. The documentary chronicles his development from being instrumental in making dolphins one of the most beloved animal species in the popular imagination to a passionate animal activist who opposes their enslavement in marine parks around the world. The moment that changed O'Barry's mind was when Kathy, one of the dolphins playing Flipper, died in his arms after closing her blowhole voluntarily in order to suffocate. "She committed suicide," he says into the camera, which then cuts to archival footage showing Kathy. "She swam into my arms, and looked me right in the eye, and . . . took a breath and didn't take another one. . . . The next day I was [put] in jail for trying to free a dolphin at the Lerner Marine Laboratory. That's how I reacted to it. I was going to free every captive dolphin I could." It was a disturbing emotional experience, then, that turned O'Barry from trainer to liberator. Having worked closely with dolphins his whole life, he has no doubts about their cognitive and emotional abilities, and he seems convinced that the dolphin swam deliberately into his arms, looking him in the eye as she decided to end her own suffering. Whether or not his interpretation of the animal's motives and emotions is correct, it led to a moment of intense empathetic distress combined with profound feelings of guilt over his implication not only in the death of this particular dolphin but also in the enslavement of dolphins in the marine parks he had helped make popular.

Psychologist Martin Hoffman differentiates between bystander guilt, which is a response to witnessing someone's distress without helping the person, and transgression guilt, "a painful feeling of disesteem for oneself, usually accompanied by a sense of urgency, tension, and regret, that results from empathic feeling for someone in distress, combined with awareness of being the cause of that distress" (2000, 114). It is different from bystander guilt in that the person experiencing it has actually harmed the victim. Like anger and fear, guilt is a moral emotion, and according to Hoffman, it can lead to several actional outcomes: "To keep from feeling guilty, a person can avoid carrying out harmful acts, or, having committed such an act, he can make reparation to the victim in the hope of undoing the damage and decreasing the feeling of guilt" (114). This is why Hoffman conceptualizes it as a prosocial emotion that can inhibit harmful behavior toward others and instead further helping behavior. In O'Barry's case, this is what seems to have happened, and the objects of his helping behavior are nonhuman animals that are either captured for display or killed for consumption. When he talks about Kathy's suicide, he is visibly moved, his facial features and voice showing his emotions and thereby cueing viewers to share his feelings through processes of emotional contagion. They remain aligned with O'Barry throughout much of the film, learning about his life and his commitment to face Japanese authorities and fishermen alike to stop the capturing and harvesting of dolphins. As Belinda Smaill has pointed out, O'Barry and the filmmakers themselves, who also take part in the action, "are the speaking subjects of the documentary, asking the viewer to see as they see and feel as they feel. Alignment with and immersion in the momentum of the activist movement is a key strategy of *The Cove* and documentary that seeks social change more broadly" (2014, 108).

This is the outsider dimension, then, of the film's use of strategic empathizing in order to make a moral and ethical argument about animal abuse and exploitation. Viewers are invited to feel along with the human protagonist O'Barry and his fellow activists, to share their affection for dolphins and their moral outrage about dolphin slaughter, and to hope that they will succeed in making the atrocities public. The other dimension of strategic empathy in the film involves the many scenes featuring dolphins, be it in captivity or in the wild, which cue *direct* trans-species empathy and a range of emotional responses to the animals. When O'Barry remembers Kathy's suicide in his arms, viewers are likely to feel both with him, sharing his horror and mourning, and with the dolphin who was so unhappy that she swam into the arms of her trainer to kill herself. The fact that trans-species empathy bears a significant risk of *empathetic inaccuracy* (Keen 2010, 88) makes such moments prone to misjudgment if they are not accompanied by critical anthropomorphism and the inclusion of "the full range of available scientific data" (Rivas and Burghardt 2002, 11). O'Barry suggests that he himself had to learn to read the bodies of dolphins correctly when attributing consciousness to them, and in part the film serves the purpose of sharing that knowledge, educating viewers that "the dolphin's smile [is] nature's greatest deception" and thereby destroying the illusion of the "happy" dolphin that performs in marine shows.

Smaill argues that the film makes a case for "dolphin exceptionalism," depicting the cetaceans as "too human (and extraordinary) to be killed or harvested in the way that other animals or fish regularly are" (2014, 108). The film indeed suggests several times that, cognitively and emotionally, dolphins are in certain ways like humans.[22] However, considering the insights of cognitive ethology and affective neuroscience, one need not necessarily see this as a constructed notion of exceptionalism. One could simply consider it a statement of facts—facts that are true not only for dolphins but also for other animal species.[23] As O'Barry makes clear, "it's about consciousness. They are self-aware like humans are self-aware. . . . I don't believe that the fishermen here are aware of that." The implication behind such statements is that viewers might not be aware of it either and, if they are, that they should be morally outraged at what is happening in the cove. As Smaill points out, "The documentary seeks a recognition in the viewer of the consciousness of the dolphin who is herded into the cove—that they understand the horror they are about to confront" (2014, 107). Such recognition greatly facilitates cognitive trans-species empathy, making it much easier for viewers to "slip into the animals' shoes" and to imagine the feelings of terror and pain they must be feeling before they die; however inaccurate their approximations may be. At the same time, the graphic images presented to them, filmed secretly with cameras disguised as rocks, cue immediate and involuntary affective responses through processes of embodied simulation, further amplifying the cognitive response.

The Cove's strategic cueing of both cognitive and affective empathy serves "a scrupulously visible political interest" (Keen 2010, 83). As Psihoyos openly states to the camera, the motive behind securing the visual evidence of the slaughter is "to do something that will make people change." We must assume, however, that the film's visual and narrative strategies work in very different ways on different audiences. If we recall Melanie Joy's argument about "psychic numbing" (2010, 18), it seems likely that much of the film's display of animal suffering will fail to engage viewers who consider dolphins a source of meat rather than a charming relative of Flipper. If they watch the film at all, they may react to the scenes of dolphin slaughter much like western carnivores react to images from inside a slaughterhouse. They either have successfully inhibited their empathy as a result of cultural belief systems or they try to avoid seeing the gruesome representation of animal suffering by looking away or engaging in other ways of imaginative resistance (Flory 2013, 43). Rather than feeling transgression guilt for their involvement in in a harmful practice, such viewers may attest that the film lacks intercultural tolerance and understanding or detect hypocrisy in its rhetorical stance. As the blogger Dyske Suematsu notes, "the issue that keeps coming up among the Japanese is this: Why is it OK for the Americans to slaughter thousands of cows and pigs, but it's not OK for the Japanese to slaughter dolphins? What exactly [are] the criteria? After all, the number of dolphins they kill is a drop in a bucket compared to how many cows and pigs the Americans kill" (2010, para. 2). This is a point well taken, and it returns us to Joy's thought experiment around the hypothetical golden retriever stew. In the end, Psihoyos's film reinforces in-group/out-group divisions among humans in order to get a morally enraged in-group (western, or at least non-Japanese viewers) to take action against the immoral doings of a specific out-group: Japanese citizens who either slaughter dolphins or consume the produced meat.[24] Janet Walker rightly points out that though the film makes "nuanced distinctions between the handful of Taiji whalers and the broader Japanese public" (2015, 181), this does not change the fact that both groups participate in a cultural practice that is framed as immoral and cruel.[25]

Problematic as this framing may be because of its use of intercultural blaming and relative neglect of larger questions related to wild fish depletion and other forms of animal exploitation, it has been successful in creating awareness for the issue that is at the center of the film. Like Josh Fox's *Gasland* (2010), which I have discussed in chapter 2, *The Cove* led various involved parties to release statements in response to the film and the public discussion stirred by it.[26] And while it was not popular with Japanese audiences, the documentary received considerable positive attention elsewhere in the world.

The Academy of Motion Picture Art and Science's decision to bestow *The Cove* with the award for Best Documentary Feature in 2009 further increased its popularity and reach. While it is always difficult to quantify the social impact of a single film, it must be considered a success if a documentary manages to turn public attention to an animal rights issue that most people were previously unaware of. This is what environmental documentaries can do if they present their topic in a way that engages audiences. However, it would be reductive to attribute such transformative potential to documentaries only, or to put fiction film in the realm of "wish-fulfillment," as film scholar Bill Nichols has done (2001, 2). In chapter 3, I have been concerned with environmental justice narratives that straddle the divide that Nichols and many others have tried to establish between fiction and nonfiction. While such fictional formats do not "document" the lives of real people and places in the way nonfiction formats do, they nevertheless point to historical reality, all the while capitalizing on the creative freedom inherent in fiction.

Michael Apted's *Gorillas in the Mist* is a good example of a fiction film that, just like *The Cove,* succeeded in turning public attention to the issue of wildlife abuse and related conservation issues by displaying and cueing trans-species empathy. Chronicling the life of the American primatologist Dian Fossey up to her violent death in 1985, Apted's biopic aligns viewers with its abrasive heroine (played by Sigourney Weaver) and invites them to take on as their own Fossey's passionate concern for the mountain gorillas in the Virunga Mountains in Rwanda. As in the case of *Thunderheart,* which he filmed five years later, Apted used the creative license of the fiction film to tell a story that engages viewers emotionally not only in Fossey's life and tragic death but also in the lives of the animals she sought to protect at all costs. He shot most of the footage on location in Rwanda, convinced that in order to make the film effective he would have to take it "where the gorillas are" (*Gorillas in the Mist* DVD Featurette 1994).

In chapter 2, I explained that spatial authenticity is not necessarily a given in fiction film production and that even dramatic replacements of one environment by another will go unnoticed by most viewers. There are, however, cases in which the authenticity of cinematic environment contributes to the meaning of a film *if* viewers are aware of it. Had Apted shot *Gorillas in the Mist* in some other rainforest outside of Rwanda, most viewers probably would not have noticed the difference. But learning about the fact through the press would have modulated their response to the film. Empirical research suggests that prior knowledge has considerable influence on narrative transportation (Green 2004) and people's visual and motor processing of the events presented to them (Chow et al. 2014). It is therefore safe to assume that it will make a difference for viewers' emotional response to a biopic about Dian Fossey (whose name and story was well known at the time, not least because of the fact that she had been murdered) if they are aware that what they see is the original place in which Fossey lived. Even more crucial is viewers' previous knowledge that (most of) the animals they see in the film belong to the actual group of wild mountain gorillas that Fossey studied and for whom she risked—and gave—her life.[27]

It was only a minimal film team of six, including actors, who climbed up the Virunga Mountains in 1987 with the hope of shooting the wildlife scenes with Fossey's original group of gorillas. Since the environment was exceptionally difficult to navigate and there were strict rules in place about filming wildlife in the national park, the remaining crew had to stay in the base camp at the foot of the mountain. "We spent eight weeks shooting Sigourney with wild animals," Apted explains in an interview. "We weren't allowed to do anything to these animals, like prod them, or manipulate them in any way. If they decided to attack us, they attacked us" (Simon 2012). The situation was particularly challenging for Sigourney Weaver, who had no prior experience with gorillas—wild or tame—and who now was sitting in the forest with a 450-pound silverback, pretending to be a primatologist who knows what she is doing.

In the completed film, the scenes that show Fossey with her gorillas are central for viewers' emotional engagement in the story and the message they take away from it. Fossey comes to Virunga as an outsider, an American physical therapist and lover of animals who has convinced the renowned primatologist Louis Leakey that she can do the urgently needed census of the rapidly shrinking gorilla population. For the first six weeks, she cannot even find the gorillas, and it is with her—and with her equally ignorant local tracker Sembagare—that viewers gradually get to know the great apes' natural habitat and, after the much anticipated first sighting, the gorillas themselves. The stark contrast between the animals' fierce looks and their peaceful and often playful behavior amazes Fossey.[28] A highly empathetic researcher, she begins to imitate their sounds and movements, gaining their trust. Her fieldwork closely mirrors the methods described by Marc Bekoff: it "entails sitting back and watching, and sometimes involves indirect or direct interactions with the animals" (2007, 39). Fossey learns about the gorillas by interacting with them, eventually getting close enough to experience what no other primatologist has experienced before: voluntary physical contact with wild gorillas as the silverback she calls Digit touches her hand. While the gorillas and the other wildlife in the forest are different from her in their sensual and cognitive capacities, Fossey recognizes that they are also similar in that they think, feel, and suffer.

Early on in the film, she shoots a young deer that is fatally injured after having fallen into an illegal trap placed there by the Batwa tribe. The Batwa had been hunting in the area long before it became a national park, but now they have acquired the status of poachers, hunting not only for food but also in order to sell trophies, such as ashtrays made of gorilla hands, to the United States and Europe.[29] Close-ups of Weaver's face show her character's compassion and agony as she reaches for her gun to put the deer out of its misery, while her POV shots show viewers the contorted limbs of the deer. Both types of shots cue a parallel empathetic response in viewers, inviting them to feel—together with Fossey—both trans-species empathy and compassion for the animal and empathetic anger at those who are responsible for its suffering.

Considering Eitzen's argument about the qualitative difference between fiction and nonfiction in terms of emotional response, this may be a moment that is indeed easier to bear in a fiction film than in a documentary because viewers can assume that the depicted deer was not *really* hurt and is also not *really* being shot by Sigourney Weaver. It is just make-believe for the purpose of storytelling. However, knowing that the film is a biopic and thus based on a true story complicates the issue, suggesting that there have been, and still are, countless *other* deer caught in real traps in much the same way. Such referential and representational relationships are quite common in politically engaged fiction films, and *Gorillas in the Mist* draws much of its emotional force from its mingling of fact and fiction.

The entrapped deer foreshadows the much more dramatic moment later on in the film when a group of gorillas is killed and dismembered with machetes by the Batwa. Fossey hears the shrieks of the animals and runs to the site of the massacre, but she comes too late. All that is left are the muti-lated bodies. For viewers who care about gorillas, or who have learned to care through the way the film has depicted them, these sensual impressions cue high levels of empathic distress. Even worse is the sight of one female gorilla, who escapes with her baby on her back, climbing up a tree to get away from the killers. Cross-cutting between Fossey and the gorilla mother, who is shrieking in panic as the poachers begin to cut down her tree, the sequence allows viewers to react to the animal's physical expression of fear through pro-cesses of embodied simulation, likely leading to emotions of sorrow, compas-sion, empathic fear and anger, and (at least in my own case) a senseless desire to help the beleaguered animal who, moments later, falls and is then hit by the tree. When Fossey arrives, she sees the Batwa—who are smiling—run away with their bags full of severed gorilla hands and the screaming gorilla baby. It is a horrifying moment that strengthens viewers' moral allegiance to Fossey and prepares them for her character development from here on, as she begins to fight the Batwa tribe like her worst enemy in order to protect the gorillas.

In terms of anthropomorphism, this passage is very complex. The female gorilla is not anthropomorphized in her physical display of fear and panic, and yet we are able to read her body and face, much like we are able to read the faces and bodies of suffering dogs, dolphins, or birds. As Welling points out with reference to a scene of animal suffering in *Winged Migration* (2001), "humans share enough innate dispositions with birds—such as the fear of being eaten—to justify the observation that the terror we may experience on viewing this scene is grounded in biology" (2014, 82). Emotional contagion can cross species lines because of a shared biology and shared existential needs. The fact that gorillas are evolutionarily closer to humans and more physically *like* them than birds may further facilitate trans-species empathy in the climactic scene of animal suffering in *Gorillas in the Mist*. And yet, the scene also demonstrates that representational authenticity is not a necessary precondition for our immediate affective response to a film scene. While most of the shots in the film show Weaver with Fossey's actual gorilla group, the massacre scene uses robots and humans in gorilla suits instead of real animals. What is behind the scene, then, is a human attempt to display animal suffering in a non-anthropomorphic way in order to cue trans-species empathy in viewers. As a result, viewers read the bodies and faces of dressed-up humans and robots who *play* gorilla emotion expressions, much like Sigourney Weaver plays the emotion expressions of Dian Fossey.

Receiving this information may make a difference in viewers' evaluation of the scene later on, but in the moment of exposure it is too immediate to allow for such reflection. As Victor Gazzola and colleagues have shown, the mirror systems in our brains are "activated strongly by the sight of both human and robotic actions, with no significant differences between these two agents" (2007, 1674). In the film, the fact that most viewers will not be able to tell the difference between authentic animals and their replacements further strengthens their emotional response to the scene. In his review for the *Chicago Sun-Times*, film critic Roger Ebert writes that

> it is hard to say who should get the most credit: those who photographed real animals in the jungle or those who used special effects to create animals, and parts of animals, for particular shots. I imagine that some of the close-ups of a gorilla's hand, clasping Weaver's, were done with Rick Baker's special effects creations. I imagine some of the gorillas in the jungle are real, and some are men inside gorilla suits. But the work is done so seamlessly that I could never be sure. Everything looked equally real to me, and

the delicacy with which director Michael Apted developed the relationships between woman and beast was deeply absorbing. There were moments when I felt a touch of awe. (1988)

Authenticity, then, remains a tricky issue even in a film like *Gorillas in the Mist,* in which the affective appeal fundamentally depends on its being based on a true story and in which the makers nevertheless regularly had to relinquish authenticity not only in the interest of animal welfare but also in order to strengthen the overall effect of the film and the persuasiveness of its conservation argument. This is perhaps most obvious when it comes to the film's depiction of Dian Fossey herself. As David Ingram points out, "the movie celebrates Fossey as a heroine of conservationism, in a narrative of heroic self-realization and sacrifice. It achieves this by being highly selective of the biographical and historical evidence available on Fossey's life and work" (2000, 132). Many commenters have criticized Apted's idealization of Fossey and his choice to tone down her extreme and violent antagonism to the local human population. Apted, however, has defended his choices, feeling that such concessions were necessary in order to make the movie commercially and politically successful. He has explained in an interview that "what [Fossey] did with her life was remarkable and tremendously symbolic, heroic and valuable, but she probably went mad there [in Rwanda] and eventually became completely uncontrollable. I think the truth of the matter was that she was raving mad by the time she was murdered, but I didn't want to make that kind of film. . . . If I had made a film about a nutter, I think it would have diminished the importance of what she did" (Apted 1993, 30). The film's overall effect, then, was more important to Apted than biographical authenticity, so he went on "to see how tough-minded I could make her without losing the audience's sympathy for her" (Easton 1988, 28).

This, too, constitutes a case of authorial strategic empathizing in the service of animal rights and nature conservation and, as in the case of *The Cove,* it involves blaming one or several groups of humans (the Batwa tribe and those who sell and buy gorilla parts) who are put into an imaginary out-group. Since, as several studies have shown (Oatley 1999; Mazzocco et al. 2010; Dan Johnson, Huffman, and Jasper 2014), empathy plays a central role in both viewer immersion and narrative persuasion, it makes sense for films with a conservationist agenda, be the films nonfiction, like *The Cove,* or fiction, like *Gorillas in the Mist,* to not only show animals in the most appealing ways but also to feature human characters who invite viewers to feel along with them as they feel for—and fight for—those animals. However, offering heroic human identification figures who fight on behalf of disenfranchised nonhumans (and often against human antagonists) is not the only way in which strategic empathy can be employed in environmental narratives about animals. The final section of the chapter will explore texts and films that put nonhuman characters—and their view of the world—at the center of their stories. Instead of aligning us with humans who passionately care for animals, such narratives offer direct access to the consciousness of their nonhuman protagonists.

FEELING THROUGH THEM: INHABITING NONHUMAN MINDS IN ENVIRONMENTAL FICTION

World literature is full of texts that use what narratologist Brian Richardson has somewhat derogatively called "bestial narrators and focalizers" (2006, 3).[30] Many of those narratives use animal focalization allegorically. While texts such as Orwell's *Animal Farm* (1945) ostentatiously invite readers to slip inside the minds of animals, they really are interested in exploring human subjectivity, using animal bodies only as very thin disguises. In such cases, as Herman has pointed out, "the specificity of the experiences of nonhuman animals is emptied out and replaced with experiences modeled after and imported from the human domain" (2011, 162). However, there are also stories that offer what Herman has labeled "Umwelt exploration," because their "emphasis is less on the translation of the nonhuman into the human than on the lived, phenomenal worlds of nonhuman animals themselves" (167). Yet, regardless of how serious and well-intended such explorative stories might be, they cannot fully get around Thomas Nagel's "bat problem": their human authors do not know enough about the subjective experience of other animals to give a truly authentic account of that experience. Even more problematic is the paradox that whatever animal narrators and focalizers sense, feel, or think has to be expressed in human language—a language that, with very few exceptions, nonhuman animals do not use in order to communicate.[31] As the narratologist William Nelles puts it, "written narratives, inherently limited to verbal representations of consciousness, quickly encounter stumbling blocks when depicting animal focalization," not least because "first-person or homodiegetic examples do pose the problem of assigning human language to animals, who by definition cannot speak" (2001, 188). And even if animals do not narrate the story, their conscious experience has to be rendered in human language. Nonhuman focalization in human literature is inherently and inescapably anthropomorphic.

In his discussion of the representation of nonhuman points of view in "realistic animal stories" (2002, 339), Allan Burns suggests that the limited

third-person point of view is best suited for mediating "the animal's experience and convey[ing] its purposiveness and emotional states," thereby allowing "readers to glimpse the world through the sensory apparatus of a different
species" (342). Limited third-person perspectives in fiction can roughly be
compared with the nonfiction writing practices used by ethologists, ethographers, and others who aim to be as truthful as possible to actual animal experience.[32] Telling a *fictional* story from the perspective of a nonhuman animal,
however, is much trickier in terms of anthropomorphization, since authors do
not only have to consider the sensory apparatus and cognition of a different
species but are also forced to invent plots for them, and therefore thoughts,
emotions, motivations, and goals. Jack London's *The Call of the Wild* (1903)
and its sequel, *White Fang* (1906), are pertinent examples of novels that focalize their story through an experiencing animal consciousness using a limited
third-person perspective. The first of the two novels align readers with Buck,
a St. Bernadine who turns from pet to service dog and then into a feral animal that roams the woods of Canada with a pack of wolves. The second novel
centers on White Fang, a wild wolfdog who ends up domesticated by the end
of the story. The following text passage from *White Fang* presents the canine
consciousness pondering the abilities of humans:

> It was this last [their capacity to change the very face of the world] that
> especially affected him. The elevation of frames of poles caught his eye; yet
> this in itself was not so remarkable, being done by creatures that flung sticks
> and stones to great distances. But when the frames of poles were made into
> tepees by being covered with cloth and skins, White Fang was astounded.
> It was the colossal bulk of them that impressed him. They arose around
> him, on every side, like some monstrous quick-growing form of life. They
> occupied nearly the whole of his field of vision. He was afraid of them. They
> loomed ominously above him; and when the breeze stirred them into huge
> movements, he cowered down in fear, keeping his eyes warily upon them,
> and prepared to spring away if they attempted to precipitate themselves
> upon him. (London [1906] 1991, 123)

White Fang serves as focalizer in this passage, relating his sensory experience as well as his cognitive processing of those sensations and his emotional
reactions to them. Nelles has argued that the focus in this passage "veers
sharply away from anthropomorphic interest toward imagining what an animal's focalization—both literally and psychologically—must be like" (2001,
191). It is indeed a good example of consistent nonhuman focalization and
the ways in which it invites readers to simulate in their minds the sensations,

thoughts, and emotions of an animal. It offers a vivid description not only of White Fang's perceptions and emotions but also of his cowering body position, which places his gaze even lower than it would normally be, making his fear more easily understandable for human readers.

And yet, there are also multiple anthropomorphic elements in the passage. While the use of human language is inevitable in written representation, the eloquence of White Fang's thoughts seems remarkable for an uneducated animal. Not only is he aware of monsters, he also knows that the "colossal" and "looming" human constructions around him are tepees. Such labeling of objects may help readers to get a better grasp on the things that the animal perceives and to therefore form a "correct" simulation of the animal's environment in their minds. However, it also compromises "literal" animal focalization, since that would have to do without human concepts when looking at the world. What is most important for readers' engagement and immersion in the tale, however, is that they are aligned with White Fang's subjective perspective and that they empathically relate to his experience of the world. Just as important, the moral structure of the novel encourages them to build allegiance with the wolfdog when he is menaced by humans or other animals.

Barbara Gowdy's much more recent novel, *The White Bone* (1999), is similar to London's mode of narration in its near-consistent employment of animal focalization, but in this case it is coupled with a plea for wildlife conservation. Using omniscient third-person narration, *The White Bone* tells its story through the minds of African elephants—mostly through that of the young female Mud and occasionally also through that of the older Date Bed and the bull Tall Time. Like London's novels, it offers insights into animals' sociality and their perspective on humans, but whereas in *The Call of the Wild* and *White Fang* the protagonists' relationship to humans is shaped by a long history of domestication, *The White Bone* is focalized through the minds of wild animals who perceive humans as a deadly threat. As Dan Wylie has observed, "Gowdy's strategy is, firstly, to depict an elephant society as complex and wonderful as the human, in order to have it accorded equal respect. Secondly, she relates with shocking and graphic economy the depredations of ivory-hunters: the novel is almost unremittingly a series of such massacres, with barely a hint of hope at the close" (2002, 123). The novel's relationship to Africa's historical reality is therefore not unlike that of *Gorillas in the Mist,* but the use of strategic empathizing is entirely different. Instead of offering a human identification figure that comes as an outsider to the situation and learns to care about a group of animals, *The White Bone* aligns readers with the animals' *insider perspective.* Gowdy's evocations of animal suffering and death are emotionally powerful: "All the faces are hacked off, the trunks tossed aside, the tusks gone and some of the feet as well. . . . On a certain cow her [Mud's] eye settles and by the line of the jaw she recognizes She-Doubts-And-Doubts. . . . Twenty-three bodies she counts before her eye dims" (1999, 26). Narrated in present tense like the whole novel, the passage describes with great immediacy one of the reoccurring visions that Mud and some of the other elephants have of slaughter. It scares Mud and it also affects readers who are simulating the situation in their minds. The *Outside Magazine* calls *The White Bone* "an unsentimental and meticulously imagined immersion into the world of the African elephant" that is "utterly believable" (1999). And yet, although it is based on extensive research, the novel also takes considerable creative license in its evocation of animal minds and emotions. Not only do the elephants converse in English, they also have a complex system of naming (female elephants change their names after their first sexual experience) and an equally complex spiritual life that involves the use of a mystical "third eye" for preternatural vision.

What makes the novel nevertheless interesting from the perspective of both critical animal studies and cognitive ethology is that it does "not hesitate to attribute 'mind,' 'thinking,' and self-awareness to the elephants" (Wylie 2002, 126) and that it invites readers to do the same. Gowdy has called her novel "an attempt, however presumptuous, to make a huge imaginative leap—to imagine what it would be like to be that big and gentle, to be that imperiled" ("An Elephant's Story" 2008). That imaginative leap cannot possibly attain any degree of epistemological accuracy. As Caracciolo points out, "literature does not provide tools to validate insights into animal experience—it can only offer imaginary reconstructions whose perceived plausibility reflects the biases (and limitations) of the human imagination" (2016, 194). And yet, focalizing the story though the minds of elephants foregrounds the fact that they are conscious and sentient beings, thereby offering a productively estranged perspective on the fate of a species whose capacity to mourn and remember their dead we are only beginning to understand.

Bold as some of her narrative strategies are, the fact that Gowdy narrates in the third person signals her awareness of the epistemological limitations involved in her project. Wylie notes that the use of "third person narration draws attention to the fact that some perceptual, cognitive, and emotional differences between human writer and nonhuman protagonist remain intractable, untranslatable" (2002, 122). Assuming a first-person perspective is an even bolder choice in that regard, one that—for better or worse—aims at collapsing those differences. It has not fared very well with critics. Burns calls the use of first-person narration in animal stories "an overtly anthropomorphic fantasy" (2002, 339). Nelles has been more nuanced but similarly dismissive. "Homodiegetic narration," he writes, "constrained to attribute the implausible capability of human language directly to a nonhuman narrator, compromises the verisimilitude required for a convincing illusion of representation" (2001, 192). We must therefore assume that both Nelles and Burns would roll their eyes at children's stories, such as Anna Sewell's *Black Beauty* (1877), or novels aimed at adults, such as Patrick Neate's *The London Pigeon Wars* (2004) and Garth's Stein's *The Art of Racing in the Rain* (2008), all of which are told by horses, birds, or dogs that sound an awful lot like humans.[33] The nonhuman insider perspective poses epistemological difficulties that simply cannot be overcome, regardless of how faithfully authors try to imagine animal embodiment and its consequences for conscious experience.[34] Perhaps they do not have to be overcome, since scores of people seem to find great enjoyment in such stories, not only in fiction and creative nonfiction literature but also in film. The question should rather be whether anthropomorphic inhabitations of animal minds can have any positive influences on how we look at real-world animals and whether there are any significant differences between literary and filmic approaches to such inhabitation.

While film gets around the central problem faced by literary animal stories that use insider perspectives—that nonhuman sensation and consciousness has to be rendered in human language—it is faced with another one: it has to enable viewers to read the bodies and faces of animals correctly in order to attribute the states of mind that are necessary for the understanding of the larger narrative.[35] In the case of live-action film, this necessitates the use of trained animal actors who can not only move from point A to point B if so directed, but who are also able to display emotional reactions when cued. From a critical animal studies perspective, such uses of animals are inherently problematic. As Randy Malamud notes, "in virtually every aspect of visual culture . . . the animals did not choose to participate" (2012, 3).[36] That this is not always entirely true becomes obvious when we recall that Michael Apted's film team was not allowed to prod or manipulate the gorillas of Virunga National Park in any way for the making of *Gorillas in the Mist,* and that the animals voluntarily chose to interact with actress Sigourney Weaver. Such cases, however, are extremely rare in feature film. The typical case involves domesticated or tamed animals and their trainers in which the former (mostly) do what they are being told by the latter. Malamud maintains that this must "not necessarily always involve exploitation and domination, [but] we must at least always be attuned to that possibility" (3). Directing our attention at the objectification of animals in many modes of filmmaking and viewing, he argues that even when we "try to tap into and connect with animal otherness . . . in films like *Whale Rider, Horse Whisperer, Dances with Wolves* and *Grizzly Man,* we are still much more interested in ourselves than in them" (75).[37] This is even true for a film such as Kornél Mundruczó's *White God* (2014), which tells the story of a girl and her dog who get separated by the girl's inconsiderate father and who try to reunite. A large part of the film aligns viewers with the dog, who, after having been caught by animal control officers, builds a downright army of dogs in order to take revenge on the humans who have mistreated them. Although the dogs cannot speak in Mundruczó's film, they convey a remarkable array of emotions through body language and facial expressions that, in combination with a David-versus-Goliath narrative, strongly engages viewer emotions. Particularly interesting from an animal rights perspective is that the film stages a revolt of animals against human exploitation and that it asks viewers to side with the revolting animals rather than with the cruel and callous humans. However, it remains an "overtly anthropomorphic" fantasy in that it imagines a pack of dogs acting with an army-like efficiency, their actions as well as their motives often paralleling those of humans (Burns 2002, 339).

The same is true for the nonhuman protagonists of "animal talkies" such as *Dr. Doolittle* (2001) and *Babe* (1995), which are less violently inclined but nevertheless human through and through. Both films add human voices to express the animals' thoughts and emotions and both use computer animation to match their facial expressions to what is being said. Manipulating real-life footage during postproduction allows for a high degree of anthropomorphization that greatly facilitates viewers' employment of cognitive and affective empathy because it makes animals a lot more like humans. This narrative strategy can no longer be said to cue trans-species empathy because it sacrifices any resemblance to the inner lives of actual animals. It nevertheless has been massively successful with both children and adult audiences.

The strategy of extreme anthropomorphism remains just as effective in engaging viewers once one does away entirely with the real thing, as is attested by the enduring popularity of animated films centering on animals. While such representation of animal minds can be accused of the "emptying out" of animal minds that is so problematic from a critical animal studies perspective, we should not immediately conclude that their effects on viewers' perceptions of animals are always detrimental. One of Walt Disney Animation Studios' earliest feature productions was *Bambi* (1942), a film that suggests that heavily anthropomorphized animals can cue strong emotions as well as forms of moral allegiance that last beyond the immediate viewing experience.[38] As Robin Murray and Joseph Heumann explain in their ecocritical study of animation film, the romantic story of the orphaned deer that is hunted by the humans who also killed its mother "had a powerful effect on its viewers, causing hunters to protest such an inaccurate presentation of nature and children to object to killing deer that could be a Bambi or Bambi's mother" (2011, 30).[39]

Over the decades, animation film—and Disney animation in particular—has become ever-more sophisticated in its use of technical means to immerse viewers in the experiential worlds of deer, dogs, cats, foxes, lions, cougars, bears, penguins, and countless other animals. The embodied simulation of these animated animals' actions and emotions sometimes also kindles feelings of sympathy for their actually existing counterparts, as the example of *Bambi* attests. While it may not aid in developing a better understanding of the actual animals' inner lives, it can help weaken viewers' empathy inhibitions toward specific species or use existing sympathies strategically in order to make a larger argument about nature conservation and sustainable development.

Little is known at this point of how exactly viewers respond to animated animals, but the historical evidence suggests that it makes sense for a film like George Miller's *Happy Feet* (2006) to combine its melodramatic story of a tap-dancing, music-loving penguin with hyper-real animation and an appeal to end global warming. As film scholar David Whitley observes, many reviewers were not enamored with that combination, or with the film's use of "dance" and "song" as metaphorical interpretations of central aspects of penguin behavior. The perceived danger was "one of tasteless commodification, the empathetic reverence towards nature displayed in *March of the Penguins* repackaged as pop in the Antarctic, with the additional celebrity allure of film star voice-overs" (2014, 151). However, as Whitley demonstrates in his astute analysis of the film, "it is by no means clear that *Happy Feet* simply abandons all claims to develop viewers' sympathetic understanding of the plight of wild creatures in taking these metaphors [of song and dance] literally as a pretext for anthropomorphized disco routines" (151). Instead of condemning the film for its unabashed anthropomorphism—which went as far as using human dancers for the motion capture that is the basis of the penguin protagonist's movements—Whitley pays attention to the ways in which it guides viewers toward its utopian and emotionally gratifying ending in which the penguin community engages in a dance that links humans and animals together in harmonious understanding.[40] Sarah McFarland sees *Happy Feet*'s narrative strategies in a much more critical light, arguing that the Hollywood "desire for 'happy endings' precludes the kind of ending that a genuinely environmental film would have—one that makes us rise and leave the theatre with a sense of urgency, a clearly defined action plan, and a desire to make a difference" (2009, 103). However, there is no empirical evidence that an alarming ending would lead to more "clearly defined action plan[s]" in the minds of viewers as they leave the theater. As Ingram has noted, the aesthetic and ethical assumptions implied in McFarland's critique suggests that ideological endings of any kind do not lead to immediate plans for action in the minds of audiences

(2014b, 462–63). Not only does such a standpoint fail to acknowledge the multiple ways in which viewers may negotiate their response to the emotional cues of a film, it also forgets that the influences of popular film (and literature) may be much more gradual and indirect.

Just like strategic empathizing, then, the use of strategic anthropomorphization in a film like *Happy Feet* invites viewers to care for nonhuman others, at least for the duration of the film. This is true not only for nonhuman animals, but also for humanoid aliens as we encounter them in James Cameron's *Avatar* (2009) and—perhaps most remarkably—for lifeless matter. Films such as John Lasseter's *Toy Story* (1995) and *Cars* (2006) as well as Andrew Stanton's *WALL-E* (2008) remind us that Genette was right when he suggested that "in fiction nothing prevents us from entrusting that role [of the narrative agent] to an animal . . . or indeed to an 'inanimate' object" (1980, 244).[41] As Heise has pointed out, animated objects are almost equally pervasive in animated film as animal protagonists, from its earliest beginnings to some of its latest works (2014, 303). Such films do not seem to have any problems creating the illusion of sentience for inanimate objects by giving them speech as well as voluntary movement and a wide range of emotions and related hopes and goals.[42] In her book *Vibrant Matter*, the philosopher Jane Bennett has called for strategic anthropomorphization in more general terms, considering it a useful way of extending the notion of agency to include the nonhuman more broadly. "We need to cultivate," she states, "a bit of anthropomorphism—the idea that human agency has some echoes in nonhuman nature—to counter the narcissism of humans in charge of the world" (xvi). It seems to me that when it comes to the stories we tell each other about animals, such forms of strategic anthropomorphism should be valued as one of several ways to invite viewers to care about nonhuman others. Ideally, they would also be critical in the sense of being aware of the inevitable limits and inadequacy of our own sensual and cognitive abilities.

CONCLUSION

In this chapter, I have explored the roles of trans-species empathy and anthropomorphism in our engagement with environmental narratives that centrally focus on the lives of animals. I have suggested that recent research in cognitive ethology and affective science explains why we do not only respond empathically to heavily anthropomorphized animals, as we find them in Disney animation and related forms of fiction, but that our biological makeup also allows us to empathize with actual and un-anthropomorphized animals.

Films such as *The Cove* and *Gorillas in the Mist* rely on these cognitive and affective abilities of viewers while also aligning them with human characters that empathize with the animal protagonists of the films. This double use of strategic empathizing aims to convince viewers of the sentient and conscious nature of nonhuman animals in order to promote conservationism and animal rights. As Burns puts it so pointedly, "Without an interest in the minds of other animals, empathy cannot exist. Without empathy, ethics cannot exist" (2002, 348). It may be logically impossible to disprove the proposition that nonhuman animals do not have thought and emotion, but as Donald Griffin, the founder of cognitive ethology notes, "we can escape from this paralytic dilemma by relying on the same criteria of reasonable plausibility that lead us to accept the reality of consciousness in other people" (1984, 28). Theory of Mind and embodied simulation may be less accurate when they cross species boundaries, but they are nevertheless of central importance if we are to develop an ethical relationship with all animals, not just with our dogs and other companion animals that are literally close to us.

I have also explored the epistemological and ethical consequences of the use of an *insider perspective* on animal experience, and the role played by anthropomorphism in such imaginings. Making the creative effort to inhabit a nonhuman mind, Wylie suggests, entails the enactment of "a real sense of community and reciprocity" (2002, 122). In this sense, the choice of an insider perspective on animal experience, and the related effort at translation, also has important moral and ethical implications, even though it always runs the risk of gross misrepresentation. As Wylie puts it, "Even though . . . limits remain, anthropomorphic writing nevertheless seems to embody the proposition that animals—or at least certain animals—are in some sense understandable, and have enough in common with us to demand an ethically equivalent response and sense of responsibility from humans" (2002, 116). The same is true for filmmaking, both live-action and animation. Trying to see things from an nonhuman point of view, to put oneself in the shoes of an animal, is an all-important step forward, even though there is no way to do this in non-anthropomorphic ways. While there is no guarantee that this will change viewers' attitudes toward nonhuman others, it may habituate them to taking the imaginative leap. We need more empirical research on these issues to get a better sense of how exactly we relate to nonhuman characters in feature film and how our relationships are mediated by anthropomorphism.

Herman has suggested that approaching animal narratives from a cross-disciplinary perspective can "foster new ways of imagining and responding to transspecies relationships within the larger biosphere," adding that this "remains an urgent task for narratology in the twenty-first century" (2014,

141). In addition to integrating neuroscientific research on reading and film viewing, such cross-disciplinary perspectives must take into account what we know about the minds and emotions of actual animals, which may lead to the recognition that much of what we consider anthropomorphic is actually not so. Bekoff suggests in *The Animal Manifesto* (2010) that "we must stop ignoring [animals'] gaze and closing our hearts to their pleas" (1). To do so would involve "expanding our compassion footprint" (3) to include nonhuman animals and to rid ourselves of the belief in human exceptionalism. Bekoff's plea for the expansion of human empathy and compassion across species lines has an idealistic and downright utopian ring to it, not only because humans have trouble even caring equally for other humans but also because most of us will never get to the point where we will truly feel for a mosquito. This does not change the fact, however, that our current relationship with nonhuman others and the planet as a whole is profoundly immoral and unsustainable. We are in dire need of alternatives and visions of better ways of being on planet earth. The texts and films I will consider in part III of *Affective Ecologies* all gauge the future outfall of our unsustainable relationships with the environment that surrounds and sustains us, suggesting that it must prompt us to consider their disastrous effects not only on nonhuman others but also on future human generations.

PART III

Experiencing the Future

CHAPTER 5

Troubling Futures

Climate Risk and the Emotional Power of Dystopia

ABOUT HALFWAY into the runtime of Roland Emmerich's *The Day After Tomorrow* (2004), the paleoclimatologist Jack Hall draws a horizontal line across a projected map of the United States. Everyone who lives south of that line, he declares with a somber face, needs to be evacuated immediately. Across the big conference table, several unbelieving faces stare at him, among them those of the president of the United States, the vice president, the secretary of state, and the joint chiefs of staff of the Army. "What about the people in the North?" the president asks voicelessly. Hall's facial features grow even more somber as he responds curtly: "I'm afraid it's too late for them. If they go outside, the storm will kill them. At his point, their best chance is to stay inside, try to ride it out, pray." It is the moment of truth in the film, the moment when a stubborn administration has to face the consequences of decades of climate change denial and a shortsighted focus on immediate economic gain. It is the moment when environmental risk turns into an actual catastrophe as the northern hemisphere shifts into another small ice age. The people in the meeting room seem supremely unprepared for this moment, despite an incessant flow of dire warnings from climate scientists such as Hall. As unreasonable as it may seem, they had not seen this coming. Only in this moment, as they realize that a substantial part of the American population is going to die in a "natural" catastrophe of epic proportions, do the politicians exhibit an emotional response to the phenomenon of climate change and an accompanying understanding that something needs to be done. It comes too late though, as Hall—and with him the viewer—is perfectly aware.

Viewers are aligned with Hall throughout much of the film. Not only are they attached to him in the sense of following his actions, they also have access to his subjectivity. Hall is a dedicated scientist and a lousy father, and because of his occupation he is more perceptive than others to climate-related environmental risks. As a climatologist, he has immediate access to the data that others in the field produce, most crucially to that of a team of researchers in Scotland who study ocean surface temperatures. Because they are aligned with Hall, viewers learn first-hand about the drastic drop of temperature in the North Atlantic that will cause the disastrous events later on in the film. In addition, they are invited to imaginatively experience through embodied simulation a spectacular and thrillingly active nature—a feature, as I have shown in chapter 2, which is typical of the disaster genre. Right after the opening credits of the film, viewers are treated with stunning computer-animated footage that allows them to witness how a chunk of ice "the size of Long Island" breaks off from the Antarctic ice shield. Like Hall, who is present during the spectacular event, they have experiential knowledge that strongly encourages them to build moral allegiance to him. Every event in the film's narrative supports that Hall is right and that those who do not believe him or oppose him are wrong, endangering—and effectively ending—the lives of millions of people.[1] While nothing of this is unusual for a disaster movie, *The Day After Tomorrow* stands out as a film that to this day is a reference point not only in public discourse on climate change but also in science communication.

In this chapter, I will investigate our embodied simulation of speculative future environments in ecodystopian narratives as well as the emotions cued by such narratives in order to engage their audiences and, in some cases, promote more sustainable lifestyles. Many of our current environmental problems, such as climate change, are too vast in their spatial and temporal dimensions and too abstract to be accessible to our senses. We cannot really see or smell or hear these problems, unless they manifest themselves in one specific event, such as a hurricane. One way to represent such vast ecological developments is through graphs and numbers. It is a language that scientists understand and that, in their communication with policy makers and the general public, they increasingly try to translate into accessible narratives.[2] As the ecocritic Scott Slovic and the psychologist Paul Slovic put it in their introduction to *Numbers and Nerves* (2015), "There is a space in all people, even in the scientists and the economists whose daily currency is the worldview we call 'quantification,' that 'cries out for words,' and for images and stories, for the discourse of emotion" (5). The first section of the chapter will be concerned with the complex relationship between discourses of emotion, climate risk perception, and narrative engagement, exploring how popular science books on climate change have made use of dystopian storytelling in order to make their arguments emotionally salient. The second section will discuss how a dystopian novel such as T. C. Boyle's *A Friend of the Earth* (2000) allows readers to imaginatively experience *what it is like* to live in a nightmarish future while also using irony and satire to alleviate the affective charge of the dystopian world. The final section of the chapter will return to *The Day After Tomorrow* and also consider the ways in which Hollywood films more generally have employed climate-related risk and catastrophe to provide audiences with entertaining and pleasurable viewing experiences, discussing whether the resulting mix of negative and positive emotions has any potential to promote social change.

PERCEIVING ANTHROPOGENIC RISK: DOOM, GLOOM, AND IRONY IN CLIMATE CHANGE NONFICTION

When we try to envision climate change, most of us rather swiftly reach the limits of our imaginary abilities. It is a phenomenon that is too abstract and too vast in its spatial and temporal dimensions to allow for easy visualization. It exists in scientific graphs and numbers and is encapsulated in iconic images such as receding glaciers, devastating storms, and drowning polar bears.[3] While the inhabitants of coastal regions and low-lying islands are already subject to its negative effects, for many people in the industrialized West, climate change is still a phenomenon that can be personally experienced only in slightly changed weather patterns, invasive animal and plant species, and occasional weather extremes. Although Americans actually live on a landmass that is more severely affected by climate change than many other regions in the world, they seem to have particular difficulties in registering the urgency of the issue. A 2015 study by psychologists Sander van der Linden, Edward Maibach, and Anthony Leiserowitz notes that "despite being one of the most important societal challenges of the 21st century, public engagement with climate change currently remains low in the United States. Mounting evidence from across the behavioral sciences has found that most people regard climate change as a non-urgent and psychologically distant risk—spatially, temporally, and socially—which has led to deferred public decision making about mitigation and adaptation responses" (758). As long as people believe that they will not be affected by climate change, they are unlikely to support changes on policies or to their own lifestyles because such decisions are directly dependent on their perception of risk.

Risk, explains the German sociologist Ulrich Beck in *World at Risk* (2009), "is *not* synonymous with catastrophe. Risk means the *anticipation* of the catastrophe. Risks concern the possibility of future occurrences and developments; they make present a state of the world that does not (yet) exist" (9). This differentiation between risk and catastrophe underlines the uncertainty and future-oriented temporality of risk. "Risks are always future events that *may* occur" (9), writes Beck. Despite this inherent futurity, they can have considerable effects on our present because our awareness of and emotional reactions to them shape our expectations and, potentially, our actions.[4] As Paul Slovic and other psychologists in the field of decision research have found, emotions matter at least as much as analytical thinking in both risk perception and decision making. Building on the work of Antonio Damasio, Slovic explains in *The Perception of Risk* (2000) that over time he and his colleagues "have come to recognize just how highly dependent [risk perception] is upon intuitive and experimental thinking, guided by emotional and affective processes" (xxxi). Although deliberation and analysis are important factors in many decision-making circumstances, writes Slovic, "reliance on affect and emotion is a quicker, easier, and more efficient way to navigate in a complex, uncertain, and sometimes dangerous world" (xxxi). In a later article, Slovic and his collaborators go even further, stating that analytic reasoning cannot be effective unless it is guided by emotion and affect and that "we cannot assume that an intelligent person can understand the meaning of and properly act upon even the simplest of numbers such as amounts of money or numbers of lives at risk . . . unless these numbers are infused with affect" (2010, 34). This builds directly on Damasio's claim that "emotion and feeling, along with the covert physiological machinery underlying them, assists us with the daunting task of predicting an uncertain future and planning our actions accordingly" (1994, xxiii). How we feel about a certain risk, then, will in part determine how we act when it comes to the issue of climate change.

This is why the British climatologist Mike Hulme has argued that we must get away from understanding climate only as a physical reality and begin to see it also as "an imaginative idea—an idea constructed and endowed with meaning and value through cultural practice" (2009, 14). Thus understood, anthropogenic climate change is not only a scientific but also a cultural problem. How we address it depends in part on cultural values and economic priorities and in part on our species' very capacity to sense, process, and understand information. As long as we do not believe that climate change concerns us directly, we are unlikely to engage in or support any action to curb greenhouse gas emissions more effectively. Van der Linden, Maibach, and Leiserow-itz therefore suggest that "instead of a future, distant, global, nonpersonal, and analytical risk that is often framed as an overt loss for society," climate change should be framed "as a present, local, and personal risk" in ways that "facilitate more affective and experiential engagement" (2015, 758).

But how should one facilitate such engagement for people who are not yet presently, locally, or personally affected? As Julie Doyle has noted, one of the inescapable conundrums of climate change campaigning is that it necessitates "action to prevent climate change *before its effects* [can] *be seen*" (2009, 280). One potential way out of the conundrum that has been considered by clima-tologists, psychologists, sociologists, and cultural studies scholars alike is to offer people affective and experiential engagement with climate change on the imaginary level through images and narratives.[5] Such strategies make sense from the perspective of cognitive science. Slovic and Slovic remind us that "we as a species think best when we allow numbers and narratives, abstract information and experiential discourse, to interact, to work together" (2015, 4).[6] With reference to the work of psychologist Seymour Epstein, they argue that "humans apprehend reality, including risk and benefit, by employing two interactive modes of processing information: the deliberative, logical, evi-dence-based 'rational system' . . . and the 'experiential system' which encodes reality in images, metaphors, and narratives associated with feelings, with affect" (5). Mirror neuron-enabled processes of "liberated embodied simula-tion" (Gallese and Wojciehowski 2011), as I have described them in previous chapters, may be considered an important component of the experiential sys-tem since they allow us to understand the content of metaphors, images, and narratives by activating the respective regions in our brains. The past fifteen years have produced a steadily rising number of cultural texts that attempt to engage both cognitive systems in their evocation of the potential future consequences of climate change and related anthropogenic processes in what we have come to call the Anthropocene.[7] Such texts use a number of narra-tive strategies to make their cautionary tales more immediate and emotionally engaging by framing climate change "as a present, local, and personal risk" (van der Linden, Maibach, and Leiserowitz 2015, 758).

One narrative strategy that has become common in popular science books is to write about future risks as if they were already a present reality. The renowned climatologist James Hansen, for example, insists in *Storms of My Grandchildren* (2009) that "Planet Earth is in imminent peril" (xi) because of human activity, which is why "it is crucial for all of us . . . to get involved" (277). Bill McKibben's *Eaarth* (2010) strikes a similar tone, suggesting that planet Earth is *already* "a different place" than it was for the past ten thousand

years, which is why it "needs a new name: Eaarth" (1). Rather than offering
an apocalyptic perspective, in which, as ecocritic Ursula Heise has explained,
"utter destruction lies ahead but can be averted" (2008, 142), McKibben presents a risk scenario in which "crises are already underway all around and
while their consequences can be mitigated, a future without their impact has
become impossible to envision" (Heise 2008, 142). The current environment
on his planet Eaarth is what literary scholar Frederick Buell has described
as "a horror people hopelessly dwell within, a horror that goes on and on
all around them" (2004, 251). But even as McKibben vehemently insists that
"global warming is . . . no longer a future threat, *no longer a threat at all*. It
is our reality" (2010, xiii), he still tries to alert his readers to the even greater
risks in the future so that they can adapt to the changing climate and build
"communities and economies that can withstand what's coming" (xi). James
Lovelock sounds even more alarmed in *The Revenge of Gaia* (2007), where he
speaks about his concern about "the Earth's declining health," urging his readers to do something about anthropogenic climate change because "the living
Earth's response to what we do will depend not merely on the extent of our
land use and pollutions but also on its current state of health" (1–2).

   These are just three examples of how scientists and environmentalists have
used temporal framing to make the abstract and distant risks of the Anthropocene—and in particular climate risk—more immediate for the readers of
their popular science texts in order to engage them emotionally and scare
them into action.[8] In order to convey the severity of the risks they describe on
an experiential level, such texts describe future risks as if they were *already*
an ongoing catastrophe (which may very well be the case). In doing so, they
often do not shy away from creating completely fictional dystopian narratives.
Peter Ward's *The Flooded Earth* (2010), for example, opens with a description
of Miami in the year 2120 CE, when carbon dioxide is at 800 ppm and the
city is an island "because the level of the world's oceans had risen 10 feet" (1).
Mark Lynas's *Six Degrees* (2007) also takes considerable creative liberty in its
detailed description of a future world that is one to six degrees hotter than
in the present.[9] The most daring attempt to make the potential future catastrophes tangible for readers, however, can be found in Hansen's book, which
includes a science fiction story set in the year 2525 in which a humanoid alien
species unsuccessfully tries to resettle its people to a planet Earth that now
has surface temperatures of one hundred degrees Celsius and is devoid of life.

   After dedicating the first 260 pages of the book to the memory of his long
career in climate science and the risk of a future climate catastrophe he hopes
to help avert, Hansen radically changes his mode of narration, diving into

a dialogue between the aliens as they approach the Earth and realize that it looks very different from what they had been expecting:

"It's not Earth! It's not Earth!"

"What do you mean it's not Earth?"

"The whole planet is covered by haze! It can't be Earth. The guidance system must have gone haywire. Maybe it's Venus, but it doesn't look like Venus."

"Calm down, Spud. It has to be Earth. We checked the coordinates as we were slowing down, as we approached the solar system. Mayflower II was on track to the third planet from the Sun, just as it was programmed." [. . .]

"There. It's not the blue marble. The atmosphere is full of a yellowish dust or haze [. . .]

"We are supposed to be looping in over the South Pole, right? That must be Antarctica."

"Yes, it seems to have more or less the right shape. It must be Antarctica. But I don't see any ice. What should we do Pa?" (2009, 261)

From this opening dialogue, the narrative shifts into telling mode, relating the lengthy backstory of the "five humanoid creatures and two robots" on board the Mayflower II, who left their own Earth-like planet Claron almost 500 years ago in order to search for a new home. Because the sun in their own solar system is on its way to becoming a red giant, the Claronians need a new place to stay and the Earth is their last and only hope for a new beginning. But their hopes are based on outdated data. The Earth has turned into a Venus-like planet that no longer sustains human or humanoid life. The poor Claronians thus decide to check out Mars and find several abandoned structures there with American, Chinese, Indian, European, and Japanese flags. The Chinese structure is the largest, but since they only speak English, the aliens land at the American base where they learn from old recordings that humans "had the perfect planet and they blew it" (267). Spud gets so mad that he leaves the others behind in order to crash the spaceship "where the biggest big-shot coal CEO lived" (267). They then engage in a lengthy discussion via their intercom about who is to blame, how the democratic system failed, and why no one prevented the catastrophe. Eventually, Spud runs his spaceship into where Washington, DC, used to be, leaving behind "a puff of yellow dust" (269).

While this scenario "may read like far-fetched science fiction," writes Hansen, "its central hypothesis is a tragic certainty—continued unfettered burning of all fossil fuels will cause the climate system to pass tipping points, such that we hand our children and grandchildren a dynamic situation that is out of

control" (269). In order to illustrate the book's scientific hypothesis, he turns
to post-apocalyptic science fiction in the hope that the shared imagination of
future devastation will make his discourse of anthropogenic climate risk more
tangible. However, it seems doubtful that the story will have the desired effect,
simply because it fails to engage readers' imaginations and emotions. Not only
is the dialogue wooden and the characters devoid of any individuality, there is
also not a single sentence in the story that invites readers to simulate in their
minds the characters' actions and emotions or the worlds that they behold
through the use of vivid sensory and motor imagery. Hansen is ready to admit
that "science fiction isn't [his] area of expertise" (2009, 260), so we might
forgive him that he cannot create fictional characters and storyworlds that
excite our minds and bodies. His dystopia sounds like a dry didactic trea-
tise that does not allow readers to viscerally experience the horrific result of
unmitigated climate change. And even if it did, it is questionable whether such
an approach would yield the desired results. As ecocritic Sylvia Mayer has
pointed out, "neither reliance on the expert languages of science nor reliance
on a 'fear' appeal' . . . in reporting about the various threats climate change
entails have been able to communicate its present manifestation and possible
future developments in ways that would arouse a more powerful engagement
with the problem" (2014, 22). For these reasons, Hansen's resorting to science fiction as a tool of climate change communication must be considered an
unsuccessful attempt to use fictionality in support of an analytical argument.

More interesting in that regard is the slim book that science historians
Naomi Oreskes and Erik Conway have published with the evocative title: *The
Collapse of Western Civilization: A View from the Future* (2014). Whereas the
tone of Hanson's book is quite literally dead serious, Oreskes and Conway
invent a future Chinese historian who, across a temporal distance of more
than 300 years, looks back to our present with a mixture of laconicism, irony,
and sarcasm. In 2023, we learn, "the infamous 'year of perpetual summer'
lived up to its name, taking 500,000 lives worldwide and costing nearly $500
billion in losses due to fires, crop failure, and the deaths of livestock and companion animals" (Oreskes and Conway 2014, 8). It is the beginning of what
people, in retrospect, call "the Period of the Penumbra"—the shadow age (9).
The collapse of western civilization as a result of climate change is related by
the historian as a mere statement of facts, another example of those abstract
numbers that stand for unfathomable disaster and suffering by human and
nonhuman animals alike. While the text does not "facilitate . . . affective and
experiential engagement" (van der Linden, Maibach, and Leiserowitz 2015,
758), any more than Hansen's does, it works in a different, and much more

distant, affective register, using irony as a rhetorical weapon to confront readers with the utter stupidity of their generations' collective decisions.

Ecocritic Nicole Seymour has suggested that such an ironical stance may
in fact be more effective than the "serious affective modes" (2014, 61) we find
not only in the popular science books of McKibben, Ward, Lynas, Lovelock,
and Hansen but also in many environmental documentary films.[10] Taking
her cue from Heise, who has argued that "a steady drumbeat of gloom-and-
doom rhetoric is liable to discourage and alienate individuals more than it
incites them to action" (2008, 142), Seymour suggests that irony "can address
the problems posed by serious affective modes—and foster a self-critical attitude that does not hinder but in fact enables environmentalist work" (2014,
62).[11] In her view, "the most basic element of irony is incongruity; incongruity
between, say, what is defined as possible or true, and what appears to be possible or true. Thus, for example, irony both emerges from, and can highlight,
the gap between scientific evidence of global warming and political pundits'
denials that such a phenomenon exists" (63). In *The Collapse of Western Civilization,* such incongruity is crystalized in the historian's amazement at the
curious phenomenon of "human adaptive optimism" (Oreskes and Conway
2014, 13), which throughout the twenty-first century led people to believe that
they will somehow find ways to live well within radically new environments
on what McKibben would call planet *Eaarth.* Irony, suggests literary theorist
Linda Hutcheon, "is a 'weighted' mode of discourse in the sense that it is
asymmetrical, unbalanced in favor of the silent and unsaid" (1994, 35). What
remains unsaid in the historian's account is later expressed in the "Lexicon
of Archaic Terms" that Oreskes and Conway have added to their little book.
Human adaptive optimism, we learn there, is "the the belief that there are no
limits to human adaptability—that we can either adapt to any circumstances,
or change them to suit ourselves" (2014, 58). In other words, it is pretty stupid,
given the state of the planet presented in the book.

How thick the irony is laid on both in our contemporary reality and in
Oreskes and Conway's fictional look back at that reality becomes clear when
we consider the following passage: "Legislation was passed (particularly in
the United States) that put limitations on what scientists could study and
how they could study it, beginning with the notorious House Bill 819, better
known as the "Sea Level Rise Denial Bill," passed in 2012 by the government
of what was then the U.S. state of North Carolina (now part of the Atlantic
Continental Shelf)" (2014, 12).[12] Given that the Atlantic Continental Shelf is an
underwater landmass, this parenthetic information is ripe with cosmic irony,
reminding current North Carolina legislators of what their state might be in
for as a result of their decision to ignore the latest scientific projections on

future sea level rise.[13] Ironies abound when the Chinese historian informs us in his ever-equanimous tone that "the Sea Level Denial Bill would become the model for the U.S. National Stability Protection Act of 2025, which led to the conviction and imprisonment of more than three hundred scientists for 'endangering the safety and well-being of the general public with unduly alarming threats.' . . . When the scientists appealed, their convictions were upheld by the U.S. Supreme Court under the Clear and Present Danger doctrine, which permitted the government to limit speech deemed to represent an imminent threat" (12). This openly mocks American attitudes toward climate science, suggesting that the highest legal authorities will not hesitate to muzzle climatologists in the most rigorous ways in order to ensure a status quo that directly leads to global disaster.

Oreskes and Conway thus use the fictional perspective of a future historian to comment on the politics and culture of their contemporaries in mostly scathing ways. While the narrative strategies of their text display remarkable similarities to those of Franny Armstrong's climate-change documentary, *The Age of Stupid* (2009), it cues very different emotional responses.[14] In *The Age of Stupid*, it is an old American archivist who, from a thoroughly apocalyptic 2055, looks back to the time of his own youth, filled with feelings of guilt and remorse about what he and his contemporaries have done. The narrator of *The Collapse of Western Civilization* belongs to a different, non-western civilization and is also much further removed in time. While it must be noted that actually very little in the text suggests a non-western perspective, the purported Chinese identity of the narrator likely does make a difference, at least for western readers. While *The Age of Stupid* invites viewers to empathize with its despairing archivist, cueing parallel emotions of guilt and remorse, the culturally and temporally distant narration in Oreskes and Conway's book more likely cues grim amusement and vague feelings of shame at one's own stupidity. Asked how she wrestles with the "mordant quality of the writing," Oreskes explains in the interview section of the book that "writing in hindsight gives you emotional distance" (64). Such distance, Seymour has suggested, has "self-critical and -reflexive potential" (2014, 74), precisely because it frees us from feeling the full force of the negative emotions that are cued by ecodystopian and post-apocalyptic worlds. The assumption behind this argument is that an overabundance of what Heise has called "gloom-and-doom rhetoric" (2008, 148) might overwhelm us rather than move us if it is not tempered by ironic distance and a dose of comic relief.

The Collapse of Western Civilization is indexed by its publisher, Columbia University Press, not as nonfiction (as is the case for Hansen or McKibben) but as "science-based fiction."[15] While this makes sense, given the fictionality of its narrating agency, the book misses many elements that we would consider typical or even defining for a fictional text, among them one or several characters who experience the storyworld as well as the narrated events and who invite readers to feel along with them.[16] The question that poses itself is whether narrative fiction that contains experiencing agents can offer something to the experiential systems of our brains that makes it valuable for a better understanding of climate risk. Ironically, Oreskes and Conway themselves suggest that it can, as their narrator informs us that "the most enduring literary work of this [our] time is the celebrated science 'fiction' trilogy by . . . American writer Kim Stanley Robinson—*Forty Signs of Rain, Fifty Degrees Below,* and *Sixty Days and Counting*" (13). The scare quotes around the word 'fiction' suggest that the trilogy envisages a scenario that, in hindsight, turned out to be quite true. Like the fictional formats I have discussed in previous chapters, many dystopian novels in the so-called climate fiction or "cli-fi" genre stand in a complex relationship to historical reality. In this case, however, it is a reality that has not yet happened and that therefore is still in the realm of risk.[17]

FEELING THE RISK: EXPERIENCING ECO-CATASTROPHE IN THE DYSTOPIAN NOVEL

As a speculative mode of narration, science fiction imagines possible alternative and future worlds that can be either utopian or dystopian in nature. It is "a fictive practice" that, in the words of Tom Moylan, "has the formal potential to re-envision the world in ways that generate pleasurable, probing, and potentially subversive responses in its readers" (2000, 4). Not least because of their investment in the building of alternative worlds, a good number of science fiction writers have concerned themselves with environmental issues. As Heise has pointed out, "science fiction is one of the genres that have most persistently and most daringly engaged environmental questions and their challenge to our vision of the future" (1999, 1097).[18] Arguably, the earliest science fiction novels that focus on climate change date all the way back to the 1960s. Although the scenarios they evoke are not anthropogenic in nature, books such as Brian Aldiss's *Hothouse* (1962), J. G. Ballard's *The Drowned World* (1962), and Philip K. Dick's *The Three Stigmata of Palmer Eldritch* (1965) all envision a radically different planet Earth that is the result of an increase in surface temperature. The drastically changed ecological worlds they depict, however, are driven by an altered radiation of the sun and thus by factors that lie beyond the agential reach of humans. It is only since the late 1990s that anthropogenic climate change becomes a topic in dystopian American fiction, from Norman Spinrad's *Greenhouse Summer* (1999) and T. C. Boyle's *A Friend of the Earth* (2000) to Michael Crichton's *State of Fear* (2004) and Kim Stanley Robinson's Science in the Capital series (2004, 2005, 2007). More recent publications include Steven Amsterdam's *Things We Didn't See Coming* (2009), Dale Pendell's *The Great Bay* (2010), Nathaniel Rich's *Odds Against Tomorrow* (2013), and Paolo Bacigalupi's *The Water Knife* (2015).[19]

All of these climate change novels deal with what Mayer calls "narrative[s] of catastrophe" (2014, 26), and yet they are also, and at the same time, concerned with complex risk scenarios and therefore with the anticipation of even worse catastrophes.[20] Oreskes and Conway suggest that Robinson's trilogy is particularly visionary when it comes to the risks that climate change might pose to Americans. As literary scholars Adam Trexler and Adeline Johns-Putra state in their overview of climate change in Anglophone literature, "Robinson has emerged as science fiction's most important writer to deal explicitly with the problem of climate change, not simply as the premise for an otherworldly setting but as a social, cultural, and political phenomenon and problem, requiring unusual methods of characterization and plot" (2011, 187). I will engage with Robinson's fiction in the next chapter, but for now I want to focus my attention on another novel that is interesting for its vivid evocation of climate risk and related catastrophes: Boyle's *A Friend of the Earth*. The novel is set in a near-future California, one that at the time of my writing is only ten years away. As Nils Zumbansen and Marcel Fromme observe in their treatment of the text, the novel "appears to be quite reliable and authentic in terms of its scenario, notwithstanding that the book exaggerates when it comes to the description of rapid seasonal changes, for instance" (2010, 279–80). It is narrated in the first person and in present tense by Tyrone O'Shaughnessy Tierwater, whose tragic development from committed environmental activist to disillusioned and apolitical zookeeper parallels the inexorable disintegration of his natural surroundings between the 1980s and the mid-2020s. By 2025, Tierwater is a "young-old" man of seventy-five, and, like the rest of the world, California is devastated by climate change. El Niño brings winds so strong that whole forests are destroyed and people have to fortify their houses. What resists the assault might just be washed away by the next wet season, and in the dry season people barely dare to leave their shelters as temperatures rise to 120 degrees and the formerly muddy ground turns to something very much like concrete. As Tierwater puts it dryly, this is the time when "the whole world's a pizza oven, a pizza oven that's just exploded" (Boyle 2000, 237).

Unlike Hansen's and Oreskes and Conway's fictional stories, *A Friend of the Earth* therefore features an experiencing consciousness, someone who is physically present in a storyworld that is brimming with vivid sensual imagery. "The parking lot is flooded," Tierwater informs his readers as he arrives at the bar where he is supposed to meet his ex-wife Andrea, "two feet of gently swirling shit-colored water, and there go my cowboy boots—which I had to wear for vanity's sake, when the gum boots would have done just as well" (2000, 10). Tierwater instantly regrets his decision, which was fueled by his deeply buried feelings for the woman who left him many years ago. Being too poor to sacrifice his only good footwear, he has no choice:

> I figure what price dignity, jerk off the boots, stuff my socks deep in the pointed toes of them and roll my pants up my skinny legs. The water creeps up my shins, warm as a bath, and I tuck the boots under my slicker, tug the beret down against the wind and start off across the lot. It's almost fun, the feel of it, the splashing, all the water out of its normal bounds, and the experience takes me back sixty-five years to Hurricane Donna and a day off from school in Peterskill, New York, splash and splash again. (And people thought the collapse of the biosphere would be the end of everything, but that's not it at all. It's just the opposite—more of everything, more sun, water, wind, dust, mud). (10–11)

Everything up to the parenthesis is what Marco Caracciolo calls an "instruction manual" (2014, 83) for readers' processes of embodied simulation. It does not take much cognitive effort to construct the situation and Tierwater's subjective experience of it in one's mind. Boyle's careful attention to the sensual qualities of that storyworld—the way it looks, sounds, and feels—allows readers to experience on the imaginary level *what it is like* to live in a future California that has become a place that is hostile to human life. They are cued to feel along with Tierwater as he jumps into the water not only by the sensory imagery provided but also by his mentioning of a historical hurricane, which serves as both an analytical and an affective point of reference.[21]

Just as important for readers' overall understanding of the passage, however, is the parenthetical addition. The mentioning of the collapsed biosphere reminds readers that this is not actually an exceptional and relatively rare occasion, as was Hurricane Donna, but part of everyday life in a climate-changed world.[22] In his typical, caustic manner, Tierwater reminds readers that the apocalyptical concept of the end of the world is actually quite misleading. Even if it really comes to the point of collapse, the Earth—and the life on its surface—will continue to exist. It is just a lot less conducive to the survival of large mammals such as humans and to most of the animals that they used to eat, and it has a very different experiential feel to it, one that is mostly marked by extremes. The tone here and elsewhere in the novel is not only ironic but also decidedly satirical. As Paul Simpson has observed, "Satirical texts are understood as utterances which are inextricably bound up with the context of a situation, with participants in discourse and with frameworks of knowledge" (2003, 1). Here and elsewhere, Boyle relies on and plays with readers' preconceptions about both climate change and (post-)apocalyptical discourse. There is no end of the world in sight in his tale, and there also is no clean slate that would allow for a fresh start after the collapse. Instead, it is a long, slow emergency and a dwelling in perpetual crisis. *A Friend of the Earth* is a risk narrative in that sense, a dystopian world in which countless catastrophes have happened already and new ones are showing up daily on the horizon. As Frederick Buell has observed, such narratives represent "environmental crisis as a context in which people dwell and with which they are intimate," deliberately blurring "the boundaries between dilemmas in fiction and dilemmas still very much in progress in the surrounding world" (2004, 322).

Boyle frequently engages in such blurring, making his future California easily relatable and yet disturbingly different through the use of cognitive estrangement, one of the defining features of science fiction according to Darko Suvin (1979, 4).[23] In typical dystopian fashion, he extrapolates current trends into the future, but he does not bother to give a "big picture" overview of the world he is creating, leaving it to the reader to flesh out the details of American society in 2025.[24] And yet, he gives a number of hints that facilitate this task. Clearly, the gap between rich and poor has become even greater, and the always-scanty social security system is now almost nonexistent. As most animal species have become extinct, and agriculture and land-use patterns have vastly changed, many foods are no longer available. The only crop that grows on the (outdoor) fields of California is now rice, and sake is the only alcoholic beverage available to the average American. Only the rich and super-rich can afford the foods and drinks that once formed the staple diet of the common people. Older Americans, such as Tierwater, are left to fend for themselves, without a regular income or health insurance and often also without shelter. He paints a haunting picture of life in a place that is continually drenched by rain and beaten by storms, where everything is humid and rotting and moldy and nothing is ever comfortable. He accepts the state of affairs with grim resignation. The former radical activist is now content to be employed by one of the extremely rich of the country who seems to be able to afford everything, which includes a few specimens of soon-to-be extinct animal species.

The history of Tierwater's fateful career in the environmental organization Earth Forever!—a thinly disguised fictional version of its historical counterpart, Earth First!—is the novel's most overt connection to historical reality, a reality that must have been quite present to American readers at the time of the novel's publication in the year 2000. Throughout the 1990s, the Earth Liberation Front, a radical group that grew out of Earth First!, made head-lines with spectacular actions involving not only sabotage (as it was used by Earth First!) but also arson, causing the U.S. government to prosecute some of its members as eco-terrorists.[25] We learn that Tierwater was radicalized that way in his younger years, with disastrous results. Geographer David Pepper has argued that radical environmentalist projects that blindly cling to uto-pian ideals "do not adequately and accurately take into account the socioeco-nomic dynamics of the capitalist system they are meant to reform" and are thus doomed to fail (2005, 18). This seems a perfect description of Tierwa-ter's experience. He is haunted by painful memories of political struggle and humiliating defeat, among them the greatest defeat of all: the tragic death of his daughter, another committed Earth Forever! activist. In the end, his radical environmentalism cost him everything: his freedom, his daughter, and even-tually also his beloved wife when he went into prison to serve his sentence. While Tierwater narrates the events of 2025 in the first person, he switches to third-person narration in the sections that are set in the 1980s and 1990s, as if to distance himself from his own painful memories and from his former self. We learn that he eventually gave up, after having been jailed repeatedly and after becoming ever more desperate, watching the natural world turn "to shit" (Boyle 2000, 9). The result is his present ironic stance, which creates a safe emotional distance between him and the environmental catastrophe he could not prevent despite his passionate and burning desire to do so.

As James Knudsen has observed in his review of the book, the dust jacket of the hardcover edition of *A Friend of the Earth* does not denote the book as a "novel" but as "fiction?" with a question mark, which promises "that Boyle's portrait of the future will be amazingly accurate" (2001, 330). In Knudsen's view, "Boyle has done an extraordinary job of evoking the world that may well evolve from our current one, twenty-five years down the line" (330). The felt realism of *A Friend of the Earth* is indeed the most haunting and power-ful aspect of the book, not only in terms of the degraded environment of the future but also in terms of the exhaustion of utopianism and the dangerous collapse of citizenship participation. Fighting a losing battle, Tierwater hopes to save at least a few animals in the private zoo of his boss, Mac, and to "keep them from extinction until we're gone" (Boyle 2000, 281). But the narrative disappoints even this very humble utopian project, as Mac's violent death puts an end not only to Tierwater's employment but also to the zoo itself. Tierwater is forced to release the remaining animals and can only hope that they will fend for themselves. The only animal he takes with him is a Patagonian fox, who in the end becomes a dog-like companion when he and his activist ex-wife return to the cabin in the (now devastated) woods where they were once in hiding from the authorities.

I will return to the relationship between environmentalism and utopianism in the final chapter of the book, where I consider the affective appeal of ecotopian narratives. Although *A Friend of the Earth* does end with a glimmer of hope as Tierwater sees "the shoots of . . . new trees rising up out of the graveyard of the old" and realizes that "our woods . . . are coming back" (348), the tone of the novel is profoundly dystopian. It is a scathing critique of radical environmentalism, and it also does not leave much space for hope that mainstream environmentalists will be able to save the Earth from the devastating effects of anthropogenic climate change. Like Oreskes and Conway's *The Collapse of Western Civilization,* Boyle's novel uses irony and satire in its relation of the sad future of a civilization that is unable to read the writing on the wall, but it does so with a much higher level of immediacy. Not only is the narrative set in the very near future, it also aligns readers with a character who was born in 1950 and who therefore has witnessed first-hand the degradation of the Earth's biosphere. Tierwater's present-tense homodiegetic narration and vivid language greatly facilities embodied simulation, inviting readers to stand in moral allegiance with a character who is quirky and flawed but who nevertheless deserves our sympathy because he often suffers greatly (though not necessarily always undeservedly) and at the same time cares passionately (if at times misguidedly) about the Earth and nonhuman animals. At the same time, the narration also provides a shielding layer of distancing irony, not only for Tierwater himself, but also for readers who share his experience. The doom-and-gloom of the novel's future California is also thoroughly amusing at times, a narrative strategy that might help avoid alienating readers with an overload of negative and, therefore, uncomfortable emotions.

Tom Moylan has argued that science fiction narratives "not only delight but also teach" (2000, xvi) and that they do so through "an enlightening triangulation between an individual reader's limited perspective, the estranged re-vision of the alternative world on the pages of a given text, and the actually existing society" (xvi–xvii). This triangulation is of particular importance to dystopian narratives dealing with climate change because they can engage the experiential systems of our brains in particularly vivid ways and therefore contribute to our understanding of what is at stake. While Moylan clearly has literary texts in mind, the same might be said of movies. Often considered less "seriously environmentalist" than novels because of the conceptual compromises that come with the need for a big budget, science fiction film can show us concrete images of future environments, allowing us to experience those environments on the visual and visceral level.[26] In the opening paragraphs of this book, I have offered a brief glance at John Hillcoat's *The Road* (2009) and the ways in which it brings to life on the screen the thoroughly depressing post-apocalyptical world of McCarthy's novel.[27] In the final section of this chapter, I want to turn to another strategy of narrating the potential future consequences of human adaptive optimism, one that is not only disturbing but also profoundly entertaining.

RISK, PLEASURE, AND CATASTROPHE IN *THE DAY AFTER TOMORROW*

In his 2007 address to the Intergovernmental Panel on Climate Change (IPCC), United Nations Secretary-General Ban Ki-moon expressed his concerns about the risks associated with climate change in perhaps somewhat unexpected terms. The scenarios outlined in the 2007 IPCC report, Ban declared, "are as frightening as a science fiction movie, but they are even more terrifying, because they are real" (Ban 2007). Ban thus introduced his call for a new environmental ethics with an allusion to popular culture, offering a seemingly concrete referent for an abstract scientific scenario while at the same time insisting that the reality is even worse because it is consequential.[28] The "science fiction movie" he had in mind is in all likelihood Emmerich's *The Day After Tomorrow*, a film that aptly combines features of the melodrama and the disaster narrative to engage viewers in a spectacular story about climate risk. Produced by Emmerich's company Centropolis and the Canadian studio Lionsgate with a budget of $125 million, it earned $652 million at the box office. According to Box Office Mojo, this currently makes it the fourth-highest grossing film of all times in the category "environmentalist."[29] It also still ranks third in the category "controversial," beaten only by *The Passion of Christ* (2004) and *The Da Vinci Code* (2006).[30] This latter achievement reflects the wide attention the film received not only from journalists but also from climatologists, sociologists, environmentalists, and American government officials, who either lauded or vilified the film. While certainly not the first cultural text with a significant effect on the general public in the United States and beyond, it was the first popular film to be credited with—and chastised for—turning public awareness to the issue of climate change.[31]

I am going to argue that this social and political impact is to a large degree due to the fact that, like Boyle's *A Friend of the Earth*, *The Day After Tomorrow* transforms an abstract scientific scenario into a concrete story about likeable and trustworthy people, and that this story is combined with a number of audio-visual spectacles that have a direct *visceral* and highly thrilling effect on viewers. In chapter 2, I have suggested that rather than being separate or even autonomous from narrative, as Martin Lefebvre has claimed (2006, 22), spectacular and active cinematic environments must be seen in relationship to both plot and character development. As Geoff King has put it so pointedly, "spectacle . . . has the potential to reinforce, almost physiologically, whatever the narrative asserts" (2000, 34). *The Day After Tomorrow* illustrates the validity of this claim particularly well, not only because climate change emerges as the primary driver of plot and character development, but also because the film has been the subject of five different reception studies that were conducted more or less simultaneously in four different countries, examining the attitudes of audiences toward global warming before and after seeing the film.[32] It is extremely valuable to have such studies to put into relation with a theoretical reading of the film's narrative and visual strategies and a related assessment of its capacity to involve viewers on the experiential level in a story about climate risk.

As I have mentioned at the beginning of this chapter, Emmerich's film opens in the vast white expanse of Antarctica. The first few minutes of a film set the mood for the rest of the story, and so the opening sequence of *The Day After Tomorrow* serves several narrative purposes: firstly, a long high-angle tracking shot—basically a simulated helicopter shot—introduces us to the spectacular beauty of the polar region, a "natural" beauty which is wholly computer-animated. When we finally see a group of (equally animated) humans, they look tiny and insignificant in this vast white landscape, but as we get closer we realize that they are not, actually, lost. As the prominent American flag indicates, the isolated humans on the Larsen B Ice Shelf are a group of U.S. scientists doing ice core drillings. The second purpose of these first minutes of the film is the introduction of Jack Hall (Dennis Quaid), a paleoclimatologist who combines in himself the qualities of the melodramatic victim and the action hero.[33] While an inexperienced colleague does the drilling, a gigantic fracture suddenly forms in the ice, leaving the scientists' camp at the edge of an enormous abyss and their extracted ice cores on the other side. Without hesitation, Jack jumps across the abyss, salvages the ice cores and with another, even riskier leap, returns to his comrades. As the camera zooms out we witness the spectacular breaking off of the ice shelf which foreshadows the coming disaster—the third narrative purpose of this opening sequence.

The first and third of these purposes are fulfilled brilliantly: as spectators, we feel the emotional impact of both the beauty of nature (aided by the music score) and its destruction (aided by our previous knowledge about the effects of climate change on the Polar Regions).[34] The evocation of a spectacularly beautiful but suddenly also threatening and threatened environment cues awe for the sheer beauty of the images and sadness in relation to a vulnerable ecological space that is at risk. The second purpose of the opening scene, the introduction of the scientist as action hero, is arguably rather less successful. When Jack jumps heroically across the expanding crevasse in the ice cap to save the ice cores, most viewers are likely closer to laughter than awe. As paleoclimatologist William Hyde scathingly remarked in a blog after seeing the film, "the movie is at its most stunningly accurate in its portrayal of paleoclimatologists. Paleoclimatologists are notoriously brave and of course very fit. Nary a one of us would hesitate to jump a widening crevasse—twice—while wearing arctic gear—to recover some ice cores which would take 2–3 hours to re-drill" (Hyde 2004). Even if we find the unrealistic nature of Jack's actions amusing rather than stunning, however, we will engage in a thrilling embodied simulation of them since our "eyes and ears are telling [us] that something exciting is happening in front of [us] and [our] brain is preparing to react" (Zacks 2015, 4). On the cognitive-analytical level, the scene succeeds in establishing Jack as a dedicated man who does not hesitate to go to physical extremes if he deems it necessary. And not only is the hero of *The Day After Tomorrow* handsome, righteous, and "notoriously brave," as Matthew Nisbet has observed, he also has a number of other qualities: "He drives a hybrid car . . . shares a strong bond with his co-workers, and risks his life . . . to save his colleague. . . . The only downside to Quaid's character is that he is a workaholic. He is completely devoted to climate science while missing out on his family life" (Nisbet 2004). He is thus presented as a morally righteous hero in the face of human ignorance and greed, inviting viewers to empathize with his position and to build moral allegiance to him.[35]

After his daring stunt in the melting ice of Antarctica, we next see Jack in the confined political space of a UN conference, explaining the scientific scenario of a potential stalling of the North Atlantic Conveyor Belt and the resulting abrupt climate change to the assembly members.[36] This is the moment in which the film establishes a rational notion of risk, one that is very similar to the climate change risk scenarios viewers might have heard about in the real world. However, Jack is confronted with ignorance and a strong belief in short-term profits, and he thus cannot succeed in warning the politicians of the world about the catastrophe that they are bringing about. With these first two sequences, his two vastly more powerful opponents are established: the American government—personified by a vice president who bears a striking resemblance to Dick Cheney—and "nature," which, following the genre conventions of the disaster movie, will from now on become increasingly more active and hostile. It does not take long until viewers realize, together with Jack, that the process he described to the UN Assembly will not in fact happen in 100 or 1000 years, but right now and very quickly. Thus the much more commanding of his two opponents begins to determine the direction of the story, first with vicious tornadoes, and later with towering flood waves and enormous storm systems that allegedly suck down from the stratosphere air so cold that it freezes everything it touches.

These scenes of disaster are the "money shots" of the film. They come with powerful images and sound, and thus have a strong visceral effect on viewers, regardless of the fact that the depicted future environments are not "authentic" in any way. King has suggested that one theme common to many disaster films "is that of 'natural' or elemental force breaking into the paved, built-up and 'civilized' . . . worlds created by humans" and that "the principal targets for destruction are symbols of luxury, decadence [and] arrogance" (2000, 146). To witness the annihilation of famous cultural landmarks—the first twister in *The Day After Tomorrow* swiftly erases the Hollywood sign—seems to be immensely pleasurable for a large number of moviegoers. King hypothesizes that this pleasure may be related to the emotional effects of such scenes on viewers, and in chapter 2 I have explained that effect in terms of liberated embodied simulation: not only do viewers quite literally feel the protagonists' struggle against what Maurice Yacowar has called a "Nature Attack" (2012, 313) as they map the protagonists' actions onto the respective parts of their own brains, they are also likely to simulate the swift movement of the twisters and storm surges themselves.[37] The combination of direct sensual and emotional responses to the displayed environment and empathetic responses to that same environment through character identification is what makes watching the film's money shots so exciting.

One complaint that has been leveled at *The Day After Tomorrow* from various parties is that these spectacular disaster scenarios depart significantly from the predictions of climate science, and that they generally violate notions of scientific plausibility. However, as David Ingram has pointed out, we miss the point of Emmerich's film if we simply dismiss it for its scientific inaccuracies. As a science fiction movie, it uses "realist elements of climate science as a starting point for melodrama and fantasy, so that it can dwell on the spectacle of extreme weather . . . and also invite the audience's emotional engagement with the human interest story that becomes the main focus of narrative" (2008, 55). Since the unleashed natural forces are depicted as too powerful an opponent to be stopped or beaten, Jack's goals must focus on something that he actually *can* try to accomplish, albeit against tremendous odds: the timely

evacuation of a part of the American population, and the highly melodramatic
rescue of his son Sam (Jake Gyllenhaal). Both of these goals are related, since
Sam is in New York and thus above the line that Jack draws on the map of
the United States, indicating to the American government the divide between
those that can be saved and those that must be sacrificed. As Robin Murray
and Joseph Heumann have pointed out, the main plot of *The Day After Tomorrow* "revolves around Jack's quest to save his son and his son's evolution into
a new eco-hero like his father" (2009, 10). The narrative invites viewers to
empathize also with Sam, who is protecting a group of people in the New York
Public Library from the disaster by listening to the advice of his expert father.
Carl Plantinga has argued that sympathetic emotions typically "arise when the
spectator assesses the narrative situation in response to a favored character's
predicament and goals. When the viewer develops a concern that the goals of
the character be met, this creates a desire for the attainment . . . of the character's desired state or the escape from or avoidance of an aversive state" (2009,
88). *The Day After Tomorrow* asks us to care for Sam's goal of survival and of
saving the girl he is in love with, and for Jack's goal to save as many Americans from the storm as he can and to keep his promise to his son. In face of a
disaster of enormous proportions, Jack learns from his old mistakes and thus
creates a new basis for his relationship with his son.

　　"Learning from one's mistakes" is a recurring theme in the film, both in
the private and the political sphere, and it is clearly the message that viewers
are supposed to grasp as the film develops from an initial risk scenario into
epic and uncontrollable catastrophe. Catastrophes are often said to have transformative effects, and in *The Day After Tomorrow,* this certainly is the case.
The greatest personal transformation and learning experience is, surprisingly,
not accomplished by Jack or his son, but by the man who so much looks like
Dick Cheney, and who is now the new President of a United States that is as
much changed as he himself is. In his first TV address to the nation after the
disaster, he displays a new sense of humility and environmental ethics. "For
years," he states, "we operated under the belief that we could continue consuming our planet's natural resources without consequences. We were wrong.
I was wrong. The fact that my first address to you comes from a consulate
on foreign soil is a [testimony] to our changed reality." This is the narrative's
moment of catharsis and recognition, the moment that the film insists most
blatantly on its environmentalist message. Emmerich juxtaposes the presiden-
tial address with high angle tracking shots, which—as in the opening scene—
show a white landscape (to the same musical score), with the difference that
that landscape now is New York City and the beautiful white cover functions
as a shroud that hides the millions of people lying dead underneath it. Like

most makers of disaster movies, Emmerich makes sure that viewers do not dwell too much on the victims of the catastrophe and instead empathize with those who struggled and survived. As Plantinga has shown, melodramatic films use a number of techniques to balance negative emotions with positive ones to create a satisfying viewing experience (2009a, 2009b), and *The Day After Tomorrow* demonstrates well how this can be done through the use of music, aestheticized images, and narrative framing. Even as the film thus reaches its problematic happy ending, however, some things are shown to have drastically changed. The monstrous nature at work in the middle of the film is stable again, but the United States and the rest of the world are permanently transformed and order is not reestablished. Only utter devastation, Emmerich seems to suggest, can finally give humanity the ability to learn from its mistakes and change its unsustainable practices.

It was a suggestion that created quite a stir in the U.S. media before and after the film's release, giving researchers reason to think about the value of engaging storytelling in science communication. A study conducted by Yale psychologist Anthony Leiserowitz reveals that *The Day After Tomorrow* generated "more than 10 times the news coverage of the 2001 IPCC report," and, given that "a key component of the risk amplification process is media attention" this is an important factor in the film's social impact (2004, 34).[38] Another important factor was the controversial nature of that public attention. Leiserowitz notes that

> some commentators feared that the catastrophic plotline of *The Day After Tomorrow* would be so extreme that the public would subsequently dismiss the entire issue of global warming as fantasy. . . . Others spun a scenario in which, panicked by the movie, the US public would force Congress to pass climate change legislation, President George W. Bush would subsequently veto the bill, and challenger John Kerry would exploit public hysteria over global warming to win the U.S. presidential election. (23)

There is reason to believe, however, that the most "hysterical" reactions were actually those of the Bush administration itself. Leiserowitz mentions a memo from NASA administrators that was later leaked to *New York Times* journalist Andrew Revkin and that stated that "no one from NASA is to do interviews or otherwise comment on anything having to do with" the film, and that "any news media wanting to discuss science fiction vs. science fact about climate change will need to seek comment from individuals or organizations not associated with NASA" (Revkin 2004). Regardless of this attempted muzzling of federal climate scientists (which was later partially retracted), the impending release of Emmerich's film received ample public attention from climatologists around the world. As David Kirby has noted, the scientific inaccuracies that riddle *The Day After Tomorrow* can be "problematic for the scientific community because the majority of errors are exaggerations of scale that are designed to heighten drama" (2013, 179). And yet, some scientists were quick to embrace the film.

The climatologist Stefan Rahmstorf at the Potsdam Institute for Climate Impact Research, for example, called the film's depiction the *politics* of climate science "chillingly realistic" (2004). Even more interesting, from today's perspective, is Rahmstorf's assessment of the film's spectacular evocation of abrupt climate change: "Clearly this is a disaster movie and not a scientific documentary; the film makers have taken a lot of artistic license. But the film presents an opportunity to explain that some of the basic background is right: humans are indeed increasingly changing the climate and this is quite a dangerous experiment, including some risk of abrupt and unforeseen changes. After all—our knowledge of the climate system is still rather limited, and we will probably see some surprises as our experiment with the atmosphere unfolds" (2004). Rahmstorf frames his assessment of the film in terms of risk and considers the film—regardless of its at times wild exaggerations—as an opportunity for climate scientists to use the attention created by the film to educate the public about the real risks associated with climate change.[39] Although he could not yet know it at the time, the reception studies that were conducted at in the United States, Great Britain, Germany and Japan also demonstrated that the film itself had a significant impact on viewers' climate risk perceptions.

The American study, which was conducted by Leiserowitz and his team, examined viewers' attitudes toward climate change before and after seeing the movie. All parameters considered, Leiserowitz summarizes the results of the study as follows:

> *The Day After Tomorrow* had a significant impact on the climate change risk perceptions, conceptual models, behavioral intentions, policy priorities, and even voting intentions of moviegoers. The film led moviegoers to have higher levels of concern and worry about global warming, to estimate various impacts on the United States as more likely, and to shift their conceptual understanding of the climate system toward a threshold model. Further, the movie encouraged watchers to engage in personal, political, and social action to address climate change and to elevate global warming as a national priority. (2004, 34)

The international impact of the film, as Fritz Reusswig notes (2004), was some-what but not entirely different. The changes in attitudes of the German audi-ences that Reusswig and his collaborators surveyed, were less drastic, which he ascribes to the fact that a large portion of the audience was already sensi-tized to the issue of climate change, so much so that it was one of their main reasons for watching the film (this was different for the American audience, which was primarily interested in seeing Emmerich's latest disaster movie). Nevertheless, Reusswig concludes that the film did have significant effects on its German viewers and that "the entertainment industry seems to have done quite a lot for the public awareness of climate change" (2004, 43). The two British studies came to similar conclusions. "Overall," Andrew Balmford et al note, "our findings confirm that intense dramatizations have real potential to shift public opinion" (2005, 1713). Lowe at al., the authors of the second British study, conclude that "our research shows that seeing the film, at least in the short term, changed people's attitudes; viewers were significantly more concerned not only about climate change, but also about other environmental risks such as biodiversity loss and radioactive waste disposal" (2005, 2).[40]

Impressive as they are, the short-lived nature of such attitudinal changes is a point that seems to offset any positive effects a film might have on viewers' risk perceptions. Evaluating the results of the five studies, Mike Hulme writes that "overall, the film . . . cannot be said to have induced the sea-change in public attitudes or behaviour that some advocates had been hoping for" (2009, 214). All the more interesting, then, is a recent article by Michael Svoboda (2014) on "the long melt" of *The Day After Tomorrow*. Svoboda interviewed several people involved in climate change communication who confirmed that, more than ten years after its release, the film continues to facilitate their work. Sunshine Menezes from the Metcalf Institute on Marine and Environmental Reporting credits Emmerich's film "with at least making a wider audience think about climate change as a globally and locally important phenomenon, rather than something that was only relevant to scientists" (quoted in Svoboda 2014). Other interviewees made similar statements, suggesting that—next to *An Inconvenient Truth*—Emmerich's film remains helpful for climate change communication to the general public. This may in part be the case because to this day, it is the only Hollywood movie that centrally focuses on a climate risk scenario, featuring a climate scientist as protagonist. While, as we have seen, there are numerous climate change novels on the market, most contem-porary feature films deal with the issue only in a cursory manner. Christopher Nolan's *Interstellar* (2014) and the latest incarnation of the Mad Max Series *Fury Road* (2015) both feature dead and dusty landscapes that are parched by the sun, but their climate-changed worlds mostly function as drivers for narratives about the colonization of outer space or post-apocalyptical struggles over the remaining resources. On the other end of the climatic spectrum, there is a range of films that exploit the aesthetic qualities of ice, among them Jeff Renfroe's *The Colony* (2013) and Bong Joon-ho's science-fiction thriller *Snowpiercer* (2013). The spectacular frozen worlds of these films are the unintended outcome of misguided climate engineering efforts, but their narratives would hardly be helpful in science communication.

While there is much to criticize about *The Day After Tomorrow's* depiction of climate risk, then, the film continues to hold a unique position in terms of popular depictions of climate science, a position that is only rivaled in the documentary realm by *An Inconvenient Truth,* a similarly "dated" climate change film. As Svoboda puts it dryly, "Hollywood is still stuck in the Holocene" when it comes to the narrativization of anthropogenic climate change (2014) and we can only hope that it will creatively arrive in the Anthropocene in the years to come. Another remarkable fact about the "long melt" of *The Day After Tomorrow* is that even its daring risk scenario no longer seems as farfetched as it did at the time of its release. Like other climatologists, Rahmstorf believed in 2004 that "luckily it is extremely unlikely that we will see major ocean circulation changes in the next couple of decades," adding that "this will only become a more serious risk towards the end of the century" (2004). Recent data on a persistent "cold blob" of water in the North Atlantic has led journalists and scientists alike to reevaluate the visionary power of the movie. In a comment to the *Washington Post,* climatologist Michael Mann acknowledges that he "was formerly somewhat skeptical about the notion that the ocean 'conveyor belt' circulation pattern could weaken abruptly in response to global warming. Yet this now appears to be underway" (quoted in Mooney 2015).[41] Ironically, those who have seen Emmerich's film already have very concrete—if very exaggerated—images in their minds of what this might mean for the inhabitants of the northern hemisphere. Whether such virtual experience of abrupt climate change will make any difference in terms of their attitudes and actions remains to be seen.[42]

CONCLUSION

In this chapter, I have been concerned with a range of cultural texts that use dystopian framing in order to make climate risk scenarios more tangible and emotional salient for readers and viewers. In addition to providing graphs and numbers, some authors of popular science books have made use of temporal foreshortening and dystopian fiction in the hope that this will allow readers to relate to their scientific scenarios on an experiential level. Given that, as Slovic and Slovic have put it, "we need numbers and we need nerves" (2015, 5) in order to fully understand an environmental risk and to make rational decisions in the face of it, the integration of storytelling into scientific discourse may be a good rhetorical strategy when speaking to the general public. One of the most influential environmentalist books in the history of the United States—Rachel Carson's *Silent Spring* (1962)—famously opens with a "A Fable for Tomorrow" that evokes the transformation of a "town in the heart of America" from idyllic paradise to a "stricken world" because of "a strange blight" (21). The strange blight alluded to is the use of DDT and other pesticides by the human population, which kills off insects and birds alike, leading to the ominous "silent spring" that gives the book its title. It is a cautionary tale that, as Eric Otto has observed, cleverly uses the pastoral trope in combination with cognitive estrangement to make its message emotionally salient for readers (2012, 9).[43] Carson's "fable" is only two pages long, but it provides what many more recent examples of popular science writing fail to provide— vivid sensory imagery that allows readers to simulate the described world in their minds and therefore experience it on the imaginary level. As many other producers of creative nonfiction—among them John Muir and many other American nature writers—have demonstrated, such vivid evocation of literary environments is not the privilege of fiction. When it comes to the evocation of future worlds, however, fictional tales might indeed be at a strategic advantage, for the simple fact that they can invent future experiencing agents in ways that nonfiction discourse cannot.

Boyle's *A Friend of the Earth* is a good example of the immediacy that can result from homodiegetic present-tense narration in a speculative novel, regardless of the fact that the narrated worlds and actions do not yet exist in the historical reality of the reader. Tierwater's narrative not only gives us a vivid sense of what it feels like to live in a climate-changed world, it also invites us to share his feelings of sadness and mourning about the mass extinction of animals in general and every single additional loss that he experiences personally in his zoo.[44] As a radical environmentalist, he cares deeply about what has remained of nonhuman life and—through the "enlightened triangulation" that Moylan sees at heart of science fiction's ability to teach (2000, xvi)—the novel implicitly asks readers whether they really want to let it come to that point. All this is very serious and sad, precisely because it feels so utterly realistic and possible, and yet the ironical tone saves the tale from becoming depressing. Cueing negative emotions such as fear, anger, sadness, mourning and regret is an often-tried and yet risky strategy for environmental narratives, because an overload of negative emotions might either lead to debilitating pessimism or to various forms of denial.

As the sociologist Kari Marie Norgaard demonstrates in her study of climate change attitudes in Norway and the United States, *Living in Denial* (2011), there are at last three different forms of denial that people practice in order to shield themselves from painful emotions: literal denial of the existence of climate change, or what we call climate skepticism; interpretive denial, which involves framing the change in such a way as to make it positive and full of opportunity; and implicatory denial of climate change's political, social and moral implications (10). All three forms of denial cause us to turn our attention away from the risks associated with climate change and their dangerous implications. The same is true for pessimistic "doomster views," as psychologists Deborah du Nann Winter and Susan Koger have shown (2004, 20). Both denial and overwhelming pessimism can be debilitating rather than enabling, and so it is important for those who want to bring about social change to keep their cueing of negative emotions at a bearable level. Narratives that mix negative emotions with positives ones, be they pleasure, amusement, or physical excitement as we feel it in response to an action film, may be best suited to involve audiences on an experiential and emotional level in narratives of environmental risk.

Another narrative strategy that has been used by nonfiction and fiction writers alike is to add a hopeful silver lining to their otherwise dystopian tales. How important it is to have such silver-linings to even the most gruesome views into the future becomes clear when we consider that the writers of young adult fiction tend to consider it deeply unethical to leave their teenage readers without a glimmer of hope at the end of their stories.[45] But the "principle of hope" as the German philosopher Ernst Bloch has called it (1989), is not reserved for the writers of young adult fiction. Geographer Robert Kates has argued that "hope is simply necessary if we as a species, now conscious of the improbable and extraordinary journey taken by life in the universe, are to survive" (1994, 122). In the next and final chapter of this book, I will explore the strategies of cultural texts that aim to offer more than just a glimmer of hope or a thoroughly disingenuous happy ending. As full-fledged utopias, these texts work in the affective registers of hope and desire, presenting us with future worlds that not are depressing but instead so enticing that they might lead us to yearn for a new way of being.

CHAPTER 6

Alluring Visions

Hope, Desire, and the Affective Appeals of Ecotopia

KIM STANLEY ROBINSON'S *Pacific Edge* (1988) opens with a panoramic view of the open expanse of Orange County: "The air was cool, and smelled of sage. It had the clarity that comes over Southern California only after a Santa Ana wind has blown all haze and history out to sea—air like telescopic glass, so that the snowtopped San Gabriels seemed near enough to touch, though they were forty miles away. The flanks of the blue foothills revealed the etching of every ravine, and beneath the foothills, stretching to the sea, the broad coastal plain seemed nothing but treetops: groves of orange, avocado, lemon, olive; windbreaks of eucalyptus and palm; ornamentals of a thousand different varieties, both natural and genetically engineered. It was as if the whole plain were a garden run riot, with the dawn sun flushing the landscape every shade of green" (1). This evocative description of a light-suffused pastoral landscape—compromised only by the casual mention of genetically engineered crops—introduces readers to the world of a narrative that is set in 2065 and, thus, in a near future that makes today's Orange County look rather dystopian. Packed with visual imagery that allows readers to simulate in their minds the intensity of the light, the clarity of the air, and the colorful pattern of fertile groves and orchards, the passage—not by coincidence—is reminiscent of John Muir's description of the Central Valley in *The Mountains of California* (1894).[1] Not much reminds readers of California's historic droughts, of climate change, traffic jams, and suburban sprawl. It is a scene that almost instantly induces longing and desire, thus setting the mood for what Edward James has called "perhaps the most convincing (and attractive) utopian novel written since the 1970s" (1996, 23). Unlike the flooded and parched environments we find in T. C. Boyle's *A Friend of the Earth* (2000) and Paolo Bacigalupi's *The Water Knife* (2015), *Pacific Edge* immerses readers into a world that is both aesthetically pleasing and politically progressive.

Pacific Edge is the third part of Robinson's Orange County trilogy, but while the first two novels—*The Wild Shore* (1984) and *The Gold Coast* (1988)—confront their readers with dystopian visions of California, the third part of the trilogy imagines a near-future in which the citizens of the fictional community of El Modena have learned from the mistakes of the past and try to live more in harmony with nature. Robinson's novel is indeed one of very few contemporary texts that—in the vein of Ernest Callenbach's *Ecotopia* (1975)—seriously attempt to envisage future modes of ecological citizenship.[2] Unlike Callenbach's book, however, it is an ecotopia with a critical edge. A *critical utopia*, in Tom Moylan's definition of the term, rejects utopia as a static and perfect blueprint, focusing instead "on the continuing presence of difference and imperfection within the utopian society itself and thus render[ing] more recognizable and dynamic alternatives" to existing societies that surround both writer and reader (1987, 17). This kind of utopian literature, in Moylan's view, does not try to determine its readers' visions of the future; rather, it "serves to stimulate in its readers a desire for a better life and to motivate that desire toward action by conveying a sense that the world is not fixed once and for all" (35).

In this chapter, I will be concerned with hope, desire, and a range of other positive emotions that are cued when ecotopian narratives imagine new modes of ecological citizenship and manage to avoid the much more problematic feeling of boredom. The latter is an emotion that scholars have frequently mentioned in the context of utopian writing, simply because the imagination of a perfect and perfectly static world almost by definition runs the risk of lacking drama. Yet, as Robinson's novel demonstrates, ecological utopia does not have to be static in order to imagine what Moylan calls "a better life." The first section of the chapter will explore the emotional dimensions of ecotopian thought, exploring the differences between abstract and concrete utopias and their relationship to emotions of hope and desire. It will also consider the role of embodied simulation in the creation and sharing of the "unfinished forward dream[s]" that the German philosopher Ernst Bloch saw at the heart of the utopian impulse (1986, 157). Neuroscientist Anjan Chatterjee reminds us that "there is no thought, no desire, no emotion, no dream, no flight of fancy that is not tethered to the activity of our nervous system" (2013, xi). Whether authors use their imagination to create frightening dystopias or alluring alternative worlds—whenever we engage in social dreaming or any other kind of creative imagination, we necessarily make use of our brain–body system to make such dreams feel tangible and real.[3]

The second section of the chapter will then turn to Robinson's *Pacific Edge*, exploring what—if anything—such a critical ecotopian scenario, and readers' embodied simulation of it, can contribute to environmentalist political imaginations and the hope for a more sustainable future. Andrew Dobson's concept of *ecological citizenship* will serve as a touchstone for a consideration of the potential value of ecotopian narratives in instigating social change. The third section of the chapter will then turn to a popular film that follows the genre conventions of the classical rather than the critical utopia, using state-of-the-art cinematic technology to immerse viewers into a storyworld that instigates desire: James Cameron's science fiction epos *Avatar* (2009). Although the film's alternative world is both perfect and static, Cameron makes viewers' virtual experience of it exciting by putting that perfect world at risk. The fact that *Avatar* went on to become the most successful film in history invites an exploration of the exact nature of the enticing world it depicts and the technical means it uses to provide viewers with an emotionally salient virtual experience.

THE POLITICS OF HOPE AND DESIRE: EMOTION, UTOPIA, AND ECOLOGICAL CITIZENSHIP

Hope and desire are generally considered key components of the utopian impulse. Bloch famously dubbed the utopian tradition the "principle of hope" in his book of the same title (1986) and the sociologist Ruth Levitas suggests in *The Concept of Utopia* (2010) that "the essence of utopia seems to be . . . the desire for a different, better way of being" (209). Desire is a term that is well known to scholars in utopian studies, but Levitas belongs among those who struggle with the fact that the term has become firmly linked to Freudian and Lacanian discourses and cannot be easily disentangled from those. Lacanian psychoanalysis, she freely admits, makes her "lose the will to live, which seems a dystopian rather than utopian effect" (xiv).[4] Levitas's own definition of desire, like Bloch's, has a much "broader existential reach," describing an urge not unlike hunger or longing, the longing to reach a state that seems attractive, satisfying, and pleasurable.

Many cognitive scholars of literature and film share Levitas's desire to be able to use the term *desire* and related expressions without simultaneously evoking the complete Freudian and/or Lacanian psychoanalytical universe. Carl Plantinga, for example, dedicates a whole chapter of *Moving Viewers* (2009a) to "pleasures, desires, and fantasies" in the viewing of film, explaining that "Freudian psychoanalysis differs from cognitive-perceptual approaches to emotion in an important way. For Freud, the root cause of an emotion was primarily within the individual rather than in a relationship between the individual and her or his environment" (40). The proponents of cognitive-perceptive approaches, by contrast, consider the individual's embodiment (in a physical body) and embeddedness (in a physical environment) as constitutive of the emotional response. Referring to the term's use in folk psychology, Plantinga suggests that desire "is best taken to denote a psychic state in which the individual wants, wishes for, or craves something. Thus, a desire only becomes interesting from a narrative standpoint in relation to its object, which may be specific or diffuse" (42). As we have seen in previous chapters, the embodied and embedded nature of our minds enables us to engage in vivid mental simulations of the storyworlds, situations, and events we encounter in literature and film, mental simulations that have both cognitive and affective components. Desire, like hope, curiosity, and suspense, is what psychologist Ed Tan has called a "tonic emotion" (1996, 199). Such emotions, Tan explains, "are based on prospects and retrospects" and they have "a longer life span" than phasic emotions such as surprise or enjoyment, which come and go very swiftly (199). Together with general moods, they are what keeps our eyes riveted to the screen not only in thrillers and other suspense-laden films but also in love stories and drama films more generally, when we desire and hope for a pleasurable outcome. If the "feeling of risk," as psychologist Paul Slovic has called it (2010, xix), involves the anticipation or apprehension of catastrophe, then feeling hope and desire involves the *anticipation of pleasure* in real life as well as in our engagement with narratives of all kinds. "The evocation of conflicting desires and pleasures," Plantinga explains, "is one of the dynamic tools of the scenarist and filmmaker," because "a pleasure is experienced in the present while a desire is oriented toward the future" (2009a, 43). As such, it is of central importance for our engagement in stories because it is our desire to find out what will happen that makes us turn the pages of a novel or sit motionless in our theater seats, our eyes glued to the screen.

Beyond this immediate narrative curiosity and desire, there are other desires that can be awakened by an engagement with literature and film. It may be as simple as desiring the haircut of the protagonist or a dress she wears, or the desire to be able to afford the same house, the same car, or the same lifestyle. That cultural texts can awaken such desires is the reason why any major Hollywood film is brimming with product placement. It is also the reason why proponents of the Frankfurt School and other critical thinkers came to see such media products as part of a "culture industry" (Horkheimer and Adorno [1944] 2007) that interpellates subjects into capitalist ideology.[5] Such thinkers saw very little potential that mass culture, including Hollywood film, could contribute anything at all to a utopian "education of desire" (Levitas 2010, 123). In their view, only experimental and difficult "high art"—such as modernist literature and music—could have such emancipatory effects because it is not driven by a capitalist impulse. Looking at the merchandise-spewing marketing campaigns that tend to accompany even inherently eco-topian Hollywood films such as Andrew Stanton's *WALL-E* (2008), there is no doubt that the influential critique of the Frankfurt School has a point. It remains a fact, however, that it is not only material desires that are elicited by literature or even Hollywood film but also the hope, desire, and longing for romantic love, deep friendship, and a better way of being.

Such desires are, of course, not only awakened by literature and film. We also experience them in our day-to-day lives in the form of imagining or day-dreaming—what Bloch called *Tagträume*. "Everybody's life," he writes in *The Principle of Hope*, "is pervaded by daydreams: one part of this is just stale, even enervating escapism . . . but another part is provocative, is not content just to accept the bad which exists, does not accept renunciation. This other part has hoping at its core, and is teachable. . . . Thinking means venturing beyond. . . . The future dimension contains what is feared or what is hoped for; as regards human intention, that is, when it is not thwarted, it contains only what is hoped for" (1986, 3). Hope and desire, then, are goal-directed emotions that are at the very heart of the utopian impulse. Bloch differentiates between "abstract" and "concrete" utopias. While the former is a form of escapism and has compensatory functions, the latter is a form of social dreaming that has "the power of anticipation" and functions as a potentially transformative "methodical organ for the New, an objective aggregate state for what is coming up" (157). While both forms of utopian daydreaming can be fueled by desire, only the concrete utopia can truly involve the emotion of hope. As Diana Fritz Cates points out, "we hope only in what we regard as possible," so our utopian projects are always circumscribed by "limits of knowledge and imagination, partial perspectives, self-interest biases, [and] the consequences of previous, poor choices" (2015, 25). This may not stop us, however, from letting our imagination run wild with desire.

The differentiation between hope and desire, and the roles they play in the abstract or concrete utopian impulse, becomes particularly interesting once we begin to think about sharing our utopian dreams with others. Given the central importance of such impulses for alternative, critical, or resistant practices, it is not surprising that David Pepper locates utopianism within various forms of environmentalism. In "Utopianism and Environmentalism" (2005), he argues that eco(dys)topianism—which he sees emerging in the context of post-1950s utopian thought and later being fueled by popular science books such as Paul Ehrlich's *The Population Bomb* (1970) and the Club of Rome's *Limits to Growth* (Meadows et al. 1972)—today reflects "contemporary fears of . . . risk society" and is marked by technological and social pessimism (6).[6] In his "assessment of the potential of ecotopianism to assist social change," Pepper detects a fatal weakness in environmentalism's general tendency to rely on what he considers highly abstract and even nostalgic utopian horizons. "The transgressiveness of ecotopianism," he writes, "is ambiguous and limited because of its inherent tendency towards regression," a tendency that he locates especially in deep ecology and bioregional approaches, and in what he considers their unhelpful idealism (3).[7] Pepper not only includes sociopolitical theory and political projects in his criticism but also fictional texts, arguing that "taken together, ecotopianism and eco-dystopianism represent ecologism's 'good cop/bad cop' approach to admonishing us for our ecological transgressions" (6).

As we have seen in the previous chapter, Pepper is right to point out that the fear of global environmental risks is a theme in much of recent American literature and film and that the narrative strategies of such cultural texts include a good deal of admonishing. Yet his evaluation of both contemporary environmentalism and environmental fiction nevertheless seems unduly pessimistic. Boyle's *A Friend of the Earth*, which Pepper mentions in his article, cannot be reduced to an "underlying 'deep ecology' philosophy" that is "riddled with a palpable hatred of development and modernity, which are blamed for the anticipated global ecological collapse in 2025" (Pepper 2005, 11). Such a reading misses the novel's ironic and satirical overtones as well as its unflattering depiction of radical environmentalism. If anything, *A Friend of the Earth* can be read as a critique of precisely the kind of "unhelpful idealism" that Pepper finds problematic. It confronts readers with much more ambiguity than Pepper acknowledges, both on the political and on the emotional level, not only because Boyle is not his narrator-protagonist Tierwater but also because Tierwater himself looks back at his past actions with a mixture of irony, sadness, and disillusionment. Saving the last remaining animals on the planet, he at some point claims, is "our only hope" (Boyle 2000, 281). At least, it is the only hope he still clings to and, as I have shown, even that hope is disappointed by the narrative. "As an emotion," explains Diana Cates, "hope can pull us in different directions. Inasmuch as we have an attractive possibility in view. . . . We are drawn to that possibility emotionally and we anticipate the pleasure of uniting with it. However, inasmuch as we are confronted by difficulties. . . . We also feel disturbed" (2015, 25), and, if we sense that the obstacles are too strong, or we too weak, we are likely to withdraw. As a result, "we might suffer the end of hope, and let that be the end of it" (25). Subsequently, we might direct our hope at other, more achievable, goals, as Tierwater does, or we might fall into despair. The latter is the collapse of the concretely utopian impulse, and if it concerns a political project in defense of the Earth, as it is in the case for Tierwater, it is also the end of ecological citizenship. Boyle's novel arguably is a meditation on the precarious condition of the concretely ecotopian impulse in the face of unsurmountable obstacles.

Such concretely ecotopian impulses, I would argue, do also inform contemporary theoretical concepts of ecological citizenship, even as the creators of these concepts do not always acknowledge it. Utopia does not even have an entry in the index of Andrew Dobson's *Citizenship and the Environment* (2003), although the utopian desire for a better world lies at the heart of the author's political project.[8] Only "ecological citizens," Dobson believes, "will make democracies more responsive to sustainability demands" (2003, 8). He differentiates between *environmental* and *ecological* citizenship, which— although by no means oppositional—operate on different scales and aim for different things. *Environmental citizenship* is "the claiming of environmental rights against the state in a traditionally conceived public sphere and through the political mechanisms associated with that sphere" (206). As such, it is the basis for intranational environmental justice claims as well as for other legal cases that involve the claiming of environmental rights against the state or against other citizens.[9] *Ecological citizenship*, by contrast, is "the exercise of ecologically related responsibilities, nationally, internationally, and intergenerationally, rooted in justice, in both the public and private spheres" (206). In Dobson's view, it is a "specifically ecological form of post-cosmopolitan citizenship that shares with notions of cosmopolitanism an emphasis on nonterritoriality (which distinguishes it from liberal and republican citizenship), but not "cosmopolitanism's reluctance to entertain care and compassion as potential citizenship values" or "the belief that citizenship is carried out exclusively in the public sphere" (80).[10] In this context, the emphasis on citizen *responsibilities*—and on the affective and personal aspects of these responsibilities—is essential because only individuals who see themselves as ecological citizens in this understanding will harbor a personal commitment to ecological principles and "do good because it is the right thing to do" (4). There are, thus, deeply affective and moral components to Dobson's concept of ecological citizenship, which is all the more remarkable because he has argued elsewhere that empathy, compassion, and other affective processes do not make a good basis for the recognition of citizen responsibilities.

In "Thick Cosmopolitanism" (2006), Dobson suggests that an "appeal to the mechanism of empathy" will not be enough to motivate people to act in the interest of others within and beyond the nation (170). To produce a cosmopolitan sense of solidarity, he argues, one needs "less empathy" and "more causal responsibility" (172). As I have discussed in chapter 3, philosophers such as Jesse Prinz have voiced similar concerns, suggesting that empathy "is so vulnerable to bias and selectivity that it fails to provide a broad umbrella of moral concern" (2011, 227). Due to various forms of imaginative resistance (fueled by economic, cultural, and deeply egoistical concerns), the citizens of affluent societies might find it quite difficult to truly empathize with the people who suffer from floods in Bangladesh. This is why Dobson argues that cosmopolitan responsibility is *not* an issue of empathy but, instead, of the obligations that emerge from causal relationships: if the floods in Bangladesh "are in part a result of the lifestyle of (some) members of those very same affluent societies, then 'sympathy' and 'identification' are anyway redundant responses" (174).[11] "Thin" forms of cognitive and affective empathy are thus replaced by "thick" moral obligations in Dobson's account of ecological citizenship. And yet, he fails to explain by what mechanism we come to understand the suffering of others and to acknowledge our obligations to them. Environmental justice scholar Julie Sze quotes Enoch Adams Jr., the chair of the Relocation Planning Committee of the low-lying island of Kivalina, who states that his people "get a lot of *sympathy* from a lot of people . . . but we need more than sympathy, we need *empathy*. . . . To empathize with another, you've got to really put yourself in their shoes for an extended period of time. . . . To really empathize with someone in our situation you really have to experience what we experience" (Sze 2015, 9). This suggests that there is a political value to embodied simulation since cognitive and affective empathy—and the resulting imaginary experience of another's situation—are the very basis for recognition and a resulting desire for the improvement of that situation. According to psychologist Martin Hoffman, processes of simulation and perspective taking are constitutive for pro-social feelings of bystander and transgression guilt (2000, 114)—feelings that may lead to considerable empathetic distress and related helping behavior.[12]

Although Dobson does not acknowledge the importance of empathetic perspective taking in his thoughts on "thick" forms of cosmopolitanism, his utopian concept of ecological citizenship does so through an inclusion of a feminist ethics of care and compassion (2003, 65–66). Ursula Heise's concept of *eco-cosmopolitanism* (2008, 8) similarly acknowledges the importance of affect in the attempt to "envision how ecologically based advocacy on behalf of the non-human world as well as on behalf of greater socioenvironmental justice might be formulated in terms that are premised no longer primarily on ties to local places but on ties to territories and systems that are understood to encompass the planet as a whole" (10). The eco-cosmopolitan project, Heise makes clear here, entails the transformation or widening of already existing affective ties not only to other humans but also to the nonhuman environment.

Whether they acknowledge it or not, Dobson, Heise, and other environmental thinkers who concern themselves with potential better and more sustainable ways of being on planet Earth are always working with concretely ecotopian horizons. And since all utopian projects are, as Lucy Sargisson reminds us, "invariably fictions" (1999, 6), it is hardly surprising that American novelists, too, have endeavored to imagine new modes of ecotopian citizenship. Because they write fiction, such authors can offer on an imaginary level the kind of empathetic engagement that Adams considers fundamental for true understanding and the desire for change. To date, there has been only limited interest in analyzing the narratives of such ecotopian fiction from an econarratological or cognitivist perspective. Sociologist Lisa Garforth is right when she bemoans that "there has been little attention to the ways in which the reflexive and critical strategies of recent utopian narratives can make a distinctive contribution to . . . the process of imagining more environmentally cautious forms of society" (2005, 393). This is unfortunate since ecotopian novels have contributed their share to the cultural discourse around these issues. While Pepper argues that the apparent transgressiveness of eco(dys)topian fiction is at best "ambiguous" (2005, 18), his criticism not only overlooks the complexity of ecodystopian novels such as *A Friend of the Earth,* it also omits ecotopian texts that are more reflexive, and critical in their approach than what he describes. In order to stimulate hope and desire for a better way of being, such critical ecotopias must engage readers emotionally in the storyworlds they present while at the same time making their fictional scenarios plausible enough to convince them that a better world *is* indeed possible.

EXPERIENCING A BETTER WAY OF BEING: HOPE AND DESIRE IN *PACIFIC EDGE*

Although it opens with an outlook onto a light-suffused landscape, the storyworld of *Pacific Edge* has its dark spots. Not all is perfect or even well in

Robinson's ecotopian future. While hardly anybody ever uses cars anymore in El Modena, and sustainable architecture has become the norm, capitalism is not dead and some citizens still prefer profitable old-style urban development over nature conservation. This means that Robinson does not make the mistake that Pepper believes to be so detrimental for the political project of ecotopian literature: his novel does not fall back on "future primitivism" and "environmentalist myths about pre-Columbian America" (Pepper 2005, 10). *Pacific Edge* in fact challenges, as Garforth has noted, "the closed binary of forward-looking progress versus backward-looking rural idyll" (2005, 393), envisioning instead a society that tries to combine the two and is willing to live with the fact that this can lead to disagreement.

The novel's main narrative, set in the ecotopian California of 2065, uses limited third-person narration and focalizes through the mind of Kevin Claiborne, a young architect and passionate nature conservationist who has recently been elected into El Modena's town council for the Green Party. The central political conflict of the narrative is Kevin's struggle to save Rattlesnake Hill—the last undeveloped wilderness area in the community—from being rezoned into land that can be developed for commercial purposes. It is a conflict that is closely intertwined with his personal life, since he is in love with the beautiful Ramona Sanchez, who has recently broken up with Alfredo Blair, the new mayor of the town and Kevin's political opponent. The second narrative, set in 2012 (and thus, at the time of the publication of the novel in 1988, in the near future), tells the story of Kevin's grandfather Tom Barnard, who, embittered by the ineffectuality of his legal work, has given up his job as a lawyer to follow his scientist wife to Switzerland and write a utopian novel that will allow him to "change the world in [his] mind" (K. S. Robinson 1988, 35). Both men are white, middle-class Americans, and both learn in the course of the story that they have, as Carol Franko calls it, a "responsibility to otherness" (1994, 204), which leads them to take on their ecological citizenship responsibilities and actively fight for the rights of human and nonhuman others in both the personal and the public sphere. Both of them are motivated by personal and often highly emotional engagements.

In Tom's case, the process begins with his realization that the beautiful and materially abundant world of the Switzerland of 2012 is a *pocket utopia*—"a little island of calm in a maddened world" (K. S. Robinson 1988, 36). The citizens of the industrialized West, he writes into his journal, are *"the aristocracy of the world"* (61), which *"stand[s] on little islands of luxury, while the rest [is] great oceans of abject misery, bitter war, endless hunger"* (36). Experiencing the parasitic nature of Switzerland's "pocket utopia" firsthand fills Tom with the strong distancing emotion of disgust. Like the wealthy California of his childhood, Switzerland can only maintain its beauty and wealth at the cost of people and landscapes elsewhere, but now it can no longer maintain its exclusive state, since the excluded others are increasingly pressing against the borders of those who are more privileged. *"Refugees are pouring in,"* Tom tells us, "Ausländer *nearly half the population they say"* (36). As a result, nationalism is on the rise and, as an unwanted *Ausländer,* Tom gets deported while his wife and daughter remain in Switzerland. Upon his entry into the United States, he is immediately arrested because his memberships in environmental and social legal groups allegedly violate a new law against advocating the overthrow of the government. With his American citizenship rights profoundly curtailed, he ends up in a detention camp.

Through this use of cognitive estrangement, Robinson paints a dystopian picture of the United States' near future that seems to anticipate the substantial loss of civil liberties following the attacks of 9/11 and the subsequent passing of The Patriot Act by the Bush administration.[13] It is not transnational terrorism, however, that is targeted by the U.S. authorities in the novel, but ecological and economic refugees as well as leftist and environmentalist American citizens. Confronted with this harsh reality, Tom becomes increasingly critical of his work as a utopian writer. *"What a cheat utopias are,"* he writes bitterly, *"no wonder people hate them. Engineer some fresh start, an island, a new continent, dispossess them, sure, give them a new planet sure! So they don't have to deal with our history. Ever since More they have been doing it: rupture, clean cut, fresh start"* (95). This is an explicit critique of the classical utopian form in the tradition of More's *Utopia,* which frequently transports a lonely traveler to a distant place or time, where he encounters a perfect society. Like Switzerland, the writers of such classical texts pretend that it is possible to have a "pocket-utopia" that is somehow disconnected from the misery elsewhere in the world, perfect in its utter isolation. But this is *"ahistorical, static,"* Tom observes, *"so why should we read them?"* (95). The idea of the pocket-utopia belongs to what Bloch has defined as the abstract realm of the utopian impulse: it is an escapist fantasy that might instill or fulfill narrative desires but that cannot give anyone genuine hope because it is utterly disconnected from the surrounding historical world and would be unsustainable in such a world. *"No more utopia for me,"* Tom decides, *"the time has passed when a utopia could do anybody any good"* (275). In a spontaneous upheaval of emotion, he destroys the manuscript of his unfinished book.

As it turns out, however, the problem is not utopianism as such but only the ahistorical and abstract version of it. The very next day, one of Tom's dorm mates in the camp provides him with a new ballpoint and notebook, telling him that he has *"got to tell them what happens here"* (276). This is the starting

point of a new and different utopian project, one that Tom takes directly from history and the people around him. *"There is a refusal to despair,"* he notes, and *"there is a place where people on the edge of death make jokes, they help each other, they share what they have, they endure. In this hell they make their own 'utopia'"* (276). The endurance, care, and compassion he observes among the inhabitants of the detention camp deeply touches Tom, and it gives him hope that perhaps something indeed can be changed if one does not give up and continues to struggle together with others. After he is released from the camp, he returns to his law practice and takes part in a concerted world-wide effort to dismantle corporate capitalism and neocolonialism, fighting for a profound change in human–nature relationships. What he and other participants in this global project share is a *concrete* utopian impulse in Bloch's understanding of the term, one that differs from abstract utopianism in that it is anticipation rather than compensation, an "unfinished forward dream" (Bloch 1986, 157) that drives an eco-cosmopolitical project in the real world.

Unlike Boyle's Tierwater, who becomes increasingly more isolated and lonely during his career as environmental activist, Tom is part of a much larger movement, one that transcends national, racial, and class boundaries. "It took everyone to do it," he later explains to Kevin, "a consensus of world opinion, governments, the press. A revolution of all the people, using the power of government—laws, police, armies—against the very small executive class that owned and ran the multinationals" (K. S. Robinson 1988, 283). Using the instruments of individual states and of international organizations, the corporate world was cut apart so that "now there's nothing but small business scattered everywhere" and "basic resources [such as energy, water, and land] were made common property . . . in the service of a more long-distance self-interest" (284). Much of what Tom recounts here sounds like a (vaguely Marxist) enactment of Dobson's concept of ecological citizenship—"the exercise of ecologically related responsibilities, nationally, internationally, and intergenerationally, rooted in justice, in both the public and private spheres" (Dobson 2003, 206). And in this case, it indeed leads to a more ecologically sustainable and just society. Readers experience Tom's thought process and the increasing desperation that eventually drives him to partake in a global revolt, mostly through the ruminations he jots down in his journal and thus through the inhabitation of his consciousness. The same is true for the moments in which an older Tom tells Kevin and others how it all came to pass. These passages offer analytical information about what happened but very little opportunity for readers to simulate in their minds any details of the exciting times of revolt, rebellion, and reconstruction. Instead, it is the world in which Kevin lives in 2065—and thus the society that is the result of Tom's personal and

political engagement for a better world—that invites embodied simulation and an *imaginative experience* of ecotopia.

Not only is El Modena surrounded by an enticing pastoral landscape, we learn that the town itself mostly "seems to consist of gardens" (K. S. Robinson 1988, 87) and of houses with "big clear walls that make it impossible to tell if you're indoors or out" (37). Kevin specializes in rebuilding and renovating older homes in ways that are both aesthetically pleasing and ecologically sensible. He also is an outdoors enthusiast and loves any kind of occupation that involves a combination of physical movement and a conscious immersion in the natural world. Early on in the novel, he and Ramona step into a man-powered glider plane weighing "less than thirty pounds" and "grind at the tandem pedals as if racing to get the craft up to two hundred feet, where the afternoon sea breeze lifted them dizzily" (15). Once they are up in the sky, the narrative invites readers to simulate the extremely pleasant emotions of a young man who is in love with the woman next to him as they are gazing down at a place that he loves almost as dearly:

> They relaxed the pace, settled into a long distance rhythm, swooped around the sky over Orange County. . . . From time to time Kevin glanced at Ramona's legs, working in tandem next to his. Her thighs were longer than his, her quads bigger and better defined. . . . The texture of her skin was very smooth, barely dusted by fine silky hair. . . . Kevin shook his head, surprised by the dreamlike intensity of his vision, by how well he could *see* her. He glanced down at the Newport Freeway, crowded as usual. From above, the bike lanes were a motley collection of helmets, backs, and pumping legs, over spidery lines of metal and rubber. The cars' tracks gleamed like bands of silver embedded in the concrete, and cars hummed among them, blue roof red roof blue roof. As they cut curves in the air Kevin saw buildings he had worked on at one time or another: a house reflecting sunlight from canopies of cloudgel and thermocrete; a garage renovated to a cottage; warehouses, offices, a bell tower, a pond house . . . His work, tucked here and there in the trees. It was fun to see it . . . to remember the challenge of the task met and dealt with, for better or worse. (16–17)

The worlds that emerge in individual readers' minds as they scan this passage are bound to be very different, depending on their familiarity with the area, the time when they are picking up the book, and their own personal predilections and preferences. Not everyone enjoys strenuous physical activity or flying, but those who do will most likely enjoy the idea of propelling a light plane into the air and then gazing down on an attractive landscape. Environ-

mentalists and the fans of speculative fiction might also appreciate the nearly unimaginable sight of Southern California freeways with moving traffic, not to mention the fact that what moves on them are mostly bikes. They will also take note of the mentioning of "cloudgel," "thermocrete," and other innovative building materials that ensure ecologically sustainable and aesthetically pleasing comfort.

The other imaginary dimension of this passage, however, is almost universally pleasing. As Patrick Colm Hogan has shown, the "romantic tragicomedy" (2003, 11) is one of several literary universals that can be found in cultures around the world because they are based on universals in human emotion. And one of the "most intense happiness goals"—in life as well as in fiction—"combines attachment with sexual desire in romantic love" (P. Hogan 2011a, 182). When Kevin gazes at Ramona's beautiful, and quite powerful, legs, and when he then is "surprised by the dreamlike intensity of his vision," most readers will be able to relate, either because they have been in similar situations before or because they would like to be. And so it is with a grain of salt that they soon after process the information that Ramona still has feelings for Alfredo. For Kevin, it very much feels like a punch in the gut when he realizes that she is crying. Adding an additional physical experience to the moment, Robinson has her at first hitting the fragile frame of the plane a few times and then has her stop pedaling altogether. Kevin is too nice to say anything, so he begins to "pedal like a fiend. Their flyer dropped anyway . . . toward the hills behind Tustin. Directly at them, in fact" (K. S. Robinson 1988, 20). Kevin's emotional up and down is thus mirrored on the physical level as their plane threatens to crash because he is the only one who is pedaling to keep it flying. When they finally make it safely back on the ground and stretch their legs, he feels "his voice quiver" as he tells Ramona he wants to be her friend (21).

This moment above the ecotopian expanse of El Modena not only engages readers in exciting simulations of motion and emotion; it also cues the desire that Kevin shall reach his happiness goal and the hope that he will. As the psychologist Keith Oatley observes, "We are creatures of desire, so the desire and intentions of story characters resonate in us" (2012, 23). It is precisely because we simulate the pleasure of moments of romantic happiness in our minds and bodies that we are keen on characters reaching them. In this context, it is instructive to consider Gregory Currie's differentiation between "character desire" and "narrative desire" and his observation that the two can, and often do, stand in conflict (1999, 183). While we might be sympathetic to a character's happiness goal, desiring and hoping that he will be able to reach it, we at the same time have a narrative desire that the story not be boring. Unfortunately, happy people living harmoniously in perfect worlds do not make for a whole lot of conflict, and so one of the intrinsic problems of utopian writing is precisely this: boredom. Narrative tension thrives on conflict, and so readers' desire for the character's happiness is at odds with their desire for an exciting narrative. The intimate moment between Kevin and Ramona serves to raise reader expectations as well as uncertainty since they cannot know how the love story will end. This is one way in which Robinson creates narrative tension in an ecotopian world. The other way is related to the political process by which that ecotopia is maintained. Like Kevin's relationship with Ramona, it is not static or stable but subject to conflict and a constant risk of failure.

Despite massive political successes and a highly attractive, healthy, and livable environment, not everyone is happy with the new state of the world in 2065. For some, the struggle was not radical enough; for others, who do not accept "altruism for the sake of self-interest" (K. S. Robinson 1988, 284), it was fueled by the wrong motives. Others again would like to see more economic development in El Modena and react with spite to the radical demands of the Green Party. Ecotopian transformations can never be stable, which is why in Robinson's novel they are ongoing rather than completed. Like Kevin's personal love for Ramona, the main political conflict of the story—his struggle to save Rattlesnake Hill—constantly reminds readers that ecotopia *only* exists as a utopian horizon and that it takes the constant active engagement of ecological citizens to move toward it. Also, we learn that this horizon itself is neither monolithic nor stable. Rather, it needs to be negotiated and redefined in an ongoing political process.

Much of Kevin's story revolves around this often slow and painful process in which the boundaries between the public and private sphere are becoming increasingly porous. Kevin firmly believes that Rattlesnake Hill, to which he has a close emotional connection, is "worth much more as wilderness than it ever could be as any kind of business center" (267). However, this kind of reasoning does not work on Alfredo, whose passion for medical technologies helps him rationalize his unscrupulous development plans for the area. Kevin first tries to use the law against Alfredo and thus to succeed in the public sphere, but his grandfather's death prohibits the timely presentation of proofs, and Kevin's party is defeated at a decisive town meeting. In his despair, Kevin convinces the community to hold a memorial service for Tom among the trees he once planted on Rattlesnake Hill. This gathering is what eventually changes people's minds. As Franko observes, the memorial service among the trees "makes people feel their connections to each other, their community, this place," and therefore makes it emotionally impossible for them to approve the rezoning of the area that "now embodies both the 'strange' otherness of wilderness and the 'ordinary' otherness of their human utopian history" (1994,

208). The struggle over Rattlesnake Hill, like the struggle for a better, more sustainable world, thus becomes something utterly personal for Kevin and something that deeply affects his emotions.[14] Readers are cued to share his desire and his hope that it can be achieved.

However, it is not only their embodied simulation of Kevin's emotional engagements that keeps readers involved in the political plot of the novel. As Currie reminds us, "fictions engender desirings" (1999, 183) not only in relation to the fictional world and its protagonists but also beyond them. If we want a fictional story to end happily, this is in fact "as much desiring something about the real world" (184) as it is about desiring that a character will succeed. Although Kevin's hope for a life with Ramona is disappointed in the end, his struggle to save Rattlesnake Hill is successful; so upon closing the book, readers leave a world that, for now at least, continues to be healthy and attractive. While it seems to Kevin that he is "without a doubt the unhappiest person in the whole world," he at the same time finds solace in an environment that "pulse[s] green and amber, jumping with his heart, glossy, intense, vibrant, awake, alive" (K. S. Robinson 1988, 326). Readers are cued to simulate that vibrant world in their minds and, by an implicit comparison, find their own world lacking. This is the kind of imaginative engagement that ecotopian novels and other literary texts can provide because, within certain boundaries, they give readers the freedom to envision what they find desirable.

Cinematic ecotopias are much more limited and limiting when it comes to the worlds they create because they have to transform utopian ideas into concrete images and sounds and because their audiences tend to have much higher expectations when it comes to their entertainment value. In a 2007 article on the dystopian imagination in American film, Thomas Halper and Douglas Muzzio observe that "in place of the ordinary, where we live our ordinary lives, [speculative] movies present the extreme" (379). They then go on to wonder, "why . . . the extremes [are] almost never positive—that is, utopias?" (379). Their answer to this question is as follows: "Utopias represent ideals . . . endpoints, where nearly everything that ought to be done has been done. The problem with all utopias is stasis; the problem with all utopian movies is boredom. Movies need movement, change, and conflict, whether emotional or physical. Hence, the appeal of the standard dystopian scenario of a brave band of brothers . . . in combat with their hellish world" (379). This is a rehashing of the by-now familiar argument about the inherent dullness of the classical utopian tale. While Halper and Muzzio are right that over the past decades Hollywood has produced a lot more dystopias than utopias—presumably for some of the reasons they mention—film history has proven them wrong in assuming that this is a general rule. Whatever criticism one may want to hurl at James Cameron's *Avatar*—at the time of my writing, the most commercially successful film of all times—one thing it certainly is not is boring. Instead, it is highly attractive visually and highly engaging on an emotional level, providing viewers with an overabundance of "movement, change, and conflict." Unlike *Pacific Edge*, Cameron's epic tale about a fateful human-alien encounter in the year 2154 on the resourceful moon Pandora is a *classical* utopia. And yet it avoids the classical utopian problem of boredom by first introducing its hero—and its viewers—to a gorgeous and perfect ecotopian world and by then putting that world *at risk*.

PERFECTION WITHOUT BOREDOM? THE THRILLS OF ECOTOPIA ENDANGERED

It is indeed quite remarkable how closely Cameron's film follows the conventions of the classical utopia. If we care to look closely, *Avatar* exhibits all the elements that we typically associate with a classical utopian text such as Thomas More's *Utopia* (1516). Pandora in many ways recalls the Garden of Eden; its indigenous population has built a self-sufficient and well-functioning society that lives in harmony with nature. Also, the protagonist of the story— the paraplegic ex-marine Jake Sully (Sam Worthington)—is a traveler, transported across both space and time from the Earth to the highly attractive environment of Pandora. As in the classical utopian tale, this traveler soon meets a native guide—the Na'vi woman Neytiri (Zoe Saldana)—who teaches him, the ignorant stranger, about the ways of the local people. Gradually, the initially skeptical traveler is converted to this attractive and much better way of being. At the end of the classical utopian tale, the traveler must choose whether he will leave or stay—return to the society he came from and tell his story or remain and become a member of the society he now admires. In most cases, the traveler makes the first choice in order to be able to tell others about the wonderful place he has experienced and, ideally, get them to adopt some of the features of its vastly superior society. In some cases, however, as for example in Charlotte Perkins Gilman's feminist utopia *Herland* (1915) and in Callenbach's *Ecotopia* (1975), the traveler somewhat egoistically chooses to leave his native society behind, preferring to lead the good life himself rather than sacrificing his own pleasure for the opportunity to improve the lives of his ignorant compatriots. This is also the choice made by *Avatar*'s Jake Sully. In fact, his final decision is even more radical than that, and it is one that has given human viewers of the film considerable amounts of narrative pleasure.

Cameron is a master of the cinematic pleasure machine. As Plantinga has shown in his writings on the director's previous blockbuster *Titanic* (1997), he is particularly apt at the mixing of negative and positive emotions, evoked by a highly melodramatic narrative in combination with a sensory spectacle that affects viewers on the visual and visceral level (Plantinga 2009a, 2009b). In *Avatar*, Cameron uses a similar mix, presenting viewers with a Manichean universe in which good fights against evil in a cinematic environment that could not be more breathtaking. As Adrian Ivakhiv has pointed out, "The film is spectacular on multiple fronts: there are its immersive 3-D effects, CGI and advanced motion-capture technology; there are the thrills-and-chills of its lengthy, high-tech and rapid-fire battle scenes; and, of greatest interest for an ecocritical reading, there is the film's scintillating portrayal of the biotic life of Pandora, perhaps the most seductive and alluring vision of another planet ever presented in cinema" (2014, 162). However, just who is good and who is evil in the battle over this alluring world changes in the course of the story and so does the narrative's predominant affective tone. Whereas its first half cues mostly positive emotions of pleasure, fascination, admiration, and excitement in response to Jake's embodied exploration of the Pandora forest and his initiation into an alien form of ecological citizenship, the second half plunges viewers into a bath of negative emotions as the beautiful world of Pandora erupts in flames, leaving them desiring a happy ending against all odds and hoping that they will receive it. The hook of the narrative is that the Na'vi's Hometree, as well as their sacred Tree of Souls, sits on top of large amounts of the precious mineral unobtanium, which the human colonizers desire very badly and which they will try to get by all means. Sully's mission on Pandora is complicated, as several involved parties expect different things from him: the group of scientists led by Grace Augustine (Sigourney Weaver) has hired him after the death of his twin brother so that he can use his brother's genetically matching avatar to find out more about the Na'vi; the corporation that runs the mining operation on Pandora wants to use this information to convince the Na'vi to move elsewhere; and the military that protects the whole endeavor wants him to find the weak point of the forest people so that they can be attacked more effectively if diplomacy should fail.

Early on, the film establishes its notion of environmental risk when the always-menacing Colonel Quaritch (Stephen Lang) warns his men that not only is Pandora's air deathly for humans, but that, in fact, "every living thing that crawls, flies, or squats in the mud wants to kill you." In his words, Pandora's rainforest emerges as a teeming jungle, something that sounds familiar to the ex-marine Sully. However, when Sully makes his first trip into this hostile world in his brand-new Na'vi avatar, he—and with him the viewer—cannot help but be fascinated by its lush and wondrous beauty.[15] The very first scene of the film is an animated bird's-eye view of a similarly lavish forest that is almost immediately revealed to be Sully's dream of flying, while his actual body is not only paralyzed but also locked into a tiny compartment in cryosleep on board the spaceship that brings him to Pandora. Now, for the first time in years, he is able to walk again in the woods with the help of his avatar, and he is excited like a little boy, fooling around and touching plants until he is suddenly attacked by one of the moon's fierce predators. While it is suggested at this point that for Sully pleasure and mortal danger are just one false step apart, for the viewer the entire sequence is pleasurable and exciting. Not only is it more than unlikely that the narrative will kill off its main protagonist this early in the film, but technically speaking nothing can happen to Sully at all at this point, since he is lying in a chamber in the scientific wing of the mining colony, directing his Na'vi avatar with his mind. Given the immediacy of the scenes, however, this technicality will have little influence on viewers' embodied simulation of Sully's sensations, emotions, and actions, be it his physically taxing struggle with a predator or his clumsy flirting with Neytiri after she has saved his life.[16] As neuroscientist Jeffrey Zacks points out, "you can't make a movie like *Avatar* . . . without having a lot of insight into perception" (2015, viii), and this scene illustrates well how such insights inform the film's use of sophisticated motion-capture technology.[17] Although the protagonist is not even physically present in the scene, viewers will readily perceive and accept his avatar's emotion expressions as his own and will share his desire to learn more about this enticing world—a world that, like Sully's avatar, was built in a computer.

As I have mentioned in chapter 2, *Avatar* illustrates particularly well the fact that cinematic environments do not have to be in any way authentic in order to affect us emotionally. What counts is that they engage our senses and, in the case of a positive emotional response, that they strike us as beautiful. According to Anjan Chatterjee, current research in cognitive science suggests that we tend to regard as beautiful landscapes that are conducive to human survival and that "the brain's responses to beautiful landscapes involve neuronal ensembles in the visual cortex that . . . fire together with neurons in the reward systems" (2013, 52).[18] In addition, Chatterjee explains, "we respond to fitness indicators. . . . In landscapes these are trees that indicate a bountiful environment or flowers that promise rich sources of nutrition. . . . Gardens are examples of landscape enhancements. They are designed to delight and give pleasure. They often exaggerate the aspects of natural landscapes that we find beautiful, by leaving open places, open vantage points, partially hidden paths and flowers that signal the promise of bounty" (53). The computer-animated "natural" world we see in *Avatar* is presented as wilderness, not as a garden, and yet it is enhanced in exactly this sense. After his initial run-in with the less-peaceful inhabitants of Pandora's forests, Sully begins to explore the environment more carefully, under the guidance of Neytiri, discovering enormous trees, bountiful flowers, open vantage points, and partially hidden paths. Just like Southern California in Robinson's ecotopian vision, the sentient and bioluminescent nature of Pandora is—in a much more literal sense— "glossy, intense, vibrant, awake, alive" (K. S. Robinson 1988, 326).[19] Despite the remoteness of his own disabled body, Sully is able to physically experience that enticing environment through the body of his materially present Na'vi avatar, allowing viewers to do the same on the imaginary level.[20]

Viewers' sensual immersion in a strange but beautiful world is one of the great attractions of Cameron's film, one that they experience with and through its main protagonist.[21] Ivakhiv notes that "following Sully's trajectory can be a particularly immersive experience for viewers" (2014, 165), and this includes his interactions with Pandora's indigenous population and the ensuing love story. Like the protagonists of the narratives I have discussed in chapter 3, Sully offers viewers an *outsider perspective* on a case of environmental injustice. Just like *Thunderheart*'s Ray Levoi, he bears a certain physical resemblance to the indigenous community he is supposed to investigate (in *Thunderheart* because Ray is part Sioux himself, in *Avatar* because of Sully's fake Na'vi body) but his mind has no understanding of indigenous values or practices. He is thus an easy identification figure for viewers, who also do not understand the ways of the Na'vi. The forest people agree to teach Sully because they hope that, finally, one of the "sky people" will understand their way of being in and with the forest and get other humans to respect it. As Claire Molloy points out, "The principles that organise the moral structure of *Avatar* place Na'vi and human practices in opposition with the unsustainable economics of capitalism, corporate greed and advanced technologies positioned against a hunter-gather community system that operates in harmony with nature and through small social groups" (2013, 183). As they follow Sully into the forest, viewers are cued to develop a moral understanding of the Na'vi notion of ecological citizenship as they simulate his constantly increasing capacity for trans-species empathy.

Trans-species empathy is used strategically in Cameron's film, both on the level of content and on the level of narrative structure. As Lisa Sideris has noted, *Avatar* portrays empathy "in largely positive ways, as a transformative step toward enlightenment" (2010, 461), and much of Sully's education is carried out through an empathetic interaction with Pandora's animals.[22] The first task given to him by Neytiri is to ride a 'direhorse,' a docile, six-legged creature that the Na'vi have domesticated to a riding animal. It is the first time that

Sully has to make "the bond" by intertwining the neural tendrils of his avatar's braid with those of the direhorse. This bond, or queue, "allows a Na'vi to sense the energetic and kinetic signals broadcast by creatures, plants and even the moon itself" (Wilhelm and Mathison 2009, 29). In terms of accuracy, it certainly is a step up from ordinary, unbonded forms of embodied simulation, and it also allows the humanoid Na'vi to mentally control some of the moon's nonhumanoid animals.[23] Sully's difficulties mastering the task create moments of comedy, and they also invite viewers' respect for the superior abilities of the native population. At the same time, these moments also prepare for the second half of the film, when the close collaboration of humanoid and non-humanoid animals will be essential for an anticolonial struggle against the human oppressors.

Another key scene in this development is Sully's first flight on a banshee. After he has managed to make the bond, the animal lunges forward off a cliff and then downward like a stone into what looks like an endless abyss. While, on the level of content, this is another initiation ritual on Sully's way to becoming a Na'vi, it also treats viewers to a thrilling virtual experience of flying. Constantly moving POV shots suggest that the camera itself is positioned on one of the banshees, flying above, behind, and, sometimes, in front of Sully. As Gallese and Guerra have demonstrated in an empirical, high-density EEG neuroscientific study, viewers' brain motor responses to different forms of camera movement suggest that the camera has the capacity "to simulate the virtual presence of the viewer inside the movie" (2014, 103).[24] We must assume that the same is true—perhaps to an even higher degree—for animated 3-D shots that simulate camera movement. Accompanied by a musical score that cues feelings of elation, the spectacular flying scene educates viewers' desire for another way of being, exploiting their capacity for affective empathy and embodied simulation strategically for that education.[25] Since they are aligned with Sully and encouraged to build moral allegiance to him, they are likely to share not only his growing love for the natural world of Pandora but also his changing notion of risk. While, at the beginning of the film, it was the Na'vi and their sentient environment that were framed as dangerous, Sully now realizes that it is the humans who pose a deadly danger to that ecotopian world.

The second half of the film counters the positive emotions cued in its first half with an abundance of *negative* emotions for both Sully and the viewer. The difference is that for Sully the experience is wholly negative while viewers' emotional responses will likely be more ambivalent, depending on their personal tolerance or predilection for the depiction of suffering and gun-blazing violence. One of the central scenes that evoke negative emotions in viewers— feelings of compassion, regret, and loss—is the vicious human attack on the

Na'vi's Hometree. The climactic scene shows the forest giant at first trembling and tilting under the blows of the explosives and then crashing down on the life on the ground. In its intense and sustained focus on the slow death of the old tree, the scene demonstrates that we, indeed, have the capacity to feel "empathy for objects" (Currie 2011, 82). Aided by a highly melancholic musical score, it exploits both the admiration and awe that many people experience in the presence of particularly tall, old, and beautiful trees and the moral allegiance they might feel at this point to the Na'vi and their relationship to their Hometree. Confronted with powerful images of destruction, suffering, and death, viewers are likely to desire some kind of revenge for this ruthless act. That is what the film delivers in its violent showdown in which Sully leads the entire ecosystem of Pandora into a defensive war against the human aggressors. In the end, the enemy is beaten and forced to leave Pandora altogether. Like Cameron's earlier blockbuster *Titanic,* then, *Avatar* culminates in an emotionally satisfying ending. Not only do the good guys win (for now) and the bad guys lose (for now), but the lovers Sully and Neytiri also reach their romantic union, according to Patrick Hogan, the ultimate happiness goal of the romantic tragi-comedy (2003, 102). Plantinga suggests that the gradual replacement of negative, painful emotions with more positive, pleasant emotions is a typical narrative strategy of the Hollywood melodrama (2009b, 248), and *Avatar* is no exception. After long minutes of empathetic suffering, viewers are rewarded with the emotionally satisfying triumph of the protagonist and the sight of disheveled humans, who seem to have lost their hubristic attitude somewhere in the vibrant expanse of the Pandoran jungle.

Often compared to *Pocahontas* and *Dances with Wolves, Avatar's* storyline may seem to offer nothing that is really new or original. A number of commentators have complained that it is, once again, a Hollywood story in which "noble savages" are dependent on a white man for their defense. However, such comments overlook the truly original world building of the film as well as its neuroscientific implications from the perspective of embodied cognition. Not only does *Avatar* present us with a *visibly* sentient and interconnected environment, it also features a protagonist who, during large parts of the film, experiences that environment through a nonhuman (though humanoid) body. More important still, it is suggested that Sully's cognitive understanding of the situation on Pandora is changed as a result of experiences that are both embodied (in a Na'vi body) and embedded (in the Pandora environment). Those who have similar embodied experiences—i.e. Grace Augustine and the other scientists who also use Na'vi avatars—share this deeper understanding, while those humans who never experience Pandora with the sensory apparatus of a Na'vi body remain ignorant and callous. Sully ventures most deeply into the strange world of the forest, falling in love with Neytiri and making the physical queue with her and several of its other inhabitants. As a result, his mind is the one that is most radically changed, to the point that he not only begins to think like a Na'vi but also to communicate with their deity, Eywa, who then mobilizes the whole ecosystem in order to defend Pandora against destruction. In the terms of James Lovelock, we might dub the second part of the film "the revenge of Gaia" (2007), and one of the film's narrative achievements is that it invites viewers to stand in moral allegiance with *her* rather than with their own invasive human species.[26] As Russell Moore concludes in his review of the film, "if you can get a theater full of people in Kentucky to stand and applaud the defeat of their country in war, then you've got some amazing special effects" (2009). This is exactly what *Avatar* has been able to do with some audiences.[27] And because it is not *Dances with Wolves,* and thus not bound by the constraints of historical reality, it can end its utopian tale with the *victory* of the indigenous people and the temporary salvation of ecotopia from the risk of anthropogenic exploitation and destruction. Moreover, it can allow its utopian traveler to genuinely switch sides by moving permanently into his Na'vi body.

This brings us back to the political potential of ecotopian storytelling. Ruth Levitas has suggested that "what has weakened in recent decades" is not so much the utopian impulse as such, as has often been argued, but its capacity "to perform a transformative function" (2010, 228). It is fatalism that Levitas sees as the key issue. "In situations where there is no hope of changing the social and material circumstances," she claims, "the function of utopia is purely compensatory" and thus solely in the cueing and imaginary fulfilment of desire (222). Looking at the current state of the world, her line of argument is rather convincing, and there have been audience responses to *Avatar* that support it. In 2010, Jo Piazza noted that "Cameron's completely immersive spectacle . . . may have been a little too real for some fans who say [in online posts that] they have experienced depression and suicidal thoughts after seeing the film because they long to enjoy the beauty of the alien world of Pandora" (2010, para. 1). In his analysis of the audience response to the film, Matthew Holtmeier calls this phenomenon "Post-Pandoran Depression" and notes its occurrence on several websites in addition to the one named by Piazza, adding up to "a total of well over 3,000 posts" (2010, 415). Looking at the content of such posts, Holtmeier notes that "the typical reaction reported by those feeling post-*Avatar* depression was that of seeking ways to re-immerse themselves in the Pandoran world, in other words, to prolong the *dream*" (416). Suggested remedies from other posters included listening to the soundtrack and watching the film again and again. "Rather than enabling these individuals to take ethical action in the world," concludes Holtmeier, "the viewers who are affected by Post-Pandoran Depression are unable to act because they desire participation with a fictional universe" (418).

Without doubt, such expressions of utopian desire are to a considerable degree the result of high levels of viewer immersion in Cameron's alluring 3-D world.[28] The narrative, writes David Edelstein in his review for *New York Magazine,* "would be ho-hum without the spectacle. But what spectacle! *Avatar* is dizzying, enveloping, vertiginous. . . . [Cameron] has created a living ecosystem—and You (and Your 3-D Glasses) Are *There*" (2009, para. 2 and 4). Edelstein, I believe, is correct in insisting on the importance of the visual and visceral impact of Cameron's film and on the resulting high levels of transportation and immersion. *Avatar's* powerful evocation of a beautiful and threatened ecological space elicits in us what Plantinga calls *artifact* and *meta* emotions—in this case awe for the sheer beauty of the images and sadness for a vulnerable ecological space that is at risk.[29] As Plantinga notes, movies draw on "the structures of response spectators bring from their extra-filmic lives" (2009a, 62), so one of the reasons why viewers got depressed after seeing the film might have been that their emotional response to the beauty of the portrayed world was mixed with their knowledge about the state of the actual world. As a fictional, computer-animated fantasy, Pandora thus is indeed a classical utopian space in the sense of being the 'good place' and 'no place' at the same time.[30]

However, before we decide too quickly that an ecotopian tale like *Avatar* can be no more than an escapist and compensatory fantasy, we should consider another range of responses to the film.[31] Holtmeier calls this response "Na'vi Sympathy" and relates it to the recognition that "while the Na'vi and Pandoran nature are fictional, many viewers recognize that they symbolize nature and indigenous people on Earth" (2010, 419). This form of sympathy was expressed by viewers around the world, including several postcolonial and indigenous communities. As Joni Adamson notes, "what *was* surprising about some of the first responses to the film were the number of cautiously positive responses from indigenous groups, political figures, community leaders and scholars" (2012, 145). Although they often objected to Cameron's choice of making a "white guy" the hero of his story, such groups and individuals used the film politically in order to turn public attention to environmental justice issues and to the endemic disregard for indigenous world views.[32] In this context, we should also consider a somewhat unlikely event that took place in April 2010 in Volta Grande do Xingu in Brazil, where James Cameron met with the indigenous leaders of thirteen Amazon tribes who had contacted him to tell them about their struggle against the Belo Monte Dam planned by the Brazilian government (Adamson 2012, 154).[33] One might argue that this probably was not exactly what Cameron bargained for when making the film, but he ended up writing a letter to President da Silva in support of the indigenous movement. Although Levitas is right when she writes that in compensatory utopias such as *Avatar* "the transformative element is no longer primary" (2010, 226), this must not mean that such texts cannot end up having some real-world effects. The sheer popularity of *Avatar* and the controversial responses it has triggered across the world indicate that we should pay more attention to the ways in which not only critical but also compensatory ecotopias resonate with their global audiences.

CONCLUSION

In this chapter, I have explored the narrative strategies of ecotopian texts and interrogated their capacity to inspire thinking, feeling, and acting beyond their fictional worlds. I have paid particular attention to the emotions of hope and desire, which many theorists consider to be both the driving motivation behind the utopian impulse and the primary affects that utopian narratives can elicit in audiences that are not resistant to the narrative itself. As Dan Flory has pointed out, "imaginative resistance . . . does not depend on any fundamental cognitive incapacity on our part, but rather a certain unwillingness that makes it difficult or at times even impossible for us to imagine in the way the narrative directs us" (2013, 44). This is why it is so crucial for the producers of ecotopian narratives to make those narratives attractive by creating an enticing world and relatable characters that might help readers and viewers to overcome an initial unwillingness to imagine an alternative to the status quo. Clearly, this is not always going to be successful, and just as clearly, not all successful imagining is going to lead to a desire to change the situation in the real world, let alone to becoming active in order to bring that change about. And yet, there are good reasons to keep on trying. "Without ecotopian dreaming," Eric Otto reminds us, "damaging systems are allowed to flourish at the expense of sustainable ecological and social possibilities" (2012, 73), and we only have to look at the most recent projections of climate science to know that we are in dire need of alternative visions.

Currie suggests that there are at least three ways in which fiction might change the desires people have with regard to the world they live in: "By making available thought-contents that were not previously available to the subject; by vividly depicting a state of affairs and thus giving specifity to a previously inchoate desire; by depicting a certain state of affairs and eliciting a pleasurable sensation from the viewer [or reader], causing the viewer [or reader] to desire a state of affairs relevantly similar to the depicted one" (1999, 197). Both *Pacific Edge* and *Avatar* attempt to do all of this, and Cameron's film also has been read as advocating more empathic engagement with the victims of (post-)colonial violence and subjugation. Recalling Enoch Adams Jr.'s insistence that people affected by climate change "need *empathy*" from those who are in part responsible for their suffering (quoted in Sze 2015, 9), we might wonder whether even more is at stake in such imaginary empathic engagement. Hoffman would argue that compassion and care—emotions that Dobson considers central to meaningful ecological citizenship—will not develop without empathetic engagement (Hoffman 2000, 3). Ecotopian narratives cannot make their readers and viewers better ecological citizens, but they may be able to contribute their share to an education of desire for a more just and more sustainable world.

It could be argued that what we need most to bring about such a world are political visions, but as Oreskes and Conway insinuate in *The Collapse of Western Civilization* (2014, 18), sometimes it is fiction that is the most visionary, precisely because its imagination is liberated from everyday politics and concerns of immediate feasibility. This might be its greatest value in our current global ecological crisis because, as Currie notes, our imagination "is a capacity not wholly divorced from our capacity to act" because "imagining doing things can make it easier for us actually to do those things" (1999, 197). From the perspective of embodied simulation theories, this totally makes sense, and we might consider ecotopian narratives as an imaginary training ground where we can habituate ourselves to experiencing more sustainable lifestyles. Zacks suggests that whenever we witness a particular situation, we will build what he calls "event models" in our brains. Such a model is "a representation of what the situation is about, not of how you learned about the situation. It ought to be more or less the same whether you witnessed the situation yourself, watched it in a movie, or read about it in a newspaper or novel" (2015, 27). It is in this way that ecotopian narratives might be able to break up our imaginary limitations and help us develop a desire for a better way of being. At the time of my writing, we are awaiting the release of four additional films in the *Avatar* series (B. Lang 2016), ecotopian narratives that Cameron has said are "meant to create a sense of wonder and connection to the natural word" (Wagstaff 2014, question 3). It remains to be seen whether these films—and their various intermedia accompaniments and spinoffs, as well as the general media hype they create—will have any impact on how humans imagine themselves on planet Earth and with our fellow creatures. What we might really need is more critical ecotopias that imagine the way from here to there, eliciting not only desire for a more just and sustainable world, but also the hope that we can achieve it.

Environmental Narrative Across Media

IN THE PRECEDING chapters I have analyzed a range of environmental narratives from what I have called a cognitive ecocritical perspective. My focus has been on the emotionalizing strategies of such narratives, on how they use empathy and our capacity for embodied simulation strategically in order to invoke in our minds immersive environments and emotionally salient human–nature relationships. The three parts of the book have been dedicated to different aspects of such narrative strategies. Part I has explored how both literary texts and films rely on the mirror neuron system and on related simulation processes to evoke natural environments in our embodied minds in vivid and emotionally salient mental images. The second part of the book has looked at the use of strategic empathy in environmental narratives that are concerned with cases of environmental injustice between humans or with the exploitation, mistreatment, and slaughter of nonhuman animals. The third and final part of the book has built on all of these insights in its consideration of ecodystopian and ecotopian narratives that try to warn their audiences of the ecological risks inherent in current cultural and economic practices or try to awaken desire for a more sustainable world and more ethical human–nature relationships.

My aim with this book was to show that a cognitive ecocritical approach can help elucidate how environmental narratives engage viewers sensually and emotionally in the stories they tell. At the same time, I have tried to show that literary and cinematic environments also deserve more attention from scholars interested in cognitive approaches to literature and film because they are a central component of the storyworlds that surround characters and therefore limit or enable what they can do. I am well aware that there is an indefinite number of aspects that I have neglected, both from an ecocritical and from a cognitivist point of view. It is impossible to do full justice to any of the issues that I have addressed in such limited space. Rather than offering a comprehensive or even sufficient treatment of environmental justice narratives, animal stories, or ecodystopian and ecotopian storytelling, I have attempted to demonstrate that a cognitive ecocritical approach has much to offer for a critical analysis of such texts and films and that it can be combined with more politically and ethically oriented forms of literary and film criticism. As Nancy Easterlin has pointed out, acquiring knowledge of human cognitive predispositions "is valuable in a potentially wide variety of ways, since it may well illuminate the relationships between modes and forms and their depiction of places, between minds and nonhuman nature, and between urban and natural environments, to give only a few examples" (2010, 259). Easterlin's research demonstrates well how fruitful this kind of investigation can be, and the same is true for the work of Erin James, Markku Lehtimäki, and a range of other scholars who are interested in the interface between ecocriticism and narrative theory.[1] I hope that *Affective Ecologies* will contribute its share to this much larger endeavor.

In these final pages of the book, I want to point out two directions that strike me as particularly relevant for future development within the emerging field of cognitive ecocritical studies and narratological approaches to environmental narrative more generally. The first direction has to do with the kind of media texts that are in the focus of such approaches. In this book, I have limited my analytical focus to literary texts and films, thereby ignoring, for the sake of practicality, a whole range of other media texts that are of equal interest to such analysis. This not only includes television formats of all kinds but also graphic narratives, music, audiobooks, stage performances, social media, and a whole range of digital formats—most importantly, computer games. Colin Milburn has drawn our attention to the fact that, like the equally wasteful medium of film, computer games must always be seen in the context of the "environmental risks and humanitarian dilemmas involved" in their production, consumption, and disposal (2014, 203). Although these are serious concerns for any ecocritical consideration of what Milburn somewhat hesitantly calls "green gaming," he encourages us to consider "the possibility that games . . . might contribute to green politics [by] engaging players to recognize the precarious situation of our planet, and perhaps even providing the cognitive resources for actually doing something about it" (204). Hans-Joachim Backe has gone so far as to propose a "greenshift" in game studies, which would entail not just an "increased attention towards the ways digital games partake in environmentalist discourses" but also to the ways in which games can "simulate ecosystems" in ways that literature and film cannot (2014). From the perspective of cognitive ecocriticism, at least two questions immediately arise: do computer games evoke ecosystems and other narrative environments in ways that are more immersive than those of literature and film? And what, exactly, are the effects of the medium's participatory and interactive nature?

The latter is a question that scholars with an interest in the cognitive dimensions of our engagement with narrative have asked for more than a decade. Toward the end of his essay on "Narrative Desire" (1999) Gregory Currie wonders about what happens to desire when we actively engage in "narratives in which we play roles" (198). Unless they are alternate reality games using the real world as a platform and involving the embodied presence of the player in the alternate world, such narratives will share a number of features with traditional audiovisual storytelling. Greg Smith has pointed out that although the cognitive film community "has payed relatively little attention to games and gameplay thus far," it is obvious that video games "can call upon the range of classical suturing film techniques that invite spectators to imaginatively participate in the diegetic world" (2014, 292). What makes them different from a film is "the added advantage of 'interactivity,' of direct cybernetic feedback between text and player. . . . In gaming, the linkage between player and avatar is the basic condition for the medium and is a central pleasure for participants" (292).[2] This is what differentiates *Avatar,* the film, from *Avatar,* the video game, which was put on the market by Ubisoft shortly after the release of the film and that aims to immerse players in the same alluring environment and in the same narrative universe. However, unlike the film, the video game allows players to fight either on the side of the indigenous Na'vi or on that of the RDA Corporation and its armed-to-the-teeth military forces. This differs considerably from the narrative strategy of the film, which aligns viewers with a protagonist who starts out working for the RDA only to become its worst enemy after experiencing the ways of the Na'vi with the help of his avatar body. As Dan Flory has noted, narrative resistance might complicate viewers' emotional response to the film who object to its moral stance or its racial or environmental politics (2013, 44), but in the case of the game there is not even any narrative that such viewers would have to resist. They can simply choose the side of the RDA and bomb the indigenous people and their forest into oblivion.

On the one hand, then, a cognitive ecocritical approach to video games would have to consider the analytical and emotional implications of the somewhat greater freedom of choice that comes with interactivity, a freedom that may lead players to engage with virtual environments and nonhuman others in ways that are exploitative and/or destructive. On the other hand, it would have to explore the ways in which such games immerse players in their narrative environments and what consequences this might have for embodied simulation. Andreas Gregersen and Torben Grodal have proposed a model for player experiences that is based on Shaun Gallagher's enactivist analysis of the structure of embodied experience. One problem that they detect in existing game interfaces is that they "primarily support agency and thus possibly feelings of active ownership and efficacy in relationship to avatars and tools" (2009, 81). The experience of being the *object* of embodied actions is greatly curtailed, and the same is true for players' sensory experience more generally. Just how much it is curtailed becomes clear when we compare the flesh-and-bone Na'vi avatar that Jake Sully inhabits with the help of far-advanced technology in Cameron's science fiction film with those that are available to the players of the corresponding game. Whereas the film suggests that Sully has full material agency inside his Na'vi body, allowing him to direct it in any way he wants within the limits of the physical capabilities of that body and to feel all aspects of the world around him to the full extent, the player is highly restricted in his choices, and his direct sensory experiences remain, as in the case of film viewing, limited to sight and sound. All other senses, including touch and pain, are only engaged on the imaginary level. This presumably makes the risk of being the object of embodied actions—like that of being severely physically injured—a very different one.

In a more recent article, Gregersen has suggested that games that encourage "isomorphism between player and avatar embodiment (that is, the similarity between actual player movements and avatar representations)" might be more conducive to a full-fledged embodied experience of the game's storyworld (Gregersen 2014, 261). Even that, however, will not change any of the above-mentioned limitations. As Gregersen and Grodal put it, "players can dance, swordfight, and fish the nights away in the comfort of their living room, but they still get no hugs or kisses" (2009, 81). In fact, moving their actual bodies might lessen the vivacity and intensity of the imagined kiss because the respective brain regions cannot be fully re-used for an embodied simulation of the sensation of being kissed. Nor will players feel the full extent of pain, panic, and existential dread if their avatar is fatally hit by an opponent. Although video games immerse us in their worlds in ways that are different from those of films, the condition that Carl Plantinga has called "conditional realism" (2009b, 240) remains: we experience real sensations and emotions during exposure, but we also know, on the cognitive level, that the events we witness or even participate in are not really happening to us. The difference lies not least in our attitude toward and cognitive processing of the represented world. As Marco Caracciolo points out, "playing a game is a competitive practice where the emphasis is placed on player's agency and strategic planning against the background of a set of rules; engaging with an act qua narrative, by contrast, involves piecing together events and existents in a way that foregrounds specific emotional interests" (2015, 233).[3] Caracciolo argues that what he calls "narrative-focused" games encourage play and narrativization at the same time, but even such games will not provide an experience that is in any way akin to that of Sully in Cameron's future world or even to the immersion that viewers of *Avatar* experience when simulating Sully's embodied experience in their minds.

Such differences and similarities between narrative engagement in films and video games lead us to the larger issue of media convergence.[4] That the translation from one medium into another always bears the risk of losing the emotional force of the original story is a phenomenon that is well known to the producers and consumers of film adaptations of literary texts, one of the most common forms of intermedia conversion. Similar issues arise when narratives are exported from and imported into other media. As Trevor Elkington notes, "video games based on film and television licenses must attempt to appease two audiences: fans of the original license, who expect a certain adherence to its details, and fans of video games who expect adherence to common notions of gameplay" (2009, 215). This explains the often-hostile reception of such games from reviewers and players as well as the disappointment voiced by fans of the respective films. It remains a fact, however, that popular Hollywood movies such as *Avatar* increasingly become multimedia events that not only come with sophisticated marketing and merchandising campaigns but also with a whole range of accompanying media formats, from video games to companion books, novels, graphic narratives, and audiobooks. Such conversions involve complex translations and transpositions. In the words of Marie-Laure Ryan and Jan-Noël Thon, each added media text necessarily "rewrites an existing narrative, modifying the plot and ascribing different features or destinies to the characters," thereby creating "a new storyworld that overlaps to some extent with the old one" (2014, 5). If we are truly interested in the potential or actual cultural impact of transmedia environmental narratives, we must pay attention to all of these modes of storytelling and to the different ways in which they offer their recipients immersion in virtual environments and emotional engagement with human and nonhuman others.[5]

Because it involves a range of disciplinary competences and methodologies, such research necessitates what David Herman has called "transdisciplinary convergence" (2012, xi).

This brings me to the second direction I consider important for cognitive ecocritical studies within the environmental humanities: the need for empirical research. As Frederick Luis Aldama has noted, cognitive narratology can be useful in providing "concepts and instruments through which we can study the blueprints created by authors, artists, and directors that circumscribe the phenomena of narrative fiction making and consuming" (Aldama and Hogan 2014, 28). Ideally, these theoretical concepts and instruments will be complemented, and indeed substantiated, by relevant empirical research, either in the form of neuroscientific and psychological studies that examine the brain-body system of individual readers and viewers or in the form of audience response studies as they are being conducted by scholars in social psychology, media and communication studies, sociology, and other relevant fields. As Aldama explains, "the advances in the cognitive and neurosciences of memory, empathy, theory of mind, causal and counterfactual social and physical mappings, and much more can offer a foundational analysis of how an author or artist is able to create effective blueprints—effective in the sense of being able to have an impact on an audience" (28). Recent years have produced a remarkable amount of empirical research on literary and audiovisual texts that directly engages with questions of narrative transportation, immersion, and emotional engagement on the one hand and narrative impact on the other.[6]

Cognitive approaches in the humanities have "always borrowed the methods and explanations of cognitive science" (Nannicelli and Taberham 2014, 2), treating empirical research in the human sciences more generally "as a valuable source of insight, rather than a fundamentally wrong-headed enterprise" (G. Smith 2014, 295). It thus seems a logical development that such researchers also engage in inter- and transdisciplinary collaborations that involve empirical work in order to test hypotheses and confirm their significance beyond an interpretative close reading. As I have mentioned in the introduction, we see more and more of such collaborative research and even literary and film scholars who themselves have begun to engage in empirical research (Bortolussi and Dixon 2003; Hakemulder and Koopman 2010; Koopman and Hakemulder 2015; Kuijpers and Miall 2011; Miall 2008; Miall and Kuiken 2001; Reinhard and Olson 2016; Sklar 2009, 2013). These researchers meet at conferences such as the ones hosted by the International Society for the Empirical Study of Literature (IGEL) and the Society for Cognitive Studies of the Moving Image (SCSMI), and at interdisciplinary research centers such as the Max Planck Institute for Empirical Aesthetics in Frankfurt. It is a thriving field that stands to contribute important insights in our multifaceted engagement with all kinds of cultural artifacts. Vittorio Gallese has recently coined the term *experimental aesthetics* (2015, 2) for empirical work that draws on neuroscientific research on embodied simulation in order to help answer some of the questions humanities scholars tend to ask about representation, aesthetics, and reception.[7]

Such research—which explores the narrative engagement of actual readers and viewers—has been of central importance to my arguments throughout this book. My own contribution has been solely theoretical, as is the case for many cognitive narratologists and film scholars. I believe, however, that the cognitive ecocritical investigation of environmental narratives would greatly profit from empirical studies that are conducted in addition to—and ideally in conjunction with—such theoretical work. Partners for such investigations might be found in the neighboring field of environmental communication or among psychologists and social science scholars with an interest in environmental and ecological issues. They would require considerable funding to pursue, and such funding is not always easy to secure for interdisciplinary projects. And, of course, they would have to wrestle with the inevitable methodological problems involved in all such endeavors.[8] But in my opinion they are not only worth pursuing but in fact urgently needed in a research field that is so centrally concerned with the question of how environmental narratives interact with their human producers and consumers and with the larger world in which they exist. Empirical research might help answer such questions and also give us a better understanding of the mediating role of individual and cultural differences. In recent years, the pressing concerns around global ecological issues such as climate change have led researchers outside the environmental humanities to increasingly turn their attention to environmental narratives. There is a growing understanding that narratives are of central importance not only to science communication (Olson 2015) but to our relationships with all other humans and nonhumans as well as the larger environment. I hope that this will open up new possibilities for interdisciplinary cooperation and transdisciplinary convergence, and that we will explore further, in both the theoretical and the empirical realm, what environmental narratives of all kinds and in all kinds of media might contribute to our understanding of the world around us and our place in it.

NOTES

NOTES TO THE INTRODUCTION

1. The five human senses, as Francesca Bacci and David Melcher remind us in *Art and the Senses*, "are our source for vital knowledge about objects and events in the world, as well as for insights into our private sensations and feelings" (2011, 1). While each sense is unique and comes with its own set of information, they work together to create a rich subjective experience.

2. For a discussion of readers' physical responses during literary reading, see Kuijpers and Miall (2011). I will discuss this process in more detail in chapter 1.

3. Affective mimicry is the process by which we unwillingly "catch" others' emotions merely by looking at their facial expression. The mirror neuron system—to which I will turn in chapter 1—is centrally involved in this process.

4. The terms *computationalism* and *connectionism* were coined by Francisco Varela, Evan Thompson, and Eleanor Rosch in *The Embodied Mind* (1991). The terms refer to historically older (but still prevalent) strands within cognitive science that treat the mind as an entity that is not connected to the body in ways other than receiving signals and giving impulses. Computationalism developed in the 1950s and assumed that the mind is "something akin to a digital computer processing a symbolic language" (Garson 2015). Connectionism became popular in the 1980s and understands mental phenomena as the emergent processes of interconnected neural networks.

5. In *Philosophy in the Flesh* (1999), George Lakoff and Mark Johnson classified both computationalism and connectionism as "first-generation" cognitive science, labeling the more recent research that emphasized embodiment and interaction between organisms and their environments as second-generation cognitive science.

6. The discourse of enactivism goes back to the publication of Francisco Varela, Evan Thompson, and Eleanor Rosch's *The Embodied Mind* in 1991 and centers on concepts such as autonomy, sense-making, emergence, embodiment, and experience. Unlike most researchers in neuroscience and cognitive psychology, enactivists reject the notion that the mind is located in the brain or even the body of an agent. Instead, it is extended into the environment and "defined as meaningful activity in the world; it is an autonomous process of sense-making embodied in self-sustaining neural, bodily, and sensorimotor dynamics under precarious far-from-equilibrium conditions" (Froese 2015, 1). This leads to a rejection of internal mental representations in favor of investigations of the complex dynamics that structure a subject's lived existence. Evan Thompson's *Mind in Life* (2007) offers a very good introduction into enactivist philosophy. For an introduction into radical enactivist thought, see Hutto and Myin's *Radicalizing Enactivism* (2013). For a good overview of research on embodied cognition that showcases the diversity of the field, see Di Paolo and Thompson's contribution to *The Routledge Handbook of Embodied Cognition* (2014).

7. For a 4E approach that focuses on emotional and affective dimensions of experience, see Colombetti (2013). For the presentation of "A Moderate Approach to Embodied Cognitive Science," see Goldman (2012).

8. For an introduction to second-generation approaches in the cognitive study of literature, see Kukkonen and Caracciolo (2014).

9. For a detailed critique of the interrelated claims that the mind is enactive and extended, see John Michael's "Interactionism and Mindreading" (2011), in which he concludes that "rather than interpreting interactionism as an alternative to mindreading approaches to social cognition, it is possible to regard it as a modest contribution which can in fact generate empirically testable hypotheses about the individual cognitive processes underlying mindreading" (578).

10. For cognitive approaches to art history, see Solso (1996), Zeki (1999), and Livingstone (2002). On music and cognition, see Temperley (2004). See also Jenefer Robinson (2007).

11. According to David Herman, the shift from classical to postclassical narratology entails "a shift from text-centered or formal models to models that are jointly formal and functional—models attentive both to the text and to the context of stories" (1999, 8). For a good overview of the field, see Alber and Fludernik's edited volume *Postclassical Narratology* (2010).

12. Iser's *The Act of Reading* is an important precursor to contemporary cognitivist approaches to literature, not least because of its insight that reading "sets in motion a whole chain of activities that depends both on the text and on the exercise of certain basic human faculties" (1978, ix).

13. In *Literary Reading* (2006), David Miall notes that cognitive poetics "has adopted a model of cognition that, surprisingly at the present stage of psychological research, is restricted almost entirely to information processing issues: in other words, the role of feeling has been neglected" (41).

14. In a similar vein to Young and Saver, the evolutionary scholar Jonathan Gottschall writes in *The Storytelling Animal* (2013) that "human life is so bound up in stories that we are thoroughly desensitized to their weird and witchy power" (1). Yet, a few pages earlier he attests to the fact that we are actually quite sensitive to that power, marveling at "how bizarre it is that when we experience a story—whether in a book, a film, or a song—we allow ourselves to be invaded by the teller. The story maker penetrates our skulls and seizes control of our brains" (xv). Gottschall does not shy away from making large, and largely unsubstantiated, claims about the societal effects of such penetration, attesting that "fiction subtly shapes our beliefs, behaviors, ethics" and "powerfully modifies culture and history" (xvii).

15. Hogan bases his theory of simulation of connectionist theories in cognitive science (2013, xiv) rather than on embodiment theory. Many of his insights are nevertheless relevant to my deliberations here.

16. This claim is consistent with recent research in a range of disciplines that profiles narratives and storytelling as contributing to sense-making activities across multiple experiential domains. Herman points to relevant developments in narrative therapy, in which clients are encouraged to create new, more positive and life-enhancing stories of self and other and work in the philosophy of history that explores how narrative scaffolds efforts to situate events in an unfolding time-course (2013, loc. 144–48).

17. There is a long tradition of eco-phenomenological enquiries that draw on the work of Martin Heidegger. See, for example, Foltz (1995), Howarth (1995), and Zimmerman (2002). For explicitly ecocritical work that engages Heideggerian thought, see Garrard (2010) and Norris (2011).

18. See in particular Hannes Bergthaller's "Limits of Agency" (2014), which traces materialist visions of agency in the work of Varela and Humberto Maturana and brings these in conversation with Niklas Luhmann's systems theory.

19. For a book-length study outlining the principles of cultural ecology, see Zapf (2016).

20. Material ecocriticism's references to quantum physics are mostly derived from Karen Barad's *Meeting the Universe Halfway* (2007).

21. James considers cognitive narratology "a fruitful contact zone for narrative theory and material ecocriticism, given their shared interest in the human body and the capacity of that body to generate cultural and social meaning" (2015, 54). I agree that there are some interesting points of connection. The problem I see, however, is for the two approaches to find a common terminology and methodology. Material ecocriticism's commitment to semiotics and its lack of interest in the empirical insights of psychological research might make the "contact zone" of cognitive narratology a somewhat contested area.

22. For evolutionary approaches to literary narrative, see also Boyd (2009), Joseph Carroll (2004), and Jonathan Gottschall (2005, 2013).

NOTES TO CHAPTER 1

1. Narratologists have used related terms to describe the subjective impression of transportation into a storyworld. Wolfgang Iser describes the sensation as *being in the midst* of things in *The Act of Reading* (1978). Other scholars have called the same process *absorption* (Nell 1988) or *immersion* (Ryan 2001; Jacobs and Schrott 2011).

2. This is in keeping with psychologist Rolf Zwaan's more general argument that "language is a set of cues to the comprehender to construct an experiential (perception plus action) simulation of the described situation" (2004, 36).

3. For an empirical analysis of how readers' life experiences affect the knowledge they bring to bear on narrative experiences, see Gerrig (2011). A 2015 fMRI study by Chow et al. found that when listening to stories, subjects' "past experience with the scenes and actions described in the narratives selectively modulated functional connectivity between lower- and higher-level areas within the neural systems for visual and motor processing, respectively" (1494). Previous personal experiences with something described in a narrative affect how vividly we imagine it.

4. There are exceptions to the rule, of course: for example, when a person's experience of the world—be it actual or literary—is divergent from the norm because of a neurodevelopmental disorder, as in autism. The literary scholar Ralph James Savarese (2013, 2015) has collaborated with Tito Mukhopadhyay, a nonspeaking autist, in a number of literary readings. He has developed the concept of "neurocosmopolitanism" to account for the ways in which different minds might read the same text in very different ways.

5. For an insightful inquiry into the development of neurophenomenology, see Bayne (2004). For a neurophenomenological account that challenges simulation theory in favor of the concept of an "extended body" see Froese and Fuchs (2012).

6. Tom Froese has singled out Luiz Pessoa's *The Cognitive-Emotional Brain* as an integrative neuroscientific approach that converges with the enactivist approach in several respects (2015, 2). Pessoa himself understands his research as a continuation of Damasio's work (2013, x).

7. Damasio engages with phenomenology in *The Feeling of What Happens* (1999). His later work also includes research on mirror neurons in its deliberations. Gallese (2005) has suggested that the concept of embodied simulation is consistent with some of the perspectives offered by phenomenology, referring to the work of Edmund Husserl.

8. For more information on mirror neurons, see Rizzolatti and Craighero (2004). Helpful books on the topic include Rizzolatti and Sinigaglia's *Mirrors in the Brain* (2008) and Marco Iacoboni's *Mirroring People* (2009). For a critique of the research on mirror neurons from a neuroscience perspective, see Hickok (2013). Hickok's main argument against mirror neurons is that they do not seem to be selectively mirroring specific movements and that humans understand actions they cannot perform. He concludes that mirror neurons cannot explain the complexity of human simulation processes and argues for the primacy of the sensorimotor system in such simulation.

9. That linguistic representations of movement activate the same neurons that are also involved when the body performs the same movement has been explained with the hypothesis

of *neuronal recycling*. As Jacobs and Schrott explain, that hypothesis postulates that "structures in the brain eventually adapt so well to their environment that culturally determined processes such as reading end up operating through them, even though they had not evolved for this purpose" (2014, 130). An fMRI study conducted by Speer et al. found that "readers dynamically activate specific visual, motor, and conceptual features of activities while reading about analogous changes in activities in the context of narrative" (2009, 995). See also Gallese and Lakoff (2005); Goldman (2006, 2009); Tettamanti et al. (2005); Iacoboni (2008); and Aziz-Zadeh et al. (2006). For an overview of fMRI findings related to embodied semantics theory, see Aziz-Zadeh and Damasio (2008).

10. See Keysers and Gazzola (2009). According to Goldman and Jordan, there are at least three types of mental states that we constantly impute to others: "emotions (e.g., fear, anger, disgust), sensations (pain, touch, tickle), and propositional attitudes (belief, desire, intention)" (2013, 448).

11. Enactivist philosophers have repeatedly criticized this claim, stating that mirror neurons do not offer a convincing explanation of intersubjectivity and that the concept of embodied simulation is a thinly concealed version of the classic computationalist paradigm in cognitive science, treating the mind as a solipsistic entity that is located in the brain (De Bruin and Gallagher, 2011). Gallese and Sinigaglia have defended their account of the mirror neuron system as a specific kind of embodied simulation, one that is "characterized by one's reuse of one's own bodily formatted representations in functionally attributing them to others" (2012, 100). For a discussion of both simulation/mindreading theories and enactive approaches, see also Michael (2011). For a proposal of a "moderate approach to embodied cognition science," see Goldman (2012).

12. For an informed investigation of the differences between experience as conveyed in literature and experience as apprehended through scientific method, see Caracciolo and Hurlburt (2016).

13. Reading researchers like Maryanne Wolf confirm the relevance of brain research to the study of reading. Wolf states that "the brain's design made reading possible, and reading's design changed the brain in multiple, critical, still evolving ways" (2007, 216).

14. For studies of the relationship between gesture, thought, and language processing, see Bolens (2003), Goldin-Meadow (2003) and McNeill (2005).

15. In Miall's view, "literariness is manifested by the special nature of the interaction between reader and text" (2006, 3). I will come back to this point later on in this chapter.

16. Appraisal theorists understand emotions as the outcome of goal-related judgments elicited by inferences about changes in the likelihood of goal achievement rather than being directly elicited by perceptual experiences. The philosopher Robert Solomon, for years one of the most eloquent advocates of understanding emotions as judgments, has admitted that the appraisal account "lacks the keen sense of *engagement*" he now sees as essential to emotions (2004a, 77). Solomon's *Thinking about Feeling* (2004b) offers a good overview of contemporary theories of emotion.

17. An fMRI experiment designed by Chow et al. to test the embodied comprehension of stories showed that the activity of neural systems in the brain associated with motor processing, visual-spatial, and affective processing are selectively modulated by relevant story content (2013, 279).

18. Theory of Mind is the ability to impute mental states to oneself and others. In Zunshine's account, it is a form of cognitive play that is central to our enjoyment of literature. Zunshine claims that "cognitive cravings . . . are satisfied—and created!—when we read fiction" (2006, 4).

19. The enactivist philosopher Shaun Gallagher (2007) has argued that neural representation is a form of pretense since otherwise it would be a realization and not a "simulation."

20. On the latter point, see also Caracciolo's "The Reader's Virtual Body" (2011).

21. On the relationship between qualia and the nonverbal properties of fictional consciousnesses, see also Alan Palmer's *Fictional Minds* (2004, 97–98).

22. Muir chronicles his traumatic childhood in *The Story of My Boyhood and Youth* (1913).

23. The words Muir uses in this passage almost all exhibit what Jacobs et al. call a high embodiment, or "E-index" (2015, 5). Empirical studies conducted at the Dahlem Institute for Neuroimaging of Emotion at the Freie Universität Berlin established that words can be differentiated by the attributes "body-object-interaction" and "sensory experience": words such as *sea* or *honey* exhibit a high "embodiment index" while *purpose* or *accident* have a low one.

24. Starr notes that when visual imagery is processed during reading, it will activate the sensorimotor cortex in the reader's brain in much the same way as if she would perceive that environment directly. In addition to a simulation of the object's visual qualities, it "may feed into or build on motor imagery because vision allows for (and in sighted persons is preparatory to) motion: to use the term invented by James J. Gibson, the visual world allows affordances—action possibilities" (2013, 80).

25. Kaplan's study summarizes research on human preferences for grassland ecosystems such as savannahs. He concludes that what becomes apparent when reading such research comparatively is "that in their rapid assessment of what they liked, participants were drawing inferences based on the spatial information in the scene. More specifically, there seemed to be an implicit assessment of how one could function in the space represented by the scene" (1992, 587). On this point, see also chapter 8 in Anjan Chatterjee's *The Aesthetic Brain* (2013).

26. In *Imperial Eyes* (1992), Pratt argues that the colonial traveler is a "seeing man . . . whose imperial eyes passively look out and possess" (7).

27. On this point, see Olmstead and Rhode (2003).

28. Muir's continued passion for science and intimate knowledge of the Yosemite Valley led him to claim that Yosemite, and similar valleys around it, was the product of glacial activity. His theory was in contradiction to the accepted view of his time, propagated by the head of the California Geological Survey, Josiah Whitney, that the geological formation was the result of an earthquake. Muir's theory is by now generally accepted as correct.

29. Material agency is a concept within new materialist theories, and it also has informed the work of environmental historians such as Linda Nash. While much of nonhuman nature does not have agency in the sense of intentionality or choice, argues Nash, we must recognize that "so-called human agency cannot be separated from the environments in which that agency emerges" and therefore acknowledge that these environments have agency, too (2005, 69).

30. Empathists such as Theodor Lipps used the German term *Einfühlung* (the literal translation of *einfühlen* is to "feel into") for what in the English translation became empathy. As Currie points out, "einfühlen was, for the Romantics, a general means of knowing" (2011, 83), and it was therefore not restricted to the empathic relationship with another human being.

31. On this point, see also Gallese and Wojciehowski (2011).

32. Aziz-Zadeh and Damasio cite research that demonstrates that metaphorical use of action words does *not* activate the premotor cortex if the metaphor is so well established that it has become ordinary language use. They speculate that "in conventional metaphors, such as 'grasp the situation,' the metaphorical meaning (to understand) is more salient than the literal meaning (a grasping action)" and that therefore the premotor cortex is not activated (2008, 38). In the case of the metaphors used by Muir here, we must assume that premotor cortex is activated because readers' brains respond to the literal meaning (which indicates movement). On the role of metaphors in our understanding of everyday life see Lakoff and Johnson ([1980] 2003).

33. Kuzmičová insists that readers may simulate a given scene in a literary text either from an *inner* (subjective) or from an *outer* (objective) stance (2014, 282). The two stances roughly correspond to the differentiation I have drawn earlier: that readers are likely to imagine the storm scene both from Muir's subjective perspective (inner stance) and from a third-person, on-looking perspective (outer stance). Although she acknowledges that the two stances "in fact [constitute] a continuum of sorts" (282), Kuzmičová seems to suggest that readers can do one and not the other. This would involve conscious effort and is unlikely to happen in natural reading.

34. See Green and Brock (2000) and Green (2004).

35. On this point, see Finch and Elder's introduction to the 2002 edition of *Nature Writing: The Tradition in English,* which acknowledges that "any tradition, if it is to remain vital, must continue to change and incorporate new elements" (17). For a recent study that rediscovers forgotten female representations of American wilderness, see Kilcup (2013).

36. In interviews, Nadzam frequently has been asked to comment on the ambiguous nature of her narrator, but she has always insisted that she does not know who her narrator is or why she created him or her in that ambiguous way.

37. Such distinctions have been made by several narratologists, but Shaw is directly responding to Seymour Chatman's *Coming to Terms* (1990). Chatman later responded to Shaw, defending the separation of discourse and story in narratological analysis.

38. For an empirical study on the effects of free indirect discourse, see Hakemulder and Koopman (2010). The study confirms that the technique gives readers a greater sense of immediate access to the inner life of a character than other modes of third-person narration, but it also finds that some readers grow confused about the moral stance of the character.

39. See Patoine (2015) for a cognitive study of "sensationalist" literary texts that encourage empathetic reading of morally transgressive characters in ways that engage the body of the reader.

40. Humbert narrates his story in the first person. It is the story of a literature professor who is obsessed with a twelve-year-old girl and who later becomes sexually involved with her after becoming her stepfather. The book is now a classic of American literature, but it was highly controversial at the time of its publication and banned in several U.S. states.

NOTES TO CHAPTER 2

1. In his 1916 study *The Photoplay,* the psychologist Hugo Münsterberg suggested that film mimics natural visual perception. Cognitive researchers frequently draw on Münsterbeg's pioneering work, among them Bordwell (2012), Plantinga (2009a), and Zacks (2015).

2. Experimental aesthetics, as Gallese defines it, is related to the larger field of neuroaesthetics but centrally relies on the model of embodied simulation for its conceptual framing. Neuroaesthetics "is committed to investigating the neural mechanisms underpinning humans' perceptual analysis of the formal visual features of art works and the explicit aesthetic judgment they report" (Gallese 2015, 2). For an overview of neuroaesthetics, see also Dio Cinzia and Gallese (2009).

3. When Deleuze writes that cinema "puts movement in the mind" (2000, 366), he suggests that instead of linguistics and psychoanalysis, it is "the biology of the brain" that explains why we can be so captivated by motion pictures.

4. Muybridge's zoopraxiscope used a rapidly rotating glass disk to give the impression of motion.

5. Invented by Thomas Edison in 1888, the kinetoscope was a device that allowed customers to view short film strips individually through a peephole viewer window that was located at the top of the wooden device.

6. Just as in the case of reading, the actual viewing environment can demand varying degrees of attention and therefore disturb or facilitate the degree of immersion into the storyworld of a film. That is why, at least in the context of western exhibition traditions, everything about viewers' actual environments—the dark room of the theater, the big screen that fills out most of the visual field, the comfortable seats—is geared toward keeping their eyes focused and the rest of their bodies motionless, making them the perfect sounding boards for the embodied simulation of what is happening on the screen.

7. On the development of continuity editing techniques in early film, see Bordwell, Staiger, and Thompson (1985) and Bordwell and Thompson (2001).

8. Chapter 7 of Zacks's *Flicker* (2015) offers a detailed overview of possible neurological explanations for why most viewers tend to not notice cuts between shots, ranging from the blinks and saccades that are typical for human vision to various attentional phenomena.

9. Experimental film, on the other hand, often foregrounds the filmic means, thereby disrupting the illusion of transparency and calling attention to the film as film.

10. For a study of the influence of continuous film narrative on viewers' attention and goal pursuit, see Cohen, Shavalian, and Rube (2015). For a study on the relationship between editing and viewer attention, see Shimamura et al. (2015).

11. Theory of Mind (ToM) is the ability to impute mental states to oneself and others through mental inferences.

12. For a range of ecocritical essays dealing with the affective dimensions of film, see Weik von Mossner (2014i). Adrian Ivakhiv's ecocritical study *Ecologies of the Moving Image* (2013) draws on Deleuze (among a number of other philosophers) in its conceptualization of the moving image as a medium that is "moving" in multiple ways, from the actual physical movement of the images to the way in which it "immerses us into the flow of sensations felt or imagined in the viewing" and the "process that moves from minerals to photographic chemicals, plastics, and silicon chips, to shooting locations and sets, to editing suites and film distributors, who deliver images to screen and desktop, where they resonate within us so that we subsequently insinuate them into conversations, symbolic narratives, figures of speech, and bodily gestures modelled on screen heroes and heroines" (loc. 264–67). The theoretical approach developed by Ivakhiv in his book aims to encompass all of those various forms and meanings of movements. My aims are much more modest here, focusing on the much smaller question of how filmic environments come to life in the minds of viewers and how they engage them emotionally. Among the few ecocritical film scholars who have considered film emotion from a cognitive perspective are David Ingram (2014a), Bart Welling (2014), and Salma Monani (2014). See also Weik von Mossner (2014b).

13. See, for example, N. Carroll (2003), Grodal (2009), Plantinga (2009a), G. Smith (2003), and M. Smith (1995).

14. Cynthia Freeland explains that "the sublime object presents us with a sensory and emotional experience of some sort that is so extreme, unsettling, or intense that it would be disturbing on its own. But in its context it forces us to shift into another mental mode, cognition, or thought," with the result that "we become more able to handle the deep feelings evoked by the work" (1999, 68).

15. On the use of arid landscapes in the American Western film, see Carmichael (2006) and Murray and Heumann (2012).

16. Berila's essay also discusses Redford's 1998 film adaption of Nicholas Evans's novel *The Horse Whisperer* (1995), but I will concentrate here on the earlier film.

17. Plantinga gives the example of "a soft curving line or an elegantly paced camera movement" that is "associated with soothing sounds rather than grating or pounding noises that viewers might hear" (2013, 103). On the emotional effects of film music scores, see also J. Smith (1999) and Hoeckner et al. (2011). On the relationship between film music and embodied experience, see Chattah (2015) and Ward (2015).

18. The filmic depiction of landscapes has been the explicit topic of three different essay collections, all of them published within the last ten years: Lefebvre (2006), R. Fish (2007), and Harper and Rayner (2010).

19. Landscapes are not uncontested and objective environment that are simply "out there." Instead, the term denotes, as human geographer Denis Cosgrove reminds us, "the external world mediated through subjective human experience. . . . It is a construction, a composition of that world" and, as such, "possesses an affective meaning" (1998, 13).

20. A study by Mital and colleagues uses high-speed infrared eye tracking to measure viewer attention in the observation of dynamic scenes and finds that "temporal features such as flicker, motion, and their respective contrasts were the most predictive of gaze location" (2011, 5). A study

by Levin and Varakin (2004) demonstrates that a sudden onset of motion—such as a character's head turn or hand movement—attracts viewers' attention. For an argument regarding the importance of eye tracking studies for cognitive film theory, see Tim Smith (2013).

21. An eye-tracking study conducted by Antoine Coutrot et al. found "that sound impacts on eye position, fixation duration and saccade amplitude," thereby guiding visual attention (2012, 1). On the influence of sound on our understanding of actions, see Kohler et al. (2002). On the creation of suspense more generally, see Smuts (2009).

22. Empirical research by communication scholars Busselle and Bilandzic suggests that logical inconsistencies can interfere with viewers' mental processing and thus compromise their sense of transportation and immersion into the narrative world (2008, 256). Busselle and Bilandzic distinguish between viewers' perceived *internal realism* (related to the internal logic of the narrative world) and the perceived *external realism* (related to the narrative world's relationship to the actual world) (256). Their research suggests that "violations of both types of realism result from an inconsistency between the mental models that represent the narrative, general knowledge structures, and incoming narrative information" (256). See also Bilandzic and Busselle (2011).

23. Bacon most likely takes the notion of ecological "affordances" from ecological psychologist J. J. Gibson (1979). Joseph Anderson and Barbara Fisher Anderson are cognitive film scholars who have more explicitly brought Gibson's work on visual perception into the study of film in their introduction to *Moving Image Theory* (2005).

24. Ingram reports that the preview of the film "in Bozeman, Montana, was held in aid of the restoration of the Big Blackfoot River, the river on which Maclean's novel was set, but which was so polluted that the movie was actually filmed on the nearby Gallatin, near Livingstone" (2000, 29).

25. On the history of American disaster film, see Keane (2001).

26. The other "Basic Types" of disaster film that Yacowar mentions are "The Ship of Fools," "The City Falls," "The Monster," "Survival," "War," "Historical," and "The Comic."

27. A Steadicam is a camera stabilizer mount for film cameras that is worn by an operator. It mechanically isolates it from the operator's movement, producing very steady images instead of the shaky footage that a hand-held camera would produce. On the effect of camera movements on motor cortex activation, see also Heimann, Umiltà, Guerra, and Gallese (2014).

28. A 2008 fMRI study conducted by Uri Hasson et al. further supports these findings. It used inter-subject correlation analysis (ISC) to assess similarities in the spatiotemporal responses across viewers' brains during movie watching. Summarizing their findings, the authors state that "some films have the potency to 'control' viewers' neural responses" through the ways in which they are shot and edited (2). The embodied simulation thesis offers a good explanation for these findings. Citing Crick (1994), Damasio (1999), and LeDoux (1996) for support, Hasson et al. explain that "under the assumption that mental states are tightly related to brain states . . . controlling viewers' brain states, for our purposes, is the same as controlling their mental states including their percepts, emotions, thoughts, attitudes, etc." (2–3).

29. For empirical studies on the role of sound in guiding viewer attention, see Tim Smith (2014, 2015); Robinson, Stadler, and Rassell (2015); and Rassell et al. (2016).

30. On the importance of high-speed tracking shots for viewers' sense of motion, see Thomson-Jones (2013).

31. Undercranked footage is filmed at a slower speed than the speed at which it is later projected, leading to a speeding up of the actions seen. It is the opposite of slow motion.

32. There were several attempts to add scents to the film viewing experience, among them Smell-O-Vision and Odorama, but they remained mostly unsuccessful.

33. Coming at the issue from a phenomenological perspective with her concept of "haptic visuality," Laura Marks suggests in *The Skin of the Film* (2000) that "vision itself can be tactile, as though one were touching the film with one's eyes" (xii). The notion of touch, just like the notion that films have "skins," is employed metaphorically here to denote a subjective experi-

ence. Neuroscientific research suggests that vision can indeed have such tactile dimensions for the experiencer because it engages the respective brain areas.

34. On the sensation of touch in film viewing, see also Barker (2013).

35. Münsterberg worried already in his 1916 *The Photoplay* that actors may have trouble reproducing the complexity of authentic facial emotion expressions ([1916] 1970, 48). Psychologists Thalia Goldstein and Paul Bloom point out that "the two leading Western theories of how best to act can be classified as 'technique,' 'outside-in' or 'physical-based' acting versus 'method or system,' 'inside-out,' or 'emotional-based' acting" (2011, 142). Technique-based acting mimics the physical expression of an emotion and thus pretends to have an emotion without feeling the emotions of the character or manipulating one's own emotions. By contrast, inside-out-based acting (also called "method acting") depends on the actor diving deeply into his or her role in order to feel the feelings of the character and thus genuinely produce the according emotional expression. Well-known method actors include Dustin Hoffman, Al Pacino, Robert De Niro, and Daniel Day-Lewis. Many actors use a mixture of the two techniques.

36. See Adam O'Brian's *Transactions with the World* for a recent study that explores "the presence pro-filmic material reality" (2016, 3) in New Hollywood film from a material ecocritical perspective.

37. On the protagonists' complex relationship to the environment of Alaska, see Goldberg (2015).

38. Wadi Rum has in fact been repeatedly used in science fiction films that are set on Mars. Antony Hoffman's *Red Planet* (2000) and Brian de Palma's *Mission to Mars* (2000) also include scenes that were shot in Jordan's "Valley of the Moon." Desert areas in Utah, New Mexico, and Arizona have also been used as shooting locations for films set on Mars.

39. Michael Renov has argued that it is difficult to draw an exact line between feature films and documentaries because "nonfiction contains any number of 'fictive' elements" (1993, 3). Bill Nichols turns the argument on its head by claiming that "every film is a documentary" because "even the most whimsical of fictions gives evidence of the culture that produced it and reproduces the likenesses of the people who perform within it" (2001, 1).

40. There are, of course, fiction films that pretend to be documentaries—so-called mockumentaries—and that take part of their appeal precisely from the fact that they mimic the formal conventions of documentary film (typical examples are Christopher Guest's *Waiting for Guffman* [1997] and *Best in Show* [2000]). In most cases, however, such films are nevertheless indexed as fiction films and taken as such by the audience.

41. On the importance of indexing in viewers' understanding of fiction and nonfiction film, see also Eitzen (1992).

42. Hydraulic fracturing is a means of natural gas extraction employed in deep natural gas well drilling. Once a well is drilled, several millions of gallons of water, sand, and chemical substances are injected under high pressure, fracturing the shale and propping open fissures that enable natural gas to flow out of the well. The process has been discussed controversially because of the actual and potential danger it poses to ecosystems, animals, and humans. Gus Van Sant's *Promised Land* (2012) was one of the first fiction films to engage the issue.

43. In her reading of *Gasland,* Helen Hughes conceptualizes the image of flaming water as an example of what Delicath and DeLuca have called an "image event" (Delicath and DeLuca 2003, 315). Image events "have the capacity to gain attention, ignite debate" (Hughes 2014, 129).

44. The film can be watched online at www.truthlandmovie.com.

45. Another documentary that directly engages with *Gasland*—Phelim McAleer and Ann McElhinney' *Frack Nation* (2013)—also takes pains to convince viewers that the visual evidence presented in Fox's film is not the result of fracking. It bears mentioning that McAleer and McElhinney have also directed *Not Evil, Just Wrong* (2009), a film that attacks the truth claims of Guggenheim's *An Inconvenient Truth.*

46. Burning springs, also called natural gas springs, are water-fed springs that percolate enough natural gas to be set on fire with some kind of ignition device. They are the product of

natural geological processes. On *Gasland*'s website, the filmmakers respond to the accusation that they have made false inferences by stating that "the flaming faucets documented in *Gasland* are the product of natural gas migration into water supplies in most cases due to fracking right next door. Numerous investigations have confirmed this fact, including studies by the United States Environmental Protection Agency, the Pennsylvania Department of Environmental Protection, and many others" ("Fracking FAQs" 2016).

47. Energy In Depth's letter to the Academy of Motion Pictures is no longer available online, but Rebecca Keegan's 2010 article on the incident in the *Los Angeles Times* quotes the relevant passage (quoted in Keegan 2010).

48. In 2012, Fox made the documentary short *The Sky Is Pink* to react to some of the complaints of Energy In Depth and other interested parties. In 2013, he released a second feature documentary—*Gasland II*—that looks at the most recent developments around natural gas fracking.

49. I have discussed Currie's notion of "empathy for objects" in the previous chapter. On this point, see also Freedberg and Gallese (2007).

NOTES TO CHAPTER 3

1. The American environmental justice movement started in the 1980s, one of its key events being the 1982 direct action in a poor, predominantly black community in Warren County, North Carolina, when the affected community protested the building of a Polychlorinated Biphenyl (PCB) disposal site near their homes. It has "its historic roots in civil rights activism" (Melosi 1995, 5), and while there has been a significant amount of tension between environmental justice advocates and traditional environmentalists, the movements have increasingly attempted to find common ground in recent years.

2. For critical discussions of the American literature on environmental injustice, see Adamson (2001) and Myers (2005) and Adamson, Evans, and Stein (2002).

3. Novels such as John Steinbeck's *The Grapes of Wrath* (1939) and Sanora Babb's *Whose Names Are Unknown* (2004) remind us that it is not only ethnic minorities that historically have had to bear disproportionate environmental risks. Recounting the fates of poor homesteaders during the Dust Bowl era of the 1930s, both novels follow their white protagonists from windswept Oklahoma to the orchards of California where they face different kinds of hardship and exploitation.

4. While ToM allows us to reconstruct the minds and intentions of other people through our own mental meta-representational processes, FoB crucially relies on processes of embodied simulation. Gallese and Wojciehowski describe it as "a basic functional mechanism," that allows "a more direct and less cognitively-mediated access to the world of others" (2011).

5. For related empirical evidence see Hoffman (2000) and Eisenberg and Miller (1987). See also Oliner and Oliner (1988).

6. The study confirms the results of an earlier study (Mar et al. 2006) and also parallels results from a 2010 study conducted by Mar, Tackett, and Moore on the effect of fiction reading on children. On the influence of literary reading on readers' Theory of Mind, see Kidd and Castano (2013).

7. This form of inaccuracy can most easily happen in the reading of literature and involves imagining a character to be more "like oneself" than the character actually is by overlooking or ignoring some of the information given in the text. I am grateful to Salma Monani for bringing to my attention the controversy around the casting of black actors in Gary Ross's 2012 film adaption of Susan Collins's *The Hunger Games* (2008). The novel specifies the skin color of two characters, Rue and Thresh, as "dark brown" (45), and yet, despite this explicit information (which is only given once), some readers have complained that they imagined the characters to be white and therefore were disturbed and angered by the black cast in the film adaptation. Rather than

empathizing with an out-group other, then, these readers falsely imagined an in-group member while reading the novel. See Stewart (2012). On the white normativity and its consequences for reader empathy, see also note 22.

8. Spivak's concept of strategic essentialism refers to the "strategic use of positivist essentialism in a scrupulously visible political interest" ([1985] 1996, 214). It is a political tactic employed by minority groups, usually in a postcolonial context, that involves emphasizing a shared identity for political reasons even though strong differences may exist between members of these groups.

9. According to Keen, empathetic inaccuracy can manifest itself as *failure* or as *falsity*. In the first case, the author's empathetic imagining of a fictional world does not "transmit to readers without interference," evoking empathy in readers in ways that are against the author's "apparent or proclaimed representational goals" (2010, 81). In the second case, "narrative empathy short-circuits the impulse to act compassionately or to respond with political engagement" (81).

10. Howard Sklar notes that empathy implies "a reduction of the sense of distance between the empathizer and the object of empathy, in other words, the minimizing of the 'observer role,' which is a form of aesthetic distance. By contrast, sympathy requires a degree of distance for readers to observe and then judge a character's situation" (2009, 584). Sympathy therefore necessitates a greater degree of cognitive reflection. Both forms of relation are involved in readers' emotional response to fictional characters, often at the same time or in quick succession.

11. It should be noted that Adullah is a Pakistani-American author, and the novel's protagonist is a Pakistani immigrant and thus not Arab-American. Unfortunately, this fact is not mentioned anywhere in the study or in the follow-up studies, and it also does not seem to have made a difference for the subjects (who may have been unaware of the ethnic difference), which is interesting in itself. The conflation of ethnicities nevertheless puts a question mark behind some of the results of the studies. Among other things, it tells us a lot about processes of racialization and the frequent misattribution of ethnic identities.

12. Johnson reports that "individuals who were more transported into the story rated Arab-Muslims significantly lower in stereotypical negative traits (Study 1, N = 67) and exhibited significantly lower negative attitudes toward Arab-Muslims (Study 2, N = 102) postreading than individuals who were less transported into the story" (2013, 77). On this point, see also Johnson, Huffman, and Jasper (2014).

13. The realist novel first developed in the nineteenth century with writers such as Stendhal and Honoré de Balzac in France; Alexander Pushkin and Leo Tolstoy in Russia; and George Eliot in England. It was a reaction against Romantic idealism and aimed to represent its subject truthfully, focusing on everyday occurrences and eschewing grandiose events and plot turns.

14. Viramontes's choice to put a love story at the heart of her narrative facilitates such moral judgments because the narrative prototype of the "romantic tragi-comedy" (P. Hogan 2003, 19) rests on universals in human emotions. Much of Hogan's work over the past decade has been dedicated to the isolation of three cross-cultural prototype narratives—the heroic, the sacrificial, and the romantic tragi-comedy—which are "literary universals" in the sense that they are "generated from the prototypical structure of our emotion concepts" and therefore bound up with universals in human emotion (11). Hogan argues that the romantic love story has antidivisive and incorporative tendencies because it tends to pit two desperate lovers against a social system that opposes their love—Shakespeare's *Romeo and Juliet* being a prime example—and because it usually invites us to empathize and sympathize with the lovers, not with the system that threatens to destroy their love (P. Hogan 2009, 20–21). The same narrative structure can be found in Viramontes's novel.

15. Linda Hogan's *Solar Storms*, for example, is told through the eyes of a young indigenous woman who returns to her community, an island town on the boundary waters between Minnesota and Canada, after several years of absence. Because of her personal history, the protagonist is something of an insider-outsider who is personally affected by the flooding of indigenous lands.

16. James Phelan reminds us that simultaneous present-tense narration constitutes a radical break from the mimetic code because "the impossibility of living and telling at the same time

means that there is no plausible occasion for the narration" (2013, 180). Readers nevertheless have no problem accepting such narration because "just like we have a convention that permits a noncharacter narrator to violate real-world rules about knowing other people's minds . . . we have a convention, developed in response to authors' practices, that authorizes a narrator's telling to a narrate while simultaneously acting in ways that would in the real world preclude such narration" (181).

17. This principle, explains Jace Weaver, "creates a hierarchy of users based upon the date each began to first withdraw water from a given source. Those that are first in time are first in right" (1996, 85). By contrast, the water law east of the hundredth meridian in the United States is "borrowed from England. The governing principle is one of riparian rights. Simply stated, whoever owns land adjacent to a stream or lake is entitled to the reasonable use of water from it as long as it does not interfere with the rights of other riparian uses. The right runs with the land and may not be sold separate from it" (85).

18. Indian American ownership of water rights has frequently been contested over the centuries. "The fight for water rights," explains Phyllis Young, "is an ongoing struggle for Indian people all over the Americas" (1996, 88). Because of the scarcity of water in the western United States, there have been countless attempts to take away the old rights of Indian tribes that continue into the present. On this issue, see also Healy (2013) and Leslie (2015).

19. During the 1973 Wounded Knee Incident, followers of the American Indian Movement occupied the town of Wounded Knee in the Pine Ridge Reservation in protest against the U.S. government. The occupation led to a seventy-one-day standoff with U.S. Marshals, the FBI, and other law enforcement agencies, until the AIM activists finally surrendered. The 1975 Pine Ridge Shootout refers to another armed confrontation between AIM activists and the FBI, one that cost the lives of two FBI agents and one AIM activist. The subsequent investigation led to the arrest of three Native Americans suspected to have been involved in the shootout. Two of them were acquitted, one of them, Leonard Peltier, was convicted. The evidence used for Peltier's conviction, however, remains the subject of much controversy to this day. In his acknowledgments in the novel, Everett thanks Ward Churchill and Jim Vander Wall, the authors of *Agents of Repression* (1988) for sending him "some documents I found helpful" (Everett [1996] 2003, 202).

20. For more information on environmental hazards on Native American reservations, see Brook (1998), Weaver (1996), Small (1994), and Lynch and Stretesky (2012).

21. Sociologists Gregory Hooks and Chad Smith explain that "the geopolitical demands of the world's remaining leading military power pushed the United States to produce, test, and deploy weapons of unprecedented toxicity" (2004, 558), and that it is particularly Native American lands, "which are positively associated with the count of extremely dangerous sites" (567). The U.S. military, Hooks and Smith argue, has "systematically used and damaged Native American lands" in their choices of location for dangerous military facilities (563).

22. A particularly important figure in the history of the American environmental justice movement is Rev. Benjamin Chavis, the former head of the NAACP, who coined the term "environmental racism" to denote what he recognized as the strategic targeting of minority communities—in particular black communities—for the location of toxic waste dumps. His study *Toxic Wastes and Race* (1987) for the United Church of Christ (UCC) Commission for Racial Justice found a strong correlation between race and hazardous waste dumping and a deliberate targeting of minority communities for waste facilities.

23. In Everett's novel *Glyph* (1999), the first-person narrator addresses the reader directly on page 54 with the words "Have you to this point assumed that I am white?" thereby directing their attention to their underlying assumptions (the protagonist is black, but this wasn't specifically mentioned). According to the results of the Kaufman and Libby study (2012), we might expect that at this point readers already feel enough allegiance to the character to continue to vividly simulate his thoughts and feelings, even as they now have learned that he belongs to a different racial group than perhaps previously assumed.

24. Scholars have interrogated the prejudice that African Americans do not care for the environment and have no particular relationship to it. Sylvia Mayer reminds us of the "severe psychological damage" that was the result not so much of plantation slavery but of the Great Migration to the urban centers of the North and the resulting "collective loss of [a] close relationship to nature" (2003, 1). Kimberley Smith has investigated "how humans' relationship to the environment is affected—and often distorted—by racially oppressive political, social, and legal institutions and practices" (2007, 6). The opposite is true also. Ian Finseth has argued that "racial subjectivity matters to how human beings perceive, narrate, and interact with nature" (2009, 12).

25. Interestingly, despite Everett's resistance to racial stereotyping when it comes to his characters' relation to nature, his protagonist's personal journey fits surprisingly well into the "recurring pattern" that Finseth has detected in nineteenth-century African American novels that include a temporary retreat of the main character into nature. Finseth observes in these texts the following development: a move from culture to nature that interrupts the flow of daily existence; an intimate sensory encounter of the perceiving mind with its natural surroundings; the stimulation of self-reflective awareness, particularly of the personal past and future; the reevaluation of social relations and knowledge prompted by the *irrealization* of the ordinary; and then the individual's return to the cultural sphere but in a shifted relation to it (2009, 20). This very closely describes Robert Hawks's development in *Watershed*.

26. Examples of film that consist solely of POV shots, simulating a first-person perspective, include Robert Montgomery's *The Lady in the Lake* (1947) and Franck Khalfoun's *Maniac* (2012).

27. Such performative authenticity matters in a cinematic tradition that is notorious for casting white actors as Indians. Some reviewers have nevertheless been critical of the choice of Kilmer for the role of Levoi. Steven Hunter, for example, writes, "though Kilmer's own Indian heritage seems somewhat cynically calculated to dispute the charge, the movie still feels like one of those earnest liberal crusades" (1992, last para.). Calling *Thunderheart* a "big Hollywood extravaganza," Hunter suggests that a movie without Kilmer that focuses on Native American actor Graham Greene, John Trudell, and Sheila Tousey "would have been a better one" (1992, last para.).

28. On the depiction of typical Western landscapes versus reservation landscapes, see also Murray and Heumann's discussion of Chris Eyre's *Smoke Signals* (1998) in chapter 6 of *Gunfight at the Eco-Corral* (2012).

29. Informed viewers might recognize that this, once again, corresponds to historical reality, since on the very day of the Pine Ridge Shootout, tribal president Wilson was in Washington, DC, offering the American government part of the reservation land for uranium mining.

30. With the American Indian Revolution activist Tyrone Bisset, Everett's *Watershed* also features a fictionalized Leonard Peltier figure.

31. See Hunter (1992).

32. Sam Pack has argued that although "in many respects, *Thunderheart* is a refreshing departure from its predecessors in the Native American film genre" it "still relies upon too many Hollywood crutches in depicting Native Americans, which is particularly evident in its utilization of three tropes: the construction of the 'other,' the appropriation of native spirituality, and the formation of identity" (2001, 97). On Hollywood's frequent misrepresentation of Indians, see Rollins and O'Connor (2003) and documentaries made by Native American filmmakers, such as Victor Masayesva Jr.'s *Imagining Indians* (1992) and *Reel Injun* (2009) by Cree filmmaker Neil Diamond.

33. The film not only received numerous awards—among them an Academy Award for Best Actress for Julia Roberts—but also has earned a lifetime gross of over $125 million domestic and $130 million abroad, suggesting that it was popular with film audiences around the world.

34. This does not mean that there are no fiction films centering on American Indians and questions of environmental justice. On emotional appeals in indigenous filmmaking that focuses on environmental issues, see Monani (2014).

35. The film's protagonist, the personal injury lawyer Jan Schlichtmann (John Travolta), makes a number of imprudent decisions that in the end forces the affected community to accept

a settlement with the responsible corporations that barely covers its legal expenses. Schlichtmann also loses his firm and is forced to file for bankruptcy. The only small triumph that the film offers is a postscript informing viewers of the (historical) fact that the Environmental Protection Agency (EPA) later used the evidence Schlichtmann had collected in its own enforcement action against the offending corporations, forcing them to pay millions of dollars for a cleanup of the contaminated area. For ecocritical discussions of the film, see Ingram (2000, 5–6) and Murray and Heumann (2014, 28–29). See also Pezzullo (2006).

36. Ecocritic Paula Willoquet-Maricondi has argued that *Erin Brockovich* does not qualify as politically minded ecocinema because "by the end of the film, the contamination of soil, water, and human life that should have remained the focus of the narrative is upstaged by the individual courage and heroism of the main character" (2010, 48). There is no doubt a good deal of truth to this critique, but it should not stop us from seeing the potential value of a film that uses melodramatic and/or emotionally uplifting narrative strategies.

37. Fiction films are almost always shot out of sequence. Their shooting schedule follow the needs of production, determined by needs intrinsic to the script, location constraints, availability of actors, and availability of special equipment.

38. The film's fictional island of "Isle de Charles Doucet"—known to its residents as the Bathtub—was inspired by several isolated and independent fishing communities threatened by erosion, hurricanes, and rising sea levels in Louisiana's Terrebonne Parish, most notably the rapidly eroding Isle de Jean Charles.

39. See, for example, Bradshaw (2012) and Robey (2012).

40. See, for example, Hackett (2013) and Brown (2013).

41. Hume explores the paradox of tragedy in his "Of Tragedy" ([1793] 1965).

42. Plantinga develops his notion of an emotional spillover-effect with reference to psychologist Dolf Zillman's *Exitation Transfer Theory* (1983).

43. Collapsing the boundary between Hushpuppy and her animals in this scene of *Beasts of the Southern Wild* is not without its representational risks. As Graham Huggan and Helen Tiffin have observed, "human individuals and cultures at various times have been and are treated 'like animals' by dominant groups" and that "animal metaphors and animal categorizations frequently [have been] deployed to justify exploitation and objectification, slaughter and enslavement" compromises any serious consideration of the status of the animal (2010, 135).

NOTES TO CHAPTER 4

1. For an overview of research work on critical animal studies, see Nocella et al. (2013).

2. In the words of the Canadian sociologist John Sorenson, critical animal studies "is part of the contemporary animal rights movement and supports a range of diverse tactics, including direct action to rescue animals, civil disobedience, and vegan education" (2014, xxi).

3. Herman turns to enactivism and the work of Andy Clark (2010), Shaun Gallagher (2005), and Alva Noë (2004), although he does not really incorporate enactivist insights in his readings of graphic narratives in the second part of the article (Herman 2011).

4. In *The Companion Species Manifesto* (2003) and *When Species Meet* (2008) Haraway makes the claim that some species—in particular humans and dogs—are companion species in the sense that they are bonded in "significant otherness."

5. See Hal Herzog's *Some We Love, Some We Hate, Some We Eat* (2011) for another highly insightful book-length study on our complex emotional relationships to various animals.

6. For philosophical, political, and legal approaches to animal rights, see Singer (1975) and Sunstein and Nussbaum (2004). Charles Darwin's *Expression of the Emotions in Man and Animals* (1872) already showed awareness of the continuity between human and nonhuman cognition. As Marc Bekoff, Colin Allen, and Gordon Burghardt point out in their introduction to *The Cognitive*

Animal (2002), Darwin "systematically set out to show that the gap between humans and other animals was smaller than previously thought, and even more important, how the gap could be bridged by natural selection and sufficient time. Darwin's notebooks from the 40 years preceding *The Descent of Man* showed how influenced he was by the similarities of monkeys and apes to human beings" (x). For analyses of Darwin's influence on Anglophone literature, see Gottschall (2005) and Richter (2011).

7. Cognitive ethology was founded by the zoologist Donald Griffin in the late 1970s. It is a rapidly growing interdisciplinary field of science that is attracting much attention from researchers in numerous and diverse disciplines, including those interested in animal welfare. See, for example, Cheney and Seyfarth (1990); Ristau (1991); Griffin (1992); Allen and Bekoff (1997); Bekoff and Allen (1997); and Bekoff and Jamieson (1996).

8. For a detailed study of empathy in human and nonhuman animals, see De Waal (2009). For critical animal studies perspectives on the use of animals in scientific experiments, see McCance (2013) and Sorenson (2014).

9. On our entangled empathetic relationship with animals, see also Gruen (2015).

10. For ecocritical approaches to the representation of animals in literature and film, see, for example, Armbruster (2013), Garrard (2011a), Hediger (2013), Huggan and Tiffin (2010), Tuur and Tonnesen (2014), Welling (2009), Welling and Kapel (2012), and a 2010 special issues of the journal *Safundi* on "Animal Studies and Ecocriticism" edited by Dana Phillips. See also Cary Wolfe (2003, 2006), whose philosophical work on animals and posthumanism has been quite influential in ecocritical thought. For a collection of essays located at the intersection of critical animal studies and media studies, see Almira and Cole (2015). For an argument on animal compassion as trans-species entanglement from a posthumanist perspective, see Chiew (2014).

11. Balcombe notes that the bat mothers also use their sense of smell in order to find their young (2010, 10).

12. As Thom van Dooren and Deborah Bird Rose have noted, "ethographies invite readers into a sense of curiosity about the intimate particularities of others' ways of life: how they hunt or reproduce, how they relate to and make sense of their particular place" (2016, 9).

13. For an astute criticism of the considerable danger of unreflected, crude, or chauvinistic anthropomorphism in scientific research, see also Louise Barrett's *Beyond the Brain* (2011).

14. For additional explorations of the rich and varied uses of anthropomorphism, see the contributions to Lorraine Daston and Gregg Mitman's edited volume *Thinking with Animals* (2005).

15. In *Regarding Life*, Belinda Smaill points out that in recent years the representation of animals in documentary film is becoming "markedly more complex and multilayered," including "a range of wildlife natural history film and television, advocacy documentary, avant-garde nonfiction and developments in new media" (2016, 2).

16. A 2010 fMRI study conducted by Massimo Filippi and colleagues suggests that there are significant differences in brain activity among omnivores, vegetarians, and vegans who are exposed to images of human and animal suffering. The authors conclude that "empathy toward non conspecifics has different neural representation among individuals with different feeding habits, perhaps reflecting different motivational factors and beliefs" (2010).

17. In a parallel emotional response, the empathizing person feels the same kind of response as the person she empathizes with (for example, fear if she perceives the person to be afraid). In a complementary emotional response, the empathizing person reacts with an emotion that complements the perceived emotion. For example, a person might feel afraid when she senses that the other person is very angry.

18. Foer's book even turned some vegetarians into vegans. For one of the best-known autobiographical accounts, see actress Natalie Portman's 2010 article "Jonathan Safran Foer's *Eating Animals* Turned Me Vegan" in the *Huffington Post*.

19. The authors speculate that these results may nevertheless be influenced by their decision to use dogs for their experiment, precisely because they enjoy a special status in the eyes

and hearts of many Americans and other western cultures. They refer to Scott Plous's "similarity hypothesis" (1993), which suggests that humans show greater empathy for animals that are perceived as closer and more similar to them, regardless of whether their depictions are anthropomorphized or not.

20. On dogs in film and other media, see McLean (2014), McMahon and Lawrence (2015), and Cudworth and Jensen (2016). On the history of the representation of animal agency in American literature, see Susan McHugh (2011). Films like Lasse Hallström's *Hachi: A Dog's Tale* (2009) and Steven Spielberg's *Warhorse* (2011), which center on suffering, nonhuman protagonists, have been commercial successes, but they are by far outnumbered by films in which such animals seem virtually untouchable, regardless of what happens to the humans around them.

21. On documentary wildlife film, see Mitman (1999) and Bousé (2000). For a more recent consideration of the genre in relation to ecocinema studies, see Rust (2014).

22. In the film, Dr. John Potter from the Tropical Marine Science Institute in Singapore reinforces the intrinsic value of dolphins by pointing to their ability to respond to American Sign Language and connect with humans on an emotional level.

23. On the emotional lives of animals, see Balcombe (2006) and Bekoff (2003, 2010).

24. It should be noted that the film also addresses itself to Japanese audiences who consume dolphin meat, warning them of the fact that they might put themselves and their children at risk. Because of the high content of mercury in their prey, consuming dolphins might lead to mercury poisoning. See Walker (2015) and Murray and Heumann (2014) on this point as well as on the film's use of animal rights discourses.

25. Smaill observes that *The Cove*'s rhetorical arc supports "a binarisation between the West and the non-West. Japanese individuals are, for the most part, represented by physically and verbally aggressive fishermen, evasive and wary officials or self-interested representatives on the IWC [International Whaling Commission]" (2014, 114). Walker recounts that "in academic settings, conversations [about the film] have concentrated on whether the depiction of the [Japanese] coastal fishermen in this US film is ethnocentric, anti-Japanese or even racist" (2015, 181).

26. On the effects of the film on dolphin fishing in Taiji, see Masters (2009), O'Barry (2009, 2011), and Murray and Heumann (2014).

27. Recent research suggests that preexisting knowledge does indeed modulate emotional responses to a fictional narrative considerably. See Chow et al. (2014).

28. In their critique of the ideological underpinnings of the film, Nash and Sutherland note that *Gorillas in the Mist* "addresses the moral relationships between humans and animals in carefully selected visual images. Whenever gorillas appear in the film, they are portrayed as natural, pure, clean, loving, non-violent and innocent. They never once do anything cruel to each other or to humans. People, on the other hand, are depicted as destructive, violent, selfish, egotistical, dirty and disdainful, or at best oblivious to nature. The symbolic message is of nature (animals: gorillas) as morally pure and culture (humans, both from developed and underdeveloped countries) as morally corrupt. In this tragic encounter between nature and culture, only Dian Fossey stands out as a heroine" (1991, 114).

29. The Batwa are one-dimensionally represented as antagonists in the film. As Ingram points out, Fossey's hostile and racist attitude toward the local African population "may be interpreted as arrogant and colonialist, but it is also motivated by righteous indignation and a desire for justice for the gorillas" (2000, 133). Ingram also reminds us of the fact that Fossey's swiftly deteriorating relationship with the locals led to her replacement as head of her research center, a development that the film omits.

30. For a number of examples of such nonhuman narrators in literary traditions outside the United States, see Lars Bernaerts et al. (2014). On literary nonhuman agency more generally, see Susan McHugh (2009, 2011).

31. One such potential exception has been reported by the cognitive ethologist Irene Pepperberg who, after years of working with the parrot Alex, gave the bird a grape instead of a nut and found herself confronted with the following demand: "Want a nut. N-U-T." The animal never

had learned to spell words. On other occasions, he would use human speech to talk to another parrot at the research center, demanding that he speak more clearly or to be more precise in his responses. This points to some degree of understanding and conscious use of human language by a nonhuman animal. On this issue, see Warter (2015).

32. Burns mentions Rachel Carson as an example of a writer whose nonfiction work "attained greater naturalistic accuracy and more consistently avoided anthropomorphizing" (2002, 339) than earlier animal stories by Ernest Thompson Seton and Charles G. D. Roberts.

33. Stein's bestselling novel opens with its canine first-person narrator lying on the kitchen floor in "a puddle of [his] own urine" (1), and waiting for his owner to come home. "Gestures are all I have," he explains to the reader, "sometimes they must be grand in nature. . . . I have no words I can rely on because, much to my dismay, my tongue was designed long and flat and loose, and therefore, is a horribly ineffective tool . . . for making complicated and polysyllabic sounds that can be linked to form sentences" (1). While that may be the case, the long and flat and loose tongue clearly is no obstacle to forming highly complicated and polysyllabic thoughts in human language. The (self-)ironic tone notwithstanding, this is yet another human in animal guise with a slightly altered perceptive apparatus. The dog may not be used allegorically here, but its look at the world is nevertheless indistinguishable from that of a clever human, cueing readers' allegiance much in the way a human first-person narrator would. For a critical discussion of canine first-person narrators, see Harel (2013).

34. See chapter 5 of Caracciolo's *Strange Narrators in Contemporary Fiction* (2016) for an astute reading of Andrej Zaniewski's novella *Rat* (1994), which attempts to capture the existence of a rat "from the rat's own perspective," foregrounding the "animal's embodied consciousness" and "putting the reader in contact with an animal body—its size, sensorimotor affordances, and (as we will see) its often disturbing needs and deeds" (Caracciolo 2016, 195).

35. For an overview of different modes of representing animal minds in narrative film, see Porter (2010).

36. On this point, see also Freeman and Merskin (2016).

37. Malamud mentions YouTube videos of dressed-up pets and major Hollywood productions "including stars such as Lassie, Flipper, Old Yeller, Sounder, Elsa, Rin Tin Tin, and Francis the talking mule" and "monstrous others" such as "King Kong, the shark in *Jaws* . . . and Hitchcock's *Birds*" (2012, 75).

38. Disney's animation film is an adaptation of *Bambi: Eine Lebensgeschichte aus dem Walde* (1923) by the Austrian writer Felix Salten. On the depiction of animals and nature more generally in Disney animation, see Whitley (2012).

39. Ralph Lutts has used the terms *Bambi complex, Bambi factor,* and *Bambi syndrome* to denote the deeply sympathetic attitudes toward deer and wildlife more generally that were cued by the film (1992, 161). Lutts is highly critical of the "sentimental" view of nature that many viewers adopted after seeing the film, but that this happened at all gives us an idea of the emotional power of an animated film that aligns viewers with a nonhuman character that can express his thoughts and feelings. On the "Bambi syndrome" and the film's impacts on attitudes toward hunting in the United States, see also chapter 9 in Cartmill (1996).

40. On the film's use of motion-capture technology, see Yacov Freedman (2012).

41. On the role of anthropomorphism in the narrative strategies of *WALL-E*, see Whitley (2012) and Weik von Mossner (2014c). Research by Gazzola et al. (2007) on viewers' brain activity during the perception of robotic movements suggests that it is not only anthropomorphism that allows the vivid simulation of WALL-E's motions and emotions.

42. Heise notes that the nonhuman protagonists of animated film cannot be reduced to anthropomorphic fantasies since "even in those cases when animals, plants, or objects behave like humans, their bodies quite often do not. Animated bodies, human and nonhuman, are notorious for their seemingly infinite ability to expand, contract, stretch, bulge, flatten, implode, explode, fragment, and yet return to their original shapes" (2014, 304). Such capacities differentiate them in quite obvious ways from actually existing humans.

NOTES TO CHAPTER 5

1. I have discussed Murray Smith's (1995) differentiation between alignment and allegiance in chapter 3.

2. The scientist-turned-filmmaker Randy Olson suggests that most scientists "do not have enough comprehension of narrative and how it works" and that this constitutes a serious problem in science communication (2015, 8).

3. For an exploration of visual communication of science findings, see Dobrin and Morey (2009) and Wilson (2000).

4. Beck's *World at Risk* focuses on three kinds of global risks in particular: climate change, the financial system, and "transnational suicide terrorism" (2009, 9). In Beck's view, these are three different "'logics' of global risks" (9) that together shape the world risk society.

5. See, for example, Hulme (2009), Leiserowitz (2004), Posner (2004), and Reusswig (2004a, 2004b).

6. On this point, see also Marshall (2014).

7. As an informal scientific term, the *Anthropocene* denotes a geological epoch that follows the Holocene, an epoch that is marked by a new scale of human activity and agency. Those who are interested in the social and cultural dimensions of the Anthropocene tend to look not only at its present challenges but also at its potential risks for ecosystems and humans alike. On the importance of climate change to this new era and the inequalities and vulnerabilities is creates or exacerbates, see Chakrabarty (2009).

8. On the complex relationship between environmental literature and science, see Heise (2015).

9. Based on the scientific literature on climate change, *Six Degrees* is organized into six chapters, with each chapter describing the possible impacts at a specific average temperature, starting with a rise of one degree and ending at a rise of six degrees Celsius. Lynas acknowledges that he "would be foolish to expect these predictions to come true in any literal sense" (2007, xxii).

10. American documentary films focusing on climate change include Davis Guggenheim's *An Inconvenient Truth* (2006), Michael Nash's *Climate Refugees* (2010), Jon Shenk's *The Island President* (2011), and Jeff Orlowski's *Chasing Ice* (2012). I have written about these films elsewhere (Weik von Mossner 2012b, 2014b, 2014g, 2015, 2017).

11. For an overview of research work on irony in cognitive science, see Gibbs and Colston (2007).

12. House Bill 819 is an actual law that bans state agencies from reporting that sea-level rise is accelerating. It states that future sea level rise rates "shall only be determined using historical data, and these data shall be limited to the time period following the year 1900. Rates of seas-level rise may be extrapolated linearly." The law was passed by the North Carolina senate in June 2012.

13. Cosmic irony is an irony of fate. It builds on the idea that fate, destiny, or a god controls and toys with human hopes and expectations.

14. *The Age of Stupid* is a British documentary-feature hybrid that combines six documentary film strands with a fictional dystopian frame narrative in which an old archivist looks back to the years up to 2009, wondering how humanity could be so stupid as to ignore the risks associated with climate change. For an analysis of the film that also takes into account the findings of Rachel Howell's 2011 reception study on the film, see Weik von Mossner (2013).

15. The publisher indicates the genre on the book's dustcover.

16. While narrators can be experiencers, as Phelan has noted (2001), this is not the case for the Chinese narrator of *The Collapse of Western Civilization*, who has not experienced anything that he describes; he has just learned about it from various historical sources.

17. *Cli-fi* is a relatively recent term that was first used by the journalist Dan Bloom and that since has become regularly used to refer to novels that deal with issues of global warming and climate change. Such novels do not have to be speculative or dystopian, but they often are. For an overview on climate change fiction, see Johns-Putra (2015). See also Trexler (2015).

18. On science fiction's environmentalist potential, see also Murphy (2001) and Otto (2012). I will return to this issue in chapter 6 when I discuss ecotopian fiction.

19. For a discussion of climate risk in *Things We Didn't See Coming,* see Mehnert (2014). For a discussion of the depiction risks of the Anthropocene, including climate change, in *The Great Bay,* see Weik von Mossner (2014h).

20. Mayer differentiates between the "narrative of catastrophe" and the "narrative of antici-pation" within the genre of climate fiction. Novels such as Barbara Kingsolver's *Flight Behavior* (2012) or Susan Gaines's *Carbon Dreams* (2001) belong to the latter category because they remain at the level of anticipation, focusing "on the moment of uncertainty in the present when aware-ness of the risk figures prominently and controversially in a culture, but has not yet led to a catas-trophe" (Mayer 2014, 26). Narratives of catastrophe tend to be set in dystopian futures, allowing readers to experience imaginatively what it would be like to live through the disasters that might be the result of unmitigated climate change. Such narratives, however, are almost always also nar-ratives of risk, and therefore anticipation, since they tend to create new, additional risks that have not materialized in addition to those that already have, risks that are discussed controversially in the future culture. For other discussions of climate change novels, see Goodbody (2014), Heise (2008, 2015), Horn (2014), and S. Slovic (2015).

21. The other point that is interesting about the passage is that it demonstrates that physical experience can trigger memories. It is Tierwater's stepping into the floodwater and the sounds caused by his movements that trigger his memory of the hurricane he lived through as a child.

22. Hurricane Donna affected the East Coast of the United States in 1960. The first major hurricane of the season, it made landfall on September 10, 1960, near Marathon, Florida, with winds of 130 mph, killing thirteen people and leading to severe property damage and coastal flooding.

23. In Suvin's view, science fiction breaks the rules of our habituated understanding of a certain environment by introducing "a strange newness" or what he calls "*novum*" into the story-world (1979, 4). The result, in the words of Carl Freedman, is "an alternative fictional world that . . . [does not] take our mundane environment for granted" (2000, 16–17). On the use of cognitive estrangement in environmental science fiction, see Otto (2012).

24. Raffaella Baccolini and Tom Moylan explain that "unlike the 'typical' eutopian narrative with a visitor's guided journey through a utopian society which leads to a comparative response that indicts the visitor's own society, the dystopian text usually begins directly in the terrible new world," letting the reader slowly find out what happened to make it so terrible (2003, 5).

25. For an enlightening and balanced documentary film on the history of the Earth Libera-tion Front (ELF) and the U.S. government's decision to classify the acts of the ELF as eco-terror-ism, see Marshall Curry's *If a Tree Falls* (2013).

26. Not only do big-budget feature films often have to make concessions when it comes to environmentalist content in order to make a profit at the box office, they are also notoriously wasteful during the production, distribution, and exhibition phase. For detailed analysis of the ecological footprint of films, see Bozak (2012). For a critical discussion of the concessions that popular films have to make on the level of content, see Ingram (2000), Murray and Heumann (2009), Willoquet-Maricondi (2010), and Ivahkiv (2013).

27. For a detailed discussion of Hillcoat's *The Road,* see Weik von Mossner (2014f).

28. I have discussed the consequential nature of nonfiction discourse with reference to an argument by Dirk Eitzen (2005) in Chapters 2, 3, and 4 of the book.

29. *Box Office Mojo,* accessed November 15, 2015. http://boxofficemojo.com/genres/chart/?id =environment.htm.

30. *Box Office Mojo,* accessed November 15, 2015. http://boxofficemojo.com/genres/chart/?id =controversy.htm.

31. Davis Guggenheim's *An Inconvenient Truth* was only released in May 2006, more than a year after the release of *The Day After Tomorrow.* Many commentators have speculated on *The Day After Tomorrow*'s effect on the global success of Guggenheim's documentary. Fact is that

Guggenheim reuses some of the spectacular computer-animated footage from the opening of Emmerich's blockbuster showing Antarctica. It is an unusual choice for a nonfiction film that demonstrates the connection between the two filmmakers.

32. Reusswig (2004b) gives the following information about the five studies: all but the American study were based on questionnaires. The American study made use of a web-based survey. Two studies (Reusswig et al and Lowe et al) also used focus groups. The size of the sampling was N = 1118 (only filmgoers) for Reusswig et al's study in Germany, N = 384 (only filmgoers) for Aoyagi-Usui's study in Japan, N = 301 for Lowe et al's study in the UK, N = 200 (only filmgoers) for Balmford et al's study in the UK, and N = 529 (filmgoers & general public) for Leiserowitz's study in the U.S.

33. The screen-filling American flag not only eases the cut from animation to partial animation combined with life action, it also tells us clearly that this is going to be a story about the U.S. The rest of the world only exists as a cipher in Emmerich's film, despite its attempts to add a global dimension through the inclusion of a few scenes in Ireland, Japan, and India.

34. For a cognitive perspective on the emotional effects of film music see Jeff Smith, "Movie Music as Moving Music: Emotion, Cognition, and the Film Score" (1999).

35. For detailed accounts of melodrama in film narratives, see Robert Lang (1989), Mercer and Shingler (2004) and Linda Williams (1998). For an interesting discussion of the function of melodrama in disaster films see Kakoudaki (2002).

36. For a detailed explanation of the function of the North Atlantic Conveyor Belt and the danger of its potential slowing down or stalling, see Rahmstorf et al. (2015).

37. In chapter 1 and 2, I have explained the phenomenon with reference to neuroscientific research on embodied simulation (Keysers et al. 2004) and Currie's notion that we can have "empathy with objects" (2012).

38. Even as that sounds considerable, Leiserowitz notes that "relative to other news stories, global warming is a rarely reported issue" (2004, 34). At the time when he collected his data, "the Abu Ghraib prison scandal had in turn more than 10 times the coverage of *The Day After Tomorrow*" (34) and thus 100 times the news coverage of the 2001 *IPCC Report*.

39. In their essay on "Millennial Ecology" (1996), Jimmie Killingsworth and Jaqueline Palmer make clear that strategic exaggeration is in fact a typical feature of apocalyptical environmental narratives since Rachel Carson's *Silent Spring*. If the "predicted devastation is extreme in the apocalyptic narrative," they argue, "then the change in consciousness of political agenda recommended by the narrator is correspondingly extreme or radical" (41). In the author's view, such exaggeration is in fact required in order to shock people into awareness and bring about social change. From this perspective, holding apocalyptical narratives to their predictions simply misses the point because it fails to recognize the rhetorical strategies of such narratives.

40. The Japanese study, which was conducted by Midori Aoyagi-Usui, has remained unpublished, but Reusswig reports in his overview that Japanese interviewees actually perceived abrupt climate change scenarios as *less* likely after seeing the film, while showing at the same time a higher motivation to take individual action to prevent it (2004, 2).

41. Mann is one of the coauthors in a study that was led by Rahmstorf and published in *Nature Climate Change* (Rahmstorf et. al 2015). Rahmstorf himself is quoted in the same *Washington Post* article as saying that "the fact that a record-hot planet Earth coincides with a record-cold northern Atlantic is quite stunning. There is strong evidence—not just from our study—that this is a consequence of the long-term decline of the Gulf Stream System, i.e. the Atlantic ocean's overturning circulation AMOC, in response to global warming" (quoted in Mooney 2015). Mooney goes on to assert that "This won't lead to anything remotely like *The Day After Tomorrow* (which was indeed based—quite loosely—on precisely this climate scenario). But if the trend continues, there could be many consequences, including rising seas for the U.S. East Coast and, possibly, a difference in temperature overall in the North Atlantic and Europe" (2015). For other media coverage of the issue, see Elena Nichols (2015), Simons (2015) and Grenoble (2015).

42. For a study of the long-term impacts of climate change communications on individuals' attitudes and behavior, see Howell (2014).

43. On Carson's use of the pastoral trope in the opening of *Silent Spring,* see also Garrard (2011).

44. In *Imagining Extinction* (2016), Heise argues that extinction narratives frequently rely on the template of the elegy as they nostalgically look back to a better time when animal species were plentiful (13). Boyle's novel participates in that tradition while, at the same time, ironizing it.

45. Monica Hughes, herself a writer of dystopian fiction for young adults, has argued that such texts must retain hope in order to be attractive to young readers and socially responsible (2003, 157). Kay Sambell sees a problematic tension between this literature's intention to "caution young readers about the probable dire consequences of current human behavior" and their impulse "to counsel hope and present the case for urgent social change" (2003, 163).

NOTES TO CHAPTER 6

1. In an interview with Jon Christensen, Jan Goggans, and Ursula Heise for the magazine *Boom,* Robinson explains that he has "read all of Muir now and studied his life" (2014).

2. Callenbach's *Ecotopia* (1975) is a classical utopia in the sense that it aims to describe a perfect, "blue-print" society that has formed after the Pacific Northwest has ceded from the rest of the United States to found the ecological sustainable country of Cascadia. Set in 1999, the narrator is William Weston, a (fictional) American journalist who is at first skeptical about this alternative society but quickly learns to see its many advantages. Six years later, Callenbach published the prequel, *Ecotopia Emerging* (1981), which describes the political process that led to the formation of an independent Cascadia. Both texts were influential on American counterculture and the environmentalist movement in the late 1970s and thereafter. For critical discussions of Callenbach's novels, see De Geus (1999), Katerberg (2008), and Otto (2012).

3. This is in keeping with Vittorio Gallese's claim that embodied simulation is a "nonconscious, pre-reflective functional mechanism of the brain–body system, whose function is to model objects, agents and events" (2014, 3–4).

4. For an influential text that relies on a Freudian/Lacanian notion of desire in its discussion of utopian thought, see Fredric Jameson's *Archaeologies of the Future* (2005).

5. Horkheimer and Adorno's chapter on "The Culture Industry," subtitled "Enlightenment as Mass Deception," is part of their book *Dialectic of Enlightenment* ([1944] 2007). The inherent danger of the culture industry, they argue, is the cultivation of false psychological needs that can only be met and satisfied by the products of capitalism.

6. Ehrlich's *The Population Bomb* was an influential nonfiction book that described the detrimental future repercussions of a rapid worldwide population growth. The authors of the *Limits to Growth* study, Donella Meadows, Dennis Meadows, Jørgen Randers, and William Behrens III, used computer simulation to predict the future consequences of exponential economic and population growth with finite resource supplies.

7. Deep ecology is an ecological philosophy that recognizes an inherent worth in all living beings without privileging human life over other forms of life. The term was coined by the Norwegian philosopher Arne Næss. Bioregionalism is a concept that recognizes the importance of naturally defined areas, called bioregions, over "artificial" boundaries. These bioregions are defined by natural features such as watershed boundaries as well as by soil and terrain characteristics.

8. From its inception, utopian writing has been concerned with notions of citizenship and the creation of a better society. Early texts such as Thomas More's *Utopia* (1516) and Tommaso Campanella's *The City of the Sun* (1602) envision new societal formations that ensure the material and spiritual well-being of its members. Political theorist Marius de Geus has argued that More's text must be considered as the first ecological utopia because it "gives an outline for an ecologi-

cally responsible society, albeit of an authoritarian and puritan kind that would not be advocated by contemporary greens" (1999, 70). Later ecotopian texts include Henry David Thoreau's *Walden* (1854), William Morris's *News from Nowhere* (1890), Ebenezer Howard's *Garden Cities of Tomorrow* (1902), B. F. Skinner's *Walden Two* (1948), and Callenbach's *Ecotopia*.

9. On environmental justice issues, see chapter 3.

10. Dobson differentiates liberal, republican, and post-cosmopolitan citizenship as follows: Liberal citizenship focuses on rights and entitlements. It is contractual, exercised in the public sphere, virtue-free, and territorial in nature. Republican citizenship, by contrast, focuses on duties and responsibilities. It also is contractual, exercised in the public sphere, and territorial, but it emphasizes (masculine) virtues. Post-cosmopolitan citizenship emphasizes both duties and responsibilities, and it is enacted in both the public and the private spheres. Rather than "masculine" virtues if emphasizes "feminine" virtues (such as care). Unlike both liberal and republican citizenship, it is non-territorial (Dobson 2003).

11. The postcolonial scholar Rob Nixon has used the term "slow violence" (2011, 2) for the, often oblique, relationship between those who are responsible for the lion's share of global CO_2 emissions and those who, in some other part of the world, are the victims of a changing climate.

12. I have discussed Hoffman's argument in more detail in chapters 3 and 4.

13. Passed by the U.S. Congress in October 2001, shortly after the terrorist attacks of 9/11, The USA Patriot Act is a piece of legislation that widens the definition of "domestic terrorism" and greatly extends the authority of the government's ability to conduct secret surveillance and to search and arrest suspects.

14. As Tom Moylan has noted, Kevin's emotionality and "openness to diversity and equality" make him an unusual science fiction character in a time that was dominated by cyberpunk (1995, 2).

15. As Huhndorf has shown, jungle landscapes have often been used as a place where idealized masculinities that have been softened by civilization can be tested or rediscovered (2001, 104). Molloy points out that the Pandoran jungle participates in this tradition while also undermining it, since "in Avatar the nature space does not remain a hostile force and its protection becomes a key motivation for Jake to lead the Na'vi into battle with the corporate security forces" (2013, 186).

16. Sideris notes that studies with virtual body transfers show a strong sense of ownership and identification with one's avatar body well after one has "returned" to one's own body (2010, 465).

17. Yacov Freedman explains that the use of motion-capture technology should not really be considered a form of animation and reminds us that studios have repeatedly attempted "to position motion capture as an extension of the actor. Twentieth Century Fox launched a full-fledged campaign to nab an Oscar nomination for actress Zoe Saldana, whose performance was recorded entirely via motion capture" (2012, 46)

18. On this point, see also Easterlin (2012) and Kaplan (1992).

19. And yet, the designers were very careful when deciding on the level of cognitive estrangement. Pandora's enormous trees have familiar-looking trunks, branches, and leaves, although it is suggested that due to the moon's lower gravity, the proportions are different.

20. For a consideration of the neuroscience of *Avatar*, see Hutton (2010).

21. Several books have been published on the imaginative flora and fauna of Pandora, some of them coordinated with the release of the film to give those who desire to learn more about the moon's complex ecology an opportunity to do so. Wilhelm and Mathison's *Avatar: A Confidential Report on the Biological and Social History of Pandora* (2009) was published together with the release of the film and includes a remarkable combination of simple "facts" about Pandora's ecology and an "ADR Weapons Guide" that details every firearm used in the film. Popular science journalist and science fiction author Stephen Baxter has published a book on *The Science of Avatar* (2012) that purports to explain the science behind the film and also offers a brief "scientific"

explanation for the Earth's ecocide at the time when the film is set, framing it as "sudden climate collapse."

22. For a collection of essays that consider the religious significance of the film and its representation of nature spirituality, see Taylor (2013). For a critical discussion of the film's depiction of ecocentric identification, see Bergthaller (2012).

23. Molloy has sharply criticized both the element of control involved in the bond between the Na'vi and the nonhumanoid animals of Pandora and the fact that feeling those animals' feelings does not seem to keep the Na'vi from killing or eating them. She points out that "the narrative goes as far as to normalize violence toward animals as part of the Na'vi customs and, in doing so, appropriates a western fantasy of native-animal relations to maintain the moral legitimacy of such actions" (2013, 188).

24. I discuss this issue in more detail in chapter 2.

25. On the role of music in viewer attention and emotional response, see Jeff Smith (1999), Tim Smith (2014, 2015), and Hoeckner et al. (2011). For fMRI evidence of music's modulating activity in brain structures that are known to be crucially involved in emotion, see Koelsch (2014).

26. In *Gaia: A New Look at Life on Earth* ([1979] 2000) and several subsequent book publications (2007; 2009), Lovelock proposed that the Earth's biosphere forms a complex interacting system that must be thought of as a single organism.

27. For a discussion of "resistant spectatorship" to *Avatar,* conceived "as a form of not wishing to imagine a fictional world in which presumptions or values deeply held by the viewers must be thought of as otherwise," see Flory (2013).

28. On the relationship between 3-D technology and viewer immersion, see Zacks (2015, 264–68).

29. In Plantinga's definition, artifact emotions "take as their object the film as a constructed artifact, whereas meta emotions "take as their object the spectator's own responses or the responses of other spectators" (2009a, 69).

30. The Greek term utopia is ambiguous in that it can mean both "good place" and "no place."

31. On the argument that utopian imaginings function mainly as an affective compensation during times of crisis, see also Jameson (2005, 232–33).

32. Adamson reports that "in eastern India, the Dongria Kondh tribe posted a YouTube video titled 'The Real Avatar' that narrates their (successful) battle to stop mining giant Vedanta Resources from siting a bauxite mine on their sacred mountain, Niyam Raja. At an Ecuadoran fundraising event posted on YouTube, Shuar, Achuar, and Waorani tribal members enter a movie theater decked out in their plumes, feathered crowns, and jewelry, then watch Avatar wearing 3-D glasses" (Adamson 2012, 154–55).

33. On Cameron's visit to Brazil, see also Barrionuevo (2010).

NOTES TO THE EPILOGUE

1. Erin James and Eric Morel's forthcoming book on *Ecocriticism and Narrative Theory* showcases a wide range of such critical investigations.

2. On the role of embodiment in players' engagement with videogames, see also Fahlenbrach and Schröter (2016).

3. On this point, see also Fromme (2007) and Ryan (2009).

4. On the history of media convergence, see Staiger and Hake (2009) and Tryon (2009).

5. Jenkins has suggested that such "transmedia storytelling represents a process where integral elements of a fiction get dispersed systematically across multiple delivery channels for the purpose of creating a unified and coordinated entertainment experience" (2006, 1), but in practice, such unification will hardly be possible. Different media require very different modes of

storytelling, but there are only very few people who are willing to engage with all of the of those delivery channels in order to finally find out what the story was all about.

6. Greg Smith notes that researchers have also "begun to use the modern empirical cognitivist toolbox to examine real-time gameplay, including fMRI, EEG, skin conductance, eye tracking, pupil size, heart rate and so on" (2013, 293). On immersion and presence in video games, see also McMahan (2003).

7. Experimental aesthetics, as Gallese defines it, is related to the larger field of neuroaesthetics, which "is committed to investigating the neural mechanisms underpinning humans' perceptual analysis of the formal visual features of art works and the explicit aesthetic judgment they report" (Gallese 2015, 2). For an overview of neuroaesthetics, see Dio Cinzia and Gallese (2009).

8. On the point of methodological differences and how they might be overcome, see Caracciolo and Hurlburt (2016).

BIBLIOGRAPHY

12 Angry Men. 1957. Directed by Sidney Lumet. United Artists.

1408. 2007. Directed by Mikael Håfström. Dimension Films.

2012. 2009. Directed by Roland Emmerich. Columbia Pictures.

Abdullah, Shaila. 2009. *Saffron Dreams.* Ann Arbor: Modern History Press.

Abram, David. 2014. "Afterword: The Commonwealth of Breath." In *Material Ecocriticism*, edited by Serenella Iovino and Serpil Oppermann, 301–12.Bloomington: University of Indiana Press.

Adamson, Joni. 2001. *American Indian Literature, Environmental Justice, and Ecocriticism.* Tucson: University of Arizona Press.

———. 2012. "Indigenous Literatures, Multinaturalism, and *Avatar:* The Emergence of Indigenous Cosmopolitics." *American Literary History* 24 (1): 143–62.

Adamson, Joni, Mei Mei Evans, and Rachel Stein, eds. 2002. *The Environmental Justice Reader: Politics, Poetics, and Pedagogy.* Tucson: University of Arizona Press.

The Age of Stupid. 2009. Directed by Franny Armstrong. Spanner Films.

Ahmed, Sarah. 2004. *The Cultural Politics of Emotion.* London: Routledge.

Alaimo, Stacy. 2010. *Bodily Natures: Science, Environment, and the Material Self.* Bloomington: Indiana University Press.

Alber, Jan, and Monika Fludernik, eds. 2010. *Postclassical Narratology: Approaches and Analyses.* Columbus: The Ohio State University Press.

Aldama, Frederick Luis, and Patrick Colm Hogan. 2014. *Conversation on Cognitive Cultural Studies.* Columbus: The Ohio State University Press.

Aldiss, Brian. 1962. *Hothouse.* New York: Faber and Faber.

Alexie, Sherman. 1996. Introduction to *Watershed,* by Percival Everett, vii–xii. Boston: Beacon.

Allen, Colin, and Marc Bekoff. 1997. *Species of Mind: The Philosophy and Biology of Cognitive Ethology.* Cambridge, MA: MIT Press.

Almiron, Núria, and Mathew Cole. 2015. "Introduction: The Convergence of Two Critical Approaches." In *Critical Animal and Media Studies: Communication for Nonhuman Animal*

Advocacy, edited by Núria Almiron, Mathew Cole, and Carrie P. Freeman, 1–9. New York: Routledge.

Amsterdam, Steven. 2009. *Things We Didn't See Coming.* London: Random House.

Anderson, Joseph D., and Barbara Fisher Anderson, eds. 2005. *Moving Image Theory: Ecological Considerations.* Carbondale: Southern Illinois University Press.

"An Elephant's Story: Gowdy Reflects on *The White Bone*" (radio broadcast). 2008. *Animal Voices.* http://animalvoices.ca/2008/01/29/an-elephants-story-gowdy-reflects-on-the-white-bone/.

Aoyagi-Usui, Midori. 2004. "*The Day After Tomorrow*: A Study on the Impact of a Global Warming Movie on the Japanese Public." National Institute for Environmental Studies (NIES) Working Paper (unpublished).

Apted, Michael. 1993. *A Conversation with Michael Apted.* New York: Columbia College, Department of Film and Video.

Armbruster, Karla. 2013. "What Do We Want from Talking Animals? Reflections on Literary Representations of Animal Voices and Minds." In *Speaking for Animals: Animal Autobiographical Writing,* edited by Margo DeMello, 17–33. New York: Routledge.

Avatar. 2009. Directed by James Cameron. 20th Century Fox.

Aziz-Zadeh, Lisa, and Antonio Damasio. 2008. "Embodied Semantics for Actions: Findings from Functional Brain Imaging." *Journal of Physiology–Paris* 102: 35–39.

Aziz-Zadeh, Lisa, and Stephen M. Wilson, Giacomo Rizzolatti, and Marco Iacoboni. 2006. "Congruent Embodied Representations for Visually Presented Actions and Linguistic Phrases Describing Actions." *Current Biology* 16 (18): 1818–23.

Babb, Sanora. 2004. *Whose Names Are Unknown.* Norman: University of Oklahoma Press.

Babe. 1995. Directed by Chris Noonan. Universal Pictures.

Bacci, Francesca, and David Melcher. 2011. "Editors' Introduction." In *Art and the Senses,* edited by Francesca Bacci and David Melcher, 1–8. New York: Oxford University Press.

Baccolini, Raffaella, and Tom Moylan. 2003. "Introduction: Dystopias and History." In *Dark Horizons: Science Fiction and the Dystopian Imagination,* edited by Raffaella Baccolini and Tom Moylan, 1–12. London: Routledge.

Bacigalupi, Paolo. 2015. *The Water Knife.* London: Orbit.

Backe, Hans-Joachim. 2014. "Greenshifting Games Studies: Arguments for an Ecocritical Approach to Digital Games." *First Person Scholar* (March 19). http://www.firstpersonscholar.com/greenshifting-game-studies/.

Bacon, Henry. 2011. "The Extent of Mental Completion of Films." *Projections* 5 (1): 31–49.

Balcombe, Jonathan. 2006. *Pleasurable Kingdom: Animals and the Nature of Feeling Good.* Basingstoke, UK: Palgrave Macmillan.

———. 2010. *Second Nature: The Inner Lives of Animals.* Basingstoke, UK: Palgrave Macmillan.

Ballard, J. G. (1962) 2008. *The Drowned World.* New York: Harper Perennial.

Balmford, Andrew, Percy FitzPatrick, Andrea Manica, Lesley Airey, Linda Birkin, Amy Oliver, and Judith Schleicher. 2004. "Hollywood, Climate Change, and the Public" *Science* 17: 1713.

Bambara, Toni Cade. 1980. *The Salt Eaters.* New York: Random House.

Bambi. 1942. Directed by David Hand. Walt Disney Productions.

Ban, Ki-moon. 2007. "Secretary-General's address to the IPCC upon the release of the Fourth Assessment Synthesis Report (November 17, 2007)."

Barad, Karen. 2007. *Meeting the Universe Halfway: Quantum Physics and the Entanglement of Matter and Meaning.* Durham, NC: Duke University Press.

Barker, Jennifer M. 2011. "Touch and the Cinematic Experience." In *Art and the Senses,* edited by Francesca Bacci and David Melcher, 149–60. New York: Oxford University Press.

Barrett, Louise. 2011. *Beyond the Brain: How Body and Environment Shape Animal and Human Minds.* Princeton, NJ: Princeton University Press.

Barrionuevo, Alexei. 2010. "Tribes of the Amazon Find an Ally Out of 'Avatar.'" *New York Times,* April 10. http://www.nytimes.com/2010/04/11/world/americas/11brazil.html?_r=0.

Barthes, Roland. 1974. *S/Z.* New York: Hill and Wang.

Batra, Nandita. 2003. "Dominion, Empathy, and Symbiosis Gender and Anthropocentrism in Romanticism." In *The ISLE Reader: Ecocriticism, 1993–2003,* edited by Michael P. Branch, 155–71. Athens: University of Georgia Press.

Baxter, Steven. 2012. *The Science of Avatar.* New York: Orbit.

Bayne, Tim. 2004. "Closing the Gap: Some Questions for Neurophenomenology." *Phenomenology and the Cognitive Sciences* 3 (4): 349–64.

Beasts of the Southern Wild. 2012. Directed by Benh Zeitlin. Fox Searchlight Pictures.

Beck, Ulrich. 2009. *World at Risk.* Cambridge, UK: Polity Press.

Bekoff, Marc. 2003. *Minding Animals: Awareness, Emotions, and Heart.* New York: Oxford University Press.

———. 2007. *The Emotional Lives of Animals: A Leading Scientist Explores Animal Joy, Sorrow, and Empathy—and Why They Matter.* Novato, CA: New World Library.

———. 2010. *The Animal Manifesto: Six Reasons for Expanding Our Compassion Footprint.* Novato, CA: New World Library.

Bekoff, Marc, and Colin Allen. 1997. "Cognitive Ethology: Slayers, Skeptics, and Proponents." In *Anthropomorphism, Anecdote, and Animals,* edited by Robert W. Mitchell, Nicholas S. Thompson, and H. Lyn Miles, 313–34. Albany: State University of New York Press.

Bekoff, Marc, Colin Allen, and Gordon Burghardt, eds. 2002. *The Cognitive Animal: Empirical and Theoretical Perspectives on Animal Cognition.* Cambridge, MA: MIT Press.

Bekoff, Marc, and Dale Jamieson, eds. 1996. *Readings in Animal Cognition.* Cambridge, MA: MIT Press.

Bennett, Jane. 2010. *Vibrant Matter: A Political Ecology of Things.* Durham, NC: Duke University Press.

———. 2014. "Of Material Sympathies, Paracelsus, and Whitman." In *Material Ecocriticism,* edited by Serenella Iovino and Serpil Oppermann, 239–50. Bloomington: Indiana University Press.

Benston, Kimberly W. 2009. "Experimenting at the Threshold: Sacrifice, Anthropomorphism, and the Aims of (Critical) Animal Studies." *PMLA* 124 (2): 548–55.

Bergthaller, Hannes. 2012. "A Sense of No-Place: *Avatar* and the Pitfalls of Ecocentric Identification." *Dislocations and Ecologies,* edited by Alexa Weik von Mossner and Christoph Irmscher. Special issue of the European Journal of English Studies 16 (2): 151–62

———. 2014. "Limits of Agency: Notes on the Material Turn from a System-Analytics Perspective." In *Material Ecocriticism,* edited by Serenella Iovino and Serpil Oppermann, 37–50. Bloomington: Indiana University Press.

Berila, Beth. 2010. "Engaging the Land/Positioning the Spectator: Environmental Justice Documentaries and Robert Redford's *The Horse Whisperer* and *A River Runs Through It.*" In *Fram-*

ing the World: Explorations in Ecocriticism and Film, edited by Paula Willoquet-Maricondi, 116–32. Charlottesville: University of Virginia Press.

Berlant, Lauren. 2008. *The Female Complaint: The Unfinished Business of Sentimentality in American Culture.* Durham, NC: Duke University Press.

Bernaerts, Lars, Marco Caracciolo, Luc Herman, and Bart Vervaeck. 2014. "The Storied Lives of Non-Human Narrators." *Narrative* 22 (1): 68–93.

Berns, Gregory. 2013. *How Dogs Love Us: A Neuroscientist and His Adopted Dog Decode the Canine Brain.* New York: Amazon New Harvest.

Best in Show. 2000. Directed by Christopher Guest. Warner Bros.

Bezdek, Matthew A., Richard J. Gerrig, William G. Wenzel, Jaemin Shin, Kathleen Pirog Revill, and Eric H. Schumacher. 2015. "Neural Evidence that Suspense Narrows Attentional Focus." *Neuroscience* 303: 338–45.

Bilandzic, Helena, and Rick Busselle. 2011. "Enjoyment of Films as a Function of Narrative Experience, Perceived Realism and Transportability." *Communications: The European Journal of Communication Research* 36: 29–50.

Birth of a Nation. 1915. Directed by D. W. Griffith. Epoch Producing Company.

Bloch, Ernst. 1986. *The Principle of Hope.* Translated by Neville Plaice, Stephen Plaice, and Paul Knight. Cambridge: The MIT Press.

Bolens, Guillemette. 2012. *The Style of Gestures: Embodiment and Cognition in Literary Narrative.* Baltimore: Johns Hopkins University Press.

Booth, Wayne. 1961. *Rhetoric of Fiction.* Chicago: The University of Chicago Press.

Bordwell, David. 2012. "The Viewer's Share: Models of Mind in Explaining Film." *David Bordwell's Website on Cinema.* Last modified May 2012. http://www.davidbordwell.net/essays/viewersshare.php.

Bordwell, David, Janet Staiger, and Kathleen Thompson. 1985. *The Classical Hollywood Cinema: Film Style and Mode of Production to 1960.* New York: Routledge.

Bordwell, David, and Kathleen Thompson. 2001. *Film Art: An Introduction,* 6th ed. New York: McGraw-Hill.

Bortolussi, Marisa, and Peter Dixon. 2003. *Psychonarratology: Foundations for the Empirical Study of Literary Response.* Cambridge: Cambridge University Press.

Bousé, Derek. 2000. *Wildlife Films.* Philadelphia: University of Pennsylvania Press.

Boyd, Brian. 2009. *On the Origins of Stories: Evolution, Cognition, and Fiction.* Cambridge, MA: Belknap Harvard.

Boyle, T. C. 2000. *A Friend of the Earth.* New York: Penguin.

Bozak, Nadia. 2012. *The Cinematic Footprint: Lights, Camera, Natural Resources.* New Brunswick, NJ: Rutgers University Press.

Bradshaw, Gay A., and Mary Watkins. 2006. "Trans-species Psychology: Theory and Praxis." *Spring Journal* 75: 69–94.

Bradshaw, Peter. 2012. Review of *Beasts of the Southern Wild,* directed by Benh Zeitlin. *The Guardian,* October 18. https://www.theguardian.com/film/2012/oct/18/beast-southern-wild-review.

Brereton, Pat. 2005. *Hollywood Utopia: Ecology in Contemporary American Cinema.* Bristol, UK: Intellect.

———. 2015. *Environmental Ethics and Film.* London: Routledge.

Brook, Daniel. 1998. "Environmental Genocide: Native Americans and Toxic Waste." *American Journal of Economics and Sociology* 57 (1): 105–13.

Brown, Jayna. 2013. "*Beasts of the Southern Wild*—The Romance of Precarity II." *Social Text,* September 27. http://socialtextjournal.org/beasts-of-the-southern-wild-the-romance-of-precarity-ii/.

Buell, Frederick. 2004. *From Apocalypse to Way of Life: Environmental Crisis in the American Century.* London: Routledge.

Buell, Lawrence. 1995. *The Environmental Imagination: Thoreau, Nature Writing, and the Formation of American Culture.* Cambridge, MA: Harvard University Press.

Bullard, Robert D. 1990. *Dumping in Dixie: Race, Class, and Environmental Quality.* Boulder, CO: Westview.

Buried. 2012. Directed by Rodrigo Cortés. Lionsgate.

Burns, Allan. 2002. "Extensions of Vision: The Representation of Non-Human Points of View." *Papers on Language and Literature: A Journal for Scholars and Critics of Language and Literature* 38: 339–50.

Burt, Jonathan. 2002. *Animals in Film.* London: Reaktion Books.

Busselle, Rick, and Helena Bilandzic. 2008. "Fictionality and Perceived Realism in Experiencing Stories: A Model of Narrative Comprehension and Engagement." *Communication Theory* 18: 255–80.

Callenbach, Ernest. 1975. *Ecotopia: The Notebooks and Reports of William Weston.* Berkeley, CA: Banyan Tree Books.

———. *Ecotopia Emerging.* 1981. Berkeley, CA: Banyan Tree Books.

Campanella, Tommaso. (1602) 2009. *The City of the Sun. Project Gutenberg.* http://www.gutenberg.org/files/2816/2816-h/2816-h.htm.

Caracciolo, Marco. 2011. "The Reader's Virtual Body: Narrative Space and Its Reconstruction." *Storyworlds* 3: 117–38.

———. 2013a. "Blind Reading: Toward an Enactivist Theory of the Reader's Imagination." In *Stories and Minds: Cognitive Approaches to Literary Narrative,* edited by Lars Bernaerts, Dirk de Geest, Luc Herman, and Bart Vervaeck, 81–106. Lincoln: University of Nebraska Press.

———. 2013b. "Embodiment at the Crossroads: Some Open Questions between Literary Interpretation and Cognitive Science." *Poetics Today* 34: 1–2.

———. 2014. *The Experientiality of Narrative: An Enactivist Approach.* Berlin: De Gryter.

———. 2015. "Playing Home: Videogame Experiences between Narrative and Ludic Interests." *Narrative* 23 (3): 231–50.

———. 2016. *Strange Narrators in Contemporary Fiction: Explorations in Readers' Engagement with Characters.* Lincoln: University of Nebraska Press.

Caracciolo, Marco, and Russell T. Hurlburt. 2016. *A Passion for Specificity: Confronting Inner Experience in Literature and Science.* Columbus: The Ohio State University Press.

Carmichael, Deborah A., ed. 2006. *The Landscape of Hollywood Westerns: Ecocriticism in an American Film Genre.* Salt Lake City: University of Utah Press.

Carroll, Joseph. 2004. *Literary Darwinism: Evolution, Human Nature, and Literature.* New York: Routledge.

Carroll, Noël. 1996. "Nonfiction film and Postmodern Skepticism." In *Post-Theory: Reconstructing Film Studies,* edited by David Bordwell and Noël Carroll, 283–305. Madison: University of Wisconsin Press.

———. 1999. "Film, Emotion, and Genre." In *Passionate Views: Film Cognition, and Emotion,* edited by Carl Plantinga and Greg M. Smith, 21–47. Baltimore: Johns Hopkins University Press.

———. 2003. *Engaging the Moving Image.* New Haven: Yale University Press.

Carroll, Noël, and William P. Seeley. 2013. "Cognitivism, Psychology and Neuroscience: Movies as Attentional Engines." In *Psychocinematics: Exploring Cognition at the Movies,* edited by Arthur Shimamura, 53–75. New York: Oxford University Press.

———. 2014. "Cognitive Theory and the Individual Film: The Case of *Rear Window.*" In *Cognitive Media Theory,* edited by Ted Nannicelli and Paul Alexander Taberham, 235–52. New York: Routledge.

Cars. 2006. Directed by John Lasseter. Buena Vista Pictures.

Carson, Rachel. 1962. *Silent Spring.* New York: Houghton Mifflin.

Cartmill, Matt. 1996. *A View to a Death in the Morning: Hunting and Nature Through History.* Cambridge, MA: Harvard University Press.

Cates, Diana Fritz. 2015. "Hope, Hatred and the Ambiguities of Utopic Longing." In *Hope and the Longing for Utopia: Futures and Illusions in Theology and Narrative,* edited by Daniel Boscaljon, 23–40. Cambridge, UK: James Clark and Co.

Chakrabarty, Dipesh. 2009. "The Climate of History: Four Theses." *Critical Inquiry* 35: 197–222.

Chasing Ice. 2012. Directed by Jeff Orlowski. Submarine Deluxe.

Chatman, Seymour. 1990. *Coming to Terms: The Rhetoric of Narrative in Fiction and Film.* Ithaca: Cornell University Press.

Chattah, Juan. 2015. "Film Music as Embodiment." In *Embodied Cognition and Cinema,* edited by Maarten Coëgnarts and Peter Kravanja, 81–113. Leuven: Leuven University Press.

Chatterjee, Anjan. 2013. *The Aesthetic Brain: How We Evolved to Desire Beauty and Enjoy Art.* New York: Oxford University Press.

Cheney, Dorothy L., and Robert M. Seyfarth. 1990. *How Monkeys See the World: Inside the Mind of Another Species.* Chicago: University of Chicago Press.

Chiew, Florence. 2014. "Posthuman Ethics with Cary Wolfe and Karen Barad: Animal Compassion as Trans-Species Entanglement." *Theory, Culture & Society* 31 (4): 51–69.

Chow, Ho Ming, Raymond A. Mar, Yisheng Xu, Siyuan Liu, Suraji Wagage, and Allen R. Braun. 2013. "Embodied Comprehension of Stories: Interactions between Language Regions and Modality-specific Neural Systems." *Journal of Cognitive Neuroscience* 26 (2): 279–95.

———. 2015. "Personal Experience with Narrated Events Modulates Functional Connectivity within Visual and Motor Systems during Story Comprehension." *Human Brain Mapping* 36 (4): 1494–505.

Christensen, Jon, Jan Goggans, and Ursula Heise. 2014. "Planet of the Future: The *Boom* Interview with Kim Stanley Robinson," edited by Jon Christensen and Kim Stanley Robinson. *Boom* 3 (4). http://www.boomcalifornia.com/2014/01/kim-stanley-robinson/.

Churchill, Ward, and Jim Vander Wall. 1988. *Agents of Repression: The FBI's Secret Wars Against the Black Panther Party and the American Indian Movement.* Boston: South End Press.

A Civil Action. 1998. Directed by Steven Zaillian. Touchstone Home Entertainment.

Clark, Andy. 2005. "Intrinsic Content, Active Memory and the Extended Mind." *Analysis* 65 (1): 1–11.

———. 2010. *Supersizing the Mind: Embodiment, Action, and Cognitive Extension.* New York: Oxford University Press.

Clark, Andy, and David J. Chalmers. 1998. "The Extended Mind." *Analysis* 58: 7–19.

Clay, Zanna, and Marco Iacoboni. 2011. "Mirroring Fictional Others." In *The Aesthetic Mind: Philosophy and Psychology,* edited by Elisabeth Schellekens and Peter Goldie, 313–30. New York: Oxford University Press.

Climate Refugees. 2010. Directed by Michael Nash. LA Think Tank.

Cohen, Anna-Lisa, Elliot Shavalian, and Moshe Rube. 2015. "The Power of the Picture: How Narrative Film Captures Attention and Disrupts Goal Pursuit." *PLoS ONE* 10 (12). doi:10.1371/journal.pone.0144493.

Collins, Susan. 2008. *The Hunger Games.* New York: Scholastic Press.

Colombetti, Giovanna. 2013. *The Feeling Body: Affective Science Meets the Enactive Mind.* Cambridge, MA: MIT Press.

The Colony. 2013. Directed by Jeff Renfroe. Entertainment One.

Cosgrove, Denis E. (1984) 1998. *Social Formation and Symbolic Landscape.* Madison: University of Wisconsin Press.

Coutrot, Antoine, Nathalie Guyader, Gelu Ionescu, and Alice Caplier. 2012. "Influence of Soundtrack on Eye Movements during Video Exploration." *Journal of Eye Movement Research* 5 (5): 1–10.

The Cove. 2009. Directed by Louie Psihoyos. Lionsgate.

Crane, Mary Thomas. 2000. *Shakespeare's Brain: Reading with Cognitive Theory.* Princeton, NJ: Princeton University Press.

Crichton, Michael. 2004. *State of Fear.* New York: Harper Collins.

Crick, Francis. 1994. "The Astonishing Hypothesis." *The Journal of Consciousness Studies* 1 (1): 10–16.

Cronon, William. 1996. "The Trouble with Wilderness." In *Uncommon Ground: Rethinking the Human Place in Nature,* edited by William Cronon, 69–90. New York: W. W. Norton & Company.

Cudworth, Erika, and Tracy Jensen. 2016. "Puppy Love? Animal Companions in the Media." In *Critical Animal Media Studies: Communication for Nonhuman Advocacy,* edited by Nuria Almiron and Matthew Cole, 185–202. New York: Routledge.

Currie, Gregory. 1999. "Narrative Desire." In *Passionate Views: Film, Cognition and Emotion,* edited by Carl Plantinga and Greg M. Smith, 183–99. Baltimore: Johns Hopkins University Press.

———. 2011. "Empathy for Objects." In *Empathy: Philosophical and Psychological Perspectives,* edited by Peter Goldie and Amy Coplan, 82–95. New York: Oxford University Press.

Damasio, Antonio. 1994. *Descartes' Error: Emotion, Reason, and the Human Brain.* London: Vintage.

———. 1999. *The Feeling of What Happens: Body and Emotion in the Making of Consciousness.* London: Hartcourt.

———. 2003. *Looking for Spinoza: Joy, Sorrow, and the Feeling Brain.* London: Vintage.

———. 2010. *Self Comes to Mind: Constructing the Conscious Brain.* New York: Pantheon.

Dances with Wolves. 1990. Directed by Kevin Costner. Orion Pictures.

Dante's Peak. 1997. Directed by Roger Donaldson. Universal Pictures.

Darwin, Charles. (1872) 2009. *The Expression of the Emotions in Man and Animals.* Oxford, UK: Oxford University Press.

Daston, Lorraine, and Gregg Mitman, eds. 2005. *Thinking With Animals.* New York: Colombia University Press.

The Da Vinci Code. 2006. Directed by Ron Howard. Columbia Pictures.

The Day After Tomorrow. 2004. Directed by Roland Emmerich. 20th Century Fox.

De Bruin, Leon, and Gallagher, Shaun. 2011. "Embodied Simulation: An Unproductive Explanation: Comment on Gallese and Sinigaglia." *Trends in Cognitive Science* 16 (2): 98–99.

Decety, Jean, and Jason M. Cowell. 2014. "The Complex Relation between Morality and Empathy." *Trends in Cognitive Sciences* 18 (7): 337–39.

———. 2015. "Empathy, Justice, and Moral Behavior." *AJOB Neuroscience* 6 (3): 3–14.

De Geus, Marius. 1999. *Ecological Utopias: Envisioning the Sustainable Society.* Utrecht: International Books.

Deleuze, Gilles. 2000. "The Brain Is the Screen: An Interview with Gilles Deleuze." *The Brain Is the Screen,* edited by Gregory Flaxman, 365–74. Minneapolis: Minnesota University Press.

Delicath, John W., and Kevin M. DeLuca. 2003. "Image Events, the Public Sphere, and Argumentative Practice: The Case of Radical Environmental Groups." *Argumentation* 17 (3): 315–33.

De Waal, Frans. 2009. *The Age of Empathy: Nature's Lessons for a Kinder Society.* New York: Three Rivers Press.

Dick, Philip K. 1965. *The Three Stigmata of Palmer Eldritch.* New York: Double Day.

Dio Cinzia, Di, and Vittorio Gallese. 2009. "Neuroaesthetics: A Review." *Current Opinion in Neurobiology* 19: 682–87.

Di Paolo, Ezequiel, and Evan Thompson. 2014. "The Enactive Approach." In *The Routledge Handbook of Embodied Cognition,* edited by Lawrence Shapiro, 68–77. New York: Routledge.

Dobrin, Sidney, and Sean Morey, eds. 2009. *Ecosee: Image, Rhetoric, Nature.* Albany: State University of New York Press.

Dobson, Andrew. 2003. *Citizenship and the Environment.* Oxford, UK: Oxford University Press.

———. 2006. "Thick Cosmopolitanism." *Political Studies* 54: 165–84.

Doctor Zhivago. 1965. Directed by David Lean. Metro-Goldwyn-Mayer.

Dogville. 2003. Directed by Lars von Trier. Lions Gate Entertainment.

Doyle, Julie. 2009. "Seeing the Climate? The Problematic Status of Visual Evidence in Climate Change Campaigning." In *Ecosee: Image, Rhetoric, Nature,* edited by Sidney Dobrin and Sean Morey, 279–98. Albany: State University of New York Press.

Dr. Dolittle. 1998. Directed by Betty Thomas. 20th Century Fox.

Earthlings. 2005. Directed by Shaun Monson. Nation Earth.

Earthquake. 1974. Directed by Mark Robson. Universal Pictures.

Easterlin, Nancy. 2010. "Cognitive Ecocriticism: Human Wayfinding, Sociality, and Literary Interpretation." In *Introduction to Cognitive Cultural Studies,* edited by Lisa Zunshine, 257–75. Baltimore: Johns Hopkins University Press.

————. 2012. *A Biocultural Approach to Literary Theory and Interpretation.* Baltimore: Johns Hopkins University Press.

Easton, Nina J. 1988. "Film Makers in the Mist: Bringing Dian Fossey Story to Screen Proves to Be a True High Adventure." *Los Angeles Times,* September 16. http://articles.latimes.com/1988-09-16/entertainment/ca-2300_1_dian-fossey.

Ebert, Roger. 1988. Review of *Gorillas in the Mist,* directed by Michael Apted. *Chicago Sun-Times,* September 28. http://www.rogerebert.com/reviews/gorillas-in-the-mist-1988.

Eco, Umberto. 1979. *The Role of the Reader: Explorations in the Semiotic of Texts.* Bloomington: Indiana University Press.

Edelstein, David. 2009. "Gigantic, Gigantic, a Big Big Love: Falling for *Avatar*." *New York Magazine,* December 17. http://nymag.com/daily/movies/2009/12/gigantic_gigantic_a_big_big_lo.html.

Ehrlich, Paul. 1970. *The Population Bomb.* New York: Ballantine Books.

Eisenberg, Nancy, and Paul A. Miller. 1987. "The Relation of Empathy to Prosocial and Related Behaviors." *Psychological Bulletin* 101 (1): 91–119.

Eitzen, Dirk. 1992. "When Is a Documentary? Documentary as a Mode of Reception." *Cinema Journal* 35: 81–102.

————. 2005. "Documentary's Peculiar Appeals." In *Moving Image Theory,* edited by Joseph D. Anderson and Barbara Fisher Anderson, 183–99. Carbondale: Southern Illinois University Press.

Elkington, Trevor. 2009. "Too Many Cooks: Media Convergence and Self-Defeating Adaptations." In *The Video Game Theory Reader 2,* edited by Bernard Perron and Mark J. Pl. Wolf, 213–35. New York: Routledge.

Erin Brockovich. 2000. Directed by Steven Soderbergh. Universal Studios.

Evans, Mei Mei. 2002. "'Nature' and Environmental Justice." In *The Environmental Justice Reader: Politics, Poetics, and Pedagogy,* edited by Joni Adamson, Mei Mei Adams, and Rachel Stein, 181–93. Tucson: University of Arizona Press.

Evans, Nicholas. 1995. *The Horse Whisperer.* New York: Delacorte Press.

Everett, Percival. 1999. *Glyph.* Minneapolis: Graywolf Press.

————. (1996) 2003. *Watershed.* Boston: Beacon Press.

Evernden, Neil. 1996. "Beyond Ecology." In *The Ecocriticism Reader,* edited by Cheryl Glotfelty and Harold Fromm, 92–104. Athens: University of Georgia Press.

Fahlenbrach, Kathrin, and Felix Schröter. 2016. "Embodied Avatars in Video Games: Audiovisual Metaphors in the Interactive Design of Player Characters." In *Embodied Metaphors in Film, Television, and Video Game*s, edited by Kathrin Fahlenbrach, 251–67. New York: Routledge.

Filippi, Massimo, Gianna Riccitelli, Andrea Falini, Francesco Di Salle, Patrik Vuilleumier, Giancarlo Comi, and Maria A. Rocca. 2010. "The Brain Functional Networks Associated to Human and Animal Suffering Differ among Omnivores, Vegetarians and Vegans." *PLoS ONE* 5 (5). doi:10.1371/journal.pone.0010847.

Finch, Robert, and John Elder. 2002. Introduction to *Nature Writing: The Tradition in English,* edited by Robert Finch and John Elder, 15–25. New York: W. W. Norton & Company.

Finseth, Ian F. 2009. *Shades of Green: Visions of Nature in the Literature of American Slavery, 1770–1860.* Athens: University of Georgia Press.

Fish, Robert, ed. 2007. *Cinematic Countrysides: Inside Popular Film*. Manchester: Manchester University Press.

Fish, Stanley. 1980. *Is There a Text in This Class?: The Authority of Interpretive Communities*. Cambridge, MA: Harvard University Press.

Flory, Dan. 2008. *Philosophy, Black Film, Film Noir*. University Park: Penn State University Press.

———. 2013. "Race and Imaginative Resistance in James Cameron's *Avatar*." *Projections: The Journal for Movies and Mind* 7 (2): 41–63.

Foer, Jonathan Safran. 2009. *Eating Animals*. New York: Little, Brown & Company.

Foltz, Bruce V. 1995. *Inhabiting the Earth: Heidegger, Environmental Ethics and the Metaphysics of Nature*. Atlantic Highlands, NJ: Humanity Books.

Food, Inc. 2008. Directed by Robert Kenner. Magnolia Pictures.

Forest of Bliss. 1985. Directed by Robert Gardner. Documentary Educational Resources.

"Fracking FAQs." 2016. *Gasland*. Accessed October 7, 2016. www.gaslandthemovie.com/whats -fracking.

FrackNation. 2013. Directed by Ann McElhinney and Phelim McAleer. Magnet Releasing.

Francione, Gary L. 2010. "The Abolition of Animal Exploitation. In *The Animal Rights Debate: Abolition or Regulation?*, edited by Gary L. Francione and Robert Garner, 1–100. New York: Columbia University Press.

Franklin, Robert G., Anthony J. Nelson, Michelle Baker, Joseph E. Beeney, Theresa K. Vescio, Aurora Lenz-Watson, and Reginald B. Adams. 2013. "Neural Responses to Perceiving Suffering in Humans and Animals." *Social Neuroscience* 8 (3): 217–27.

Franko, Carol. 1994. "Working the 'In-Between': Kim Stanley Robinson's Utopian Fiction," *Science Fiction Studies* 21: 191–211.

Fraser, Caroline. 1999. "Far from Babar." Review of *The White Bone*, by Barbara Gowdy. *The New York Review of Books,* September 23. http://www.nybooks.com/articles/1999/09/23/far-from -babar/.

Freedberg, David, and Vittorio Gallese. 2007. "Motion, Emotion and Empathy in Esthetic Experience." *Trends in Cognitive Sciences* 11 (5): 197–203.

Freedman, Carl. 2000. *Critical Theory and Science Fiction*. Hanover, CT: Wesleyan University Press.

Freedman, Yacov. 2012. "Is it Real . . . or is it Motion Capture? The Battle to Redefine Animation in the Age of Digital Performance." *The Velvet Light Trap* 69: 38–49.

Freeland, Cynthia A. 1999. "The Sublime in Cinema." In *Passionate Views: Film, Cognition, and Emotion,* edited by Carl Plantinga and Greg M. Smith, 65–82. Baltimore: Johns Hopkins University Press.

Freeman, Carrie P., and Debra Merskin. 2016. "Respectful Representation: An Animal Issues Style Guide for all Media Practitioners." In *Critical Animal Media Studies: Communication for Nonhuman Advocacy,* edited by Nuria Almiron and Matthew Cole, 205–20. New York: Routledge.

Froese, Tom. 2015. "Enactive Neuroscience, the Direct Perception Hypothesis, and the Socially Extended Mind." *Behavioral and Brain Science* 38: 1–6.

Froese, Tom, and Thomas Fuchs. 2012. "The Extended Body: A Case Study in the Neurophenomenology of Social Interaction." *Phenomenology and the Cognitive Sciences* 11: 205–35.

Frome, Jonathan. 2007. "Eight Ways Videogames Generate Emotion." In *Proceedings of the 2007 Digital Games Research Association Conference,* edited by Baba Akira, 831–35. Tokyo: University of Tokyo.

Fudge, Erica. 2002. *Animal.* London: Reaktion.

Gaines, Susan. 2001. *Carbon Dreams.* Berkeley, CA: Creative Arts Books Company.

Gallagher, Shaun. 2005. *How the Body Shapes the Mind.* Oxford, UK: Oxford University Press.

———. 2007. "Simulation Trouble." *Social Neuroscience* 2 (3–4): 353–65.

Gallese, Vittorio. 2005. "Embodied Simulation: From Neurons to Phenomenal Experience." *Phenomenology and the Cognitive Sciences* 4: 23–48.

———. 2011. "Mirror Neurons and Art." In *Art and the Senses,* edited by Francesca Bacci and David Melcher, 441–49. New York: Oxford University Press.

———. 2014. "Bodily Selves in Relation: Embodied Simulation as Second-person Perspective on Intersubjectivity." *Philosophical Transactions of the Royal Society B* 369: 1–10. doi.org/10.1098/rstb.2013.0177.

———. 2016. "Bodily Framing." In *Experience: Culture, Cognition and the Common Sense,* edited by Caroline Jones, David Mather, and Rebecca Uchill, 1–15. Cambridge, MA: MIT Press.

Gallese, Vittorio, and Michele Guerra. 2012. "Embodying Movies: Embodied Simulation and Film Studies." *Cinema: Journal of Philosophy and the Moving Image* 3: 183–210.

———. 2014. "The Feeling of Motion: Camera Movements and Motor Cognition." *Cinéma & Cie* 14 (22/23): 103–12.

Gallese, Vittorio, and Georg Lakoff. 2005. "The Brain's Concepts: The Role of Sensory-Motor System in Reason and Language." *Cognitive Neuropsychology* 22: 455–79.

Gallese, Vittorio, and Corrado Sinigaglia. 2012 "Response to de Bruin and Gallagher: Embodied Simulation as Reuse is a Productive Explanation of a Basic Form of Mind-reading." *Trends in Cognitive Sciences* 16 (2): 99–100.

Gallese, Vittorio, and Hannah Wojciehowski. 2011. "How Stories Make Us Feel: Toward an Embodied Narratology." *California Italian Studies* 2 (1). http://escholarship.org/uc/item/3jg726c2.

Garforth, Lisa. 2005. "Green Utopias: Beyond Apocalypse, Progress, and Pastoral." *Utopian Studies* 16 (3): 393–427.

Garrard, Greg. 2010. "Heidegger, Nazism, Ecocriticism." *Interdisciplinary Studies in Literature and Environment* 17 (2): 251–71.

———. 2011. *Ecocriticism: The New Critical Idiom.* New York: Routledge.

Garratt, Peter. 2016. *The Cognitive Humanities: Embodied Mind in Literature and Culture.* Basingstoke, UK: Palgrave Macmillan.

Garson, James. 2015. "Connectivism." *Stanford Encyclopedia of Philosophy.* Last modified February 19. http://plato.stanford.edu/entries/connectionism/.

Gasland. 2010. Directed by Josh Fox. New Video Group.

Gasland 2. 2013. Directed by Josh Fox. HBO.

Gazzola, V., L. Giacomo Rizzolati, B. Filcker, and C. Keysers. 2007. "The Anthropomorphic Brain: The Mirror Neuron System Responds to Human and Robotic Actions." *Euroimage* 35: 1674–84.

Gendler, Tamar Szabó. 2000. "The Puzzle of Imaginative Resistance." *Journal of Philosophy* 97 (2): 55–81.

———. 2006. "Imaginative Resistance Revisited." In *The Architecture of Imagination: New Essays on Pretence, Possibility, and Fiction,* edited by Shaun Nichols, 149–73. Oxford, UK: Clarendon Press.

Genette, Gérard. 1980. *Narrative Discourse: An Essay in Method.* Oxford, UK: Blackwell.

Gerrig, Richard J. (1993) 1998. *Experiencing Narrative Worlds: On the Psychological Activities of Reading.* Boulder, CO: Westview.

———. 2010. "A Moment-by-Moment Perspective on Readers' Experience of Characters." In *Characters in Fictional Worlds: Understanding Imaginary Beings in Literature, Film and Other Media,* edited by Jens Eder, Fotis Jannidis, and Ralf Schneider, 357–76. Berlin: De Gruyter.

———. 2011. "Individual Differences in Readers' Narrative Experiences." *Scientific Study of Literature* 1 (1): 88–94.

Gibbs, Raymond W., and Herbert L. Colston, eds. 2007. *Irony in Language and Thought: A Cognitive Science Reader.* New York: Lawrence Erlbaum Associates.

Gibson, J. J. 1979. *The Ecological Approach to Visual Perception.* Boston: Houghton Mifflin.

Gifford, Terry. 2006. *Reconnecting with John Muir: Essays in Post-Pastoral Practice.* Athens: University of Georgia Press.

———. 2011. "John Muir's Literary Science." *The Public Domain Review.* Accessed on May 6, 2015. http://publicdomainreview.org/2011/06/09/john-muirs-literary-science/.

Gilman, Charlotte Perkins. (1915) 2009. *Herland.* New York: Penguin Classics.

Goldberg, Sylvan. 2015. "'What is it about You . . . that so Irritates Me?' *Northern Exposure*'s Sustainable Feeling." *New International Voices in Ecocriticism,* edited by Serpil Oppermann, 55–70. Lanham, MD: Lexington Books.

Goldin-Meadow, Susan. 2003. *Hearing Gesture: How our Hands Help Us Think.* Cambridge, MA: Harvard University Press.

Goldman, Alvin. 2006. "Imagination and Simulation in Audience Responses to Fiction." In *The Architecture of the Imagination: New Essays on Pretence, Possibility, and Fiction,* edited by Shaun Nichols, 41–56. Oxford, UK: Oxford University Press.

———. 2009. "Mirroring, Mindreading, and Simulation." In *Mirror Neuron Systems,* edited by J. A. Pineda, 311–30. New York: Humana Press.

———. 2012. "A Moderate Approach to Embodied Cognitive Science." *Review of Philosophy and Psychology* 3 (1): 71–88.

Goldman, Alvin, and Lucy Jordan. 2013. "Mindreading by Simulation: The Role of Imagination and Mirroring." In *Understanding Other Minds,* 3rd ed., edited by Simon Baron-Cohen, Michael Lombardo, and Helen Tager-Flusberg, 448–65. Oxford, UK: Oxford University Press.

Goldstein, Thalia R., and Paul Bloom. 2011. "The Mind on Stage: Why Cognitive Scientists Should Study Acting." *Trends in Cognitive Sciences* 15 (4): 141–42.

Goodbody, Axel. 2014. "Risk, Denial and Narrative Form in Climate Change Fiction: Barbara Kingsolver's *Flight Behavior* and Illja Trojanow's *Melting Ice.*" In *The Anticipation of Catastrophe: Environmental Risk in North American Literature and Culture,* edited by Sylvia Mayer and Alexa Weik von Mossner, 59–58. Heidelberg, Ger.: Universitätsverlag Winter.

Gorfinkel, Elena, and John David Rhodes. 2011. "Introduction: The Matter of Places." In *Taking Place: Location and the Moving Image,* edited by John David Rhodes and Elena Gorfinkel, vii–xxix. Minneapolis: University of Minnesota Press.

Gorillas in the Mist. (1988) 2003. Directed by Michael Apted. Warner Home.

Gottschall, Jonathan. 2005. *The Literary Animal: Evolution and the Nature of Narrative*. Evanston, IL: Northwestern University Press.

———. 2013. *The Storytelling Animal: How Stories Make Us Human*. Boston: Mariner Books.

Gowdy, Barbara. 1999. *The White Bone*. Toronto: HarperCollins.

Green, Melanie C. 2004. "Transportation into Narrative Worlds: The Role of Prior Knowledge and Perceived Realism." *Discourse Processes* 38: 247–66.

Green, Melanie C., and Timothy C. Brock. 2000. "The Role of Transportation in the Persuasiveness of Public Narratives." *Journal of Personality and Social Psychology* 79: 701–21.

Green, Melanie C., Christopher Chatham, and Marc A. Sestir. 2012. "Emotion and Transportation into Fact and Fiction." *Scientific Study of Literature* 2 (1): 37–59.

Gregersen, Andreas. 2014. "Cognitive Theory and Video Games." In *Cognitive Media Theory*, edited by Ted Nannicelli and Paul Taberham, 253–66. New York: Routledge.

Gregersen, Andreas, and Torben Grodal. 2009. "Embodiment and Interface." In *The Video Game Theory Reader 2*, edited by Bernard Perron and Mark J. Pl. Wolf, 65–83. New York: Routledge.

Gregg, Melissa, and Gregory J. Seigworth, eds. 2010. *The Affective Theory Reader*. Durham, NC: Duke University Press.

Grenoble, Ryan. 2015. "Scenario That Opens 'The Day After Tomorrow' Actually Not That Far-Fetched, Research Finds." *Huffington Post,* October 12. http://www.huffingtonpost.com/entry/day-after-tomorrow-reseach-climate-change_561bd2a2e4b0e66ad4c88cfd.

Grewe-Volpp, Christa. 2005. "'The Oil Was Made from Their Bones': Environmental (In)Justice in Helena Maria Viramontes's *Under the Feet of Jesus*." *ISLE: Interdisciplinary Studies in Literature and Environment* 12 (1): 61–78.

Griffin, Donald R. 1984. *Animal Thinking*. Cambridge, MA: Harvard University Press.

———. 1992. *Animal Minds*. Chicago: University of Chicago Press.

Grodal, Torben. 2009. *Embodied Visions: Evolution, Emotion, Culture, and Film*. Oxford, UK: Oxford University Press.

Gruen, Lori. 2015. *Entangled Empathy: An Alternative Ethic for Our Relationships with Animals*. Brooklyn: Lantern Books.

Guerra, Michele. 2015. "Modes of Action at the Movies, or Re-thinking Film Style from the Embodied Perspective." In *Embodied Cognition and Cinema,* edited by Maarten Coëgnarts and Peter Kravanja. 139–53. Leuven: Leuven University Press.

Hachi: A Dog's Tale. 2009. Directed by Lasse Hallström, Stage 6 Films.

Hackett, Thomas. 2013. "The Racism of *Beasts of the Southern Wild*." *New Republic*, February 19. https://newrepublic.com/article/112407/racism-beasts-southern-wild.

Hakemulder, Jèmeljan, and Emy Koopman. 2010. "Readers Closing in on Immoral Characters' Consciousness: Effects of Free Indirect Discourse on Response to Literary Narratives." *Journal of Literary Theory* 4 (1): 41–62.

Halper, Thomas, and Douglas Muzzio. 2007. "Hobbes in the City: Urban Dystopias in American Movies." *American Culture* 30 (4): 379–90.

Handley, William R. 2005. "Detecting the Real Fictions of History in *Watershed*." *Callaloo* 28 (2): 305–12.

Hansen, James. 2009. *Storms of My Grandchildren: The Truth about the Coming Climate Catastrophe and Our Last Chance to Save Humanity*. London: Bloomsbury.

Happy Feet. 2006. Directed by George Miller, Warner Bros.

Haraway, Donna. 2003. *The Companion Species Manifesto: Dogs, People, and Significant Otherness.* Chicago: University of Chicago Press.

———. 2008. *When Species Meet.* Minneapolis: University of Minnesota Press.

Harel, Naama. 2013. "Investigations of a Dog, by a Dog: Between Anthropocentrism and Canine-Centrism." In *Speaking for Animals: Animal Autobiographical Writing,* edited by Margo DeMello, 49–60. New York: Routledge.

Harper, Graeme, and Jonathan Rayner, eds. 2010. *Cinema and Landscape.* Bristol, UK: Intellect.

Hart, Elizabeth F. 2001. "The Epistemology of Cognitive Literary Studies." *Philosophy and Literature* 25: 314–34.

Hasson, Uri, Ohad Landesman, Barbara Knappmeyer, Ignacio Vallines, Nava Rubin, and David J. Heeger. 2008. "Neurocinematics: The Neuroscience of Film." *Projections* 2 (1): 1–26.

Healy, Jack. 2013. "Water Rights Tear at an Indian Reservation." *New York Times,* April 21. http://www.nytimes.com/2013/04/22/us/bitter-battle-over-water-rights-on-montana-reservation.html?_r=0.

Hediger, Ryan. 2013. "Our Animals, Ourselves: Representing Animal Minds in *Timothy* and *The White Bone.*" In *Speaking for Animals: Animal Autobiographical Writing,* edited by Margo DeMello, 35–47. New York: Routledge.

Heimann, Katrin, Maria Alessandra Umiltà, Michele Guerra, and Vittorio Gallese. 2014. "Moving Mirrors: A High-density EEG Study Investigating the Effect of Camera Movements on Motor Cortex Activation during Action Observation." *Journal of Cognitive Neuroscience* 26 (9): 2087–101.

Heise, Ursula K. "Letter." *PMLA* 114, no. 5 (1999): 1096–97.

———. 2008. *Sense of Place and Sense of Planet: The Environmental Imagination of the Global.* Oxford, UK: Oxford University Press.

———. 2014. "Plasmatic Nature: Environmentalism and Animated Film." *Public Culture* 26 (2): 301–18.

———. 2015. "Environmental Literature and the Ambiguities of Science." *Anglia* 133 (1): 22–36.

———. 2016. *Imagining Extinction: The Cultural Meanings of Endangered Species.* Chicago: University of Chicago Press.

Herman, David, ed. 1999. *Narratologies: New Perspectives on Narrative Analysis.* Columbus: The Ohio State University Press.

———. 2005. "Storyworld." In *Routledge Encyclopedia of Narrative Theory,* edited by David Herman, Manfred Jahn, and Marie-Laure Ryan, 569–70. New York: Routledge.

———. 2007a. "Introduction." In *The Cambridge Companion to Narrative,* edited by David Herman, 3–20. Cambridge: Cambridge University Press.

———. 2007b. "Cognition, Emotion, and Consciousness." In *The Cambridge Companion to Narrative,* edited by David Herman, 245–58. Cambridge: Cambridge University Press.

———. 2011. "Storyworld/Umwelt: Nonhuman Experiences in Graphic Narratives." *SubStance* 40.1 (124): 156–81.

———. 2012. "Editor's Column: Transmedial Narratology and Transdisciplinarity." *StoryWorlds: A Journal of Narrative Studies* 4: vii-xii.

———. 2013. *Storytelling and the Sciences of Mind.* Cambridge, MA: MIT Press.

———. 2014. "Narratology beyond the Human." *Diegesis* 3 (2): 131–43.

Herzog, Hal. 2011. *Some We Love, Some We Hate, Some We Eat: Why It's So Hard to Think Straight About Animals*. New York: Harper Perennial.

Hickok, Gregory. 2013. "Do Mirror Neurons Subserve Action Understanding?" *Neuroscience Letters* 540: 59–61.

Hoeckner, Berthold, Emma W. Wyatt, Jean Decety, and Howard Nusbaum. 2011. "Film Music Influences How Viewers Relate to Movie Characters." *Psychology of Aesthetics, Creativity, and the Arts* 5 (2): 146–53.

Hoffman, Martin. 2000. *Empathy and Moral Development: Implications for Caring and Justice*. Cambridge: Cambridge University Press.

———. 2011. "Empathy, Justice, and the Law." In *Empathy: Philosophical and Psychological Perspectives*, edited by Amy Coplan and Peter Goldie, 230–53. New York: Oxford University Press.

Hogan, Linda. 1995. *Solar Storms*. New York: Scribner.

Hogan, Patrick Colm. 2003. *The Mind and Its Stories: Narrative Universals and Human Emotion*. Cambridge: Cambridge University Press.

———. 2009. *Understanding Nationalism: On Narrative, Cognitive Science, and Identity*. Columbus: The Ohio State University Press.

———. 2011a. *Affective Narratology: The Emotional Structure of Stories*. Lincoln: University of Nebraska Press.

———. 2011b. *What Literature Teaches Us about Emotion*. Cambridge: Cambridge University Press.

———. 2013. *How Authors' Minds Make Stories*. Cambridge: Cambridge University Press.

Holmes, Steven Jon. 1999. *The Young John Muir: An Environmental Biography*. Madison: University of Wisconsin Press.

Holtmeier, Matthew. 2010. "Post-Pandoran Depression or Na'vi Sympathy: *Avatar*, Affect, and Audience Reception." *Journal for the Study of Religion, Nature and Culture* 4 (4): 414–24.

Hooks, Gregory, and Chad L. Smith. 2004. "The Treadmill of Destruction: National Sacrifice Areas and Native Americans." *American Sociological Review* 69 (August): 558–75.

Horkheimer, Max, and Theodor Adorno. (1944) 2007. *Dialectic of Enlightenment*, translated by Edmund Jephcott. Palo Alto, CA: Stanford University Press.

Horn, Eva. 2014. *Zukunft als Katastrophe*. Frankfurt: Fischer.

The Horse Whisperer. 1998. Directed by Robert Redford. Buena Vista Pictures.

Houser, Heather. 2014. *Ecosickness in Contemporary U.S. Fiction: Environment and Affect*. New York: Columbia University Press.

Howard, Ebenezer. (1902) 1965. *Garden Cities of To-morrow*. Cambridge: The MIT Press.

Howarth, Jane M. 1995. "The Crisis of Ecology: A Phenomenological Perspective." *Environmental Values* 4: 17–30.

Howell, Rachel A. 2011. "Lights, Camera. Action? Altered Attitudes and Behaviour in Response to the Climate Change Film *The Age of Stupid*." *Global Environmental Change* 21 (1): 177–87.

———. 2014. "Investigating the Long-Term Impacts of Climate Change Communications on Individuals' Attitudes and Behavior." *Environment and Behavior* 46 (1): 70–101.

Huggan, Graham, and Helen Tiffin. 2010. *Postcolonial Ecocriticism: Literature, Animals, Environment*. New York: Routledge.

Hughes, Helen. 2014. *Green Documentary: Environmental Documentary in the 21st Century.* Bristol, UK: Intellect.

Hughes, Monica. 2003. "The Struggle between Utopia and Dystopia in Writing for Children and Young Adults." In *Utopian and Dystopian Writing for Children and Young Adults,* edited by Carrie Hintz and Elaine Ostry, 156–61. New York: Routledge.

Huhndorf, Shari M. 2001. *Going Native: Indians in the American Cultural Imagination.* Ithaca, NY: Cornell University Press.

Hulme, Mike. 2009. *Why We Disagree About Climate Change: Understanding Controversy, Inaction and Opportunity.* Cambridge: Cambridge University Press.

Hume, David. (1793) 1965. "Of Tragedy." In *Of the Standard of Taste and Other Essays,* edited by John V. Lenz, 29–37. Indianapolis: Bobbs-Merrill.

The Hunger Games. 2012. Directed by Gary Ross. Lionsgate.

Hunter, Steven. 1992. "'Thunderheart' Trips All Over Its Good Intentions." *The Baltimore Sun,* April 3. http://articles.baltimoresun.com/1992-04-03/features/1992094182_1_kilmer-thunderheart -john-trudell.

The Hurricane. 1937. Directed by John Ford. United Artists.

Hutcheon, Linda. 1994. *Irony's Edge: The Theory and Politics of Irony.* New York: Routledge.

Hutto, Daniel D. 2000. *Beyond Physicalism.* New York: John Benjamins Publishing.

Hutto, Daniel D., and Erik Myin. 2013. *Radicalizing Enactivism: Basic Minds Without Content.* Cambridge, MA: MIT Press.

Hutton, Noah. 2010. "The Neuroscience of *Avatar.*" *The Beautiful Brain,* January 5. http://thebeautifulbrain.com/2010/01/the-neuroscience-of-avatar/.

Hyde, William. 2004. "My Day After Tomorrow Review(ish) Thing." Google Groups, July 2. Accessed July 5, 2015. http://groups.google.com/group/rec.arts.sf.written/msg/6e52157aaf63775f.

Iacoboni, Marco. 2008. "The Role of Premotor Cortex in Speech Perception: Evidence from fMRI and rTMS." *Journal of Physiology–Paris* 102 (1–3): 31–34.

———. 2009. *Mirroring People: The Science of Empathy and How We Connect with Others.* New York: Picador.

If a Tree Falls. 2013. Directed by Marshall Curry. Oscilloscope Laboratories.

Imagining Indians. 1992. Directed by Victor Masayesva Jr. Native Networks.

Incident at Oglala. 1992. Directed by Michael Apted. Miramax.

An Inconvenient Truth. 2006. Directed by Davis Guggenheim. Paramount Classics.

Ingram, David. 2000. *Green Screen: Environmentalism and Hollywood Cinema.* Exeter, UK: University of Exeter Press.

———. 2005. "Hollywood Cinema and Climate Change: *The Day After Tomorrow.*" In *Words on Water: Literary and Cultural Representations,* edited by Maureen Devine and Christa Grewe-Volpp, 53–63. Trier: Wissenschaftlicher Verlag Trier.

———. 2014a. "Emotion and Affect in Eco-Films: Cognitive and Phenomenological Approaches." In *Moving Environments: Affect, Emotion, Ecology, and Film,* edited by Alexa Weik von Mossner, 23–40. Waterloo, ON: Wilfrid Laurier University Press.

———. 2014b. "Rethinking Eco-Film Studies." In *The Oxford Handbook of Ecocriticism,* edited by Greg Garrard, 459–74. New York: Oxford University Press.

Interstellar. 2014. Directed by Christopher Nolan. Paramount Pictures.

Iovino, Serenella, and Serpil Oppermann. 2014. "Introduction: Stories Come to Matter." In *Material Ecocriticism,* edited by Serenella Iovino and Serpil Oppermann, 1–19. Bloomington: Indiana University Press.

Iser, Wolfgang. 1978. *The Act of Reading: A Theory of Aesthetic Response.* Baltimore: Johns Hopkins University Press.

The Island President. 2011. Directed by Jon Shenk. Samuel Goldwyn Films.

Ivakhiv, Adrian. 2013. *Ecologies of the Moving Image: Cinema, Affect, Nature.* Waterloo, ON: Wilfrid Laurier University Press.

———. 2014. "What Can a Film *Do*? Assessing Avatar's Global Affects." In *Moving Environments: Affect, Emotion, Ecology, and Film,* edited by Alexa Weik von Mossner, 159–80. Waterloo, ON: Wilfrid Laurier University Press.

Jacobs, Arthur M., and Raoul Schrott. 2011. *Gehirn und Gedicht: Wie Wir Unsere Wirklichkeit Konstruieren.* München: Carl Hanser Verlag.

———. 2014. "Captivated by the Cinema of Mind: On Toggle Switches, Madeleine Effects and Don Quixote Syndrome during Immersion in Textual Worlds." In *Concentration,* edited by Ingo Niermann, 118–49. Accessed on June 22, 2016. http://fiktion.cc/books/concentration/.

Jacobs, Arthur M., Melissa L.-H. Võ, Benny B. Briesemeister, Markus Conrad, Markus J. Hofmann, Lars Kuchinke, Jana Lüdtke, and Mario Braun. 2015. "10 Years of BAWLing into Affective and Aesthetic Processes in Reading: What are the Echoes?" *Frontiers in Psychology* 6: 1–15.

James, Edward. 1996. "The Landscape of Mars." *Time Literary Supplement* (May 3): 23.

James, Erin. 2015. *The Storyworld Accord: Econarratology and Postcolonial Narratives.* Lincoln: University of Nebraska Press.

James, Erin, and Eric Morel. Forthcoming. *Ecocriticism and Narrative Theory.* Columbus: The Ohio State University Press.

Jameson, Fredric. 2005. *Archaeologies of the Future: The Desire Called Utopia and Other Science Fictions.* London: Verso.

James, Henry. 1884. "The Art of Fiction." *Longman's Magazine* 4 (September). Available at https://public.wsu.edu/~campbelld/amlit/artfiction.html

Jauss, Hans Robert. 1982. *Toward an Aesthetic of Reception.* Minneapolis: University of Minnesota Press.

Jenkins, Henry. 2006. *Convergence Culture: Where the Old and the New Media Collide.* New York: New York University Press.

Johnson, Dan R. 2013. "Transportation into Literary Fiction Reduces Prejudice Against and Increases Empathy for Arab-Muslims." *Scientific Study of Literature* 3 (1): 77–92.

Johnson, Dan R., Daniel M. Jasper, Sallie Griffin, and Brandie L. Huffman. 2013. "Reading Narrative Fiction Reduces Arab-Muslim Prejudice and Offers a Safe Haven From Intergroup Anxiety." *Social Cognition* 31 (5): 578–98

Johnson, Dan R., Brandie L. Huffman, and Danny M. Jasper. 2014. "Changing Race Boundary Perception by Reading Narrative Fiction." *Basic and Applied Social Psychology* 36: 83–90.

Johnson, Dan R., Daniel M. Jasper, Sallie Griffin, and Brandie L. Huffman. 2013. "Reading Narrative Fiction Reduces Arab-Muslim Prejudice and Offers a Safe Haven from Intergroup Anxiety." *Social Cognition* 31 (5): 578–98

Johnson, Mark. 1994. *Moral Imagination: Implications of Cognitive Science for Ethics.* Chicago: University of Chicago Press.

———. 2014. *Morality for Humans: Ethical Understanding from the Perspective of Cognitive Science*. Chicago: University of Chicago Press.

Johns-Putra, Adeline. 2016. "Climate Change in Literature and Literary Studies: From Cli-fi, Climate Change Theater and Ecopoetry to Ecocriticism and Climate Change Criticism." *WILEY Interdisciplinary Reviews—Climate Change* 7 (2): 266–82.

Joy, Melanie. 2010. *Why We Love Dogs, Eat Pigs and Wear Cows: An Introduction to Carnism*. San Francisco: Conari Press.

Kakoudaki, Despina. 2002. "Spectacles of History: Race Relations, Melodrama, and the Science Fiction/Disaster Film." *Camera Obscura* 17 (2): 109–53.

Kaplan, Stephen. 1992. "Environmental Preference in a Knowledge-Seeking, Knowledge-Using Organism." In *The Adapted Mind: Evolutionary Psychology and the Generation of Culture*, edited by Jerome Barkow, Leda Cosmides, and John Tooby, 581–98. New York: Oxford University Press.

Katerberg, William H. 2008. *Future West: Utopia and Apocalypse in Frontier Science Fiction*. Lawrence: University Press of Kansas.

Kates, Robert W. 1994. "Sustaining Life on Earth." *Scientific American* 174 (4): 114–22.

Kaufman, Geoff F., and Lisa K. Libby. 2012. "Changing Beliefs and Behavior through Experience-taking." *Journal of Personality and Social Psychology* 103: 1–19.

Keane, Stephen. 2001. *Disaster Movies: The Cinema of Catastrophe*. London: Wallflower.

Keegan, Rebecca. 2011. "Energy Group Targets Oscar-nominated 'Gasland.'" *Los Angeles Times* (February 15). Accessed on October 7, 2016. http://articles.latimes.com/2011/feb/15/entertainment/la-et-0215-oscar-gasland-20110215.

Keen, Suzanne. 2007. *Empathy and the Novel*. Oxford, UK: Oxford University Press.

———. 2010. "Narrative Empathy." In *Toward a Cognitive Theory of Narrative Acts*, edited by Frederick Louis Aldama, 61–94. Austin: University of Texas Press.

———. 2015. *Narrative Form*. Basingstoke, UK: Palgrave Macmillan.

Kerridge, Richard. 2014. "Ecocritical Approaches to Literary Form and Genre: Urgency, Depth, Provisionality, Temporality." In *Oxford Handbook of Ecocriticism*, edited by Greg Garrard, 361–75. Oxford, UK: Oxford University Press.

Keysers, Christian, and Valeria Gazzola. 2009. "Expanding the Mirror: Vicarious Activity for Actions, Emotions, and Sensations." *Current Opinion in Neurobiology* 19: 1–6.

Keysers, Christian, Bruno Wicker, Valeria Gazzola, Jean-Luc Anton, Leonardo Fogsi, and Vittorio Gallese. 2004. "A Touching Sight: SII/PV Activation during the Observation and Experience of Touch." *Neuron* 42 (2): 335–46.

Kidd, David Comer, and Emanuele Castano. 2013. "Reading Literary Fiction Improves Theory of Mind." *Science* 342 (6156): 377–80.

Kilcup, Karen L. 2013. *Fallen Forests: Emotion, Embodiment, and Ethics in American Women's Environmental Writing, 1781–1924*. Athens: University of Georgia Press.

Killingsworth, M. Jimmie, and Jacqueline S. Palmer. 1996. "Millennial Ecology: The Apocalyptic Narrative from Silent Spring to Global Warming." In *Green Culture: Environmental Rhetoric in Contemporary America*, edited by Carl G. Herndl and Stuart C. Brown, 21–45. Madison: University of Wisconsin Press.

King, Geoff. 2000. *Spectacular Narratives: Hollywood in the Age of the Blockbuster*. London: I. B. Tauris.

Kingsolver, Barbara. 2012. *Flight Behavior: A Novel.* New York: HarperCollins.

Kirby, David A. 2013. *Lab Coats in Hollywood: Science, Scientists, and Cinema.* Cambridge, MA: MIT Press.

Knudsen, James. 2001. Review of *A Friend of the Earth,* by T. C. Boyle. *The Free Library.* Accessed on November 12, 2015. http://www.thefreelibrary.com/A+Friend+of+the+Earth.+%28Fiction %29.-a080500233.

Koelsch, Stefan. 2014. "Brain Correlates of Music-evoked Emotions." *Nature Reviews Neuroscience* 15: 170–80.

Kohler, E., C. Keysers, M. A. Umiltá, L. Fogassi, Vittorio Gallese, and Giacomo Rizzolatti. 2002. "Hearing Sounds, Understanding Actions: Action Representation in Mirror Neurons." *Science* 297 (5582): 846–48.

Koopman, Emy, and Frank Hakemulder. 2015. "Effects of Literature on Empathy and Self-Reflection—A Theoretical-Empirical Framework." *Journal of Literary Theory* 9 (1): 79–111.

Kracauer, Siegfried. (1960) 1997. *Theory of Film: The Redemption of Physical Reality.* Princeton, NJ: Princeton University Press.

Kuijpers, Moniek M., and David S. Miall. 2011. "Bodily Involvement in Literary Reading: An Experimental Study of Readers' Bodily Experiences during Reading." In *De stralende lezer: Wetenschappelijk onderzoek naar de invloed van het lezen,* edited by Frank Hakemulder, 160–82. Delft, Neth.: Eburon.

Kukkonen, Karin, and Marco Caracciolo. 2014. "Introduction: What is the "Second Generation?" *Style* 48 (3): 261–74.

Kuzmičová, Anežka. 2012. "Presence in the Reading of Literary Narrative: A Case for Motor Enactment." *Semiotica* 189 (1/4): 23–48.

———. 2013. "The Words and Worlds of Literary Narrative: The Trade-off between Verbal Presence and Direct Presence in the Activity of Reading." In *Stories and Minds: Cognitive Approaches to Literary Narrative,* edited by Lars Bernaerts, Dirk De Geest, Luc Herman, and Bart Vervaeck, 191–231. Lincoln: University of Nebraska Press.

———. 2014. "Literary Narrative and Mental Imagery: A View from Embodied Cognition." *Style* 48 (3): 275–93.

———. 2015. "Does it Matter Where You Read? Situating Narrative in Physical Environment." *Communication Theory* 26 (3): 290–308. doi:10.1111/comt.12084.

Lady in the Lake. 1947. Directed by Robert Montgomery. Metro-Goldwyn-Mayer.

Lakoff, George, and Mark Johnson. 1999. *Philosophy in the Flesh: The Embodied Mind & its Challenge to Western Thought.* New York: Basic Books.

———. 2003. *Metaphors We Live By.* 1980. Chicago: University of Chicago Press.

Lang, Brent. 2016. "James Cameron Making Four 'Avatar' Sequels." *Variety* (April 16). http://variety .com/2016/film/news/james-cameron-avatar-1201753774/.

Langfeld, Herbert. 1920. *The Aesthetic Attitude.* New York: Hartcourt Brace.

Lang, Robert. 1989. *American Film Melodrama: Griffith, Vidor, Minnelli.* Princeton, NJ: Princeton University Press.

LaSalle, Mick. 1996. "*Twister:* Season's First Action Thriller is a Real Blast." *San Francisco Chronicle,* May 10. http://www.sfgate.com/movies/article/TWISTER-Season-s-first-action-thriller -is-a-2982112.php.

LeDoux, Joseph. 1996. *The Emotional Brain.* New York: Simon and Schuster.

Lefebvre, Martin. 2006a. Introduction to *Landscape and Film,* edited by Martin Lefebvre, xi-xxxi. London: Routledge.

———. 2006b. "Between Setting and Landscape in the Cinema." In *Landscape and Film,* edited by Martin Lefebvre, 19–60. London: Routledge.

Lehtimäki, Markku. 2013. "Natural Environments in Narrative Contexts: Cross-pollinating Ecocriticism and Narrative Theory." *StoryWorlds: A Journal of Narrative Studies* 5: 119–41.

Leiserowitz, Anthony A. 2004. "Before and after *The Day After Tomorrow:* A U.S. Study of Climate Risk Perception. *Environment* 46 (9): 23–37.

Leslie, Jaqueline. 2015. "How a Stunning Klamath Basin Water Agreement Has Been Doomed by Lawmakers." *Los Angeles Times,* December 18. http://www.latimes.com/opinion/op-ed/la-oe -leslie-klamath-river-agreement-20151218-story.html.

Levin, Daniel T., and Donald A. Varakin. 2004. "No Pause for a Brief Disruption: Failures of Visual Awareness during Ongoing Events." *Consciousness and Cognition* 13: 363–72.

Levin, Daniel T., and Caryn Wang. 2009. "Spatial Representation in Film." *Projections: The Journal for Movies and Mind* 3: 24–52.

Levin, Janet. 1999. "Qualia." In *The MIT Encyclopedia of the Cognitive Sciences,* edited by Robert A. Wilson and Frank C. Keil, 693–94. Cambridge, MA: MIT Press.

Levitas, Ruth. 2010. *The Concept of Utopia.* Berne and New York: Peter Berg.

Lipps, Theodor. 1903–1906. *Ästhetik–Psychologie des Schönen und der Kunst.* Hamburg: Leopold Voss.

Livingstone, Margaret. 2002. *Vision and Art: The Biology of Seeing.* New York: Abrams.

Lockwood, Alex. 2012. "The Affective Legacy of *Silent Spring.*" *Environmental Humanities* 1: 123–40.

London, Jack. 1903. *The Call of the Wild.* New York: Macmillan.

———. (1906) 1991. *White Fang.* Mineola, NY: Dover Thrift Editions.

Lovelock, James. (1979) 2000. *Gaia: A New Look at Life on Earth.* Oxford: Oxford University Press.

———, 2007. *The Revenge of Gaia: Earth's Climate Crisis and the Fate of Humanity.* New York: Basic Books.

———. 2009. *The Vanishing Face of Gaia: A Final Warning.* New York: Basic Books.

Lowe, Thomas, Katrina Brown, Suraje Dessai, Miguel de Franca Doria, Kat Haynes, and Katharine Vincent. 2005. "Does Tomorrow Ever Come? Disaster Narrative and Public Perceptions of Climate Change." *Tyndall Centre for Climate Change Research Working Paper* 72 (March): 1–32.

Lutts, Ralph. 1992. "The Trouble with Bambi: Walt Disney's *Bambi* and the American Vision of Nature." *Forest & Conservation History* 36 (4): 160–71.

Lynas, Mark. 2007. *Six Degrees: Our Future on a Hotter Planet.* London: HarperCollins.

Lynch, Michael J., and Paul B. Stretesky. 2012. "Native Americans, Social and Environmental Justice: Implications for Criminology." *Social Justice* 38 (3): 34–54.

Lyon, Thomas J. 2001. *This Incomparable Land: A Guide to American Nature Writing.* Minneapolis, MN: Milkweed Editions.

Maclean, Norman. 1976. *A River Runs Through It and Other Stories.* Chicago: University of Chicago Press.

Mad Max: Fury Road. 2015. Directed by George Miller. Warner Bros.

Malamud, Randy. 2012. *An Introduction to Animal Studies and Visual Culture.* Basingstoke, UK: Palgrave Macmillian.

Maniac. 2012. Directed by Franck Khalfoun. IFC Midnight.

Marks, Laura. 2000. *The Skin of the Film: Intercultural Cinema, Embodiment, and the Senses.* Durham, NC: Duke University Press.

Mar, Raymond A., and Keith Oatley. 2008. "The Function of Fiction is the Abstraction and Simulation of Social Experience." *Perspectives on Psychological Science* 3 (3): 173–92.

Mar, Raymond A., Keith Oatley, Maja Djikic, and Justin Mullin. 2011. "Emotion and Narrative Fiction: Interactive Influences Before, During, and After Reading." *Cognition & Emotion* 25: 818–33.

Mar, Raymond A., Keith Oatley, Jacob Hirsh, Jennifer dela Paz, and Jordan B. Peterson. 2006. "Bookworms versus Nerds: Exposure to Fiction versus Non-fiction, Divergent Associations with Social Ability, and the Simulation of Fictional Social Worlds." *Journal of Research in Personality* 40: 694–712.

Mar, Raymond A., Keith Oatley, and Jordan B. Peterson. 2009. "Exploring the Link between Reading Fiction and Empathy: Ruling Out Individual Differences and Examining Outcomes." *Communications: The European Journal of Communication* 34: 407–28.

Mar, Raymond A., Jennifer L. Tackett, and Chris Moore. 2010. "Exposure to Media and Theory-of-Mind Development in Preschoolers." *Cognitive Development* 25: 69–78.

Marshall, George. 2014. *Don't Even Think About It: Why Our Brains Are Wired to Ignore Climate Change.* New York: Bloomsbury.

The Martian. 2015. Directed by Ridley Scott. 20th Century Fox.

Martin, Alex, Cheri L. Wiggs, Leslie G. Ungerleider, and James V. Haxby. 1996. "Neural Correlates of Category-Specific Knowledge." *Nature* 379: 649–52.

Marubbio, M. Elise. 2012. "Ghosts and Vanishing Indian Women: Death of the Celluloid Maiden in the 1990s." In *Contested Images: Women of Color in Popular Culture,* edited by Alma M. García, 45–70. Lanham, MD: AltaMira.

Massaro, Davide, Federica Savazzi, Cinzia Di Dio, David Freedberg, Vittorio Gallese, Gabriella Gilli, and Antonella Marchetti. 2012. "When Art Moves the Eyes: A Behavioral and Eye-Tracking Study. *PLoS ONE* 7 (5): 1–16.

Massumi, Brian. 2002. *Parables for the Virtual: Movement, Affect, Sensation.* Durham, NC: Duke University Press.

Masters, Coco. 2009. "Japan Gets Its First Chance to See *The Cove.*" *Time Magazine,* September 16. http://content.time.com/time/world/article/0,8599,1923252,00.html.

Mayer, Sylvia. 2003. Introduction to *Restoring the Connection to the Natural World: Essays on the African American Environmental Imagination,* edited by Sylvia Mayer, 1–10. Münster: LIT Verlag.

———. 2014. "Explorations of the Controversially Real: Risk, the Climate Change Novel, and the Narrative of Anticipation." In *The Anticipation of Catastrophe: Environmental Risk in North American Literature and Culture,* edited by Sylvia Mayer and Alexa Weik von Mossner, 21–38. Heidelberg, Ger.: Universitätsverlag Winter.

Mazzocco, Philip J., Melanie C. Green, Joe A. Sasota, and Norman Jones. 2010. "This Story is Not for Everyone: Transportability and Narrative Persuasion." *Social Psychological and Personality Science* 1: 361–68.

McCance, Dawne. 2013. *Critical Animal Studies: An Introduction.* Albany: State University of New York Press.

McCarthy, Cormac. 2006. *The Road.* New York: Vintage.

McFarland, Sarah E. 2009. "Dancing Penguins and a Pretentious Raccoon: Animated Animals and 21st Century Environmentalism." In *Animals and Agency: An Interdisciplinary Exploration,* edited by Sarah E. McFarland and Ryan Hediger, 89–103. Leiden, Neth.: Brill.

McHugh, Susan. 2009. "Literary Animal Agents." *PMLA* 124 (2): 487–95.

———. 2011. *Animal Stories: Narrating across Species Lines.* Minneapolis: University of Minnesota Press.

McKibben, Bill. 1990. *The End of Nature.* New York: Anchor Books.

———. 2010. *Eaarth: Making a Life on a Tough New Planet.* New York: St Martin's Griffi.

McLean, Adrienne L. 2014. "Introduction: Wonder Dogs." In *Cinematic Canines: Dogs and Their Work in the Fiction Film,* edited by Adrienne McLean, 1–30. New Brunswick, NJ: Rutgers University Press.

McMahan, Alison. 2003. "Immersion, Engagement, and Presence: A Method for Analyzing 3-D Video Games." In *The Video Game Theory Reader,* edited by Mark J. P. Wolf and Bernard Perron, 67–86. New York: Routledge.

McMahon, Laura, and Michael Lawrence. 2015. *Animal Life and the Moving Image.* Basingstoke, UK: Palgrave Macmillan.

McNeill, David. 2005. *Gesture and Thought.* Chicago: University of Chicago Press.

Meadows, Donella H., Dennis L. Meadows, and Jørgen Randers. 2004. *Limits to Growth: The 30-Year Update.* White River Junction, VT: Chelsea Green.

Meadows, Donella H., Dennis L. Meadows, Jørgen Randers, and William W. Behrens III. 1972. *The Limits to Growth: A Report for the Club of Rome's Project on the Predicament of Mandkind.* New York: Universe Books.

Mehnert, Antonia. 2014. "Things We Didn't See Coming—Riskscapes in Climate Change Fiction." In *The Anticipation of Catastrophe: Environmental Risk in North American Literature and Culture,* edited by Sylvia Mayer and Alexa Weik von Mossner, 59–78. Heidelberg, Ger.: Universitätsverlag Winter.

Melosi, Martin V. 1995. "Equity, Eco-Racism, and Environmental History." *Environmental History Review* 19 (3): 1–16.

Mercer, John, and Martin Shingler. 2004. *Melodrama: Genre, Style, and Sensibility.* London: Wallflower Press.

Miall, David S. 1988. "Affect and Narrative: A Model of Response to Stories." *Poetics* 17: 259–72.

———. 1989. "Beyond the Schema Given: Affective Comprehension of Literary Narratives," *Cognition and Emotion* 3: 55–78.

———. 2006. *Literary Reading: Empirical and Theoretical Studies.* Bern, Switz.: Peter Lang.

———. 2008. "Feeling from the Perspective of the Empirical Study of Literature." *Journal of Literary Theory* 1 (2): 377–93.

Miall, David S., and Don Kuiken. 1994a. "Foregrounding, Defamiliarization, and Affect: Response to Literary Stories." *Poetics* 22: 389–407.

———. 1994b. "Beyond Text Theory: Understanding Literary Response." *Discourse Processes* 17: 337–52.

———. 2001. "Shifting Perspectives: Readers' Feelings and Literary Response." In *New Perspectives on Narrative Perspective,* edited by Willie van Peer and Seymour Chatman, 289–301. Albany: State University of New York Press.

Michael, John. 2011. "Interactionism and Mindreading." *Review of Philosophy and Psychology* 3: 559–78.

Milburn, Colin. 2014. "Green Gaming: Video Games and Environmental Risk." In *The Anticipation of Catastrophe: Environmental Risk in North American Literature and Culture,* edited by Sylvia Mayer and Alexa Weik von Mossner, 201–19. Heidelberg, Ger.: Universitätsverlag Winter.

Mission to Mars. 2000. Directed by Brian de Palma. Buena Vista Pictures.

Mital, Parag K., Tim J. Smith, Robin L. Hill, and John M. Henderson. 2011. "Clustering of Gaze during Dynamic Scene Viewing is Predicted by Motion." *Cognitive Computation* 3: 5–24.

Mitman, Gregg. 1999. *Reel Nature: America's Romance with Wildlife on Film.* Seattle: University of Washington Press.

Molloy, Claire. 2013. "Animals, Avatars, and the Gendering of Nature." In *Screening Nature: Cinema beyond the Human,* edited by Anat Pick and Guinevere Narraway, 177–92. New York: Berghahn.

Monani, Salma. 2014. "Evoking Sympathy and Empathy: The Ecological Indian and Indigenous Eco-activism." In *Moving Environments: Affect, Emotion, Ecology, and Film,* edited by Alexa Weik von Mossner, 225–48. Waterloo, ON: Wilfrid Laurier University Press.

Mooney, Chris. 2015. "Why Some Scientists Are Worried about a Surprisingly Cold 'Blob' in the North Atlantic Ocean." *The Washington Post,* September 24. https://www.washingtonpost.com/news/energy-environment/wp/2015/09/24/why-some-scientists-are-worried-about-a-cold-blob-in-the-north-atlantic-ocean/.

Moore, Russel. 2009. "*Avatar: Rambo* in Reverse." Russel Moore website, December 18. https://www.russellmoore.com/2009/12/18/avatar-rambo-in-reverse/.

More, Thomas. (1516) 1982. *Utopia.* New York: Penguin.

Morris, William. (1890) 1983. *News from Nowhere.* London: Routledge and Kegan Paul.

Moylan, Tom. 1987. *Demand the Impossible: Science Fiction and the Utopian Imagination.* London: Routledge.

———. 1995. "'Utopia Is When Our Lives Matter': Reading Kim Stanley Robinson's *Pacific Edge.*" *Utopian Studies* 6 (2): 1–24.

———. 2000. *Scraps of the Untainted Sky: Science Fiction, Utopia, Dystopia.* Boulder, CO: Westview.

Muir, John. 1894. *The Mountains of California.* Sierra Club Website. Accessed June 10, 2015. http://vault.sierraclub.org/john_muir_exhibit/writings/the_mountains_of_california/.

———. 1913. *The Story of My Boyhood and Youth.* Sierra Club Website. Accessed June 8, 2015. http://vault.sierraclub.org/john_muir_exhibit/writings/the_story_of_my_boyhood_and_youth/.

Münsterberg, Hugo. (1916) 1970. *The Photoplay: A Psychological Study.* New York: Dover.

Murphy, Patrick D. 2001. "The Non-Alibi of Alien Scapes: SF and Ecocriticism." In *Beyond Nature Writing: Expanding the Boundaries of Ecocriticism,* edited by Karla Armbruster and Kathleen R. Wallace. Charlottesville: University of Virginia Press.

Murray, Rebecca. 2013. "Exclusive Interview with 'Beasts of the Southern Wild' Director Benh Zeitlin." Accessed on October 7, 2016. *About.com.* http://movies.about.com/od/directorinterviews/a/benh-zeitlin-beasts-interview.htm.

Murray, Robin L., and Joseph K. Heumann. 2009. *Ecology and Popular Film: Cinema on the Edge.* Albany: State University of New York Press.

———. 2011. *That's All Folks?: Ecocritical Readings of American Animated Features.* Lincoln: University of Nebraska Press.

———. 2012. *Gunfight at the Eco-Corral: Western Cinema and the Environment.* Norman: University of Oklahoma Press.

———. 2014. *Film and Everyday Eco-Disasters.* Lincoln: University of Nebraska Press.

Myers, Jeffrey. 2005. *Converging Stories: Race, Ecology, and Environmental Justice in American Literature.* Athens: The University of Georgia Press.

Nabokov, Vladimir. 1955. *Lolita.* Paris: Olympia Press.

Naci, Lorina, Rhodri Cusack, Mimma Anello, and Adrian M. Owen. 2014. "A Common Neural Code for Similar Conscious Experiences in Different Individuals." *PNAS* 111 (39): 14277–82.

Nadzam, Bonnie. 2011. *Lamb.* New York: Other Press.

———. "Bonnie Nadzam." *Foyles* website. Accessed on May 3, 2016. http://www.foyles.co.uk/Bonnie-Nadzam.

Nagel, Thomas. 1974. "What Is It Like to Be a Bat?" *The Philosophical Review* 83 (4): 435–50.

Nannicelli, Ted, and Paul Taberham. 2014. "Introduction: Contemporary Cognitive Media Theory." In *Cognitive Media Theory*, edited by Ted Nannicelli and Paul Taberham, 1–23. New York and London: Routledge.

Nash, Jeffrey E., and Anne Sutherland. 1991. "The Moral Elevation of Animals: The Case of *Gorillas in the Mist.*" *International Journal of Politics, Culture, and Society* 5 (1): 111–26.

Nash, Linda. 2005. "Agency of Nature or Nature of Agency?" *Environmental History* 10 (1): 67–69.

Neate, Patrick. 2004. *The London Pigeon Wars.* New York: Penguin.

Nelles, William. 2001. "Beyond the Bird's Eye: Animal Focalization." *Narrative* 9 (2): 188–94.

Nell, Victor. 1988. *Lost in a Book: The Psychology of Reading for Pleasure.* New Haven, CT: Yale University Press.

Ngai, Sianne. 2007. *Ugly Feelings.* Cambridge, MA: Harvard University Press.

Nichols, Bill. 2001. *Introduction to Documentary.* Bloomington: Indiana University Press.

Nichols, Elena. 2015. "Cold Blob Causes Lingering Fears: Will 'Day After Tomorrow' Become a Reality?" *The Examiner,* October 2.

Nisbet, Matthew. 2004. "Evaluating the Impact of *The Day After Tomorrow*: Can a Blockbuster Film Shape the Public's Understanding of a Science Controversy?" *CSICOP On-Line: Science and the Media.*

Nixon, Rob. 2011. *Slow Violence and the Environmentalism of the Poor.* Cambridge, MA: Harvard University Press.

Nocella, Anthony J. II, John Sorenson, Kim Socha, and Atsuko Matsuoka, eds. 2013. *Defining Critical Animal Studies: An Intersectional Social Justice Approach for Liberation.* Bern, Switz.: Peter Lang.

Noë, Alva. 2004. *Action in Perception.* Cambridge, MA: MIT Press.

———. 2010. *Out of Our Heads: Why You Are Not Your Brain, and Other Lessons from the Biology of Consciousness.* New York: Hill and Wang.

Norgaard, Kari Marie. 2011. *Living in Denial: Climate Change, Emotions, and Everyday Life.* Cambridge, MA: MIT Press.

Norris, Trevor. 2011. "Martin Heidegger, D. H. Lawrence, and Poetic Attention to Being." In *Ecocritical Theory: New European Approaches,* edited by Axel Goodbody and Kate Rigby, 113–25. Charlottesville: University of Virginia Press.

Not Evil Just Wrong. 2009. Directed by Ann McElhinney and Phelim McAleer. Greener Horizon Films.

Nussbaum, Martha. 1997. *Cultivating Humanity: A Classical Defense of Reform in Liberal Education.* Cambridge, MA: Harvard University Press.

Oatley, Keith. 1992. *Best Laid Schemes: The Psychology of Emotions.* New York: Cambridge University Press.

———. 1999. "Why Fiction May be Twice as True as Fact: Fiction as Cognitive and Emotional Simulation." *Review of General Psychology* 3: 101–17.

———. 2002. "Emotions and the Story Worlds of Fiction." In *Narrative Impact: Social and Cognitive Foundations,* edited by Melanie. C. Green, Jeffrey Strange, and Timothy C. Brock, 39–69. Mahwah, NJ: Lawrence Erlbaum Associates.

———. 2012. *The Passionate Muse: Exploring Emotion in Stories.* New York: Oxford University Press.

O'Barry, Richard. 2009. "Goodbye (for now) to Taiji." *SaveJapanDolphins.org,* September 29. http://savejapandolphins.blogspot.co.at/2009/09/goodbye-for-now-to-taiji.html.

———. 2011. "Dolphins Elude Dolphin Killers in Taiji." *SaveJapanDolphins.org.* October 3.

O'Brian, Adam. 2016. *Transactions with the World: Ecocriticism and the Environmental Sensibility of New Hollywood.* New York: Berghahn Books.

Oliner, Samuel P., and Pearl M. Oliner. 1988. *The Altruistic Personality: Rescuers of Jews in Nazi Europe.* New York: The Free Press.

Olmstead, Alan L., and Paul W. Rhode. 2003. "The Evolution of California Agriculture, 1850–2000." In *California Agriculture: Dimensions and Issues,* edited by Jerry Siebert, 1–28. *eScholarship University of California,* June 1. https://escholarship.org/uc/item/9145n8m1.

Olson, Randy. 2015. *Houston, We Have a Narrative.* Chicago: University of Chicago Press.

Oreskes, Naomi, and Erik M. Conway. 2014. *The Collapse of Western Civilization: A View from the Future.* New York: Columbia University Press.

Orwell, George. 1945. *Animal Farm.* London: Secker and Warburg.

Otto, Eric. 2012. *Green Speculations: Science Fiction and Transformative Environmentalism.* Columbus: The Ohio State University Press.

Out of Africa. 1985. Directed by Sydney Pollack. Universal Pictures.

Outside Magazine. 1999. Review of *The White Bone* by Barbara Gowdy. Accessed on October 1, 2016. http://www.outsideonline.com/1829516/beastliness.

Pack, Sam. 2001. "The Best of Both Worlds: Otherness, Appropriation, and Identity in *Thunderheart.*" *Wicazo Sa Review* 16 (2): 97–114.

Palmer, Alan. 2004. *Fictional Minds.* Omaha: University of Nebraska Press.

Panic Room. 2002. Directed by David Fincher. Columbia Pictures.

Panksepp, Jaak. 1998. *Affective Neuroscience: The Foundations of Human and Animal Emotions.* New York: Oxford University Press.

Panksepp, Jaak, and Jules B. Panksepp. 2013. "Toward a Cross-species Understanding of Empathy." *Trends in Neuroscience* 36 (8): 489–96.

Park, Ondine, Tonya K. Davidson, and Rob Shields. 2011. Introduction to *Ecologies of Affect: Placing Nostalgia, Desire, and Hope,* edited by Tonya K. Davidson, Ondine Park, and Rob Shields, 1–17. Waterloo, ON: Wilfrid Laurier University Press.

The Passion of the Christ. 2004. Directed by Mel Gibson. 20th Century Fox.

Patoine, Pierre-Louis. 2015. *Pour une théorie de la lecture empathique: Cooper, Danielewski, Frey, Palahniuk.* Lyon, Fr.: ENS Éditions.

Pendell, Dale. 2010. *The Great Bay: Chronicles of the Collapse.* Berkeley, CA: North Atlantic Books.

Pepper, David. 2005. "Utopianism and Environmentalism." *Environmental Politics* 14: 3–22.

Pessoa, Luiz. 2013. *The Cognitive-Emotional Brain: From Interactions to Integration.* Cambridge, MA: MIT Press.

Pezzullo, Phaedra. 2006. "Articulating Anti-toxic Activism to 'Sexy' Superstars: The Cultural Politics of *A Civil Action* and *Erin Brockovich.*" *Environmental Communication Yearbook* 3: 21–48.

Phelan, James. 2001. "Why Narrators Can Be Focalizers—and Why It Matters." In *New Perspectives on Narrative Perspective,* edited by Willie van Peer and Seymour Chatman, 51–65. Albany: State University of New York Press.

———. 2013. "Improbabilities, Crossovers, and Impossibilities: A Rhetorical Approach to Breaks in Mimetic Narration." In *A Poetics of Unnatural Narrative,* edited by Jan Alber, Henrik Skov Nielsen, and Brian Richardson, 165–84. Columbus: The Ohio State University Press.

Phillips, Dana, ed. 2010. "Introduction: Special Issue on Animal Studies and Ecocriticism." Special issue, *Safundi* 11.

Piazza, Jo. 2010. "Audiences Experience 'Avatar' Blues." *CNN,* January 11.

Pick, Anat. 2011. *Creaturely Poetics: Animality and Vulnerability in Literature and Film.* New York: Columbia University Press.

Plantinga, Carl. 1996. "Moving Pictures and the Rhetoric of Nonfiction: Two Approaches. In *Post-Theory: Reconstructing Film Studies,* edited by David Bordwell and Noël Carroll, 307–24. Madison: University of Wisconsin Press.

———. 1999. "The Scene of Empathy and the Human Face on Film." In *Passionate Views: Film, Cognition, and Emotion,* edited by Carl Plantinga and Greg M. Smith, 239–55. Baltimore: Johns Hopkins University Press.

———. 2009a. *Moving Viewers: American Film and the Spectator Experience.* Berkeley: University of California Press.

———. 2009b. "Trauma, Pleasure, and Emotion in the Viewing of Titanic: A Cognitive Approach. In *Film Theory and Contemporary Hollywood Movies,* edited by Warren Buckland, 237–56. London: Routledge.

———. 2010. "'I Followed the Rules, and They All Loved You More': Moral Judgment and Attitudes toward Fictional Characters in Film." *Midwest Studies in Philosophy* 34 (1): 34–51.

———. 2013. "The Affective Power of Movies." In *Psychocinematics: Exploring Cognition at the Movies,* edited by Arthur P. Shimamura, 94–111. Oxford, UK: Oxford University Press.

———. 2015. "Facing Others: Close-ups of Faces in Narrative Film and in The Silence of the Lamb." In *The Oxford Handbook of Cognitive Literary Studies,* edited by Lisa Zunshine, 291–312. New York: Oxford University Press.

Plous, Scott. 1993. "Psychological Mechanisms in the Human Use of Animals." *Journal of Social Issues* 49: 11–52.

Pocahontas. 1995. Directed by Mike Gabriel and Eric Goldberg. Walt Disney Pictures.

Porter, Pete. 2010. "Teaching Animal Movies." In *Teaching the Animal: Human-Animal Studies across the Disciplines,* edited by Margo DeMello, 18–34. Brooklyn, NY: Lantern Books.

Portman, Natalie. 2010. "Jonathan Safran Foer's *Eating Animals* Turned Me Vegan." *Huffington Post,* March 18. http://www.huffingtonpost.com/natalie-portman/jonathan-safran-foers-iea _b_334407.html.

Posner, Richard. 2004. *Catastrophe: Risk and Response.* New York: Oxford University Press.

Pratt, Mary Louise. 1992. *Imperial Eyes: Travel Writing and Transculturation.* New York: Routlege.

Prince, Gerald. 2001. "A Point of View on Point of View or Refocalizing Focalization." In *New Perspectives on Narrative Perspective,* edited by Willie van Peer and Seymour Chatman, 43–49. Albany: State University of New York Press.

Prinz, Jesse J. 2011. "Is Empathy Necessary for Morality?" In *Empathy: Philosophical and Psychological Perspectives,* edited by Amy Coplan and Peter Goldie, 211–29. New York: Oxford University Press.

Promised Land. 2012. Directed by Gus Van Sant. Focus Features.

Rahmstorf, Stefan. 2004. "*The Day After Tomorrow*—Some Comments on the Movie." Home page of Stefan Rahmstorf, *Potsdam Institute for Climate Impact Research.* Accessed on November 15, 2015. http://www.pik-potsdam.de/~stefan/tdat_review.html.

Rahmstorf, Stefan, Jason E. Box, Georg Feulner, Michael E. Mann, Alexander Robinson Scott Rutherford, and Erik J. Schaffernicht. 2015. "Exceptional Twentieth-Century Slowdown in Atlantic Ocean Overturning Circulation." *Nature Climate Change* 5: 475–80.

Raiders of the Lost Ark. 1981. Directed by Steven Spielberg. Paramount Pictures.

Ramachandran, Vilayanur S. 2010. *The Tell-Tale Brain: A Neuroscientist's Quest for What Makes Us Human.* New York: W. W. Norton & Company.

Rassell, Andrea, Sean Redmond, Jenny Robinson, Jane Stadler, Sarah Pink, and Darrin Verhagen. 2016. "Seeing, Sensing Sound: Eye Tracking Soundscapes in *Saving Private Ryan* and *Monsters, Inc.*" In *Making Sense of Cinema: Empirical Studies into Film Spectators and Spectatorship,* edited by Carrie Lynn D. Reinhard and Christopher J. Olson, 139–64. New York: Bloomsbury.

Red Planet. 2000. Directed by Antony Hoffman. Warner Bros.

Reel Injun. 2009. Directed by Neil Diamond. Domino Film.

Reinhard, CarrieLynn D., and Christopher J. Olson, eds. 2016. *Making Sense of Cinema: Empirical Studies into Film Spectators and Spectatorship.* London: Bloomsbury Academic.

Renov, Michael. 1993. "Introduction: The Truth about Non-Fiction." In *Theorizing Documentary,* edited by Michael Renov, 1–11. London: Routledge.

Reusswig, Fritz. 2004a. "The International Impact of *The Day After Tomorrow.*" *Environment* 46 (9): 41–43.

———. 2004b. "Climate Change Goes Public: Five Studies Assess the Impact of 'The Day After Tomorrow' in Four Countries." Potsdam Institute for Climate Research, 5 November. http://www.upf.edu/pcstacademy/_docs/200410_climatechange.pdf.

Reusswig, Fritz, Julia Schwarzkopf, and Philipp Pohlenz. 2004. *Double Impact: The Climate Blockbuster* The Day After Tomorrow *and Its Impacts on the German Cinema Public,* PIK Report 92. Potsdam: Potsdam Institute for Climate Research.

Revkin, Andrew C. 2004. "NASA Curbs Comments on Ice Age Disaster Movie." *The New York Times,* April 25. http://www.nytimes.com/2004/04/25/national/25MOVI.html.

Rhodes, John David, and Elena Gorfinkel, eds. 2011. *Taking Place: Location and the Moving Image.* Minneapolis: University of Minnesota Press.

Richardson, Alan, and Francis Steen. 2002. "Literature and the Cognitive Revolution: An Introduction." *Poetics Today* 23: 1–8.

Richardson, Brian. 2006. *Unnatural Voices: Extreme Narration in Modern and Contemporary Literature.* Columbus: The Ohio State University Press.

Rich, Nathaniel, 2013. *Odds Against Tomorrow.* New York: Farrar, Straus and Giroux.

Richter, Virginia. 2011. *Literature after Darwin: Human Beasts in Western Fiction, 1859–1939.* Basingstoke, UK: Palgrave Macmillan.

Ristau, Carolyn A., ed. 1991. *Cognitive Ethology: The Minds of Other Animals, Essays in Honor of Donald R. Griffin.* Hillsdale, NJ: Lawrence Erlbaum Associates.

Rivas, Jesús, and Gordon M. Burghardt. 2002. "Crotalomorphism: A Metaphor for Understanding Anthropomorphism by Omission." In *The Cognitive Animal: Empirical and Theoretical Perspectives on Animal Cognition,* edited by Marc Bekoff, Colin Allen, and Gordon M. Burghardt, 9–18. Cambridge, MA: MIT Press.

A River Runs Through It. 1992. Directed by Robert Redford. Columbia Pictures.

Rizzolatti, Giacomo, and Laila Craighero. 2004. "The Mirror-Neuron System." *Annual Review of Neuroscience* 27: 169–92.

Rizzolatti, Giacomo, and Corrado Sinigaglia. 2008. *Mirrors in the Brain: How Our Minds Share Actions and Emotions.* Oxford, UK: Oxford University Press.

The Road. 2009. Directed by John Hillcoat. The Weinstein Company.

Robey, Tim. 2012. Review of *Beasts of the Southern Wild,* directed by Benh Zeitlin. *The Telegraph,* October 18. http://www.telegraph.co.uk/culture/film/filmreviews/9617493/Beasts-of-the-Southern-Wild-review.html.

Robinson, Jenefer. 2007. *Deeper than Reason: Emotion and its Role in Literature, Music, and Art.* New York: Oxford University Press.

Robinson, Jennifer, Jane Stadler, and Andrea Rassell. 2015. "Sound and Sight: An Exploratory Look at *Saving Private Ryan* through the Eye Tracking Lens." *Refractory* 25. Last modified February 6, 2015. http://refractory.unimelb.edu.au/2015/02/06/robinson-stadler-rassell/.

Robinson, Kim Stanley. 1984. *The Wild Shore.* New York: Tom Doherty.

———. 1988. *The Gold Coast.* New York: Tom Doherty.

———. 1988. *Pacific Edge.* New York: Tom Doherty.

———. 2004. *Forty Signs of Rain.* New York: Spectra.

———. 2005. *Fifty Degrees Below.* New York: Spectra.

———. 2007. *Sixty Days and Counting.* New York: Spectra.

Rollins, Peter, and John O'Connor. 2003. *Hollywood's Indian: The Portrayal of the Native American in Film.* Lexington: University of Kentucky Press.

Romero, José Jesus. 2010. "Feminism, Ethnicity, and Identity: An Interview with Helena María Viramontes." *CSULA Department of English Website,* April 4. https://www.calstatela.edu/academic/english/st-2010-viramontes.php.

Rope. 1948. Directed by Alfred Hitchcock. Warner Bros. Pictures.

Rust, Stephen. 2014. "Ecocinema and the Wildlife Film." *The Cambridge Companion to Literature and the Environment,* edited by Louise Westling, 226–39. Cambridge: Cambridge University Press.

Ryan, Marie-Laure. 2001. *Narrative as Virtual Reality: Immersion and Interactivity in Literature and Electronic Media.* Baltimore: Johns Hopkins University Press.

———. 2009. "From Narrative Games to Playable Stories: Towards a Poetics of Interactive Narrative." *StoryWorlds: A Journal of Narrative Studies* 1: 43–59.

Ryan, Marie-Laure, and Jan-Noël Thon. 2014. Introduction to *Storyworlds across Media: Toward a Media-Conscious Narratology* (Kindle edition), edited by Marie-Laure Ryan and Jan-Noël Thon, 166–532. Lincoln: University of Nebraska Press.

Sambell, Kay. 2003. "Presenting the Case for Social Change: The Creative Dilemma of Dystopian Writing for Children." In *Utopian and Dystopian Writing for Children and Young Adults,* edited by Carrie Hintz and Elaine Ostry, 163–78. New York: Routledge.

Sargisson, Lucy. 1999. *Utopian Bodies and the Politics of Transgression.* London: Routledge.

Savarese, Ralph James. 2013. "Neurocosmopolitan Melville." *Leviathan* 15 (2): 7–19.

———. 2015. "What Some Autistics Can Teach Us about Poetry: A Neurocosmopolitan Approach." In *The Oxford Handbook of Cognitive Literary Studies,* edited by Lisa Zunshine, 393–419. New York: Oxford University Press.

Scarry, Elaine. (1999) 2001. *Dreaming by the Book.* Princeton, NJ: Princeton University Press.

The Searchers. 1956. Directed by John Ford. Warner Bros. Company.

The Secret Life of Pets. 2016. Directed by Chris Renaud and Yarrow Cheney. Universal Pictures.

Seeley, William. 2016. "Neuroscience and Literature." In *The Routledge Companion to Philosophy of Literature,* edited by Noel Carroll and John Gibson, 269–78. New York: Routledge.

Sewell. Anna. 1877. *Black Beauty.* London: Jarrold & Sons.

Seymour, Nicole. 2014. "Irony and Contemporary Ecocinema: Theorizing a New Affective Paradigm." In *Moving Environments: Affect, Emotion, Ecology, and Film,* edited by Alexa Weik von Mossner, 61–78. Waterloo, ON: Wilfrid Laurier University Press.

Shaw, Harry E. 1995. "Loose Narrators: Display, Engagement, and the Search for a Place in History in Realist Fiction." *Narrative* 3 (2): 95–116.

Shimamura, Arthur P., ed. 2013. *Psychocinematics: Exploring Cognition at the Movies.* Oxford: Oxford University Press.

Shimamura, Arthur P., Brendon I. Cohn-Sheehy, Brianna L. Pogue, and Thomas. A. Shimamura. 2015. "How Attention Is Driven by Film Edits: A Multimodal Experience." *Psychology of Aesthetics, Creativity, and the Arts* 9: 417–22.

The Shining. 1980. Directed by Stanley Kubrick. Warner Bros. Company.

Shrader-Frechette, Kristin. 2002. *Environmental Justice: Creating Equality, Reclaiming Democracy.* New York: Oxford University Press.

Sideris, Lisa. 2010. "I See You: Interspecies Empathy and *Avatar.*" *Journal of Religion, Nature, and Culture.* 4 (4): 457–77.

Silko, Leslie Marmon. 1977. *Ceremony.* New York: Penguin Books.

Simon, Alex. 2012. "Michael Apted: The Hollywood Interview." *The Hollywood Interview. com,* November 24. http://thehollywoodinterview.blogspot.co.at/2008/03/michael-apted-hollywood-interview.html.

Simons, Paul. 2015. "Weather Eye: The Cold 'Blob' Phenomenon." *The Times*, October 13. http://www.thetimes.co.uk/tto/weather/article4583914.ece.

Simpson, Paul. 2003. *On the Discourse of Satire: Towards a Stylistic Model of Satirical Humor.* Amsterdam: John Benjamins Publishing Company.

Singer, Peter. (1975) 1990. *Animal Liberation.* New York: Avon Books.

Skinner, B. F. (1948) 2005. *Walden Two.* Indianapolis: Hackett Publishing Company.

Sklar, Howard. 2009. "Narrative Structuring of Empathetic Response: Theoretical and Empirical Approaches to Toni Cade Bambara's 'The Hammer Man.'" *Poetics* 30 (3): 561–607.

———. 2013. *The Art of Sympathy in Fiction: Forms of Ethical and Emotional Persuasion.* Amsterdam: John Benjamins Publishing Company.

The Sky is Pink. 2012. Directed by Josh Fox. Top Documentary Films. Accessed on October 7, 2016. http://topdocumentaryfilms.com/sky-pink/.

Slovic, Paul. 2000. *The Perception of Risk.* London: Earthscan.

———. 2010. *The Feeling of Risk: New Perspectives on Risk Perception.* London: Earthscan.

Slovic, Scott. 1992. *Seeking Awareness in American Nature Writing.* Salt Lake City: University of Utah Press.

———. 1996. "Nature Writing and Environmental Psychology: The Interiority of Outdoor Experience." In *The Ecocriticism Reader: Landmarks in Literary Ecology,* edited by Cheryll Glotfelty and Harold Fromm, 351–70. Athens: University of Georgia Press.

———. 2015. "Science, Eloquence, and the Asymmetry of Trust." In *Numbers and Nerves: Information and Meaning in a World of Data,* edited by Scott Slovic and Paul Slovic, 115–35. Corvallis: Oregon State University Press.

Slovic, Scott, and Paul Slovic. 2015. *Numbers and Nerves: Information and Meaning in a World of Data.* Corvallis: Oregon State University Press.

Smaill, Belinda. 2014. "Emotions, Argumentations, and Documentary Traditions: *Darwin's Nightmare* and *The Cove.*" In *Moving Environments: Affect, Emotion, Ecology, and Film,* edited by Alexa Weik von Mossner, 103–20. Waterloo, ON: Wilfrid Laurier University Press.

———. 2016. *Regarding Life: Animals and the Documentary Moving Image.* Albany: SUNY Press.

Small, Gail. 1994. "Environmental Justice in Indian Country." *Amicus Journal* (Spring): 38–40.

Smith, Greg M. 2003. *Film Structure and the Emotion System.* Cambridge: Cambridge University Press.

———. 2014. "Coming Out of the Corner: The Challenges of a Broader Media Cognitivism." In *Cognitive Media Theory,* edited by Ted Nannicelli and Paul Taberham, 285–301. New York: Routledge.

Smith, Jeff. 1999. "Movie Music as Moving Music: Emotion, Cognition, and the Film Score." In *Passionate Views: Film, Cognition, and Emotion,* edited by Carl Plantinga and Greg M. Smith, 146–67. Baltimore: Johns Hopkins University Press.

Smith, Kimberley K. 2007. *African American Environmental Thought: Foundations.* Lawrence: University Press of Kansas.

Smith, Murray. 1995. *Engaging Characters: Fiction, Emotion, and the Cinema.* Oxford, UK: Oxford University Press.

———. 1999. "Gangsters, Cannibals, Aesthetes, or Apparently Perverse Allegiances." In *Passionate Views: Film, Cognition, and Emotion,* edited by Carl Plantinga and Greg M. Smith, 217–37. Baltimore: Johns Hopkins University Press.

———. 2011. "On the Twofoldness of Character." *New Literary History* 42: 277–94.

Smith, Tim J. 2013. "Watching You Watch Movies: Using Eye Tracking to Inform Film Theory." In *Psychocinematics: Exploring Cognition at the Movies,* edited by Arthur P. Shimamura, 165–91. Oxford, UK: Oxford University Press.

———. 2014. "Audiovisual Correspondence in Sergei Eisenstein's *Alexander Nevsky*: A Case Study in Viewer Attention." In *Cognitive Media Theory,* edited by Ted Nannicelli and Paul Taberham, 85–104. New York: Routledge.

———. 2015. "Read, Watch, Listen: A Commentary on Eye Tracking and Moving Images." *Refractory* 25. Last modified February 7, 2015. http://refractory.unimelb.edu.au/2015/02/07/smith/.

Smith, Tim J., Daniel Levin, and James E. Cutting. 2012. "A Window on Reality: Perceiving Edited Moving Images." *Current Directions in Psychological Science* 21 (2): 107–13.

Smoke Signals. 1998. Directed by Chris Eyre. Miramax.

Smith, Tim J., and Henderson, J. M. 2008. "Edit Blindness: The Relationship between Attention and Global Change Blindness in Dynamic Scenes. *Journal of Eye Movement Research* 2: 1–17.

Smuts, Aaron. 2009. "The Paradox of Suspense." *Stanford Encyclopedia of Philosophy.* Accessed on May 2, 2016. http://plato.stanford.edu/entries/paradox-suspense/.

Snowpiercer. 2013. Directed by Bong Joon-ho. CJ Entertainment.

Sobchack, Vivian. 1982. "Toward Inhabited Space: The Semiotic Structure of Camera Movement in the Cinema," *Semiotica* 1 (4): 317–35.

Solomon, Robert C. 2004a. "Emotions, Thoughts, and Feelings: Emotions as Engagements with the World. In *Thinking about Feeling: Contemporary Philosophers on Emotions,* edited by Robert C. Solomon, 76–88. Oxford, UK: Oxford University Press.

Solomon, Robert C., ed. 2004b. *Thinking about Feeling: Contemporary Philosophers on Emotions.* Oxford, UK: Oxford University Press.

Solso, Robert. 1996. *Cognition and the Visual Arts.* Cambridge, MA: MIT Press.

Sorenson, John, ed. 2014. *Critical Animal Studies: Thinking the Unthinkable.* Toronto: Canadian Scholar's Press.

Speer, Nicole K., Jeremy R. Reynolds, Khena M. Swallow, and Jeffrey M. Zacks. 2009. "Reading Stories Activates Neural Representations of Visual and Motor Experiences." *Psychological Science* 20 (8): 989–99.

Spinrad, Norman. 1999. *Greenhouse Summer.* New York: Tom Doherty.

Spivak, Gayatri Chakravorty. (1985) 1996. "Subaltern Studies: Deconstructing Historiography." In *The Spivak Reader,* edited by Donna Landry and Gerald MacLean, 203–35. London: Routledge.

Spolsky, Ellen. 1993. *Gaps in Nature: Literary Interpretation and the Modular Mind.* Albany: State University of New York Press.

Stagecoach. 1939. Directed by John Ford. United Artists.

Staiger, Janet, and Sabine Hake, eds. 2009. *Convergence Media History.* London: Routledge.

Starr, G. Gabrielle. 2010. "Multisensory Imagery." In *Introduction to Cognitive Cultural Studies,* edited by Lisa Zunshine, 275–90. Baltimore: Johns Hopkins University Press.

———. 2013. *Feeling Beauty: The Neuroscience of Aesthetic Experience.* Cambridge, MA: MIT Press.

Steinbeck, John. (1939) 2002. *The Grapes of Wrath.* New York: Penguin.

Stein, Garth. 2008. *The Art of Racing in the Rain.* New York: Harper.

Stewart, Dodal. 2012. "Racist Hunger Games Fans Are Very Disappointed." *Jezebel* March 26. Accessed on June 27, 2016. http://jezebel.com/5896408/racist-hunger-games-fans-dont-care -how-much-money-the-movie-made.

Suematsu, Dyske. 2010. "'The Cove' Debate—From the Japanese Perspective." *AllLookSame?* March 12. http://alllooksame.com/the-cove-%E2%80%94-the-unfortunate-war-continues/?author=2.

Sunstein, Cass R., and Martha C. Nussbaum. 2004. *Animal Rights: Current Debates and New Directions.* Oxford, UK: Oxford University Press.

Suvin, Darko. 1979. *Metamorphoses of Science Fiction: On the Poetics and History of a Literary Genre.* New Haven, CT: Yale University Press.

Svoboda, Michael. 2014. "The Long Melt: The Lingering Influence of *The Day After Tomorrow.*" *Yale Climate Connections,* November 5. http://www.yaleclimateconnections.org/2014/11/the -long-melt-the-lingering-influence-of-the-day-after-tomorrow/.

Sze, Julie. 2002. "From Environmental Justice Literature to the Literature of Environmental Justice." In *The Environmental Justice Reader: Politics, Poetics, and Pedagogy,* edited by Joni Adamson, Mei Mei Evans, and Rachel Stein, 163–80. Tucson: University of Arizona Press.

———. 2015. "Environmental Justice Anthropocene Narratives: Sweet Art, Recognition, and Representation." *Resilience: A Journal of the Environmental Humanities* 2 (2): 1–16.

Tan, Ed S. 1995. "Film-Induced Affect as a Witness Emotion." *Poetics* 23 (1–2): 7–32.

———. 1996. *Emotion and the Structure of Narrative Film.* Hillsdale, NJ: Lawrence Erlbaum Associates.

Tan, Ed S., and Nico Frijda. 1999. "Sentiment in Film Viewing." In *Passionate Views: Film, Cognition, and Emotion,* edited by Carl Plantinga and Greg M. Smith, 48–64. Baltimore: Johns Hopkins University Press.

Taylor, Bron, ed. 2013. *Avatar and Nature Spirituality.* Waterloo, ON: Wilfrid Laurier University Press.

Temperley, David. 2004. *The Cognition of Basic Musical Structures.* Cambridge, MA: MIT Press.

Tettamanti, Marco, Giovanni Buccino, Maria C. Saccuman, Vittorio Gallese, Massimo Danna, Paola Scifo, and Ferruccio Fazio. 2005. "Listening to Action-Related Sentences Activates Fronto-Parietal Motor Circuits." *Journal of Cognitive Neuroscience* 17 (2): 273–81.

Thompson, Evan. 2007. *Mind in Life: Biology, Phenomenology, and the Sciences of Mind.* Cambridge, MA: Harvard Belknap.

Thomson-Jones, Katherine J. 2013. "Sensing Motion in Movies." In *Psychocinematics: Exploring Cognition at the Movies,* edited by Arthur P. Shimamura, 115–31. Oxford, UK: Oxford University Press.

Thoreau, Henry David. (1854) 1971. *Walden.* Princeton, NJ: Princeton University Press.

Thunderheart. 1992. Directed by Michael Apted. TriStar Pictures.

Titanic. 1997. Directed by James Cameron. Paramount.

Toy Story. 1995. Directed by John Lasseter. Buena Vista Pictures.

Trexler, Adam. 2015. *Anthropocene Fictions: The Novel in a Time of Climate Change.* Charlottesville: University of Virginia Press.

Trexler, Adam, and Adeline Johns-Putra. 2011. "Climate Change in Literature and Literary Criticism." *Wiley's Interdisciplinary Reviews: Climate Change* 2 (2): 185–200.

Truthland. 2011. Energy Depth and Independent Petroleum Association of America. Accessed on October 1, 2016. http://www.truthlandmovie.com/

Tryon, Chuck. 2009. *Reinventing Cinema: Movies in the Age of Media Convergence.* New Brunswick, NJ: Rutgers University Press.

Tuan, Yi-Fu. 1974. *Topophilia: A Study of Environmental Perception, Attitudes, and Values.* Englewood Cliffs, NJ: Prentice Hall.

Turner, Mark. 2006. *The Literary Mind.* Oxford, UK: Oxford University Press.

Tuur, Kadri, and Morten Tonnessen, ed. 2014. *The Semiotics of Animal Representations.* Amsterdam: Rodopi.

Twister. 1996. Directed by Jan de Bont. Warner Bros.

United Church of Christ (UCC) Commission for Racial Justice. 1987. *Toxic Wastes and Race in the United States: A National Report on the Racial and Socioeconomic Characteristics of Communities with Hazardous Waste Sites.* New York: UCC.

van der Linden, Sander, Edward Maibach, and Anthony Leiserowitz. 2015. "Improving Public Engagement with Climate Change: Five 'Best Practice' Insights from Psychological Science." *Perspectives on Psychological Science* 10 (6): 758–63.

Van Dooren, Thom, and Deborah Bird Rose. 2016. "Lively Ethography: Storying Animist Worlds." In *The Routledge Companion to the Environmental Humanities,* edited by Jon Christensen, Ursula K. Heise, and Michelle Niemann. New York: Routledge.

Varela, Francisco. 1996. "Neurophenomenology: A Methodological Remedy for the Hard Problem." *Journal of Consciousness Studies* 3 (4): 330–49.

Varela, Franciso J., Evan Thompson, and Eleanor Rosch. 1991. *The Embodied Mind: Cognitive Science and Human Experience.* Cambridge, MA: MIT Press.

Vermeule, Blakey. 2010. *Why Do We Care about Literary Characters?* Baltimore: Johns Hopkins University Press.

Viramontes, Helena Maria. 1995. *Under the Feet of Jesus.* New York: Plume.

Volcano. 1950. Directed by William Dieterle. Turner Classic Movies.

Volcano. 1997. Directed by Mick Jackson. 20th Century Fox.

Waiting for Guffman. 1997. Directed by Christopher Guest. Sony Pictures Classics.

Wagstaff, Keith. 2014. "Q&A: *Avatar* Director James Cameron Talks Climate Change." *NBC News Website* (September 23). http://www.nbcnews.com/science/environment/q-avatar-director-james-cameron-talks-climate-change-n209751.

Walker, Janet. 2015. "Eavesdropping in *The Cove*: Interspecies Ethics, Public and Private Space and Trauma under Water." In *Eco-Trauma Cinema,* edited by Anil Narine, 180–206. New York: Routledge.

WALL-E. 2008. Directed by Andrew Stanton. Walt Disney Motion Pictures.

Ward, Peter D. 2010. *The Flooded Earth: Our Future In a World Without Ice Caps.* New York: Basic Books.

Ward, Mark S. 2015. "Art in Noise: An Embodied Simulation Account of Cinematic Sound Design." In *Embodied Cognition and Cinema,* edited by Maarten Coëgnarts and Peter Kravanja, 155–86. Leuven: Leuven University Press.

Warhorse. 2011. Directed by Steven Spielberg. Walt Disney Motion Pictures.

Warter, Tanja. 2015. "Frau Pepperberg hat einen Vogel." *Salzburger Nachrichten,* October 13: 19.

Weaver, Jace, ed. 1996. *Defending Mother Earth: Native American Perspectives on Environmental Justice.* Maryknoll, NY: Orbis Books.

Weik von Mossner, Alexa. 2009. "Mysteries of the Mountain: Environmental Racism and Political Action in Percival Everett's *Watershed.*" *Journal of American Studies of Turkey* 30: 73–88.

———. 2012a. "Facing *The Day After Tomorrow*: Filmed Disaster, Emotional Engagement, and Climate Risk Perception." In *American Environments: Climate-Cultures-Catastrophe,* edited by Christof Mauch and Sylvia Mayer, 97–115. Heidelberg, Ger.: Universitätsverlag Winter.

———. 2012b. "The Human Face of Global Warming: Varieties of Eco-Cosmopolitanism in Climate Change Documentaries." *Revista Canaria de Estudios Ingleses* 64: 145–60.

———. 2013. "Troubling Spaces: Ecological Risk, Narrative Framing, and Emotional Engagement in Franny Armstrong's *The Age of Stupid.*" In "Ecology and Emotion," edited by Mick Smith, special issue, *Emotion, Space and Society* 6 (1): 108–16.

———. 2014a. *Cosmopolitan Minds: Literature, Emotion, and the Transnational Imagination.* Austin: University of Texas Press.

———. 2014b. "Emotions of Consequence? Viewing Eco-Documentaries from a Cognitive Perspective." In *Moving Environments: Affect, Emotion, Ecology, and Film,* edited by Alexa Weik von Mossner, 41–60. Waterloo, ON: Wilfrid Laurier University Press.

———. 2014c. "Love in the Times of Ecocide: Eco-Trauma and Comic Relief in Andrew Stanton's *WALL-E.*" In *The Cinematic Earth: Eco-Trauma Cinema,* edited by Neil Narine, 164–79. London: Routledge.

———. 2014d. "Melodrama, Emotion, and Environmental Advocacy: A Cognitive Approach to *Erin Brockovich.*" *Anglia: Journal of English Philology* 132 (2): 292–309.

———. 2014e. "The Stuff of Fear: Emotions, Ethics, and the Materiality of Nuclear Risk in *Silkwood* and *The China Syndrome.*" In *The Anticipation of Catastrophe: Environmental Risk in North American Literature and Culture,* edited by Sylvia Mayer and Alexa Weik von Mossner, 101–17. Heidelberg, Ger.: Universitätsverlag Winter.

———. 2014f. "Visceralizing Ecocide in Science Fiction Films: *The Road* and *Hell.*" *Ecozon@: European Journal of Literature, Culture, and Environment* 3 (2): 42–56.

———. 2014g. "Disasters Foretold: Imaging Climate Catastrophe in *Six Degrees Could Change the World.*" In *Disaster as Image: Iconographies and Media Strategies across Europe and Asia,* edited by Monica Juneja and Gerrit Jasper Schenk, 157–64. Regensburg, Ger.: Schnell & Steiner.

———. 2014h. "Science Fiction and the Risks of the Anthropocene: Anticipated Transformations in Dale Pendell's *The Great Bay.*" *Environmental Humanities* 5: 203–16.

———. Ed. 2014i. *Moving Environments: Affect, Emotion, Ecology, and Film.* Waterloo, ON: Wilfrid Laurier University Press.

———. 2015. "Small Islands in Documentary Film." *Global Environment* 8 (1): 178–95.

———. 2016. "Environmental Narrative, Embodiment, and Emotion." In *The Handbook of Ecocriticism and Cultural Ecology,* edited by Hubert Zapf, 534–50. Berlin: De Gruyter.

———. 2017. "Touching the Senses: Environments and Technologies at the Movies." In *The Routledge Companion to the Environmental Humanities,* edited by Ursula K. Heise, Jon Christensen, and Michelle Niemann, 337–45 New York: Routledge.

Welling, Bart H. 2009. "Ecoporn: On the Limits of Visualizing the Nonhuman." In *Ecosee: Image, Rhetoric, Nature,* edited by Sidney Dobrin and Sean Morey, 52–77. Albany: State University of New York Press.

———. 2014. "On 'The Inexplicable Magic of Cinema': Critical Anthropomorphism, Emotion, and the Wildness of Wildlife Films." In *Moving Environments: Affect, Emotion, Ecology, and Film,* edited by Alexa Weik von Mossner, 81–101. Waterloo, ON: Wilfrid Laurier University Press.

Welling, Bart H., and Scottie Kapel. 2012. "The Return of the Animal: Presenting and Representing Non-human Beings Response-ably." In *Teaching Ecocriticism in Green Cultural Studies,* edited by Greg Garrard, 104–16. Basingstoke, UK: Palgrave Macmillan.

Westling, Louise. 2012. "Merleau-Ponty's Ecophenomenology." In *Ecocritical Theory: New European Approaches,* edited by Axel Goodbody and Kate Rigby, 126–38. Charlottesville: University of Virginia Press.

———. 2014. Introduction to *The Cambridge Companion to Literature and the Environment,* edited by Louise Westling, 1–16. Cambridge: Cambridge University Press.

White God. 2014. Directed by Kornél Mundruczó. InterCom.

Whitley, David. 2012. *The Idea of Nature in Disney Animation.* Farnham, UK: Ashgate Publishers.

———. 2014. "Animation, Realism, and the Genre of Nature." In *Moving Environments: Affect, Emotion, Ecology, and Film,* edited by Alexa Weik von Mossner, 143–58. Waterloo, ON: Wilfrid Laurier University Press.

The Wild Bunch. 1969. Directed by Sam Peckinpah. Warner Bros.-Seven Arts.

Wilhelm, Maria, and Dirk Mathison. 2009. *Avatar: A Confidential Report on the Biological and Social History of Pandora.* New York: It Books.

Williams, Linda. 1998. "Melodrama Revisited." In *Refiguring American Film Genres: History and Theory,* edited by Nick Browne, 42–88. Berkeley: University of California Press.

Willoquet-Maricondi, Paula. 2010. "Shifting Paradigms: From Environmentalist Films to Ecocinema." In *Framing the World: Explorations in Ecocriticism and Film,* edited by Paula Willoquet-Maricondi, 43–60. Charlottesville: University of Virginia Press.

Wilson, Kris. 2000. "Communicating Climate Change through the Media: Predictions, Politics, and Perceptions of Risk." In *Environmental Risks and the Media,* edited by Stuart Allan, Barbara Adam, and Cynthia Carter, 201–17. New York: Routledge.

Wilson, Robert A., and Lucia Foglia. 2011. "Embodied Cognition." In *The Stanford Encyclopedia of Philosophy,* edited by Edward N. Zalta. Accessed May 19, 2015. http://plato.stanford.edu/archives/fall2011/ entries/embodied-cognition/.

Winged Migration. 2001. Directed by Jacques Cluzaud, Michel Debats, and Jacques Perrin. Sony Pictures Classics.

Winter, Deborah Du Nann, and Susan M. Koger. 2004. *The Psychology of Environmental Problems.* Mahwah, NJ: Lawrence Erlbaum Associates.

Wolfe, Cary. 2003. *Animal Rites: American Culture, the Discourse of Species, and Posthumanist Theory.* Chicago: University of Chicago Press.

———. 2006. "Thinking Other-Wise: Cognitive Science, Deconstruction, and the (Non)Speaking (Non)Human Animal Subject." In *Animal Subjects: An Ethical Reader in a Posthuman World,* edited by Jodey Castricano, 125–44. Waterloo: Wilfrid Laurier University Press.

Wolf, Maryanne. 2007. *Proust and the Squid: The Story and Science of the Reading Brain.* New York: HarperCollins.

Worster, Donald. 2011. *A Passion for Nature: The Life of John Muir.* Oxford, UK: Oxford University Press.

Wylie, Dan. 2002. "The Anthropomorphic Ethic Fiction and the Animal Mind in Virginia Woolf's *Flush* and Barbara Gowdy's *The White Bone*." *Interdisciplinary Studies in Literature and Environment* 9 (2): 115–31.

Yacowar, Maurice. (1977) 2012. "The Bug in the Rug: Notes on the Disaster Genre." In *Film Genre Reader IV*, edited by Barry Keith Grant, 313–31. Austin: University of Texas Press.

Young, Kay. 2010. *Imagining Minds: The Neuro-Aesthetics of Austen, Eliot, and Hardy.* Columbus: The Ohio State University Press.

Young, Phyllis. 1996. "Beyond the Waterline." In *Defending Mother Earth: Native American Perspectives on Environmental Justice*, edited by Jace Weaver, 85–86. Maryknoll, NY: Orbis Books.

Zacks, Jeffrey M. 2015. *Flicker: Your Brain on Movies.* New York: Oxford University Press.

Zacks, Jeffrey M., Nicole K. Speer, and Jeremy R. Reynolds. 2009. "Segmentation in Reading and Film Comprehension." *Journal of Experimental Psychology: General* 138: 307–27.

Zapf, Hubert. 2008. "Literary Ecology and the Ethics of Texts." *New Literary History* 39 (4): 847–68.

———. 2016. *Literature as Cultural Ecology: Sustainable Texts.* London: Bloomsbury Academic.

Zaniewski, Andrej. 1994. *Rat.* New York: Arcade Publishing.

Zeki, Semir. 1999. *Inner Vision: An Exploration of Art and the Brain.* Oxford, UK: Oxford University Press.

Zillmann, Dolf. 1983. "Transfer of Excitation in Emotional Behavior." In *Social Psychology: A Sourcebook*, edited by J. T. Capacioppo and R. E. Petty, 215–40. New York: Guilford Press.

Zimmerman, Michael E. 2002. "Heidegger's Phenomenology and Contemporary Environmentalism." In *Eco-Phenomenology: Back to the Earth Itself*, edited by Ted Toadvine, 73–101. Albany: State University of New York Press.

Zumbansen, Nils, and Marcel Fromme. 2010. "Ecocatastrophes in Recent American (Non)fictional Texts and Films." In *Local Natures, Global Responsibilities*, edited by Laurenz Volkmann, Nancy Grimm, and Ines Detmers, 274–88. Amsterdam: Rodopi.

Zunshine, Lisa. 2006. *Why We Read Fiction: Theory of Mind and the Novel.* Columbus: The Ohio State University Press.

Zwaan, Rolf A. 2004. "The Immersed Experiencer: Towards an Embodied Theory of Language Comprehension." In *The Psychology of Learning and Motivation*, edited by Brian H. Ross, 35–63. San Diego: Elsevier Academic Press.

INDEX

COGNITIVE APPROACHES TO CULTURE

Frederick Luis Aldama, Patrick Colm Hogan, Lalita Pandit Hogan, and Sue Kim, Series Editors

This new series takes up cutting edge research in a broad range of cognitive sciences insofar as this research bears on and illuminates cultural phenomena such as literature, film, drama, music, dance, visual art, digital media, and comics, among others. For the purpose of the series, "cognitive science" will be construed broadly to encompass work derived from cognitive and social psychology, neuroscience, cognitive and generative linguistics, affective science, and related areas in anthropology, philosophy, computer science, and elsewhere. Though open to all forms of cognitive analysis, the series is particularly interested in works that explore the social and political consequences of cognitive cultural study.

Affective Ecologies: Empathy, Emotion, and Environmental Narrative
   ALEXA WEIK VON MOSSNER

A Passion for Specificity: Confronting Inner Experience in Literature and Science
   MARCO CARACCIOLO AND RUSSELL T. HURLBURT